RABBINIC JUDAISM

RABBINIC JUDAISM

IN THE MAKING

A CHAPTER IN THE HISTORY OF
THE HALAKHAH FROM EZRA TO JUDAH I

by ALEXANDER GUTTMANN

Hebrew Union College–Jewish Institute of Religion · Cincinnati

WAYNE STATE UNIVERSITY PRESS

DETROIT 1970

Published simultaneously in Canada by
The Copp Clark Publishing Company
517 Wellington Street, West
Toronto 2B, Canada

Library of Congress Catalog Card Number: 69–10525
Standard Book Number: 8143–1382–5

To Manya

Contents

PREFACE

*T*his book has been in preparation
for many years. It is preceded by a number of monographs pertaining to both the history of the Halakhah and, to a lesser degree, the
history of the talmudic period. If the treatment of some phases of
legal history is too brief, the reason may be that a fuller and satisfactory discussion of them is found elsewhere. On the other hand, a
few phases of Jewish legal history are dealt with in greater depth
here as they have not previously been treated fully or satisfactorily.
These chapters may be of particular interest to specialized scholars,
whereas the book as a whole should be of more general interest. In
order to facilitate the use of the book also by non-talmudists, most
of the Hebrew and Aramaic sources are translated. Available translations were used, but with modifications. Many of the sources —
e.g., Tosefta, Palestinian Talmud — appear here in English for the
first time. Whatever the shortcomings of the book, it is unique in
that it demonstrates for the first time in English how the development of Jewish legal tradition was directed and implemented by the
Pharisaic and rabbinic leadership from the earliest times to the end
of the tannaitic period, ca. 220 C.E.

It is my great pleasure to express my thanks to my disciples and
colleagues, Drs. Stephen M. Passameneck, Jakob J. Petuchowski
and the Rev. Dr. Clyde Woods for a critical reading of the typescript,

and particularly to Dr. Elias L. Epstein for a meticulous linguistic scrutiny of the text. I owe the greatest debt to Dr. Samuel Sandmel for negotiating the publication of this volume and to Dr. Jacob R. Marcus for furthering its publication. The often difficult task of preparing the manuscript for print was in the hands of Mrs. Rissa Alex. Hearty thanks to her and her staff of devoted assistants, Mrs. Helen Lederer, Mrs. Betty Finkelstein, and others.

Less tangible but most decisive in encouraging me in my work was my wife, Manya. Dr. Henry Guttmann, my brother, expressed his views on some important phases of Jewish history which greatly helped in clarifying them. Nonetheless, all the encouragement and assistance would have been in vain were it not for the foundation in Jewish and cognate learning given me by my beloved teachers, and especially by my father, Prof. Michael Guttmann of blessed memory.

A.G.

INTRODUCTION

A nation, community, culture or religion, in an extended period of existence, experiences many significant changes. Nevertheless, even a long period may properly be considered a single epoch if it possesses throughout certain fundamental characteristics peculiar to the period in question. A case in point is the long period of Rabbinic Judaism. In the course of its history, Rabbinic Judaism underwent numerous changes. Taken as a whole, its early phases have a greater affinity in certain respects to Biblical Judaism than to the later phases of Rabbinic Judaism. For example, in the beginning of the rabbinic epoch, the laws of the sacrificial cult and of ritual purity, so important in the Torah, also played an important role in Rabbinic Judaism. The termination of the sacrificial cult, the centralized Sanctuary, the high-priesthood and many other laws and institutions due to the destruction of the Temple in Jerusalem, resulted in significant changes in the forms and ways of religious life of Palestinian and Diaspora Jewry. However, these changes did not cause an essential modification of the character of "mainstream" Judaism. The transition from Soferic to Pharisaic, then to Rabbinic Judaism is not to be regarded as indicative of fundamental differences between the three. Rather, it is merely one step in the evolution of Rabbinic Judaism, which cut across profound changes caused by wars, dispersion, and political, social, and economic revolutions.

Wherein does the great strength of Rabbinic Judaism lie? What caused it to become and remain the mainstream of Judaism from antiquity to date? What enabled it to prevail against the political, economic, cultural, social and religious forces that threatened time and again to destroy both Jew and Judaism?

Deep devotion to God and His law, while a conditio sine qua non, cannot be the only reason, since this was a quality of some other branches of Judaism as well. An analytical study of Judaism shows that rabbinism prevailed through the ages due to the clear vision and effective guidance of its leaders, the rabbis. These men possessed a deep understanding of the need for a warm and practical religious expression, genuinely Jewish, and at the same time harmonious with the spiritual and material life of the peoples surrounding them. Emerging from the ranks of the people, the rabbis spoke in terms intelligible to the populace and were therefore able to lead the people in accordance with their teachings, a feat the Prophets had been unable to accomplish. Uncompromising idealists, the Prophets demanded perfection and the establishment of God's kingdom on earth in their own time; therefore, they were doomed to failure. Prophetic Judaism never became a reality but remained only an ideal, a goal, like Plato's Republic. The rabbis were idealists, too, but they were at the same time pedagogues. In guiding their people, they took the realities of life, among them the weakness of man, into consideration. They upheld the Torah as the divine code, but at the same time recognized the need for harmonizing the Torah with the ever-changing realities of life. The success of the sages of Rabbinic Judaism is to a large extent due to the ability of its leaders to maintain a harmonious state between Judaism and a continuously changing life.

The manner of implementing change varied from time to time. In the period of transition from Biblical to Rabbinic Judaism, certain necessary adjustments were made, as a rule, by direct legislation whenever religious leadership found support in the Jewish or non-Jewish government. The Great Sanhedrin, for example, of the Second Commonwealth, vested with Hasmonean authority, solved many problems through direct legislation. However, when the Pharisaic and rabbinic leaderships were not supported by the government, they increasingly resorted to *indirect* forms of legislation. The principal method of indirect legislation employed throughout the centuries was interpretation. Since the authority of the Torah reigned supreme, laws based on the interpretation of its text were accepted by the people, provided the interpreting teacher was a recognized sage. Thus, authority supported by the government was replaced by spiritual authority.

Indirect forms of legislation have existed at all times and among all nations. The resulting laws are often as valid and enforceable as are statutory laws passed through channels of direct legislation. However, the effectiveness of the indirect legislation of the rabbis depended on the voluntary cooperation of the people, which in turn depended primarily on the prestige of the legislating sages.

Interpretation, though most important, was not the only form of rabbinic legislation. Some of the other methods employed were: issuing of ordinances (though not backed by the political government), legal fiction, declaring customs as legally binding, and introducing certain legal principles.

The rabbis, in pursuing their goal, adopted a number of customs, laws and ideas of other peoples, and so fully integrated them into Judaism that they became part and parcel of the Jewish religion. The foreign origins soon were forgotten. How many devout Jews know, even today, that a part of the Seder ritual is of Roman origin? What really concerns the religionist is the present meaning of the content of his religion. The origin of a doctrine, law, or ritual is the concern of the men of the *Jüdische Wissenschaft* who demonstrated time and again that Jewish history and religion must be studied in their relationship to world history and the religions of the world for a better scholarly understanding of the anatomy of Judaism. However, the findings of the modern scholars have no bearing on the significance of the belief or ritual under examination for the man of faith.

In their work of adjusting Judaism to the needs of the day, the rabbis proceeded steadily, but gradually. They kept away from extremes. They did not adhere slavishly to the letter of the law as did some peripheral groups. On the other hand, they did not force the Bible to conform to foreign ideas and philosophies to the extent done by philosophical and sectarian schools. Generally, it may be stated that the rabbis, in effect, judaized whatever foreign law and custom they adopted, while some philosophical schools de-judaized the Bible and consequently the Jewish religion.

To keep Judaism meaningful and livable the rabbis did not merely modify old laws and add new ones but also suspended many an out-of-date law, and shifted a number of laws and practices from the periphery to the center and vice versa.

The rabbis, believing in the eternal validity of the Torah as well as in its divine character, could not abrogate its legal prescriptions. Laws that could not be observed or had lost their significance were either re-interpreted or suspended with the proviso that they would regain their validity as a matter of course as soon as circumstances would permit.

The shifting of laws and practices from the periphery to the center was of paramount importance after the destruction of the Temple, particularly in replacing the sacrificial cult by prayer service. The latter had existed for centuries but had played a secondary role in comparison with the sacrificial cult. Moreover, the shifting phenomenon was concerned not merely with laws and practices, but also with methods employed in molding Judaism. Thus, for example, textual interpretation as a method of modifying the law played a secondary role in Pharisaic-Rabbinic Judaism, prior to the destruction of the Temple, in comparison with some other methods.

Hillel was the first Jewish leader who attempted to place exegesis in general and hermeneutic rules in particular into the foreground as a principal method of modifying law and practice. Hillel realized that the Sanhedrin of his time, lacking the support of the political government, needed another source of authority to introduce changes or to clarify and strengthen old laws and practices. This other source was the Torah as interpreted in a suitable way. Therefore he advocated the employment of certain hermeneutic rules that were in vogue among Greek and Roman students of law and orators of his day, automatically excluding methods which were not in harmony with Judaism as he understood it. Hillel was unsuccessful in this endeavor in his own day primarily because of hesitancy of the sages to accept new ways and their inability to realize, as he did, that rules are often means to justify needed legislation as well as the clarification of law. Furthermore, after Herod's death the Sanhedrin regained some of its power, including jurisdiction in capital cases, so that legislation by interpretation was not of crucial importance. However, after the fall of the Temple, the situation changed fundamentally. The Sanhedrin of old was replaced by an academy called *Beth Din Ha-Gadol* or Sanhedrin, which regulated Jewish life and sought to continue the legislative tasks of the old Sanhedrin. The sages of the academy now realized that the best available source of authority was the Torah if interpreted in the manner Hillel advocated. The resistance to the employment of hermeneutic rules vanished. This is in character with human nature. The new often meets with resistance which dissipates as time passes and an objective evaluation is made. An example of recent date would be the introduction of the sermon in the vernacular in orthodox Ashkenazic synagogues, which at first was vehemently resisted. Another example is the recognition that Judaism and Zionism are compatible, while formerly this was often denied.

The rabbis of the era following the destruction of the Temple did not merely reconsider and utilize the exegetical methods of Hillel, but went much farther than did Hillel himself. They developed what is called the *eisegesis*, the association of new laws with biblical verses, although in reality these laws are not given or implied in the Bible. This was possible not only because of the urgent need for new authoritative legislation, but also because Jewish groups such as the Sadducees, orthodox Pharisees, and Shammaites, who would have opposed such far-reaching methods, became peripheral or sectarian groups after the destruction of the Temple and took no part in the development of Rabbinic Judaism.

Pharisaic-Rabbinic Judaism begins with Hillel two or three decades B.C.E. Rabbinic Judaism proper commences with the destruction of the Temple in 70 C.E. and its end is not yet in sight. However, there is a period of transition between the time of the prophets and Hillel. This period begins at least as early as the Babylonian Exile and is well under way at the time of Ezra, four hundred years before Hillel. Those sources that describe religious life in the Babylonian Exile do not permit one to make safe conclusions in regard to the significance of this period for Rabbinic Judaism. (Divine worship without a sanctuary and without animal sacrifice may have originated in the Babylonian Exile.) Therefore we shall not discuss this period in detail. We shall concentrate on Pharisaic–Rabbinic and Rabbinic Judaism, but will first briefly survey its precursors beginning with Ezra, whose activities in connection with the development of normative Judaism are well documented.

Since the origins of Jewish laws and practices, as noted before, are from the viewpoint of Rabbinic Judaism of little importance, we shall focus our attention on the impact and dynamics of the laws throughout the history of the Jewish people, and how they kept Judaism alive and vibrant.

The best way to observe the making of Rabbinic Judaism is to follow closely the activities of its leadership who saw to it that changes be made, and particularly that new laws, ideas, and practices be introduced, irrespective of their origin or authorship. Therefore, we shall trace the evolution of Rabbinic Judaism through the activities of its leadership, be it represented by an institution, such as the Sanhedrin, or by individuals, such as the *Nesi'im* (patriarchs or princes).

We have not attempted to give an exhaustive history but have tried instead to stress the fundamentals and to point to those important details which illustrate how normative Judaism came into being and why it has remained the mainstream of Judaism throughout the centuries. We hope to shed light on the evolution of Rabbinic Judaism in a manner intelligible not only to scholars but, for the most part, to interested laymen as well.

Abbreviations

BOOKS ARTICLES PERIODICALS

Allon, *Studies*	*Studies in Jewish History* מחקרים בתולדות ישראל
Allon, *Toledoth*	תולדות היהודים בארץ ישראל בתקופת המשנה והתלמוד
Ant.	Jewish Antiquities (Josephus)
ARN I	Avoth De-Rabbi Nathan, Text I
ARN II	Avoth De-Rabbi Nathan, Text II
B.	Babylonian Talmud
Bacher, *Traditionen und Tradenten*	*Traditionen und Tradenten in den Schulen Palästinas und Babyloniens*
Ber.	Bereshith
Büchler, *Das Synedrion*	*Das Synedrion in Jerusalem*
Daube, "Rabbinic Methods"	"Rabbinic Methods of Interpretation and Hellenistic Rhetoric"
Derenbourg, *Essai*	*Essai sur l'histoire et la géographie de la Palestine*
EJ	*Encyclopaedia Judaica*
Elbogen, *Gottesdienst*	*Der jüdische Gottesdienst*
Frankel, *Darkhe*	*Darkhe Ha-Mishna*
Frankel, *Mevo*	*Mevo Ha-Yerushalmi*
Geiger, *Urschrift*	*Urschrift und Üebersetzungen der Bibel*
Ginzberg, *Commentary*	*A Commentary on the Palestinian Talmud*
Ginzberg, *Significance of the Halachah*	*The Significance of the Halachah for Jewish History*

Graetz, *Geschichte*	*Geschichte der Juden*
Guttmann, *Akiba*	*Akiba, Rescuer of the Torah*
Guttmann, *Mischna und Tosephta*	*Das redaktionelle und sachliche Verhältnis zwischen Mišna und Tosephta*
Hoffmann, *Der oberste Gerichtshof*	*Der oberste Gerichtshof in der Stadt des Heiligtums*
HTR	*Harvard Theological Review*
HUCA	*Hebrew Union College Annual*
Hyman, *Toldoth*	*Toldoth Tannaim Ve-Amoraim*
Iggereth	*Iggereth Rav Sherira Gaon*
Jahrbücher	*Jahrbücher für jüdische Geschichte und Literatur*
JBL	*Journal of Biblical Literature*
JE	*Jewish Encyclopedia*
JJS	*Journal of Jewish Studies*
JQR	*Jewish Quarterly Review*
Jüdische Zeitschrift	*Jüdische Zeitschrift für Wissenschaft und Leben*
Juster, *Les Juifs al-anwār*	*Les Juifs dans l'empire romain*
Krauss, *Lehnwörter*	*Griechische und lateinische Lehnwörter in Talmud, Midrasch und Targum*
Lauterbach, *Essays*	*Rabbinic Essays*
Levy, *Wb.*	J. Levy, *Wörterbuch über die Talmudim und Midraschim*
Life	*The Life* (Josephus)
M.	Mishnah
Magazin	*Magazin für die Wissenschaft des Judentums*
Mekhilta	*Mekhilta De-Rabbi Ishma'el*
MGWJ	*Monatsschrift für Geschichte und Wissenschaft des Judentums*
Midr.	Midrash
Midr. R.	Midrash Rabbah
Mielziner, *Introduction*	*Introduction to the Talmud*
O.L.Z.	*Orientalische Literaturzeitung*
n.s.	new series

o.s.	old series
P.	Palestinian Talmud
PAAJR	*Proceedings of the American Academy for Jewish Research*
Pauly-Wissowa	*Real-Encylopädie der klassischen Altertumswissenschaft*
Ps.	*Pseudo*
Qirqisani, *Kitab*	*Kitab al-anwār wal-marāqib*
R.	Rabbi; Rabbah
REJ	*Revue des Études Juives*
Shir R.	*Shir Ha-Shirim Rabbah*
Schürer, *Geschichte*	*Geschichte des jüdischen Volkes*
Strack, *Introduction*	*Introduction to the Talmud and Midrash*
Strack-Billerbeck, *Kommentar*	*Kommentar zum Neuen Testament aus Talmud und Midrasch*
T.	Talmud
Tchernowitz, *Toledoth*	*Toledoth Ha-Halakah*
Tos.	Tosefta
War	*The Jewish War* (Josephus)
Weiss, *Dor*	*Dor Dor We-Dorshaw*
Yer.	Yerushalmi
Zeitlin, *Judaean State*	*The Rise and Fall of the Judaean State*
Zunz, *Gottesdienstliche Vorträge*	*Gottesdienstliche Vorträge der Juden*

TRACTATES OF THE MISHNAH
TALMUD TOSEFTA

A. Z.	*'Avodah Zarah*
B. B.	*Bava Bathra*
Bekhor.	*Bekhoroth*
Ber.	*Berakhoth*
Bik.	*Bikkurim*
B. M.	*Bava Mezi'a*
B. Q.	*Bava Qamma*
'Eduy.	*'Eduyyoth*

Giṭ.	*Giṭṭin*
Ḥag.	*Ḥagigah*
Ḥul.	*Ḥullin*
Ket.	*Kethuvoth*
Kil.	*Kil'ayim*
Mak.	*Makkoth*
Meg.	*Megillah*
Men.	*Menaḥoth*
M. Q.	*Mo'ed Qatan*
Ned.	*Nedarim*
Nid.	*Niddah*
Pes.	*Pesaḥim*
Qid.	*Qiddushin*
R. H.	*Rosh Ha-Shanah*
Sanh.	*Sanhedrin*
Shab.	*Shabbath*
Sheq.	*Sheqalim*
Yad.	*Yadayim*
Yev.	*Yevamoth*
Zev.	*Zevaḥim*

I

SOFERIC PERIOD

EZRA

Although Rabbinic Judaism is the continuation of and heir to Biblical Judaism, the process of transition from the one to the other was not sudden. In fact, Biblical and Rabbinic Judaism (including its precursors, Soferic and Pharisaic Judaism) dovetailed for over 600 years, i.e., from the Babylonian Exile in 586 B.C.E. to the destruction of the Second Temple in 70 C.E. The essential differences between them lie in their respective religious leaderships and in their contrasting philosophies and ways of reacting to the impact of the ever-changing spiritual and material conditions.

The religious leadership in Biblical Judaism lay in the hands of priests and prophets. The conspicuous activities of the priests, the professional leaders were centered in the Temple and were concerned mainly with the sacrificial cult, though priests were also entrusted with teaching (which includes interpreting) the Torah. They held tenaciously to their trust of leadership while warding off their antagonists with varying success. Their earlier antagonists were the prophets, whose role need not be reviewed here. Later (after Malachi) the prophets were supplanted by lay teachers who stressed the rule of the Law (nomocracy) and advocated a larger role for laymen in religious life and in modification of beliefs and practices in order to keep religion in consonance with the changing economic, political, and cultural conditions of life.

The Babylonian Exile proved that the Jewish religion could be modified, since it flourished in Babylonia without the benefit of the Temple cult and priestly leadership. Therefore, it may be said that Rabbinic Judaism reaches back to the Babylonian Exile. However, since the sources give us very little information of the religious life during the Babylonian Exile, we shall start with the period of Ezra for which more source material is available.

In view of the uprisings of Megabyzos in Syria and Inaros in Egypt, Artaxerxes was eager to secure peace and loyalty in the province of Palestine by granting it full religious autonomy.[1] Ezra was granted the privilege of taking charge of the administration of his people in Judea and was armed with extensive power of capital punishment, confiscation, and imprisonment (Ezra 7:21–26). His title (סופר) ספרא (Sofer) *Safra* was, in his time, a designation for a Persian office but was later used by the Jews in a different sense, as a designation for certain religious leaders and also for ordinary scribes.[2]

The fundamental importance of Ezra for the development of Judaism is seen in the fact that by his actions he terminated the trend of Prophetism and replaced it by emphasizing religious precepts and practices. The first and decisive step in this direction was the enforcement of the Torah as the constitution of the Jewish people.[3] Another step in this direction was, according to talmudic accounts, the issuing of תקנות *Taqqanoth*,[4] enactments, as the need arose. B. B. Q. 82a, and P. Meg. IV,1; 75a relate ten *Taqqanoth* in the name of Ezra: 1) reading from the Torah during the Sabbath Minḥah Service; 2) reading from the Torah on Monday and Thursday; 3) holding court session on Monday and Thursday; 4) laundering of clothes on Thursday in honor of the Sabbath; 5) eating garlic on Friday night because it induces love and sexual desire; 6) baking bread early Friday morning so the poor would be supplied; 7) use of a belt or girdle by women so that they would be covered front and rear; 8) washing and combing the hair by a woman before her ritual immersion; 9) travelling of peddlers in the town because of the honor of the daughters of Israel (i.e., selling them cosmetics and adornments); 10) immersion (ritual) for men who experienced a pollution.[5]

4

The Palestinian Talmud counts 1) and 2) as one, and gives one that the Babylonian Talmud does not include: Women should talk to each other while in the toilet (lest men, unaware of their presence, enter).

It is doubtful whether every one of these enactments originated with Ezra and his circle (in which we may safely place Nehemiah). Nonetheless, as a total they point to the areas of Ezra's and his followers' deepest concern: synagogue worship, Sabbath, court procedure, family life and morals, charity, and ritual purity. For centuries to come, these areas commanded central interest in post-Biblical Judaism.

B. *Sanh.* 21b–22a and parallels relate that the Aramaic characters (called by non-scholars inaccurately "Hebrew script") were introduced to the Jews by Ezra. Since Dareios I (521–485 B.C.E.) had introduced the Aramaic language and script (for official purposes) in his empire, the Jews of Palestine, who were under Persian rule, had to follow suit as did the Jews of Elephantine in Egypt. Therefore, there is no reason to doubt the historicity of the above talmudic account.[6]

Ezra was a *kohen*, a "priest," a descendant of Zadok, the first high priest in Solomon's temple. But he was not the high priest of his time nor was Nehemiah. Ezra exercised his authority as a governor appointed by the Persian ruler and was, therefore, not subject to the authority of the high priest. The situation was certainly similar during the entire Persian period. While Joshua was high priest at the time of Darius Hystaspis, the governor of Judea was Zerubbabel. In 408 B.C.E., while Johanan was the high priest, Bagoas was the Persian governor of Judea, as proved by one of the Elephantine papyri.[7]

THE GREAT ASSEMBLY

כנסת   *O*bscurities regarding the הגדולה Great Assembly (or the Great Synagogue) are most numerous. Even its very existence is denied by some scholars.[8] Yet, many independent sources testify not only to its existence, but also to the eminence and importance it possessed. The obscurities concern such details as: when was the Great Assembly founded; how long was it in existence; what caused its termination; how was it organized; what were its functions, its authority, etc.?

According to talmudic sources, the Great Assembly existed long before Ezra. *ARN* relates that the Men of the Great Assembly received the Torah from Haggai, Zechariah, and Malachi.[9] The accuracy of this account may be doubted; yet it is quite possible that this assembly is older than Ezra. Assigning it to Maccabean times would have, in view of talmudic sources to the contrary, little justification.[10] The assembly of the Maccabean period was certainly another body.

The size of the membership of the Great Assembly is controversial. The numbers usually given are 120 (e.g., B. *Meg.* 17b) and 85 (e.g., P. *Meg.* I,5; 70d).[11] The variation of the membership given in the sources can be explained best by assuming that the membership of this assembly actually varied during the many years of its existence.

What were the functions of the *Kenesseth Ha-Gedolah*; what was the extent of its authority?

Josephus does not mention the Great Assembly of the Persian period. This is an indication that it was not a body with political powers. The *Taqqanoth* and *Gezeroth* issued by this assembly show basic similarities to those ascribed to Ezra (and Nehemiah). It is quite possible that the *Taqqanoth* of Ezra are *Taqqanoth* originated or endorsed by the Men of the Great Assembly but transmitted to posterity in the name of the great leader. On the other hand, many *Taqqanoth* issued after Ezra sail under the flag of the Great Assembly. Such *Taqqanoth* are: introduction of various prayers (B. *Ber.* 33ab; B. *Meg.* 17b); introduction of the feast of Purim and the reading of the *Megillah* on Purim (B. *Meg.* 2a); writing (i.e., fixing the text) of the biblical books of Ezekiel, the Twelve Minor Prophets, Daniel and Esther (B. *B. B.* 15a), while the same activity is ascribed to Ezra with regard to the books of Ezra and Chronicles, relating events until his time (ibid.). Also ascribed to the Men of the Great Assembly is the introduction, or invention, of halakhic and aggadic Midrashim (P. *Sheq.* V.1; 48c). The accuracy of this account is more than questionable since we find no case in which the Men of the Great Assembly used a Midrash except for aggadic passages of doubtful authenticity.[12] *Gezeroth*, prohibitive ordinances, are also transmitted in the name of the Men of the Great Assembly as well as in the name of Ezra and other great personalities or leading institutions such as: Haggai, Zechariah, Malachi (Tanḥuma, *Vayeshev*, 4; B. *Pes.* 17a; B. *Yevamoth* 16a); Zerubbabel (Tanḥuma, ibid.); Men of the Great Assembly (B. *Pes.* 50b); Ezra (B. *Yevamoth* 86b); Nehemiah (B. *Shab.* 123b). The historicity of some of these accounts of the *Gezeroth* is questionable, particularly those referring to the prophets. These have the earmarks of later times.[13]

THE SOFERIM

Z. Frankel and others have believed that the members of the Great Assembly had the title סופרים *Soferim*, usually translated "scribes," but actually meaning "sages." [14] They also maintain that after the Great Assembly ended, the designation סופרים was replaced in turn by זקנים "elders," and shortly afterwards by חכמים "wise men" or "sages." The title "scribes" was used in later times as an honorary title.[15] Differing with Frankel, I. H. Weiss and others have held that the "scribes" were sages who received instructions from their superiors, the Men of the Great Assembly, and directed Jewish life accordingly, but were not themselves members of the Great Assembly.[16] While the sources are somewhat obscure they still indicate that the members of the Great Assembly held the title *Soferim*; therefore Weiss' view is to be rejected.

In later times the designation *Soferim* was used quite loosely, even designating simple teachers and copyists; and דברי סופרים "words of the *Soferim*" is often synonymous with דרבנן "words of the rabbis," "rabbinical law." [17]

We do not know the manner in which the (early) *Soferim* issued their *Taqqanoth*, ordinances. The fact that their *Taqqanoth* are

7

never connected with a textual interpretation (Midrash) shows that they possessed great authority and were able to legislate in a direct manner without citing biblical passages for authority. This holds true for all the *Taqqanoth* (and Halakhoth) transmitted in the name of the Great Assembly and also for the *Taqqanoth* of the *Zugoth* (up to Hillel and Shammai). Conjectures to the contrary have no basis. It is noteworthy that we do not find any opposition to the *Taqqanoth* of the Great Assembly (and of the *Zugoth*) as is the case with some *Taqqanoth* issued in later times. The *Taqqanoth* of the Great Assembly cannot be dated.

The *Taqqanoth* issued by the Men of the Great Assembly and Ezra (who may have been a member of the Great Assembly, although this is nowhere explicitly stated) can justifiably be designated as ordinances of the *Soferim* because these men were *Soferim*. Yet there are *Taqqanoth* ascribed to the *Soferim* without mentioning the Great Assembly.[18] Whether these *Taqqanoth* were cleared by the Men of the Great Assembly cannot be ascertained.

Doubtless many laws anonymous in the Mishnah and other tannaitic literature actually originate with the *Soferim* including the Men of the Great Assembly but cannot be identified as such; otherwise we would be able to learn more about the importance of the *Soferim* for the history of the Halakhah. The lofty pronouncement of the Men of the Great Assembly in Mishnah *Avoth* I,1

הוו מתונים בדין והעמידו תלמידים הרבה ועשו סייג לתורה

"Be deliberate in judgement, raise up many disciples, and make a fence around the law" has little or no bearing on the history of the Halakhah. This is merely good advice to the judges and teachers (often the same persons); by no means is it comparable to an order. Therefore the word *seyag*, fence, in this passage is not to be taken in the technical sense of the word. The individual teachers and judges could not possibly be asked to issue their own *seyagim*, "fences," i.e., protective laws. This would have led to chaos.

How long did the Great Assembly continue its existence? What caused its termination? What institution, if any, succeeded it?

Accordingly to Mishnah *Avoth* I,2, Simon the Just was among the remnants of the Great Assembly. This is a clear indication that the Great Assembly terminated its existence in Simon's day. Unfortu-

8

nately, it is uncertain whether the statement refers to Simon I (who lived ca. 300 B.C.E.), Simon II (who lived 100 years later), or some other Simon. We think that the following arguments carry decisive weight: The only high priest Simon called by Josephus "the Just" ὁ δίκαιος is Simon I.[19] According to rabbinic tradition Simon the Just talked to Alexander the Great.[20] Even if the historicity of this tradition is questionable, it shows clearly that when speaking of Simon the Just, the Talmud refers to Simon I. Hence the above *Avoth* passage suggests that the Great Assembly terminated about 300 B.C.E.[21]

A central institution of great prestige, even if it possesses no political power of its own and functions either by order of a political power or with its explicit or tacit approval, as did the Great Assembly, does not vanish from the scene of history without compelling reason. Alexander's conquest of the Orient, including Persia and its province Palestine, doubtless produced sweeping changes. With the end of the Persian rule, offices and institutions established or approved by this rule had to give way to new forms and systems of administration and leadership. This is an additional support for the view that the Great Assembly terminated about 300 B.C.E.[22]

SIMON THE JUST

As a high priest, Simon the Just was not merely a member of the Great Assembly, but was undoubtedly its head. It is generally believed that this was an exceptional case since we do not find other high priests as heads of the Great Assembly. The exception may have been made because Simon's outstanding personality was recognized by the Jewish people as a whole, including the members of the Great Assembly. That Soferic-Rabbinic Judaism considered him as one of its leading representatives is proven by the fact that Simon the Just is the only high priest to be included in the various chains of transmitters of the Torah from Moses down to Hillel and Shammai. All the links in these chains are personalities or groups considered by the rabbis to be the leading religious authorities of their respective times, in the estimation of the Soferic-Pharisaic-Rabbinic position.

While Simon the Just may have been the spiritual head and representative of the entire Jewish people, he was probably not vested with political power. This is in line with the system commonly followed during the Persian rule. Ben Sira praises Simon, a high priest, only because of his endeavors for the Temple,[23] indicating that he possessed no political power. Rabbinic sources (B. *Yoma* 39a and P. *Yoma* VI.3; 43c) refer to his great religious personality and to his religious activities, and describe many miraculous matters related to his high priesthood or occurring during the forty years of his high priesthood.[24]

The historicity of these miraculous, or near-miraculous, occurrences is questionable. Their significance lies in that they emphasize the greatness of Simon, as the God-favored high priest. A Baraitha in B. *Yoma* 39b describing occurrences related to Simon's death adds further qualities to his personality. The most important among these is the prophetic talent he displayed in the year of his death.[25] The sorrow for his death was, according to this source, so deep that the priests refrained from pronouncing God's name while blessing the people.[26]

Little is known about Simon's activity in the realm of the Halakhah. This is an indication that he did not endeavor to make substantial changes in this realm. In this respect he adhered to the high priesthood tradition which objected to innovations as a matter of principle. This conservative trait of his personality made it possible that, though elected head of the Great Assembly (a basically progressive group), he was still acceptable to his priestly brethren and other conservative groups. He possessed the unique personal qualities that unified the divergent groups of the Jewish people.

Neither a *Taqqanah* nor a Halakhah is ascribed to him. An incident in Tosefta *Neziruth* IV,7 (p. 289) reveals his fundamentally negative attitude toward the institution of the *nazir*, a biblical institution, while recognizing its value in exceptional cases.[27] His attitude in the matter is followed by some rabbis of the Talmud (ibid.).

Simon's words in M. *Avoth* I,2 testify to the wide range of his concern: "The world rests on three things: on the Torah, [Temple]

service, and on deeds of loving-kindness." This comprehensive statement includes all the areas basic to Judaism throughout the ages.

ANTIGONOS OF SOKHO

According to M. *Avoth* I,3: "Antigonos of Sokho received it
[the Torah] from Simon the Just." This does not mean, however,
that Antigonos succeeded Simon in every respect. He was not a high
priest as was Simon, and it is questionable whether an institution
possessing the authority and standing of the Great Assembly still
functioned under the leadership of Antigonos. Yet, like the other
personalities enumerated in the chains of transmitters of the Torah,
he must have been the leader of the group which succeeded, directly
or indirectly, the Men of the Great Assembly and were called indi-
vidually "elder," "sage," or "wise man."

Antigonos' significance for the development of the Halakhah is
unknown, since we possess no explicit record of his halakhic activity.
His statement in M. *Avoth* I,3, "Be not like servants who minister
to the master in order to receive reward, but be like servants who
minister to the master not for the sake of receiving reward; and let
the fear of Heaven be upon you," has no halakhic implications. Nor
does the additional dictum in *ARN* II (ed. Schechter, p. 26) pointing
to a reward have other than theological significance.

The statement in Mishnah *Hallah* IV,11 that "Ben Antigonos
brought up Firstlings from Babylon and they would not accept them"
sheds no light on the attitude of Antigonos or of his associates in
this matter, since the identity of Ben Antigonos as a son of Antigonos
of Sokho cannot be ascertained. Besides, some Mishnah texts in *Hallah* read Antinos for Antigonos, a reading which would preclude
any necessary connection between the two men.

The name Antigonos shows that the subject lived during the Greek
or Hellenistic period (i.e., the period of the Diadochs). According
to Bacher[28] he lived in the first century of the Greek rule, which
is probable, though on the other hand the words "received [the
Torah] from Simon the Just" need not be taken literally, i.e., he

11

was not necessarily a direct successor to Simon and may have lived at a somewhat later time. The Hebrew term *qibbel* can be used, in a spiritual sense, as is the case with the term "disciple."

According to the testimony of *ARN* II the schism of the Sadducees originated with some of Antigonos' disciples. This implies that Antigonos lived some time prior to this schism. Unfortunately, the exact date of the schism cannot be established. According to Josephus (*Ant.* XIII.V.9), the Pharisees, Sadducees, and Essenes existed as distinct groups at the time of Jonathan, the brother of Judas Maccabeus, and there is no reason to doubt the veracity of Josephus' statement. This prompts the conclusion that the schism must have occurred earlier. Therefore, it is not probable that Antigonos extended his activities much beyond 200 B.C.E., if at all.

THE GEROUSIA

*T*he possible role of the Gerousia in the history of the Halakhah is obscure. As an institution, Gerousia is not mentioned in talmudic literature. The Hebrew designation זקנים "elders" does not denote a body or an institution, but refers to elders as individuals and corresponds to the later "sages."

Josephus refers to the Gerousia when relating the events of the times prior to the establishment of the Hasmonean rule.[29] This is taken by some scholars to mean that at the establishment of the Hasmonean rule the Gerousia was changed into an institution called Sanhedrin.[30] However, Gerousia is mentioned in the New Testament (Acts 5:21) together with the Sanhedrin, both summoned by the high priest. Yet, Gerousia here could mean "elders," i.e., Pharisaic elders whom he invited to join his Sanhedrin.[31] This conjecture is supported by the fact that the Septuagint translates זקנים in the Pentateuch and Joshua (not in the other books of the Bible) as "Gerousia." II Macc. 4:44 mentions a Gerousia as existing at the time of Judas Maccabeus. Here it is obviously the designation of a body. There are many more references to Gerousia in non-talmudic literature,[32] but they contain no information of distinct value for the history of the Halakhah and shall not be discussed here.

Why the institution of Gerousia is not mentioned in talmudic literature is a matter of conjecture. It is possible that the Gerousia is identical with an institution mentioned in talmudic literature by another name.

For example, some scholars believe that the Gerousia is identical with the Sanhedrin.[33] However, this identification meets with several difficulties which make it unacceptable. The most weighty of these is that no halakhic-legislative activities of the Gerousia are transmitted, though this was the most important function of the Sanhedrin. The only thing that is certain is that the Gerousia possessed administrative functions and some political influence, and was the officially recognized representative body of the Jewish people as evidenced in II Macc. 11:27 by the official letter sent by Antiochus V to the Jewish Gerousia in 165–164 B.C.E.;[34] and in *Ant.* XII,iii.3, where Josephus relates that after his victory at Panea (198 B.C.E.) Antiochus III wrote a letter to his general Ptolemy in which he ordains that the Gerousia, the priests and the scribes of the Temple, and the Temple-singers, be exempted from "the poll-tax and the crown-tax and the salt-tax."

A more plausible explanation for the absence of the Gerousia in talmudic literature is the assumption that it was an institution that played no role of any significance in the history of Pharisaic-Rabbinic Judaism. During the Hellenistic period it was the council headed by the high priest and recognized by the foreign overlords as the official representative of the Jewish people. It is possible that at a later period a smaller council of the high priests also bore the name "Gerousia," functioning in a capacity different from that of the high priestly Sanhedrin. Acts 5:21 may have reference to these two bodies of the high priest.

Jewish councils bearing the name "Gerousia" existed also in Egypt,[35] and probably also in Asia Minor,[36] but these Gerousias possess no importance.

II

PHARISAIC-
EARLY TANNAITIC PERIOD

THE SANHEDRIN

The Hasmonean uprising resulted in a change of leadership of the Jewish people in political, religious, and civil life. The victorious Hasmoneans assumed not only political power but also the high-priesthood. In doing so, they demoted the (Sadducean) dynasty of high priests and terminated the leadership of the aristocratic (and probably pro-Hellenistic) Gerousia. In recognition of their support of the Maccabean uprising, the anti-Hellenistic Hasideans were given a role in the leadership of the Jewish people and in the reorganization of Jewish life along non-Hellenistic or anti-Hellenistic lines. In order to carry out this task, a new body was established and charged with religious and civil leadership of the people. This body was not the spiritual heir to the Gerousia but, in effect, to the ancient Great Assembly.

The designations of this institution in talmudic literature are: סנהדרין Sanhedrin, סנהדרין גדולה Great Sanhedrin, בית דין הגדול Great Court, בית דין Court, בית דין Great Court of Seventy-One, ב״ד הגדול של שבעים ואחד שבלשכת הגזית Great Court in the Hall of Hewen Stone. Since this body was established by anti-Hellenists it stands to reason that its original name was not Sanhedrin, the hebraized form of the Greek συνέδριον synedrion. While *Beth Din Ha-Gadol*, The Great Court, may be an older designation than Sanhedrin, it is possible that the original name was חבר *ḥever*, assembly.[1]

17

The word *synedrion* is widely used in Greek literature where it may have one of the following meanings: assembly, council, or court.[2] Originally, it merely meant the gathering of several persons for a joint talk.[3] In Jewish literature written in Greek, just as in the New Testament, *synedrion* designates a conference, council, or court. Josephus uses it often, usually for a council and occasionally for a court. In the sense of "council" it is used in the Septuagint, Judeo-Hellenistic literature, and by Philo.[4] Yet, in all this literature, *synedrion* refers to the Sanhedrin described in the tannaitic literature only in Josephus and only in connection with Herod's trial (*Ant.* XIV.ix. 3–5), and even the historicity of this exception is questioned by some scholars.

When the term Sanhedrin was introduced in place of the original (or earlier) Hebrew designation cannot be determined. Josephus' record of Herod's trial in *War* (I.x.8,9) does not have the term *synedrion* as does the corresponding account in *Antiquities*. Since *Antiquities* was written twenty years after *War* (i.e., about 93 C.E.), this is taken as an indication that the term Sanhedrin or *synedrion* was not used as a designation for the supreme body referred to in tannaitic literature prior to the fall of the Temple.[5] However, there are indications to the contrary.[6] While the date of the changeover cannot be determined, it must have occurred at a time when antagonism to Greek culture subsided.

Synedrion is used to designate councils of varying importance. The most important of these, the one headed by the high priest, is to be distinguished from the Sanhedrin of the tannaitic literature, as shown by A. Büchler[7] and accepted by most scholars. The first is termed the "political Sanhedrin," the latter "the religious Sanhedrin,"[8] but these designations are not precise. The origins of the high-priestly *synedrion* cannot be traced with certainty. It is certain, however, that during the Roman rule it attained the greatest power after Judea became a sub-province of Rome in 6 C.E. as indicated by Josephus' statement, "After their (i.e., Herod's and Archelaus') death the government became an aristocracy, and the high priests were entrusted with a dominion over the nation" (*Ant.* XX.x.end). The destruction of the Temple in 70 C.E. terminated the high priesthood as well as their *synedrion*.

The institution that played an eminent role in creating and molding Rabbinic Judaism is the one established after the Hasmonean victory by the anti-Hellenistic Hasideans and known by several names. For the sake of convenience, we shall henceforth call this institution "Sanhedrin."

The history of the Sanhedrin may be divided into several periods. The first major period began with its establishment or endorsement by the Hasmonean rulers about 160 B.C.E.[9] and ended with Herod's rise to power in 37 B.C.E.

During Herod's time, after the members of the Sanhedrin that tried him were massacred, a new Sanhedrin was established that continued until, or nearly until, the destruction of the Temple in 70 C.E. Another body sometimes called "Sanhedrin" was constituted after the fall of the Temple and continued until the end of the Patriarchate in 425 C.E.

The authority and functions of the Sanhedrin were not constant throughout the entire period of its existence. They varied greatly, depending on external and internal circumstances. It possessed the greatest power under the Hasmoneans when it enjoyed official recognition. In this period, it had the right to inflict capital punishment and made use of this right. Examples showing this right are the execution of a false witness by the Sanhedrin under Simon ben Shetaḥ, the execution of eighty women by him for practicing witchcraft, and Herod's trial.

At the beginning of the second major period of the history of the Sanhedrin, Herod assumed dictatorial power. During his rule the new Sanhedrin was no more than a great academy, a *Beth Midrash Gadol*, concentrating on study and regulating religious and civil law, without the benefit of support by the political government. The source of its authority was the great prestige of its learned members. On the whole, it was able to continue the more important functions of the former Sanhedrin such as exercising religious leadership, even legislating when necessary, without possessing official executive power. After the Roman annexation of Judea in 6 C.E., the Sanhedrin regained much of its former power. This was due, on the one hand, to the voluntary support of the masses, and on the other hand, to the tolerance or indifference of the Roman rulers who never granted formal recognition to the Sanhedrin.[10]

It is quite certain that it took some time, perhaps several decades, before this Sanhedrin re-constituted at Herod's time regained its right to capital punishment in spite of Josephus' reference to Titus' statement that the Jews always retained this right (*War*, VI,II.4). If Titus' statement reflects the truth, it may have reference to high-priestly courts or to the courts of the puppet kings. The burning of a priest's daughter may have been ordered by a court other than the Pharisaic Sanhedrin. This case, therefore, cannot be cited for the recovery of jurisdiction by this Sanhedrin in capital cases. Decisive, however, is the incident related in M. Sanhedrin V.2: "Ben Zakkai once tested the evidence even to the inquiring about the stalk of figs," and this occurred when he questioned the witnesses of a murder. Since Johanan ben Zakkai was a Pharisaic-Rabbinic leader during the second half of the first century c.e., this incident proves the authority of the Pharisaic-Rabbinic Sanhedrin to exercise the right of capital punishment not long before the destruction of the Temple in 70 c.e. Whether this trial was held before the Small Sanhedrin of twenty-three members, or before the Great Sanhedrin, is immaterial. If the Small Sanhedrin possessed the authority to try capital cases, the Great Sanhedrin certainly did too. The leading role Johanan ben Zakkai played before and after the fall of the Temple suggests that the Great Sanhedrin was the court of this trial.

According to the Talmud (P. *Sanh.* 18a; 24b), the right of capital punishment was taken away (by the Romans) from the Sanhedrin forty years before the destruction of the Temple. This statement is seemingly contradicted by the incident of Johanan ben Zakkai just cited, and possibly by the one concerning the burning of the daughter of the priest and related by Eleazar ben Zadok, about the middle of the first century c.e. It is a recognized fact that here, as elsewhere in talmudic literature, forty is an often used even number and is not to be taken literally. The question is, however, whether here (P. *Sanh.*, loc. cit.) it can be somewhere close to the actual number or not. The following should be helpful in answering this question. At the time of the fall of the Temple, Johanan ben Zakkai was a revered sage. He was the recognized defender of the Pharisees

20

against the Sadducees before the fall of the Temple. This indicates that his activities commenced many years, probably decades, before the fall of the Temple, permitting us to assume that forty is not too far from the actual number, and we do not have to emend ארבעים "forty" into ארבע "four."[11] The remark of Titus (cited above) therefore has reference to the court of the high priest or that of the puppet kings.[12] The reference to these forty years occurs in several sources.[13] The assumption of a scribal error is, therefore, unlikely.

The "Sanhedrin," established after the destruction of the Temple and continuing until the end of the Nasidom in 425, differed from the previous Sanhedrins. In fact, it was not called Sanhedrin for a long time but rather *Beth Din Ha-Gadol*.

In tannaitic literature, this body is described as basically inferior to the Sanhedrin of the Temple era. For example, in *Sifre* Deut. 154 we read, "For [transgressing] a decision [or instruction] of the *Beth Din Ha-Gadol* in Jerusalem one is liable to death, but one is not liable to death for a decision of the court of Javneh."[14] The recalcitrant elder can be subjected to the death penalty only by the Sanhedrin of Jerusalem, not by the court of Javneh or a local court (Mishnah *Sanhedrin* XI,4).

Though in some respects the *Beth Din Ha-Gadol* of Javneh was inferior to the Sanhedrin of Jerusalem, it had a unique advantage over it resulting from the destruction of the Temple. Due to the termination of the centralized Temple service and along with it the high-priesthood and its Sanhedrin, the *Beth Din Ha-Gadol* of Javneh was now the sole, unrivaled authoritative guiding body of the Jewish people, and of the mainstream of Judaism. Therefore, it was able to continue the main function of the Sanhedrin, i.e., guiding Jewish life by interpreting and modifying law in order to maintain a Judaism relevant to life yet true to its historical essence.

FUNCTIONS OF THE SANHEDRIN

The fundamental importance of the Sanhedrin was that it interpreted Judaism authoritatively, modified it as the need arose,

21

and saw to it that its instructions and decisions were put into practice. This basic function remained fairly constant throughout the long history of the Sanhedrin. In addition, the Sanhedrin had other functions, which varied in accordance with changes in the political and cultural history of the people.

Tannaitic descriptions of the functions of the Sanhedrin include both actual and theoretical ones, i.e., functions which the Sanhedrin never had but which are, in the opinion of the Tannaim, among the legitimate functions of the ideal Sanhedrin.

The Mishnah describes the activities, rights, and privileges of the Sanhedrin as follows:

M. *Sanh.* I,5:
A tribe, a false prophet, or the high priest may not be tried except by the court of seventy one; they may not send forth [the people] to a war of free choice except by the decision of the court of seventy one; they may not add to the City or the Courts of the Temple . . . they may not set up sanhedrins for the several tribes . . . and they may not proclaim [any city to be] an Apostate City except by the decision of the court of seventy one.

M. *Sanh.* XI,2:
The elder that rebels against the decision of the court, as it is written, 'If there arise a matter too hard for thee in judgement, between blood and blood, between plea and plea' [Deut. 17:8–13] . . . Three courts were there [in Jerusalem]: one used to sit at the gate of the Temple Mount; one used to sit at the gate of the Temple Court; and one used to sit in the Chamber of Hewn Stone. They [the local courts seeking advice] used to come first to the court that was at the gate of the Temple Mount; and the one would say, "In this way I have expounded and in that way have my fellows expounded; in this way have I taught and in that way have my fellows taught." If they [of that court] had heard a tradition, they told it to them; otherwise they went to that court which was at the gate of the Temple Court; and the one would say, "In this way I have expounded and in that way have my fellows expounded . . . If they had heard a tradition, they told it to them; otherwise they both came in to the Great Court that was in the Chamber of Hewn Stone, whence the Law goes forth to all Israel, as it is written, "From that place which the Lord shall choose" [Deut. 17:10]. If he [the rebellious elder] returned to his own city and again taught as he was wont to teach, he is not yet cul-

pable; but if he gave a decision concerning what should be done, he is culpable, for it is written, "And the man that doeth presumptuously" . . . [Deut. 17:12]; he is not culpable unless he gives a decision concerning what should be done.[15]

M. *Sanh*. XI,4: "He was not condemned to death either by the court that was in his own city or by the court that was in Javneh, but he was brought up to the Great Court that was in Jerusalem."

P. *Sanh*. II,6; 20c: "And they corrected it [the Torah scroll of the king] in accordance with the Scroll in the *'Azarah* under the supervision [or by instruction] of the Court of Seventy-One." [16] However Tosefta *Sanh*. VI,7 has a different version: "They correct it in the Court of the Priests and the Court of the Levites and the Court of the Israelites." [17]

M. *Soṭah* I,4: "They used to bring her [the suspected adulteress] up to the Great Court that was in Jerusalem and admonished her in the same manner as they admonished witnesses in capital cases, and say to her, 'My daughter, much [sin] is caused by wine,' etc."

M. *Soṭah* IX,1: "The rite of the heifer whose neck is to be broken. . . . Three used to come forth from the Great Court in Jerusalem. R. Judah says: Five, etc." — This means that the Sanhedrin of Jerusalem was to delegate a committee for the execution of the prescribed rite [Deut. 21].

M. *Middoth* V,4: "The Chamber of Hewn Stone: there the Great Sanhedrin of Israel used to sit and judge the priesthood; and if a blemish was found in a priest, he clothed himself in black and departed and went his way; and he in whom no blemish was found clothed himself in white and veiled himself in white and went in and ministered with his brethren the priests, etc."

These Mishnah passages show that the Tannaim did not intend to describe the "Sanhedrin" of Javneh, nor to give a historical account of the Sanhedrin of Jerusalem, but rather attempted to describe the *ideal* Sanhedrin. This becomes clear when the Mishnah (*Sanh*. I,5) ascribes to the Sanhedrin the right to judge a tribe, since there were no tribes during the existence of the Sanhedrin. There is no verified instance on record in which a false prophet, or an Apostate City was tried before a Sanhedrin. It is quite certain that no war was waged by Sanhedrin decision.

On the other hand, some of the functions of the Sanhedrin listed in the Mishnah are factual and deserve full credence. M. *Middoth* V,4 is such an instance, for its historicity is well established.

While we have no case on record in which the Sanhedrin tried an "elder that rebels," the Mishnah (*Sanh.* XI,2) describing the procedure, is most important because it informs us that one of the functions of the Sanhedrin was to determine *the* authoritative interpretation of the Law.

Tosefta *Sanh.* III,4 adds the following functions of the Sanhedrin: Ordering the burning of the Red Heifer (Num. 19:1–10); ordering the congregational bullock sacrifice to atone for a certain type of guilt (Lev. 4:13–21) פר העלם דבר של צבור; appointing the king. If these were really among the prerogatives of the Sanhedrin, one wonders why the Mishnah does not mention them.

We know that the Mishnah does not include all the laws. Instead, it concentrates on laws applicable in its own time and laws to be practiced after the hoped-for re-building of the Temple at the time of the restoration of independence. Historical Halakhah is neglected and usually included only if it possessed some degree of importance.[18] If we keep this in mind, the omission of the one or the other function of the Sanhedrin, particularly if it is of questionable historicity, has no significance. However, omission of the Sanhedrin's alleged prerogative to appoint a king is hardly an accident. It reflects the conviction of the Mishnah redactors that this appointment was not among the functions of the Sanhedrin, and this is historically true. Kingship as a rule was hereditary. It is also possible that Judah I, the redactor of the Mishnah, omitted this case because according to his tradition, he was a scion of King David[19] and had, therefore, a claim to the kingship without any action by the Sanhedrin.

The Mishnah does not give a clear-cut picture of all the rights and privileges of the Sanhedrin. M. *Sanh.* I,5 is, for example, worded negatively, enumerating matters which could *not* be acted upon except by the Court of Seventy-One. This wording allows the inclusion of other cases, too. Such cases are, for example, the adjudicating of suits which are within the jurisdiction of the lower courts. An example is given in M. *Sanh.* XI,2 where the Sanhedrin functions as the highest court when the lower courts were unable to decide the case. In other instances the Sanhedrin may have functioned as a supreme court.[20] Two more instances in which the Sanhedrin functioned as the highest court are given in M. *Pe'ah* II,6;[21] and M. *Eduy.* VII,4.[22]

M. *Sanh.* XI,2 tersely denotes the principal function of the Sanhedrin (Tosefta, ibid. VII,1): "from there the Law goes forth to all Israel."

MEMBERSHIP OF THE SANHEDRIN

The sources do not reveal the composition of the Sanhedrin in its early days, i.e., whether it consisted of priests only, or also of laymen, whether of men of higher rank only or also of the lower classes. All that we may safely assume is that it was non- or anti-Hellenistic. At the time of John Hyrcanus I (135–105 B.C.E.) it was at first, predominantly, if not totally, Pharisaic. In consequence of the events related in B. *Qiddushin* 66a and Josephus, *Ant.* XIII.x.6, Sadducees took over the Sanhedrin. At the time of Alexander Jannaeus (105–78 B.C.E.) or Salome Alexandra (78–69 B.C.E.) Simon ben Shetaḥ, a Pharisaic leader (a relative, perhaps a brother, of Salome Alexandra), dismissed the Saducean members of the Sanhedrin and replaced them by Pharisees.[23] It was only at the time of Salome Alexandra that the Sanhedrin became a well-established Pharisaic institution. The Sanhedrin which was newly established at Herod's time and led by Hillel and his descendants was a Pharisaic institution and remained so until its dissolution a short time before the fall of the Temple in 70 C.E. Supporting this contention is the fact that the Sadducee-Pharisee controversies of this period were very few in contrast to the large number of disputes conducted during this time among the Pharisees themselves (e.g., Beth Shammai and Beth Hillel). Even the few Sadducee-Pharisee disputes recorded were probably held outside of the Sanhedrin.

The membership of the *Beth Din Ha-Gadol* from its beginning in 70 C.E. to its end in 425 C.E. consisted throughout of sages (rabbis).

25

Tannaitic sources do not give explicitly the qualifications for membership in the Sanhedrin except for the language requirements.[24] Instead, certain disqualifying factors are listed. A Baraitha in B. *Sanh.* 36b states that no man is appointed who is old, impotent, or has no children. Mishnah *Horayoth* I,4 enumerates several categories of men disqualified to be judges of (ordinary) courts, and therefore unquestionably also disqualified for membership in the Sanhedrin: a proselyte, a bastard, a *Nathin*, and an old man who never had children.

A positive formulation of the qualities required for membership is given by the Amora R. Johanan (third century C.E.): stature, wisdom, appearance, age (knowledge of), witchcraft, and the knowledge of seventy languages, lest the Sanhedrin have to hear (the charges) from an interpreter (B. *Sanh.* 17a). The requirement of knowledge of seventy languages shows that R. Johanan relates not history but theoretical law.

The way of selecting the members is described in Mishnah *Sanh.* IV,4:

> Before them [the members of the Sanhedrin] sat three rows of disciples of the sages, and each knew his proper place. If they needed to appoint [another member], they appointed him from the first row, and one of the second row came into the first row, and one from the third row came into the second; and they chose yet another from the congregation and set him in the third row. He did not sit in the place of the former, but sat in the place that was proper for him.

To Tosefta (*Hag.* II,9) adds the preliminary stages leading to membership in the Sanhedrin:

> From there they sent and investigated. Whosoever was wise and humble and meek and fearful of sin and of unblemished youth and popular with his fellows at first was appointed judge in his own town. From there he was promoted to sit [in court] at the Temple Mount. From there he was promoted to the [court in the] *Hel*, and from there he was promoted to sit in the *Gazith* Hall.[25]

The number of the members is most often given as 71. Mishnah *Sanh.* I,6 states, "The Great Sanhedrin had 71 members." This number is often repeated, as for example, in M. *Sanh*. I.5 which lists the cases under the jurisdiction of this court. Thus there can be no doubt that at the time of the redaction of the Mishnah seventy-one was considered the authentic number. However, some sages give the numbers seventy and seventy-two. Rabbi Judah claims that seventy was the membership of Sanhedrin (Mishnah *Sanh*. I,6; cf. Tosefta, ibid. III,9). Simon ben Azzai, on the other hand, knows of seventy-two members. (M. *Zev*. I.3; M. *Yadayim* III,5; IV,2). However, Ben Azzai refers explicitly to the Academy (=*Beth Din Ha-Gadol*) of Javneh which does not necessarily mean that he ascribes the same number of membership to the Great Sanhedrin of the past.

Some scholars go to a great length to reconcile or to explain these contradictory numbers.[26] It is quite certain that the membership varied in the course of the long history of the Sanhedrin. The method of counting has also something to do with the variation, namely, whether the Nasi and *Av Beth Din* were counted or not. Halakhic considerations may have played a role, too, such as "a court cannot have an even numbered membership." [27]

LOCATION OF THE SANHEDRIN

The seat of the Sanhedrin was Jerusalem and its official meeting place was the לשכת הגזית the *Gazith* Chamber, a part of the Temple located on the southern side of its inner court (Mishnah *Middoth* V,4). *Gazith* is usually understood as meaning "hewn stone," as is its biblical usage.[28] Some scholars[29] believe that Gazith is the Greek word ξυστός *Xystos*, used by the Greeks to designate a *gymnasium*.[30] The Septuagint uses *Xystos* in Amos 5:11 as meaning "polished" (בתי גזית polished houses). Due to inadequate source material the original meaning of *Lishkath Ha-Gazith* cannot be determined. It might be "The hall of hewn stone" as often assumed.

The location of the Sanhedrin in the Temple chamber is significant, for it indicates that the Sanhedrin had an official character and a legitimate role in certain matters concerning the Temple and the priests. Such location also increased the prestige of the Sanhedrin in the eyes of the people.

However, a number of years (forty according to talmudic sources) before the destruction of the Temple the Sanhedrin had to leave its hallowed place in the Temple, and it moved to חנות Hanuth,[31] often translated "market hall," "store hall," or "bazaar." The location of this hall is uncertain. It may have been on the Mount of Olives or on the Temple Mount outside the *Lishkath Ha-Gazith*.[32] The reason for the move is not given, but it was doubtless due to an act of persecution since at that very same time the Sanhedrin was deprived of its jurisdiction in capital cases.

In contrast to the Sanhedrin of Jerusalem the succeeding *Beth Din Ha-Gadol*, "Great Court," had no permanent location hallowed by history and tradition. During its existence it moved

גלתה סנהדרין... מלשכת הגזית לחנות ומחנות לירושלים ומירושלים
ליבנה ומיבנה לאושא ומאושא ליבנה ומיבנה לאושא ומאושא לשפרעם
ומשפרעם לבית שערים ומבית שערים לצפורי ומצפורי לטבריא.

"from Javneh to Usha, from Usha to Javneh, from Javneh again to Usha, from Usha to Shefar'am, from Shefar'am to Beth She'arim, from Beth She'arim to Sepphoris, from Sepphoris to Tiberias) (B. Rosh Ha-Shanah 31ab)."

These frequent moves were necessitated primarily by such disorders as ravaging, pillaging, persecution, economic pressures, and the like caused by Palestine's role as a Roman military base during the Parthian wars.

SESSIONS OF THE SANHEDRIN

The Jerusalem Sanhedrin held daily sessions in the *Gazith* Chamber (Tosefta *Sanh.* VII.1). No sessions were held on Sabbaths and on holidays when the members of the Sanhedrin, instead, went to the *Beth Ha-Midrash* located on the Temple Mount. No particulars are transmitted about this *Beth Ha-Midrash*.

The frequency of sessions of the *Beth Din Ha-Gadol* after 70 c.e.

is unknown and probably varied throughout its existence. The fact that some of the leading members of this *Beth Din* had their own academies outside of Javneh proves that the Javneh *Beth Din* could have been in session only at certain periods.

About those institutions that are designated as Sanhedrin, but served mainly as interim Sanhedrins or did not exercise leadership over the Jewish people, we need make only brief mention.

The five *synedria* established in 57 B.C.E. by order of Gabinius, Pompey's general, may or may not have taken over the functions of the Great Sanhedrin. It is also possible that these were not even Jewish *synedria*.[33]

Besides the Great Sanhedrin and the *Beth Din Ha-Gadol*, there existed the Small Sanhedrin of twenty-three members and other smaller courts, but these exercised no leadership over the Jewish people and played no traceable role in molding Judaism.

LEADERS OF SOFERIC, PHARISAIC, AND RABBINIC JUDAISM

"Leaders" may designate both official and unofficial leaders. Thus King Saul was the official leader of the people, David exercised unofficial leadership over a considerable number of them, and while the priests were official religious leaders, the prophets were unofficial champions of religious life and thought.

At the time of the Persian rule over Palestine, the official religious leadership of the high priest and his circle was challenged by the *Soferim*, the scribes. The scribes were more successful than the prophets, on the one hand, because of the leadership of the Great Assembly, on the other, because they set goals attainable in their own day. The title of the head of the Great Assembly (assuming he had one besides *Sofer* or *Safra*) is not transmitted.

While during the Hellentistic period the Great Assembly was either non-existent or went underground, its activities were continued after the Hasmonean victory by the newly established Sanhedrin. Although the Sanhedrin sometimes had official status and at other times only the character of a private institution, its decisions were practically always communicated by its leaders and mostly appeared under their names.

The early leaders of Judaism, after the Hasmonean victory, were the *Eshkoloth* and the *Zugoth*. Let us survey, in brief, their activities.

THE ESHKOLOTH

*M*ishnah *Soṭah* IX,9 states, "When Jose ben Joezer of Zeredah and Jose ben Johanan of Jerusalem died, the *Eshkoloth* ceased, as it is written, (Mic. 7:1) 'There is no *eshkol* [grape-cluster] to eat, my soul desireth the first ripe fig.'"

This passage informs us that Jose ben Joezer and Jose ben Johanan were the last of the *Eshkoloth*, but it does not indicate the nature of the *Eshkoloth*. The fact that the last *Eshkoloth* were also the first of the (official) *Zugoth* indicates that the institution of the *Zugoth* replaced that of the *Eshkoloth*. It is quite obvious that *Eshkoloth* and *Zugoth* were not identical, otherwise a change in designation would make no sense. As to the *Zugoth*, we know that they were the officially recognized religious (and civil) leaders, vested with authority by the Hasmonean rulers. Did the *Eshkoloth* possess more, less, or a different kind of authority? Let us look at some other sources.

1) Samuel, the Amora (first half of the third century c.e.) explains the word *eshkol* as "a man in whom there is everything." This popular etymology merely reflects Samuel's view that *eshkol* means an outstanding personality. No official standing is indicated (*Sotah* 47b).

2) This passage is repeated in *Temurah* 15b where Samuel makes a more explicit statement to the same effect: "All the *Eshkoloth*

which rose in Israel from the days of Moses until the death of Jose ben Joezer studied Torah like Moses, our master. From then on, they did not study like Moses, our Master."

As with the word *Soferim*, and other designations, *Eshkoloth* is not always used in a technical sense. This is the case here where *Eshkoloth* means outstanding sages, leading religious personalities.

3) Also in *Temurah* 15b an anonymous Baraitha states: "All the *Eshkoloth* that rose in Israel from the days of Moses until the death of Jose ben Joezer were without blemish. From then onward, they had some blemish." What is said regarding the above passage holds true for this Baraitha, which indeed may have been the basis of Samuel's statement, as he could have interpreted blemish as meaning inferiority to Moses in Torah study. Rab Joseph, a later Amora, explains "blemish" as meaning the blemish of the *semikhah* (controversy).

4) Tos. *B. Q.* VIII,13 (362) gives another version of the above Baraitha with significant variants: "All the *Eshkoloth* that arose in Israel from the *death* of Moses until Jose ben Joezer of Zeredah and Jose ben Johanan of Jerusalem were without blemish. After the death of Jose ben Joezer of Zeredah and Jose ben Johanan of Jerusalem until the rise [variant, 'death'] of Judah ben Baba, they could be blamed [they were blemished]. It was said about Judah ben Baba that all of his deeds were for the sake of Heaven. . . ."

5) A similar Baraitha is found in P. *Sotah* IX,10; 24a with a significant variant: It reads *Zugoth* for *Eshkoloth*. This (if not an erroneous version) shows that *Zugoth*, in addition to its technical meaning, was also used to designate leading sages in general.

The fourth passage indicates that the *Eshkoloth*, who lived until Jose ben Joezer's time, were known in tannaitic times as the spiritual leaders of their times, but possessed no official standing. Otherwise, Judah ben Baba, who was neither Nasi nor *Av Beth Din*, certainly would not have been compared to them.

6) An additional indication to the same effect is contained in a statement in P. *Sotah* IX,10; 24a: "No *Eshkol* rose until R. Akiba rose." Akiba was the greatest sage of his day and a spiritual leader, but held no permanent office, if any at all. He was neither Nasi nor *Av Beth Din*, though he may have been acting Nasi for a short time.

Whatever influence he possessed was due to his great spiritual stature. Considering the fact that the Tannaim compare him and Judah ben Baba to the *Eshkoloth* shows clearly that these men were, in their opinion, great spiritual leaders but held no high offices endorsed by the rulers as did, for instance, the *Zugoth*.

The continuation of the above P. Talmud passage, if understood correctly, further clarifies matters: "Were not the *Zugoth Eshkoloth*? No, the difference being that *these* served as leaders; *those*, however, did not serve as leaders."

The decisive point here is the respective antecedents of the pronouns "these" and "those." It is an undeniable fact that the *Zugoth* served as leaders, as the officially recognized heads and vice-presidents of the Great Sanhedrin. The words, "These served as leaders" therefore refer to the *Zugoth*, as properly recognized by the outstanding commentators of the Palestinian Talmud, such as David Frankel and Moses Margolies ad loc. The words "those, however, etc." refer to the *Eshkoloth* who, as spiritual leaders may have surpassed the *Zugoth*, as did Akiba, but were not vested with high office.[34]

All we said above precludes the possibility that the *Eshkoloth* headed the Gerousia, the official central council of the Greek period (300–160 B.C.E.). This council, an aristocratic institution, was headed by the high priest. None of the members of the *Eshkoloth* known by name was a high priest. We mentioned above that the comparison of the *Eshkoloth* with outstanding sages, who held no office, also speaks against the conjecture that the *Eshkoloth* were leading officials of the Greek period.

The answer to the question of the nature of the *Eshkoloth* may be stated thus: They were outstanding sages of the Greek period, probably the leaders of the *Soferim* who, after the dissolution of the *Kenesseth Ha-Gedolah*, continued its work in an unofficial capacity. Their school molded Judaism, in harmony with changing facets of life, as did the later Pharisees and rabbis. It is quite probable that the *Eshkoloth* and their school developed what later was called Pharisaic Judaism, though its origins go back at least as far as Ezra. The Gerousia, on the other hand, corresponds to the later Sadducee leadership and certainly bears spiritual responsibility for the development of Sadducean Judaism.

With the Maccabean victory, the high-priesthood and whatever political power the Gerousia possessed (this was not much, since the real political power was in the hands of the Diadochs; Judea was just a vassal province) was taken over by the Hasmoneans. Subsequently a body (later) called Sanhedrin was entrusted with leadership in religious and civil matters. It is probable that this Sanhedrin is not a newly created institution but an already existing soferic or Hasidean school, last headed by Jose ben Joezer and Jose ben Johanan, which now was recognized as an official institution. If this is so, as we believe it is, then it is safe to assume that Jose ben Joezer and Jose ben Johanan were the last *Eshkoloth* and at the same time the first *Zug*, the first pair of official leaders of the Sanhedrin.

S. Krauss and others[35] suggest that the word *Eshkoloth* represents the Hebrew plural of the Greek *skole*, "school." If so, "the *Eshkoloth* ceased" would probably mean that the two pristine soferic or Hasidean schools headed by Jose ben Joezer and Jose ben Johanan respectively ceased to exist. They were unified and established as one official body. The heads of the two previous schools were nominated president and vice-president (Nasi and *Av Beth Din*) of this new body.

THE ZUGOTH

Zugoth as a term designates the heads of the official Sanhedrin known to have existed during the Hasmonean and Herodian periods. The terminus a quo of the *Zugoth* is controversial. While I. H. Weiss points out that King Joshafat already appointed *Zugoth*, who continued from then on, though with interruptions,[36] others, among them Zunz,[37] believe that the *Zugoth* commenced at the time of John Hyrcanus (135–105 B.C.E.).

The first opinion cannot be substantiated if Zugoth is to be used in its technical sense, i.e., if *Zugoth* refers to the leaders of the official Sanhedrin.

The fact that the third *Zug*, Simon ben Sheṭah and Judah ben Tabbai, officiated under the reign of Alexander Jannaeus (105–78 B.C.E.) militates against late dating of the first *Zug*. The first pair, therefore, must have functioned much earlier.

Since the establishment of the official Sanhedrin was a consequence of the Hasmonean victory, it was, in all probability, organized during the early Hasmonean period. The sources allow no exact dating. Bacher[38] following Graetz,[39] and in accord with Z. Frankel,[40] believes that Jose ben Joezer of Zeredah died as one of the sixty Hasidim who were murdered after backing Alkimos for the high-priesthood (about 160 B.C.E.). A weakness of this view is that it would afford to the second *Zug* an unusually long period, about fifty years. Yet we must consider that there was an interim period between the second and third *Zug*, due to political unrest. Such interim periods occurred several times.

In this connection we shall examine several sources. The *Zugoth* are twice enumerated in the Mishnah. *Avoth*, Chapter I names them without using the term *Zugoth* (cf. *ARN*, ed. Schechter, pp. 27 ff.). They are listed among the transmitters of the Torah, constituting the link between an anonymous group of sages and the descendants of Hillel. Who constitutes this anonymous group?

As stated above, the *Eshkoloth* were the precursors of the *Zugoth*. It stands to reason, therefore, that the *Eshkoloth* are the constituents of this anonymous group. If so, the question of why they were not mentioned explicitly has to be raised. Perhaps it is because they possessed no official standing.[41]

The other Mishnaic reference to the five *Zugoth* is in *Ḥag.* II,2:

יוסי בן יועזר אומר שלא לסמוך; יוסי בן יוחנן אומר לסמוך. יהושע
בן פרחיה אומר שלא לסמוך; ניתאי הארבלי אומר לסמוך. יהודה בן
טבאי אומר שלא לסמוך; שמעון בן שטח אומר לסמוך. שמעיה אומר
לסמוך; אבטליון אומר שלא לסמוך. הלל ומנחם לא נחלקו. יצא מנחם
נכנס שמאי. שמאי אומר שלא לסמוך; הלל אומר לסמוך. הראשונים היו
נשיאים, ושניים להם אבות בית דין.

Jose ben Joezer says: One may not perform the *semikhah*; Jose ben Johanan says: He may. Joshua ben Peraḥyah says: He may not; Nittai the Arbelite says: He may. Judah ben Tabbai says: He may not; Simon ben Shetaḥ says: He may; Shemaiah says: He may; Avtalion says: He may not. Hillel and Menahem did not differ. Menahem left and Shammai entered. Shammai says: He may not perform the *semikhah*; Hillel says: He may. The first ones [of each pair] were Presidents, and the second ones were Fathers of the Court.

This passage includes two important pieces of information: 1) The person mentioned first in each *Zug* is the Nasi, the second the *Av Beth Din*; 2) The Nasi and his *Av Beth Din* differed in matters of *semikhah*. The only exception was the *Zug* of Hillel and Menahem; but when Menahem left,[42] his successor, Shammai, again differed with the Nasi.

The first bit of information is unequivocal and leaves no doubt as to the official standing of the *Zugoth*. They were the official heads of the *Beth Din*, or the "Sanhedrin," the central body entrusted with the conduct of religious and civil matters. Josephus' omission of a description of the institution of the *Zugoth* and the Sanhedrin they headed is a clear indication that they possessed no political power.

The meaning of the second piece of information, i.e. לסמוך "to lay," and שלא לסמוך "not to lay" (the hands on . . .), is controversial.

Tosefta *Ḥag.* II,8 states:

מימיהם לא נחלקו אלא על הסמיכה. חמשה זוגות הן; שלשה מזוגות הראשונים שאמרו שלא לסמוך היו נשיאים ושנים אבות בית דין. שנים מזוגו תהאחרונים שאמרו לסמוך הוו נשיאים ושניים אבות בית דין דברי ר' מאיר וחכ' אומרים שמעון בן שטח היה נשיא ויהודה בן טבאי אב בית דין.

They never disagreed, except in the matter of the *semikhah*. There are five *Zugoth*. Three of the first *Zugoth* who said not to perform the *semikhah* were Nesi'im, the second ones Heads of the *Beth Din*. These are the words of R. Meir. But the sages say Simon ben Shetaḥ was Nasi and Judah ben Tabbai *Av Beth Din*.

Subsequently (no. 9. p. 235), R. Jose states that originally there were no disagreements in Israel. This is explained as meaning that all the problems had been worked out within a *Beth Din* of twenty-three

35

members; or if this were not possible, the final decision was made by the Great *Beth Din*, which was located in the Chamber of Hewn Stone. If a tradition existed in the matter, it was communicated to them (the enquirers); otherwise, the decision was rendered by vote. However, this state of affairs changed and disputes multiplied when there was an increase in the number of Shammai's and Hillel's disciples who did not study properly.

Of particular interest is the following passage (Tosefta, ibid. 11,10):

איזו היא סמיכה שנחלקו עליה בית שמאי או' אין סומכין ביום טוב
שלמים שחגג בהן סומך עליהן מערב יום טוב ובית הלל אומ' מביאין
שלמים ועולות וסומכין עליהן.

"About what *semikhah* do they differ? Beth Shammai say one must not perform the *semikhah* on a holiday. He should lay [hands] upon the peace offerings he is to sacrifice [on the holiday] the day before. Beth Hillel, however, say one may bring peace and whole offerings [on the holiday] and lay his hands upon them."

A long discussion follows in which both Beth Shammai and Beth Hillel try to justify their respective views. In II:11 (p. 236), an incident is related in which Hillel himself acted in accordance with the view defended by Beth Hillel. This proves that Hillel himself understood the *semikhah* controversy as referring to the laying of the hands upon the sacrificial animal.[43]

The context of the Mishnah (ibid. 3) also shows that this is the real meaning of *semikhah* in Mishnah 2 and parallels. Both Talmudim understand it similarly. In B. Ḥag. 16b, R. Johanan understands *semikhah* as described above and is not contradicted, and so does P. T. ibid. 77d; II,2 (cf. also *Beẓah* 20a).

Since the sources clearly indicate in context that the *semikhah* of the *Zugoth* has reference to laying the hands upon certain sacrifices (on a holiday), why have modern scholars suggested so many, more or less fancy, explanations?[44]

Since the *Beth Din Ha-Gadol* decided all the other issues, among them a number of far more important matters, why did they not decide also the *semikhah* controversy? To answer this puzzling question, the scholars try to interpret this *semikhah* as being something of paramount importance.[45]

This premise is certainly correct. Yet, the importance of a matter is not necessarily inherent. A matter may become very important in a certain setting. Sometimes, an originally insignificant matter may become a shibboleth, dividing people and keeping them apart.

In other instances, the implications of an unimportant matter may be quite weighty. According to Z. Frankel this is the case in our instance. Frankel understands our *semikhah* as does the Talmud. In his opinion, the importance of the matter is that by prohibiting sacrifices without the *semikhah*, i.e., without the owner's (dedicator's) laying hands upon it, people from remote areas could not send sacrificial animals to the Temple. To prevent this, the members of the Sanhedrin refrained from deciding the issue. He makes reference to *Bezah* 20 where, according to one opinion, the real issue is whether certain sacrifices require *semikhah* or not. Further, he points out that various kinds of donations and sacrifices were sent to Jerusalem from far away during the time of the Second Temple and cites Philo's pronouncement that he himself went to Jerusalem in order to pray and sacrifice there.[46]

While this explanation seems quite plausible at first glance, it has a weakness that cannot be overlooked. If no decision was made *in favor* of compulsory *semikhah* because of reasons stated, a decision *against* such a requirement was certainly possible. This is all the more so since the first three members of the *Zugoth*, who were opposed to the *semikhah*, were the heads of the Sanhedrin and certainly would have prevailed in case of a vote. A further weakness of Frankel's theory is that it would ascribe stringency in this case to Hillel and Beth Hillel. If this were true, the Talmud would not have failed to point out this fact, as it does in all the other instances in which Beth Hillel hold a strict point of view compared with Beth Shammai.

The crucial importance of the matter is shown by the Shammaites' threatening Hillel with lynching when Hillel acted in accordance with his view on the *semikhah*, because this threat indicates that the *semikhah* question was the obvious shibboleth of the two principal Pharisaic factions, which could not be decided by a vote. A vote in this matter probably would have resulted in a withdrawal of the losing faction from the Great Sanhedrin. It is possible that when the two Pharisaic groups joined in the establishment of the Great Sanhedrin, they agreed not to force the issue of the *semikhah* which they considered to be the sine qua non of their respective factions.

Why the *semikhah* issue became *the* dividing issue of the two main Pharisaic groups is a matter of conjecture. It may have been the main issue or even *the* issue which caused the early Pharisees to split into two groups. Of course, at its beginning it must have been a significant issue in order to lead to such grave consequences. The significance of the issue may lie in the following.

If we take a close look at the implications of this controversy, we see that it resembles some of the controversies between the Sadducees and Pharisees. The controversial *semikhah* was to be performed by the owner (dedicator of the animal), usually a *layman*. The performance of the sacrificial cult was a prerogative of the *kohanim*, the priests. They were commanded to do the work constituting the sacrificial process even on the Sabbath and holidays, including acts that were otherwise prohibited. Allowing a layman to perform an act like the *semikhah*, which is an initial part of the sacrificial process, on a holiday (otherwise prohibited because of *Shevuth*, a low degree of prohibition), means that he is granted a privilege in an area in which the priests alone enjoyed privileges. This was certainly not to the liking of the priests. It is a fact that the member of the first Zug to oppose this *semikhah* was Jose ben Joezer, a priest himself (S. Mishnah *Ḥag.* II,7), though his opponent Jose ben Johanan was also a priest.

Yet, even if it is true that the *semikhah* controversy originated in an atmosphere of tension between priests and laymen, it was not kept on this level. The later opponents of our *semikhah* were also non-priests. What probably happened was that the matter developed into the principal dividing issue of two Pharisaic groups, while the original reason of the dispute had been forgotten. The conservative group opposed the *semikhah* on holidays believing this to be in line with true conservatism; the liberal and more progressive group permitted it considering it to be the true liberal point of view.[47]

Among additional problems presented by the *Zugoth* is the chrono-logical difficulty that the span of the five *Zugoth* comprises more than 160 years (ca. 160 B.C.E. to between 10 and 20 C.E.). This would lead us to the highly unlikely conclusion that a *Zug* officiated, on the average, more than thirty years; yet, we have to keep in mind that the rule of the five Pharisaic *Zugoth* was repeatedly interrupted by Sadducees[48] whom the Rabbinic-Pharisaic tradition does not care to mention. Other breaks in the line of Pharisaic *Zugoth* may have been caused by Gabinius' measure of decentralization and the es-tablishment of five Sanhedrins[49] plus Herod's massacre of the sages who participated in his trial.

The theory that the Mishnah only mentions the most distinguished *Zugoth*, who disagreed on the *semikhah* issue, [50] is not tenable. Had other *Zugoth* existed, too, their names would have been transmitted also in connection with their sayings, views, actions, etc. It would be quite absurd to suppress their names and activities just because they did not disagree on the *semikhah* issue.

More puzzling is the fact that we find no overlapping of members of the *Zugoth*. It appears as if Nasi and his *Av Beth Din* began and terminated their respective offices simultaneously. An obvious ex-ception is the last *Zug*, in which Menahem was replaced by Sham-mai during Hillel's presidency. It is natural that after an interim period, when Pharisees regained their power, Nasi and *Av Beth Din* were installed in their offices simultaneously. But when this was not the case, we face a riddle. The same problem exists with regard to the death or retirement of Nasi or *Av Beth Din*. When a Nasi or an *Av Beth Din* died (or retired), did the surviving member of the *Zug* retire to make room for a new *Zug*; or did he continue in his office with the next Nasi or *Av Beth Din*? The sources are silent on this matter.

The degree of authority vested in the Nasi and the *Av Beth Din* varied throughout the period. This matter will be discussed later. Let us now turn to the activities of the *Zugoth*.

ZUG 1

JOSE BEN JOEZER OF ZEREDA, JOSE BEN JOHANAN OF JERUSALEM

Jose ben Joezer was the Nasi, while Jose ben Johanan was the *Av Beth Din* (Mishnah *Ḥag.* II,2). Jose ben Joezer is designated as the חסיד שבכהונה (ibid. 7). This may mean "the most pious among the priests," but *ḥasid* may also imply that he belonged to the Ḥasidim, occasionally a synonym for Pharisees. Above we referred to the view that he was martyred among the sixty Ḥasidim about 160 B.C.E. His statement in regard to the (unquestionably "Pharisaic") sages speaks clearly for his attachment to the Pharisees, "Let thy house be a meeting place for the sages and sit amid the dust of their feet and drink in their words with thirst" (*Avoth* 1.4).

In the field of the Halakhah, the following views are transmitted in the name of Jose ben Joezer (M. *Eduy.* VIII,4; B. *Pes.* 16a; B. *Ned.* 19a; B. *A. Z.* 37b):

"Jose ben Joezer of Zereda testified that the Avil-locust is clean; and that the liquid [that flows] in the shambles [in the Temple] is not susceptible to uncleanness; and that he that touches a corpse becomes unclean; and they called him 'Jose the Permitter.'"

While the first two statements are clear, the last one is quite obscure and subject to interpretations. Of the reasons suggested in B. *A. Z.* 37b Frankel, for example, adopts the view that leniency in this case is that only the person touching the corpse becomes unclean, but he does not transmit this defilement to others.[51] I. H. Weiss accepts the reason that the leniency is that only the person who certainly touched the corpse becomes unclean; but in case of a doubt, the person remains clean. He considers this a ruling necessitated by the Maccabean war which was raging at the time.[52]

There are more conjectures about the matter;[53] but it is not necessary to repeat them here, since they are not superior to the two cited. No matter what conjecture we accept, the fact remains that Jose expressed a lenient view in the matter.

Except for the *semikhah* issue and these three cases, all halakhic decrees of their time are transmitted in the names of both Jose ben Joezer *and* Jose ben Johanan.

In B. *Shab.* 15a (and parallels) Jose ben Joezer and Jose ben Johanan decreed (גזרו) uncleanliness over the lands of the (non-Jewish) peoples and over the vessels of glass.

The reasons for these ordinances are not given. I. H. Weiss believes that Jose ben Joezer and Jose ben Johanan decreed defilement over foreign lands in order to discourage people from emigrating from Palestine because of wars and unrest. As to the glass vessels, Weiss believes that they were declared unclean after it was learned that glass has some qualities similar to that of clay.[54] L. Ginzberg, while concurring with Weiss in the first case assumes (as does Tchernowitz) in the second instance that there were economic reasons. Import of glass — a very expensive luxury item at the time — was economically unsound.[55] Tchernowitz tries to prove that *erez ha-ammim* does not designate foreign countries, but places in Palestine with a total or almost total gentile population.[56] The purpose of the ordinance was to boycott the foreign gentiles and to prevent Jews from living among them and learning their ways. After the Hasmonean victory, this *gezerah* lost its meaning and was therefore discontinued. Yet, eighty years before the fall of the Temple, during Herod's rule, conditions changed for the worse; and the *gezerah* concerning the land of the gentiles was revived. It was reinstituted in regard to gentile settlements within Palestine and subsequently extended to foreign countries in order to curtail emigration, which increased close to the time of the destruction of the Temple.

Whatever the true reason was, the significance of the matter is that the decrees were issued not by the Sanhedrin nor by its head (as was the case at a later period), but jointly by the two leading officers of the Sanhedrin. As soon as times changed, the ordinances lost their binding strength without a formal declaration.

As to Jose ben Joezer's further activities, only two are transmitted. In B. *A. Z.* 37b, R. Juda (ben Ilai) relates that Jose ben Joezer sank posts in the ground in order to mark the borderline between private and public domain. The Talmud understands this (ibid.) in relation to his lenient view in the matter of defilement by a corpse.

B. *B. B.* 133b records that he donated his property to the Sanctuary, thus disinheriting his unworthy son.

As to Jose ben Johanan, no halakhic view of his own has been transmitted apart from his stand on the *semikhah* issue. *Avoth* I,5 gives his saying concerning human relations and morals, "Let thy house be opened wide and let the poor be the members of your household and talk not much with women."

The first *Zug* differs from the subsequent *Zugoth* inasmuch as it is designated as the end of the *Eshkoloth*.

ZUG 2

JOSHUA BEN PERAHYAH,
NITTAI THE ARBELITE

Only one halakhic opinion is transmitted in the name of Joshua ben Perahyah.

In Tos. *Makhshirin* III,4, Joshua ben Perahyah says, "Wheat that comes from Alexandria is unclean because of their [the Egyptians'] vessels [water-drawing device]. The sages said, "If so, let them be unclean for Joshua ben Perahyah but clean for all Israel."

Frankel[57] attempts to explain the basis of this controversy as halakhic. While the formal reason may well have been a halakhic one, it is quite possible that Joshua ben Perahyah has an economic consideration in mind: curtailment of imports from Egypt.[58]

It is doubtful whether the sages opposing Joshua ben Perahyah were his contemporaries. The sages could have been of a later epoch. It is not unusual that opinions uttered in different epochs are given next to one another and appear at first glance as a dispute of contemporaries. Tchernowitz, assuming that the sages here were contemporaries of Joshua, advances another economic reason: An embargo on Egyptian imports of produce would result in high prices in Palestine and the poor would suffer.[59] I. H. Weiss presents the interesting conjecture[60] that declaring Egyptian wheat unclean would render the meal sacrifices of the Onias Temple unproper and unacceptable. Joshua's decision was, therefore, directed against the Onias Temple. If this were the case, the objection of the sages declaring Alexandria wheat clean for all Israel would not be understandable.

We note the saying of Joshua ben Peraḥyah in *Avoth* I,6, "Provide thyself with a teacher and get thee a fellow [disciple]; and when thou judgest any man, incline the balance in his favor." This shows the great importance he ascribes to disciplined, systematic study. It also points to his love of mankind and his belief in man.

In B. *Men.* 109b, a Baraitha relates a statement by Joshua ben Peraḥyah in which he says that when he was first asked to accept his high office, he objected strongly. Now, however, he would vehemently object to any attempt to depose him. He compares his predicament to that of King Saul who first fled when the high honor of kingship was to be bestowed upon him. Yet, after he had become king, he sought to kill David in defense of his high office.

The authenticity of Joshua ben Peraḥyah's authorship of this statement is questionable. In P. *Pes.* VI,I; 33a, the matter is transmitted in the name of Rabbi Joshua ben Kabsav.[61]

Except for the *semiḵhah* controversy, we do not find an halakhic view uttered by Nittai the Arbelite.

A statement of warning is transmitted in his name in *Avoth* I,7: "Keep thee far from an evil neighbor and consort not with the wicked; and lose not belief in retribution."

This statement is interpreted as having reference to political conditions of the time. Frankel[62] proposes that Nittai uttered his warning after John Hyrcanus joined the Sadducees and turned against his former friends the Pharisees.

ZUG 3

JUDAH BEN TABBAI, SIMON BEN SHETAH

According to Mishnah *Ḥag.* II,2, Judah ben Tabbai was the Nasi, while Simon ben Shetaḥ was *Av Beth Din*. *Avoth* I,8 mentions Judah ben Tabbai before Simon ben Shetaḥ, indicating the same view. Other sources, however, claim that Simon ben Shetaḥ was the Nasi, while Judah ben Tabbai was *Av Beth Din*. In B. *Ḥag.* 16b, a Baraitha records a controversy about the matter.

P. *Ḥag.* II,2; 77d cites incidents supporting both views. However none of these incidents has the weight of evidence. More significant is *Qid.* 66a, where it is stated that after the massacre of the sages by John Hyrcanus, the world was desolate until Simon ben Shetaḥ came and reestablished the Torah (Pharisaic tradition) to its pristine state.

This means that he played the leading role, if not the exclusive one, in reestablishing the Pharisaic domination of the Sanhedrin and consequently of religious and civil life. It is hardly imaginable that this great deed could have been performed by the man second in rank. The fact, assuming it is a fact, that Simon ben Shetaḥ was the brother-in-law of King Alexander Jannaeus certainly contributed to his leading role among the Pharisees. Nonetheless, the sources crediting the leadership to Judah ben Tabbai cannot be brushed aside lightly. It is quite possible that there was a change in leadership (as was the case later with Hillel and Shammai). Sources allow no safe inference as to any reason for a change. The marriage of Salome (Simon's sister) to the King may have resulted in Simon's advancement to the presidency. It is also possible that the *Av Beth Din* succeeded his colleague as Nasi after the latter's death or retirement. Moreover there are other conjectures, which we cannot discuss here.

What were the halakhic activities of this *Zug*?

The Talmud ascribes the institution of the *kethuvah* to Simon ben Shetaḥ (B. *Shab.* 16b). This claim in *Shabbath* is inaccurate. Other passages in both Babylonian and Palestinian Talmudim show that the Kethubah was an older institution; Simon ben Shetaḥ merely strengthened it by the *Taqqanah*, ordering that the property of the husband serve as security for the *kethuvah*.[63] This *Taqqanah* represents a most important step toward improving the situation of the Jewish woman and is expressed in every *kethuvah* document to date.[64]

Another *Taqqanah* ascribed to Simon ben Shetaḥ is the defilement of metal vessels (B. *Shab.* 16b; P. *Ket.* end of chapter VIII; 32c).

This *Taqqanah* is ascribed to both Judah ben Tabbai and Simon ben Shetaḥ.

Since a *Taqqanah* was, as a rule, issued by either the Nasi or jointly by Nasi and *Av Beth Din*, Simon ben Shetaḥ was Nasi when he proclaimed the *Taqqanah* concerning the defilement of vessels, if B. *Shab.* 16b gives the accurate record. Should the P. Talmud report be accurate, no safe conclusion may be drawn.

The sources attest to Simon ben Shetaḥ's participation in several cases involving capital punishment.

Regarding the controversy about the false witnesses, a bone of contention between the Pharisees and Sadducees, we may first of all cite a particular incident in which according to the majority of the sources (Tos. *Sanh.* VI,6; B. *Ḥag.* 16b; B. *Mak.* 5b; P. *Sanh.* VI,3; 23b), Judah ben Tabbai had sentenced a false witness, ordered his execution and was subsequently reprimanded by Simon ben Shetaḥ. The law requires, the latter said, that both witnesses be found false, while in this case only one witness had been convicted of falsehood. However in another source (*Mekhilta Mishpatim*, Chapter 20, ed. Horowitz-Rabin, p. 327), Simon ben Shetaḥ was the sentencing judge and Judah ben Tabbai was the man who reprimanded his colleague.

This incident is interpreted by some scholars as the cause of Judah ben Tabbai's descent to the vice-presidency and Simon ben Shetaḥ's ascent to the presidency.[65] Had this been the case, one or the other of the several versions of the incident certainly would have mentioned this important fact explicitly as in the case of Hillel. What this case clearly reveals is that only one member of the *Zug* was present at the trial and that he was held responsible by the other member of the *Zug*.

Since the duties of the Nasi went far beyond that of the heading of a court, and he could not, therefore, be regularly present at trials, the sentencing judge in this case may have been the *Av Beth Din*.[66] While most sources give Judah ben Tabbai as the head of the sentencing court, which he may have headed as the *Av Beth Din*, other incidents indicate that the office of the Nasi was unquestionably in the hands of Simon ben Shetaḥ. The importance of this case lies in the fact that Pharisaic courts of the time had original jurisdiction in legal matters, even when capital punishment was involved.[67]

The Talmud relates an enigmatic case in which Simon ben Shetaḥ ordered the hanging in Ashkelon of eighty women sentenced for witchcraft.[68] The historicity of this incident as transmitted is questionable. First of all, it is doubtful whether Ashkelon was a Jewish city at that time. Further, hanging was never a Jewish method of execution, and according to Jewish Law only one capital case may be tried in one day, not even two. (The assumption in our case is that the women hanged in one day had also been tried together.) Many attempts — more or less vague conjectures — have been made to resolve the difficulties.[69] However the significance of the incident appears to be the following.

This was a most important and exceptional case involving many persons (eighty may be an inflated number) and it concerned the violation of an important precept of the Torah. The supreme authority in this case was Simon ben Shetaḥ, obviously Nasi at that time.

Another incident of capital punishment concerns the son of Simon ben Shetaḥ. P. *Sanh.* XI,3; 23b relates that false witnesses testified against Simon ben Shetaḥ's son, resulting in a death sentence. The motive behind the false testimony is believed to be revenge on the part of the executed witches' relatives. Although the witnesses confessed prior to the execution that they had lied, and Simon wanted to revoke the sentence, his son insisted that the sentence be carried out for the following reason. He said, "Father, if you want victory תשועה [or salvation] to come through you, make me a threshold [or target אסקופה]," i.e., a martyr. The meaning of these words is obscure. "Victory" may refer to the struggle between Sadducees and Pharisees or simply to the strengthening of the accepted judicial procedure which, under the given circumstances, would not allow a reversal of the sentence.

Simon ben Shetaḥ's strict adherence to the accepted judicial procedure is also reflected in an incident related in P. *Sanh.* IV,9; 22b; and B. *Sanh.* 37b (a Baraitha). (*Mekhilta*, loc. cit. gives Judah ben Tabbai in place of Simon ben Shetaḥ.) The Baraitha in B. *Sanh.* 37b relates, "R. Simon ben Shetaḥ said: May I never see comfort if I did not see a man pursuing his fellow into a ruin, and when I ran after him and saw him, sword in hand with blood dripping from it, and the murdered man writhing, I exclaimed to him: Wicked man, who slew this man? It is either you or I! But what can I do, since thy blood [life] does not rest in my hands, for it is written in the Torah, *At the mouth of two witnesses, etc., shall he that is to die be put to death.* May He Who knows one's thoughts exact vengeance from him who slew his fellow! It is related that before they moved from the place a serpent came and bit him [the murderer] so that he died."

The quotation that two witnesses were required does not mean that here in our case the obvious murderer could not be brought before the courts because there was only one witness but that circumstantial evidence cannot be admitted (cf. *Tosafoth* ibid.). The context in the Talmud requires this interpretation since the incident is cited to illustrate the statement of the M. *Sanh.* IV,5, "How did they admonish the witnesses in capital cases? They brought them in and admonished them [saying] 'Perchance ye will say what is but supposition.'" This interpretation finds further support in the fact that Simon ben Shetah did not witness the actual crime, merely the circumstances before and after the murder.[70]

The Talmud (B. *Sanh.* 19ab) relates an incident in which Simon ben Shetah plays an eminent role. This incident so greatly resembles the account of Herod's trial conducted by the Sanhedrin under Sameas-Shemaiah as found in Josephus, that we probably have the very same case under discussion in both passages. We shall discuss this below.

A Mishnah and its parallel versions [71] report that Simon ben Shetah did not like Honi's method of asking God for rain and would have excommunicated him, were it not that Honi was a special favorite before God. This unusual incident reveals that the Nasi — Simon was obviously Nasi at this time — had the power to excommunicate sages and may have used this power in other cases. It also shows that he considered tempting God to be a sin.

We have an interesting account in *Megillath Ta'anith* describing the significance of the 28th of Tebeth. On this day, the Sadducean Sanhedrin was replaced by a Pharisaic one. This was accomplished through the halakhic excellence of Simon be Shetah, the only non-Sadducean member of the Sadducean Sanhedrin.[72]

The historicity of the reason given by *Megillath Ta'anith* — Simon's halakhic superiority over the Sadducees — is questionable. The more probable reason for the changeover was the influence Simon possessed at court after King Alexander Jannaeus had married Simon's sister Salome Alexandra. The presence of both Alexander Jannaeus and Salome Alexandra at the session in which the changeover reportedly took place supports this suggestion.[73]

Except for the case of the false witness, nothing of Judah ben Tabbai's halakhic activities has been transmitted. This may be taken as a further indication that he was Nasi, for only a short period, if at all. His saying in *Avoth* I,8 shows his deep interest in a thorough and equitable judicial procedure, "Make not thyself like them that would influence the judges [or: Make not thyself like the chief justice]; and when the suitors stand before thee, let them be as wicked men; and when they have departed from before thee, let them be in thy eyes as innocent, so soon as they have accepted the judgment."

ZUG 4

SHEMAIAH AND AVTALION

Talmudic tradition holds that both, Shemaiah and Avtalion, were proselytes (cf. B. *Yoma* 71a: B. *Git.* 57b), but the historicity of this tradition is questionable.[74] More probable is the suggestion that they lived in Alexandria, where they had studied with Judah ben Tabbai, who fled there because of John Hyrcanus' persecutions of the Pharisees.[75]

The great prestige that Shemaiah and Avtalion enjoyed is demonstrated in the following account (*Yoma* 71b, a Baraitha): "It once happened that when a high priest left the Sanctuary, all the people followed him. However when they saw Shemaiah and Avtalion, they left the high priest and followed Shemaiah and Avtalion."

In this incident, Shemaiah and Avtalion are called בני עממין, an expression usually meaning gentiles, and one considered by Weiss and others as evidence that they came from gentile stock.[76] More plausible, however, is the suggestion that these words, used in a derogatory sense, point to the fact that they came from Alexandria, or that they were only laymen. The incident also clearly shows the rivalry between high priests and Pharisaic leaders. Who the high priest was is a matter of speculation.[77]

The Talmud indicates that Shemaiah and Avtalion were not merely (Pharisaic) leaders but also heads of the Sanhedrin. In B. *Pes.* 70b a Baraitha relates that Judah ben Dortai said if Elijah were to come and reproach Israel because they did not sacrifice the Ḥagigah (a private sacrifice) on Sabbath, the answer would be that Shemaiah and Avtalion, great sages and great interpreters (or: preachers) did not tell Israel that the Ḥagigah took precedence over the Sabbath.

This means that the decision of Shemaiah and Avtalion was considered authoritative in the matter, which would not have been the case if they had spoken as private individuals. They obviously spoke in the name of the Great Sanhedrin and as its heads.

A number of halakhic activities are traced to Shemaiah and Avtalion in the sources.

M. *'Eduy.* V,6 and *Sifre*, Num. 7 relate an incident informing us that Shemaiah and Avtalion administered the bitter water (arranged a *Soṭah* Procedure) to Karkemith, a freed bondwoman. This was done according to M. *Soṭah* I,5, at the Eastern Gate of the Temple. Since the execution of the *Soṭah* process was a priestly function, and Shemaiah and Avtalion were not priests as far as we know, they were undoubtedly the authorities who ordered the process which then was performed by the priests.[78]

In M. *'Eduy.* I,3, Hillel says, "One *hin* of drawn water renders the immersion-pool unfit. [We speak of hin] only because a man must use the manner of speaking of his teacher."[79] And Shammai says, "Nine *qavs*," and the sages say, "It is not according to the opinion of either; but when two weavers came from the Dung Gate in Jerusalem and testified in the name of Shemaiah and Avtalion that three *logs* of drawn water rendered the immersion-pool unfit, the sages confirmed their opinion."[80]

This case is quite significant for the history of the Halakhah. It shows that the last *Zug*, Hillel and Shammai, had no scruples about differing with their teachers. It also shows that in establishing the

Halakhah, if justified by certain conditions, later sages gave preference to the view of the older *Zug* rather than to that of the younger one.[81]

According to a tradition of R. Jose in B. *Yev.* 67a, the sages also accepted an halakhic view of Shemaiah and Avtalion involving *Terumah*, heave offering, in the event a priest died and left his widow pregnant.[82]

B. *Bezah* 25a relates testimony (in a Baraitha) as to an halakhic view of Shemaiah and Avtalion in order to refute another opinion in regard to the circumstances under which catching and eating non-domesticated animals and birds on a holiday might be permitted.

As to Shemaiah's activities, the most controversial is his trial of Herod. It possesses not only halakhic but historical significance as well. Josephus gives two accounts of the incident. The older account is that given in *War*.[83] Here he tells us that "malicious persons at court informed Hyrcanus that without oral or written instructions from Hyrcanus, Herod, in violation of Jewish Law, had put all this large number of people to death. If he is not king but still a commoner, he ought to appear in court and answer for his conduct to his king and to his country's law, which do not permit anyone to be put to death without trial. . . . Hyrcanus summoned Herod to trial. Herod . . . went with a strong escort . . . Sextus Caesar (47–46 B.C.E.) . . . sent express orders to Hyrcanus to clear Herod . . . Hyrcanus, being inclined to take that course on other grounds, for he loved Herod, acquitted him."

The report in *Antiquities*[84] is somewhat different. Here Josephus informs us that Herod killed Ezekias and many of his men without trying them before a *synedrion*, etc.: When Herod stood in the Synedrion with his troops, he overawed them all; and no one of those who had denounced him before his arrival dared to accuse him thereafter; instead, there was silence and doubt about what was to be done. While they were in this state, someone named Samaias, an upright man and for that reason superior to fear, arose and said

". . . but it is not Herod whom I should blame for this or for putting his own interests above the law, but you and the king, for giving him such great license. Be assured, however, that God is great, and this man, whom you now wish to release for Hyrcanus' sake, will one day punish you and the king as well." And he was not mistaken in either part of his prediction. For when Herod assumed royal power, he killed Hyrcanus and all the other members of the Synedrion with the exception of Samaias; him he held in the greatest honor, both because of his uprightness and because when the city was later besieged by Herod and Sossius, he advised the people to admit Herod . . . (5) Now when Hyrcanus saw that the members of the Synhedrion were bent on putting Herod to death, he postponed the trial to another day, and secretly sent to Herod, advising him to flee from the city, for in that way, he said, he might escape danger . . . they begged him to remember his acquittal. . . .

The two versions of the incident show several differences, some of them contradictory. For example, in *War* Herod was acquitted by Hyrcanus indicating that he headed the court of trial. In *Ant.* however, Hyrcanus did not acquit Herod but instead, Hyrcanus "postponed the trial" which may mean that he requested the Sanhedrin to postpone the trial or only the decision. The same account, however, later speaks of an acquittal. The number of incongruities grows larger, if we consider the talmudic account.

B. *Sanh.* 19ab:

. . . an incident which happened with a slave of King Jannai, who killed a man. Simon ben Shetaḥ said to the Sages: "Set your eyes upon him and let us judge him." So they sent the king word, saying: "Your slave has killed a man." Thereupon he sent him to them. But they again sent him a message: "Thou too must come here, for the Torah says, *If warning has been given to its owners*, meaning that the owner of the ox must come and stand by his ox." The king accordingly came and sat down. Then Simon ben Shetaḥ said: "Stand on thy feet, King Jannai, and let the witnesses testify against thee; yet it is not before us that thou standest, but before Him Who spoke and the world came into being, as it is written, *Then both the men between whom the controversy is, shall stand.*" "I shall not act in accordance with what thou sayest, but in accordance with what thy colleagues say," he answered. Simon turned to the right and to the left, but they all looked down at the ground. Then said Simon ben Shetaḥ to them: "Are ye wrapped in thoughts? Let the Master of thoughts come and call you to account!" Instantly Gabriel came and smote them to the ground, and they died.

51

This version is so different from the Josephus passage that many scholars believe that Josephus and the Talmud refer to two unrelated incidents. The Talmud has Simon ben Shetaḥ instead of Samaias and the name of the King is Jannai, not Hyrcanus. Herod's name is substituted by "Jannai's servant" or "slave" in the Talmud.

The similarities, on the other hand, are so striking that it would be almost a miracle if history had repeated itself to such an extent. In the Talmud, the servant of a Hasmonean king killed someone. In Josephus, Herod, an officer of the Hasmonean king, Hyrcanus, killed people. In the Talmud, the accusers of the murderer, with the exception of the head of the Sanhedrin, refused to speak up at the trial. This is the same as in Josephus. In the Talmud the head of the Sanhedrin rebukes the cowards who failed to speak up at the trial. Josephus gives the same account. According to the Talmud, the cowards were punished by death. Josephus concurs again.

Except for some details in the Talmud which bear the earmark of later aggadic and halakhic amplifications, the main difference between Josephus and the Talmud lies in the names. All the other historical details are basically the same.

Assuming that both the Talmud and Josephus refer to the same event, how can the divergence in names be explained? It is a fact that the Talmud uses "Jannai" for Hasmonean kings other than Alexander Jannaeus. This explains the usage of Jannai in our passage instead of Hyrcanus II. Why the Talmud does this is a problem by itself. Let us only point to the fact that Caesar's name later became the title "Emperor," an analogy to a certain extent.

Still another problem is why the Talmud gives Simon ben Shetaḥ for Samaias. It is possible that a learned transmitter of the incident, knowing that Simon ben Shetaḥ was a contemporary of Alexander Jannaeus, changed "Samaias" to Simon ben Shetaḥ.[85] It is also possible that the similarity of the sounds in Samaias and Simon led to the error. Omission of Herod's name constitutes no real problem, since names are often omitted. Although it is unimportant whether there was a motive behind the omission of the name, there are two possibilities that could account for it following the verse, "The name of the wicked shall rot [Prov. 10:7]," or, regard for the Roman rulers with whom Herod was a favorite.

The last problem requiring a solution in the discussion of the several personalities involved in the incident is the identification of Samaias. Was it Shemaiah or Shammai? According to the talmudic dating, Hillel became Nasi 100 years before the destruction of the Temple, i.e. 30 B.C.E. While this date is probably not accurate, there is no reason to doubt that it approximates the actual date. Shammai became *Av Beth Din* at a later date, since he was preceded by Mena-hem, Hillel's *Av Beth Din*. Herod's trial took place while Sextus Caesar officiated in Syria (47 or 46 B.C.E.). Since Shammai became *Av Beth Din* about 25–20 B.C.E., he could not have headed the San-hedrin, or the *Beth Din Ha-Gadol*, even as its *Av Beth Din* in 47 or 46 B.C.E. The fact that Shammai holds a principle which was ap-plied in this trial, i.e., that the instigator of a crime is also responsible, does not make him the originator of this principle,[86] and does not make Shammai out of Samaias. In this case, decisive weight rests with the chronology which excludes Shammai's presidency at the trial, pointing to Shemaiah as the president at that time.[87]

Other incongruities in need of a clarification are the contradictory accounts about the outcome of the trial. All sources agree that the criminal was not punished or even sentenced. In *War*, Josephus says that Herod was acquitted while he claims in *Ant.* that the trial was adjourned until the next day by royal request, thus giving Herod an opportunity to flee. The Talmud, on the other hand, merely says that no member of the Sanhedrin dared to speak up at the trial, whereupon Simon ben Sheṭaḥ rebuked them. The implication here is that there was no condemnation. It leaves the question open as to whether an acquittal or an adjournment took place. Since the accu-sation was not substantiated at the trial, an acquittal would normally be in order. The circumstances, however, were unusual, permitting no safe conclusion as to the action of the court, if any. The proba-bility is that the suit ended in an acquittal. This is also suggested by the fact that Josephus' second account, claiming that the trial ended with an adjournment, makes reference to an acquittal shortly after-wards.

In the history of the Halakhah, the incident is significant because it demonstrates that the (Pharisaic) Sanhedrin possessed the right to try capital cases and made use of this right.[88] According to the

Talmud (loc. cit.), it even had the power to call the king before the court. The failure of the trial resulted, according to the Talmud, in a ruling by the sages that a king may not function as a judge, nor can he be subject to a court trial (B. *Sanh.* ibid.). The statement of the Amora Rav Joseph (ibid.) that the above ruling applies only to the kings of Israel, but not to the kings of Judah is an opinion without any basis in reality or in older sources.

In M. *Avoth* I,10, Shemaiah gives the following advice, "Love Labor and Hate Mastery and Seek not acquaintance with the Ruling Power." The last clause may reflect a sentiment arising from his experiences at Herod's trial.

In M. *Avoth* I,11 Avtalion says, "Ye sages, give heed to your words lest you incur the penalty of exile and ye be exiled to a place of evil waters; and the disciples that come after you drink [of them] and die; and the name of Heaven be profaned." It is quite probable that Avtalion had a specific incident in mind when he made this utterance. The usage of symbolic language, "water" for teaching, "drink" for study, is not uncommon in talmudic literature.

Before discussing the fifth *Zug*, Hillel and Shammai, we should like to point to some significant halakhic activities of leaders or institutions of the Hasmonean period, the period of the first four *Zugoth*, which are not related to the *Zugoth*.

HIGH PRIEST JOHANAN

M. *Ma'aser Sheni* V,15 = M. *Sotah* IX,10 relates the following about Johanan the High Priest, believed to be identical with John Hyrcanus I (ruled 135–104 B.C.E.) :

יוחנן כהן גדול העביר הודיות המעשר. אף הוא בטל את המעוררים
ואת הנוקפים. ועד ימיו היה פטיש מכה בירושלים. ובימיו אין אדם
צריך לשאול על הדמאי.

Johanan the High Priest did away with the avowal concerning the Tithe. He also put an end to the "Awakeners" and the "Stunners." Until his days, the hammer used to smite in Jerusalem. And in his days, none needed to inquire concerning *demai*-product.

The language of the Mishnah here is not only brief, but also obscure and enigmatic. The first ordinance is, in fact, the abrogation of a law of the Torah. It is justified, according to talmudic sources, because of the laxity in the observance of the laws about tithes and other prescribed offerings.[89] According to a talmudic view Ezra ordained that, contrary to the law of the Torah (Num. 18:21) the priests and not the Levites should receive the first tithe because the latter did not want to return in his day from Babylonia to Jerusalem.[90] Since the Levites did not receive the tithe the givers of the tithe could not say "I gave it to the Levite" (Deut. 26:13).

Johanan's second ordinance is of a theological nature. He abrogated the daily recital of Ps. 44:23, "Awake, why sleepest Thou, O Lord," performed by the Levites on their stage. Johanan considered a daily recital of this verse improper because taken literally (as people might do) it means that God sleeps whereas Ps. 121:4 clearly states "Behold, He that keepeth Israel doth neither slumber nor sleep."

Johanan's third ordinance, abolishing the "Stunners," is understood as a prohibition of inflicting a stupefying injury to a sacrificial animal before slaughtering it. Tos. *Soṭah* XIII,10 and B. *Soṭah* 48a explain this as follows: "Stunners are those who hit the calf between its horns as they do in [the cult of] idol worship. Johanan the High Priest said to them: "How long will you feed the altar *ṭerefoth*" (or *neveloth*; cf. talmudic versions ad loc.).

The unequivocal meaning of Johanan's words is that he abolished the practice of stunning because this would result in an injury causing *ṭerefuth*. The words "as they do in the cult of idol worship" is not Johanan's statement and quite obviously represents a later stratum. The parallel versions in P. *Soṭah* IX,11; 24a, and the one in P. *Ma'aser Sheni* V (end); 56d do not have the statement that this was a custom in the cult of idolatry.

Johanan's fourth ordinance is taken to mean that he prohibited certain metal work during the intermediate days of the festivals.

The reason for the last statement concerning Johanan in our Mishnah that "in his days, none needed to inquire concerning *demai*-produce," is understood as being rooted in his ordinance that only *Terumath Ma'aser* and second tithe have to be separated from the *demai* before it could be eaten. P. T. ad loc. V,5; 56d explains that the inquiry was not needed because he set up *zugoth*, which means here "pairs [of supervisors]" and not the *Zugoth* who were the leading officers of the Sanhedrin.[91]

With one exception, all these ordinances concern the Temple cult or dues to be given to the priests or Levites. The meaning of the one exception (smiting of the hammer in Jerusalem) is obscure, and its talmudic explanation is but a conjecture.[92]

The ordinances of Johanan the High Priest show that in his time matters relevant to the Temple, priests and Levites were within the jurisdiction of the high priest, not the *Zugoth* or Sanhedrin, though it is possible that they cooperated with him. The Talmud (loc. cit.) does not judge all of his activities favorably.

According to Josephus, John Hyrcanus possessed kingship, high-priesthood, and prophecy.[93]

COURT OF THE HASMONEANS

B. *A. Z.* 36b records an ordinance issued by the Court of the Hasmoneans prohibiting sexual relations with gentiles.

At the time when the religious and civil leadership of the Jewish people was in the hands of the Nasi in conjunction with the *Av Beth Din* and the Sanhedrin or *Beth Din Ha-Gadol*, the ordinances were proclaimed, as a rule, in the name of the Nasi. The case in B. *A. Z.* 36b is an exception as were the instances of Johanan the High Priest. The reason why the Hasmonean Court issued ordinances is unknown. It may reflect an early state of affairs when the Hasmoneans retained for themselves the right of issuing whatever ordinances they wished to make. It is also possible that the ordinance was issued at a time when there was no Nasi to take care of the matter,[94] or that the Court of the Hasmoneans was a body that followed in the footsteps of Ezra and endeavored to strengthen Jewish family life. We must not forget that the nature and real character of our ordinance is very controversial.[95]

THE EARLY ḤASIDIM

The "Early Ḥasidim" חסידים הראשונים of the talmudic
(tannaitic) literature cannot be dated. The fact, however, that they
are called "early" in tannaitic literature makes it plausible that they
were contemporaneous with the *Zugoth*. No Halakhoth are transmitted in their names, only acts of pious conduct. M. *Ber.* V,1
reads: "The Early *ḥasidim* (pious men of old) used to wait an hour
before reciting the *Tefillah*, that they might direct their heart toward God."

Tosefta *Ned.* I,1 relates that the Early Ḥasidim pledged *nazirdom* in order to be required to bring a sacrifice since God would
not allow them to sin even by error (which would obligate them to
bring a sin offering; see B. T. ibid. 10a).

B. *Niddah* 38a (a Baraitha) relates that the Early Ḥasidim would
have relations with their wives only on Wednesdays, lest they pro-
fane the Sabbath at the time of childbirth! They believed that this
habit would prevent birth on a Sabbath; therefore there would be
no need to transgress the Sabbath for the sake of childbirth.

B. *B. Q.* 30a (Baraitha) relates that the Early Ḥasidim used to
hide (bury) their thorns and glass three handbreadths deep in their
fields so they would not impede the plow. This instance reflects the
punctilious character of their practice.

These Early Ḥasidim cannot be identified with the Essenes since
the latter displayed a negative attitude toward sacrifices, while the
Early Ḥasidim were eager to bring sacrifice, as we have seen.[96]

No names of individuals in this group have been transmitted.
Frankel believes[97] that Ḥoni Ha-Meaggel[98] was one of them and
that halakhic views transmitted in the name of Prophet Ḥaggai
(Ḥaggai ha-Navi) are actually Ḥoni's views, Ḥoni's name having
been changed by mistake to Ḥaggai (חגי חני) and the designation
"prophet" having been added later. We do not have to accept this
emendation in order to suggest that Halakhoth transmitted in the
name of the prophet Ḥaggai are from an early period, probably not
later than the period of the *Zugoth*, though certainly not from Ḥaggai. We shall now cite examples of this kind of Halakhah.

In B. *Yev.* 16a, "Prophet Ḥaggai sat and related three matters: The co-wife of a man's daughter is prohibited for him [to marry], Ammon and Moab [the Jews living in their lands] tithe the Tithe for the Poor in the seventh year, and proselytes may be admitted from the Kurds and Palmyrians [i.e., we do not consider them as Jewish bastards, thus disqualifying them]."

In B. *Qid.* 43a, "Shammai the elder related in the name of Haggai the Prophet that those sending a person [in order to commit a sin] are guilty as it is written 'You killed him with the sword of the Ammonites' [II Sam. 12:9]."

The last passage is particularly significant because it shows that Halakhoth ascribed to Haggai are older than Shammai. Its author cites a biblical verse to substantiate the Halakhah, a rare occurrence before Hillel and Shammai.

This passage also shows that the opinion that the instigator of a crime is responsible does not originate with Shammai, but is much older. This fact weakens the view that Shammai headed the court which tried Herod (and made the king responsible, too), simply because he makes the instigator of a crime responsible.

In Tos. *Kelim B. B.* II,3 (591–592) R. Eleazar ben Zadok relates: "In the house of my father there were two wooden blocks. One was unclean; the other was clean. I asked my father, 'Why is the one unclean and the other clean?' He answered, 'The one which is carved [i.e., has a hollow space] is unclean; the other which is not carved, is clean and on this one Prophet Haggai sat.'" The historicity of this incident may be questioned; but even if it is true, its halakhic importance is slight.

BENE BATHYRA

The identity and character of leadership of the Bene Bathyra are quite obscure. The confusion starts with the name, which is given as Bene Bathyra (B. *Pes.* 66a; B. *B. M.* 85a) as "*Ziqne Bathyra*" (P. *Pes.* VI,1; 33a. P. *Kil.* IX,4; 33b. P. *Ket.* XII,3; 35a) and as "*Deveth Bathyra*" (*Ber. Rabbah*, Chapter 33). Even more obscure is their role as leaders. Rashi, on the *Pesahim* passage, explains that they were *Nesi'im*. The fact that they are not enumerated among the *Zugoth* militates against this explanation. On the other hand, Judah Ha-Nasi, who was certainly well acquainted with the history of the Patriarchate, considered them Nesi'im though only by implication. *Ber. Rabbah*, Chapter 33,3 relates: "Our Master [Judah Ha-Nasi] was very humble and said 'Whatever a person tells me, I shall do, except that which those of the House of Bathyra did to my ancestor [Hillel],'" i.e., they relinquished their high office (*Gedullah*) in favor of Hillel. *Gedullah* here clearly refers to a leadership, such as Hillel held subsequent to the discussion in B. *Pes.* 66a (and parallels). Here we have the clear-cut statement that "they appointed him [Hillel] as their Nasi." Yet, the Bene Bathyra could not have been *Nesi'im* of the same rank as other Nesi'im, since their names are consistently omitted from the chains of the leading transmitters of the Torah, which include the *Nesi'im*. The most plausible answer to this difficulty is that the Bene Bathyra were only interim leaders, acting presidents, holding office in the Sanhedrin that was established after Herod massacred the members of the Sanhedrin that had tried him.[99] Judah Ha-Nasi's comparison dooms the conjecture that the Bene Bathyra were heads of the Sabbath committee of the Temple.[100] Besides, we have no record of the existence of such a committee. Whatever the official standing of the Bene Bathyra may have been, we know even less about their activities, since they left no evidence of achievement.[101]

ZUG 5: HILLEL AND SHAMMAI, BETH HILLEL AND BETH SHAMMAI*

As time went on, Pharisaic Judaism became progressively diversified, some of its groups developing certain theological ideas, and others emphasizing (or de-emphasizing) other aspects of religious life, and life in general.[102] One of

* See "Foundations of Rabbinic Judaism," *HUCA* 23, Pt I (1950–51): 453 ff.

the Pharisaic groups projected law and ritual into the foreground
of Judaism and Jewish life. This group was destined to develop into
Rabbinic Judaism, the Judaism of our day. To understand the
foundations of Rabbinic Judaism fully we must examine closely its
beginnings in the Pharisaic era, particularly the activities of Hillel,
Shammai, Beth Hillel and Beth Shammai, the leadership most responsible for ushering in the period of Rabbinic Judaism.

In order to appraise properly the activities and achievements of
Hillel and Shammai, as well as the activities of the schools bearing
their names, many questions have to be answered. For instance,
what is the relationship between Hillel and Shammai, what are the
divergencies between their methods and principles? What are their
respective relationships to their schools? Are they but elected heads
of schools which existed before their participation, or are they the
founders of their schools, or were the schools bearing their names
established after their deaths? Were the schools physically separated,
or did they convene in joint sessions? How long did they exist?
What brought about their termination?

Let us first see what the sources reveal about the motives [103]
of Hillel and Shammai, explicit or implicit, in their controversies.
1) M. *Nid.* I,1 = *'Eduy.* I,1:

שמאי אומר כל הנשים דיין שעתן. והלל אומר מפקידה לפקידה.
אפילו לימים הרבה. וחכמים אומרים לא כדברי זה ולא כדברי זה,
אלא מעת לעת, ממעטת על ידי מפקידה לפקידה; ומפקידה לפקידה,
ממעטת על ידי מעת לעת.

Shammai says: For all women it is enough for them [that they
be ritually unclean only from] their time [of suffering a flow].
Hillel says: [A woman is unclean] from [the previous] examination to [the present] examination, even if [the interval is of]
many days. And the sages say: It is not according to the opinion
of either; but [she is unclean] during the preceding twenty-four
hours, if this is less than [the time] from [the previous] examination to [the present] examination if this is less than twenty-
four hours.

In this controversy, dealing with a phase of defilement by menstru-
ation, *Shammai is lenient, Hillel is strict.* Tannaitic sources reveal

no motivation for their respective views. A. Schwarz[104] suggests that Hillel rendered his decision under the influence of the strict attitude of the Persian religion of his native Babylonia but this is a mere conjecture.

The view of the sages (which was accepted as the Halakhah, see B. *Nid.* 15a) represents the middle road between the respective opinions of Shammai and Hillel.

2) M. *'Eduy.* I,2:

שמאי אומר מקב לחלה. והלל אומר מקביים. וחכמים אומרים לא
כדברי זה ולא כדברי זה, אלא קב ומחצה חייבין בחלה, וכו'

Shammai says: [Dough made] from one *qav* [of flour] is liable to Dough-offering. And Hillel says: Two *qavs*. And the sages say: It is not according to the opinion of either; but one *qav* and a half is liable to Dough-offering, etc.

In this controversy, dealing with the Dough-offering *Ḥallah*, *Hillel is lenient, Shammai is rigorous.* Tannaitic sources reveal no motive. Since the *Ḥallah* is given to the priest (*kohen*), Hillel's lenient position is advantageous to the layman, exempting him from giving *Ḥallah* when baking a small bread. Shammai's view favors the priest. The third view, as in the previous instance, is a compromise of the sages.

3) M. *'Eduy.* I,3:

הלל אומר מלא הין מים שאובין פוסלין המקוה... ושמאי אומר תשעה
קבין. וחכמים אומרים לא כדברי זה ולא כדברי זה, אלא עד שבאו
שני גרדיים משער האשפות שבירושלים, והעידו משום שמעיה ואבטליין:
שלשה לוגין מים שאובין פוסלין את המקוה. וקיימו חכמים את דבריהם.

Hillel says: One *hin* of drawn water renders the *Miqwah* [ritual pool] unfit . . . And Shammai says: Nine *qavs*. And the sages say: It is not according to the opinion of either; but when two weavers came from the Dung Gate in Jerusalem and testified in the name of Shemaiah and Avtalion that three *logs* of drawn water render the *Miqwah* unfit, the sages confirmed their opinion.

In this controversy, dealing with a certain aspect of the *Miqwah*, *Hillel is rigorous, Shammai is lenient.* Ancient sources reveal no motive, and the third view is once more a compromise.

Of particular significance is the latter part of the Mishnah, which reveals that the sages gave preference to a view related in the names of Shemaiah and Avtalion over the views of Hillel and Shammai. The respective motives are not even investigated. The question now is: Why were Shemaiah and Avtalion preferred? Is it because they were older than Hillel and Shammai? This fact alone does not have much weight, particularly when the view of a younger sage has a better foundation. As we pointed out elsewhere, the authority, based on an official endorsement, gave Shemaiah and Avtalion authority and recognition basically superior to that of Hillel and Shammai.[105]

4) B. *Shab.* 17a (Baraitha. Parallels indicated, ibid.):

הבוצר לגת שמאי אומר הוכשר הלל אומר לא הוכשר. א״ל הלל
לשמאי מפני מה בוצרין בטהרה ואין מוסקין בטהרה? א״ל אם תקניטני
גוזרני טומאה אף על המסיקה. נעצו חרב בבית המדרש אמרו, הנכנס
יכנס והיוצא אל יצא. ואותו היום היה הלל כפוף ויושב לפני שמאי
כאחד מן התלמידים, והיה קשה לישראל כיום שנעשה בו עגל.

When one vintages [grapes] for the vat [to make wine], Sham-mai says: It is made fit [to become unclean]; but Hillel says, It is not made fit. Said Hillel to Shammai: Why must one vintage grapes in purity, yet not gather olives in purity? He replied: If you provoke me, I will declare uncleanness in the case of olive gathering too. A sword was planted in the *Beth Hamidrash* and it was proclaimed, "He who would enter, let him enter, but he who would depart, let him not depart!" And on that day Hillel sat submissive before Shammai, like one of the disciples, and it was as grievous to Israel as the day when the golden calf was made.

In this discussion dealing with an aspect of defilement, *Hillel is lenient, Shammai is rigorous.* More important than this are the details of our Baraitha. To Hillel's logical objection Shammai replies with a threat. The reference to the sword at the *Beth Hamidrash* and the prohibition to leave it probably mean, as Rashi ad loc. and others explain, that the matter was to be decided by vote; and therefore, the presence of many sages was sought. This probability becomes almost a certainty if we keep in mind Tos. *Shab.* I,17, where, after Beth Hillel was defeated by *vote*, the statement was made as in our case: Hillel's defeat was as calamitous for Israel as the day on which the golden calf was made.

The following statement presents some ambiguity: "On that day

Hillel was sitting submissively in front of Shammai, like one of the disciples." If we combine this remark with Shammai's threat to issue a decree, the inference that Shammai held the presidency at that time is fully justified.[106] The apparent reason for the change in leadership was the defeat of Hillel in this one particular case.

Of equal or perhaps greater significance is the fact that Hillel and Shammai subsequently issued a joint decree — the result of the vote, upholding Shammai. Obviously the defeated party accepted the majority decision.

The Baraitha concludes with the observation that the joint decree had not been accepted (by the people). However, when the same decree was issued by Hillel's and Shammai's disciples, it was accepted.

This casual remark sheds light on the type of authority Hillel, Shammai, and their disciples possessed. The effectiveness of their decrees depended on the *willingness* of the people to accept them. Enforcement was obviously out of the question. The leaders had no executive power. They were not much more than great teachers.

5) The fifth controversy between Hillel and Shammai is the mysterious *semikhah* dispute in M. *Ḥag.* II,2. This is essentially different from the previous cases inasmuch as it is a controversy transmitted from "Pair" to "Pair." It is the only controversy of this type, and is apparently the shibboleth of two Pharisaic parties. The particular significance of this controversy for our period (the period beginning with Hillel and Shammai) is that this ancient controversy terminates with Hillel and Shammai (or perhaps with Beth Hillel and Beth Shammai).

Let us supplement what we said above and take a closer look at the exigencies of this dispute during Hillel's time.

B. *Beẓah* 20a adduces two contradictory interpretations, both Baraithoth, in regard to the controversy of Beth Hillel and Beth Shammai which we read in the Mishnah. The first Baraitha is advanced by Rabbi Jose (third generation Tanna); and the other, by R. Josse bar Jehudah (fourth generation). Their interpretations have no particular significance at this stage of our investigation. Of genuine importance is the Baraitha that follows:

ת״ר מעשה בהלל הזקן שהביא עולתו לעזרה לסמוך עליה ביו״ט
חברו עליו תלמידי שמאי הזקן; אמרו לו מה טיבה של בהמה זו אמר
להם נקבה היא ולזבחי שלמים הבאתיה כשכש להם בזנבה והלכו להם
ואותו היום גברה ידם של בית שמאי על בית הלל ובקשו לקבוע הלכה
כמותן והיה שם זקן אחד מתלמידי שמאי הזקן ובבא בן בוטא שמו שהיה
יודע שהלכה כבית הלל ושלח והביא כל צאן קדר שבירושלים והעמידן
בעזרה ואמר כל מי שרוצה לסמוך יבא ויסמוך. ואותו היום גברה ידן
של בית הלל וקבעו הלכה כמותן ולא היה שם אדם שערער בדבר
כלום.

It once happened that Hillel the Elder brought his burnt-offering
into the Temple Court on a Festival for the purpose of laying
hands thereon. The disciples of Shammai the Elder gathered
around him and asked: What is the nature of this animal? He
replied to them: It is a female and I brought it as a peace offering. Then he swung its tail for them and they went away. On that
day Beth Shammai got the upper hand over Beth Hillel and
wished to fix the Halakhah according to their opinion. But an
old man of the disciples of Shammai the Elder was there named
Baba ben Buta, who knew that the Halakhah was according to
Beth Hillel and he sent and brought all the sheep of Kedar that
were in Jerusalem and put them into the Temple Court and said:
Whoever wishes to lay on hands let him come and lay on hands;
and on that day Beth Hillel got the upper hand and established
the Halakhah according to their opinion and there was no one
there who disputed it.

This Baraitha contains the statement, "on that day Beth Shammai
gained the upper hand" over Beth Hillel. This means, no doubt,
that they outnumbered Beth Hillel. Why, then, did they not carry
out their intention to establish the Halakhah as they saw fit? The
answer of the Baraitha is that Baba ben Buta, a Shammaite, knowing
that the Halakhah was in accordance with Beth Hillel, brought many
sheep to the Temple and gave them away free to anyone who would
perform the *semikhah* as required by Beth Hillel. As a result of
this action, Beth Hillel won the argument. "There was no longer
any person who would object." This indicates that the *semikhah*
controversy had now been settled once and for all. Some individual
Shammaites may have continued to adhere to their original opinion,

as indicated by another incident (ibid.). This, however, has no bearing on the problem as such. It is possible that the incident recorded after the report on the ultimate decision actually occurred before that decision.

Tos. *Ḥag.* II,11,12(236) and P. *Ḥag.* II,3; 78a offer different versions of the above incident. Yet, on every point of importance they agree with the version of the Babylonian Talmud.

The significance of this passage becomes apparent, if we realize that it reveals the following:

1) Beth Hillel and Beth Shammai already existed during the lifetime of Hillel and Shammai.

2) Beth Hillel and Beth Shammai decided the issue in a joint session, by majority vote.

3) This act terminated the *semikhah* dispute. We hear of no continuation of the *semikhah* controversy.

4) The decision had been prompted by a Shammaite who knew that the Halakhah was in accordance with Beth Hillel. What does this mean? Knowledge of the Halakhah here certainly means knowledge and acceptance of a certain tradition or practice. But was not the *semikhah* dispute the shibboleth of the *Zugoth* and their respective parties? How could a Shammaite, and subsequently many Shammaites, accept a basic position of the opposition and still remain Shammaites?

During Hillel's time the number of differences between the "Houses," as is well known, increased. Consequently, the *semikhah* question ceased to be *the* sole dividing issue. One could remain a good Shammaite without adhering to the party view on *semikhah*, which formerly served to divide the parties.

5) This and similar instances[107] indicate that the priests, or high priest, did not regulate all phases of the sacrificial cult.[108] They must have acted, at certain times and instances, as mere practitioners, performing certain duties when called upon. In legislative matters, particularly when referring to actions to be performed by the people (e.g., the *semikhah*, or bringing certain types of sacrifices to the Temple), they obviously refrained from making decisions.

After having pointed to the *five* instances in which Hillel and Shammai disagree, the question arises: Why does the Babylonian

Talmud say that there were but *three* cases where Hillel and Shammai disagreed (B. *Shab.* 15a ff.); and why does the Palestinian Talmud give the number *four* (*Ḥag.* II,3;78a), including the *semiḵhah* controversy?

This question, raised already in the Babylonian Talmud (loc. cit.), had been answered quite satisfactorily, ibid. The *semiḵhah* controversy is not counted because it did not originate with Hillel and Shammai. Controversy 4 is not counted because Hillel (complying with the majority decision) accepted Shammai's view in this case.

If the latter reasoning is correct, we have to assume that in the first three cases Hillel and Shammai did not reach an agreement. In fact, we do not find any trace of such agreement. But, why was it not possible to resolve these controversies as was the case in the instances 4 and 5?

It stands to reason that a similar solution was not necessary in these three instances, since the sages, probably the majority comprising members of both parties, adopted rulings differing with both Hillel and Shammai and representing compromise solutions. If this is correct, we have to assume that these sages are contemporaneous or nearly contemporaneous with Hillel and Shammai, i.e., the views of the sages cannot represent an appreciably later stratum.[109]

A further question that deserves an answer is why does the Gemara not include in its answer to the *semiḵhah* controversy the answer given in case 4, since it would be valid here just as in 4?

The Gemara, quite understandably, does not always advance all possible reasons. In addition, none of the versions recording discussion and incident leading to the settlement of the *semiḵhah* controversy mentions Shammai. It stands to reason that Shammai was no longer living at that time. Consequently, the answer that Shammai conceded to Hillel (corresponding to the answer given in 4) could not be suggested in the *semiḵhah* case.

Considering these five controversies, we see that Hillel is lenient in 2 and 4, (in which he ultimately conceded to Shammai's strict decision) and 5. In 1 and 3 he is rigorous. For Shammai, the opposite holds true. He is rigorous in 2, 4, and 5, and lenient in 1 and 3. As to subject matter: instances 1, 3, and 4 deal with defilement; *Ḥallah* is the subject of 2; and *semiḵhah*, of 5.

We see that the five controversies do not permit any inference as to strictness or leniency on the part of Shammai or Hillel. In order to clarify matters further, all the instances in which Shammai or Hillel speak directly, would have to be investigated.

The same holds for the question of whether their decisions were influenced by the subject matter or any other consideration.

Let us now look at the instances where Hillel and Shammai give their respective views, though they do not oppose each other.

6) Mishnah *'Eduy.* I,7

Discussants: Beth Shammai, Beth Hillel, and Shammai. *Beth Hillel are most lenient, Shammai most rigorous,* and *Beth Shammai follow a middle road.* The passage does not reveal whether Beth Shammai, opposing Shammai (and Beth Hillel), are contemporaneous with Shammai, or are of a later generation. It shows, nonetheless, that Beth Shammai did not hesitate on occasion to oppose their head. Subject: *Defilement*

7) M. *'Eduy.* I,8 (=*Ma'aser Sheni* II,4)

Discussants: Beth Shammai, Beth Hillel, Shammai, R. Akiba. The situation here is similar to that in 1. Inclusion of Akiba's view demonstrates that the Mishnah is composed of various strata. Subject: *Terumah*[110]

8),9) M. *Kelim* XXII,4

Discussants: Beth Shammai, Beth Hillel, Shammai. Tos. *Kelim, Bava Bathra* I,12 (591) R. Meir and R. Judah disagree as to the point of difference between Beth Shammai and Beth Hillel. Subject: *Defilement*. The situation as to leniency, etc. is similar to the above cases cited.

10) B. *Pes.* 115a

A Baraitha records a practice of Hillel. R. Johanan claims that his (Hillel's) colleagues differ with him and cites a Baraitha in support of his claim. As the Baraitha does not specify Beth Hillel, the probability is that those whom R. Johanan calls the "colleagues of Hillel" are, in fact, the sages of a later generation. Accordingly, we may have to rule out this passage as being a case of disagreement between Hillel and Beth Hillel.

In this case, dealing with certain dishes for the *Seder*, Hillel follows the most literal interpretation of Scripture.

11) B. *Bezah* 35a

The words of the Baraitha הלל לעצמו אוסר are ambiguous. They may mean "Hillel himself prohibits it," "Hillel alone prohibits it," or "Hillel prohibits it for himself." If the last translation is correct, the passage reflects the notion that Hillel was more strict toward himself than he was for others. If the second possible meaning, accepted by Rashi, is correct, Hillel stands in opposition to all sages, including Beth Hillel. The implications of the first meaning will be evident after we shall have pointed to the case now following. The subject of this passage is tithe.

12)–14) Tos. *Ma'aser Rishon*, III,2,3,4.

We have here three cases obviously similar in principle to those of the Baraitha in B. *Bezah* 35a. The first Tosefta passage is quite clear and informs us that not only Beth Hillel, but also Hillel himself had already made the rigorous decision. Beth Shammai, however, rendered a lenient decision.[111] — The subject is tithe.

15) M. *B. M.* V,9; Tos. ibid. VI,10; Baraitha in P. *B. M.* V,7; 10d.

In this instance an anonymous ("sages") view is contrasted with Hillel's view. The wording of all the versions indicates that the sages were contemporaries of Hillel.

In contrast to the sages, Hillel renders here a rigorous decision. The subject is interest.

15b) Mishnah, ibid. Another rigorous decision by Hillel is unopposed. The subject is interest.

16) B. *Pes.* 66a and parallels.

This instance is similar to that of 15 inasmuch as Hillel is opposed by the sages in general, not by a particular "House" or Shammai.

Considering all these sixteen controversies, we find that Shammai, participating in nine controversies, is *lenient* in two of them (1 and 3) which deal with certain aspects of defilement (*Niddah* and *Miqwah*). He is rigorous in seven cases: 2, which deals with *Hallah*; 4, 6, 7, 8, and 9, which deal with certain aspects of defilement; 5, which treats the *semikhah* problem.

Hillel, participating in twelve controversies, is lenient in four cases (but in one of these he reverted to Shammai's view): nos. 2 (*Hallah*); 4 (defilement); 5 (*semikhah*); 16 (slaughtering the Paschal lamb on the Sabbath). He is rigorous in seven or eight instances: 1 (*Niddah*); 3 (*Miqwah*); 10 (?) (*Seder*); 11–14 (tithe); 15 (interest).

In five of the sixteen controversies Beth Shammai participate. In 5 (*semikhah*) they are in agreement with Shammai; in 6–9 they are in *disagreement* with both Shammai and Beth Hillel.

Beth Hillel participate in the same five controversies as Beth Shammai and are always *lenient*.

The sages, probably referring to the sages (i.e., majority) of both Houses, are in disagreement with both Shammai and Hillel in cases 1, 2, and 3.

These sixteen controversies in which Shammai and/or Hillel participate are significant because they point in certain directions.

1) Shammai, strict in seven out of nine cases, is justly considered the conservative leader of his time, and is in perfect harmony with his "House."

2) Hillel is lenient only in four out of eleven or twelve cases. This fact might be taken to indicate that the issue dividing the two parties was not that of conservatism and liberalism, stringency and leniency, but closer inspection shows this conclusion to be false.

The concept of leniency and strictness is often relative: a rigorous decision rendered against one litigant often amounts to a lenient decision for the other.

In talmudic terminology, however, leniency simply means that the possessor of the disputed goods does not have to surrender these goods to the other party; the economic status of the respective parties is not a factor.

In the majority of cases in which Hillel is considered strict, his stand favors the poor over the rich. In 11–14, dealing with *Ma'aser*, and 15, dealing with interest, Hillel's favoritism to the poor, with certain boundaries delineated by Torah and tradition, is obvious.

These five cases in which Hillel's "strict" decision favors the poor are not suitable instances that would point to Hillel's general attitude as per leniency and strictness. In order to find this general attitude we need more material.

We saw above that Beth Hillel and Beth Shammai existed already during Hillel's and Shammai's lifetimes. Yet, we have very few instances in which Hillel and Shammai participate in controversies in which Beth Hillel or Beth Shammai appear. Does this mean that Beth Hillel and Beth Shammai did not have more controversies during Hillel's and Shammai's time? We see that the *Semikhah* controversy in M. *Bezah* II,4 designating the discussants Beth Shammai and Beth Hillel does not give the name of Hillel. Yet we have evidence — a Baraitha in B. *Bezah* 20a (and M. *Ḥag.* II,5) — proving that Hillel was included in "Beth Hillel." This fact suggests that this was the case in many other instances. In other words, many of Beth Hillel's views were, at the same time, the views of Hillel himself. How often this was the case cannot be determined. However, it is reasonable to assume that this was so in numerous instances. The same holds true for the Halakhoth of Shammai and Beth Shammai, i.e. many views of Beth Shammai are shared by Shammai himself. Halevy even suggests that in all the instances in which Hillel or Shammai are named, they differed with their respective schools, otherwise they would not have been mentioned.[112]

The validity of the above view is indicated in some of the cases, e.g., the first three and 6, 9, and 11. It may be true in some of the other cases where matters are not so obvious. In some instances other exceptional circumstances might have caused the explicit reference to Hillel and Shammai. In brief the names of Hillel and Shammai are mentioned only when the situation was exceptional. This fact prompts the inference that normally, i.e., when Hillel and Shammai agree with their Houses, their names would not be recorded. The number of such instances was, undoubtedly, larger than was the number of the exceptions. Of course, we have no means to determine their exact number. I. Halevy's inference[113] (for which he also uses the fact that, after Shammai, no other head of the party is mentioned, proving for him that none existed) that Beth Hillel and Beth Shammai were on the whole, simply contemporaries of Hillel and Shammai is not merely an exaggeration; it is contrary to the facts as well. We know, for example, that the discussion between Beth Hillel and Beth Shammai on the "Eighteen Matters" took place shortly before the Jewish-Roman war (about 65 C.E.).

We also know that the struggle between Beth Hillel and Beth Shammai for supremacy was fought in Javneh *after* the fall of the Temple, i.e., several decades after the deaths of Hillel and Shammai.

What we wanted to demonstrate is that, in determining Hillel's and Shammai's respective attitudes as to strictness and leniency, we cannot stop at the instances in which they are mentioned explicitly. These are merely the exceptions. We have to add to these a number (though an unknown number) of views by Beth Hillel and Beth Shammai which include the views of Hillel and Shammai themselves. Under this consideration, Hillel's basically lenient attitude in comparison with that of Shammai must be considered a well-established fact.

Hillel's significance for the history of the Halakhah is evident not merely in his controversies but in other halakhic endeavors as well.

1) *Prozbul.*

M. *Shevi'ith* X,3:

ג פרוזבול אינו משמט. זה אחד מן הדברים שהתקין הלל הזקן.
כשראה שנמנעו העם מלהלות זה את זה ועוברין על מה שכתוב בתורה
(דברים ט״ו, ט) השמר לך פן יהיה דבר עם לבבך בליעל וגו׳, התקין
הלל פרוזבול.

ד זהו גופו של פרוזבול: מוסר אני לכם איש פלוני ופלוני הדיינים
שבמקום פלוני, שכל חוב שיש לי שאגבנו כל זמן שארצה. והדיינים
חותמין למטה או העדים.

"[A loan secured by] a *prozbul* is not cancelled by the seventh year. This is one of the things that Hillel the Elder ordained. When he saw that the people refrained from giving loans one to another and transgressed what is written in the Torah" (Deut. 15:9) "Beware that there be not a base thought in thy heart, etc.," Hillel ordained the *prozbul*.

Ibid. 4: "This is the text of the *prozbul*: 'I affirm to you, such-a-one and such-a-one, the judges in such-a-place, that touching any debt due to me, I will collect it whenever I will.' And the judges sign below, or the witnesses."

M. Giṭ. IV,3:   הלל התקין פרוזבול מפני תקון העולם.

"Hillel ordained the *prozbul* for the general welfare." (Cf. also *Sifre* Deut. 113; P. *Shevi'ith* IX,2;39c; Tos. *Shevi'ith* VIII,3–10 [72–73]; and Tos. *B.B.* XI,7.)

A legal fiction, perhaps the first one in the history of the Halakhah, the *prozbul* effects a fictitious transfer of a private debt to the court. No longer legally a private debt, the obligation is not cancelled by the sabbatical year.

Why did Hillel introduce this *Taqqanah*? The brief answer "for the general welfare" is but an indication. The more explicit answer in *Sifre* and M. *Shevi'ith* is unequivocal: The wealthy of Hillel's time disregarded the biblical warning of Deut. 15:9,10 and would not lend money to the poor shortly before the sabbatical year. In order to induce them to lend money to the poor before the sabbatical year Hillel, through his *prozbul*, permitted a law of the Torah to be disregarded.

The obvious intention of this *Taqqanah* seems clear. It was introduced in order to help the needy. Nonetheless, other views exist, too, based on the erroneous opinion that Hillel and his descendants were wealthy, therefore he favored the rich.[114] Accordingly, Hillel introduced the *prozbul* in order to help the wealthy. At first glance this seems to be correct, since the *prozbul* protected the money of the wealthy from loss in the seventh year. However, since taking of interest was prohibited, the lending of money was an act of charity, and the poor are the obvious beneficiaries of charity. The *prozbul* made a loan to the poor less risky and, therefore, more acceptable to the wealthy. The wealthy individual was not directly benefited, as his money was more secure in the pre-*prozbul* days, when he refrained from lending money altogether. While helping the needy improves the general economy, and thus indirectly aids the wealthy also, there can be no doubt that Hillel introduced the *prozbul* in order to help the poor, as he said.[115]

2) M. *'Arakhin* IX,4: "If the last day of the twelve months has come and it was not redeemed, it becomes his for ever, no matter whether he bought it or it was given him as a gift, for it is written,

'In perpetuity' (Lev. 25:30). Beforetime the buyer used to hide himself on the last day of the twelve months so that it [the house] might be his forever; but Hillel the Elder ordained that he [the seller] could deposit his money in the Temple Chamber and break down the door and enter, and that the other, when he would, might come and take his money."

In this *Taqqanah* Hillel permits a departure from the literal observance of the law (Lev. 25:29–30) in order to protect the right of the seller of a house in a walled city to buy it back on the last possible day in spite of the trickery of the buyer. While this *Taqqanah* may not conform to the letter of the law, it is in full harmony with its spirit.

3) B. *B. M.* 104a:

Hillel the Elder used to interpret common speech. For it has been taught: The men of Alexandria used to betroth their wives, and when they were about to take them for the wedding ceremony, strangers would come and kidnap them. Thereupon the sages wished to declare their children bastards. Hillel the Elder said to them, "Bring your mother's *kethuvahs.*" When they brought them, he found written therein, "When thou art taken for the *huppah,* be thou my wife." And on the strength of this they did not declare their children bastards.

In this instance Hillel protects the status of the children against the intent of the sages who wanted to declare them bastards. This he accomplished by a suitable literal interpretation of the text of the *kethuvah* written in the language of the common people, not in accordance with the prescribed formula (cf. *Tosafoth,* ibid.). Accepted by the sages, Hillel's humane interpretation also benefited the mothers, since their marriages to the kidnapers were now legally valid. Whether a controversy preceded the decision is not known. The context shows that the sages here were contemporaries of Hillel, but it does not indicate whether they were Beth Hillel or another group of sages.

4) B. *Pes.* 66b (Baraitha): "It was related of Hillel, as long as he lived no man ever committed trespass through his burnt offering. But he brought it unconsecrated to the Temple Court, consecrated it, laid his hand upon it, and slaughtered it."

Here Hillel introduced a new practice in order to prevent people from committing a *me'ilah* — transgression pertaining to their sacrifices. This innovation violated no existing law and apparently met no opposition.

5) Exegesis.

Talmudic sources indicate that Hillel's significance for the history of the Halakhah is rooted in the fact that he projected text interpretation into the foreground of legalistic methodology. According to P. *Pes.* VI,1;33a (cf. Tosefta *Nega'im* I,16) the very reason for Hillel's coming from Babylonia to Palestine was to expound some difficult passages from the Torah.[116] His ascent to the presidency of the Academy (Sanhedrin) is attributed to his ability to settle a hotly debated issue: Does the sacrificing of the Paschal lamb (or goat) supersede the Sabbath or not?[117] In this debate, Hillel made extensive use of the hermeneutic rules and demonstrated that the conclusion reached by the use of these rules coincided with authoritative tradition.

Hillel was the first Jewish sage officially to introduce a system of hermeneutic rules, seven in number.[118] The rules were not original with him. Some of them were employed already in the Bible, all of them had been in use among the learned men of the Roman Empire.[119]

The use of exegesis in general and hermeneutic rules in particular shows a peculiar line of development. It is prominent at the beginning of Hillel's career but slackens later and plays a minor role until the destruction of the Temple. In the second century C.E. exegesis becomes most important. What might be the reason for this?

After Herod's massacre of the sages of the Sanhedrin that tried him, the surviving sages established an unofficial Sanhedrin which, at the beginning, had the character of an academy and lacked the backing of the political authorities. Therefore, to direct Jewish life effectively, the leaders of Judaism needed a new source of authority. Hillel demonstrated that the hermeneutic rules applied to the Torah could provide this new authority. However, the broad application of these rules, being new, met natural resistance, as is so often true, particularly in the realm of religion. Also, expanded use of the hermeneutic rules became unnecessary as the power of the Sanhedrin increased after Hillel, even to the extent of possessing jurisdiction in (certain) capital cases, rendering exegesis unimportant as a source of authority.

However, after the destruction of the Temple and the termination of the authoritative Sanhedrin, exegesis became of paramount importance. The authority of the *Beth Din Ha-Gadol*, the successor to the Sanhedrin, was based on its spiritual stature. Its limited power was insufficient for introducing all the changes necessitated after the destruction of the Temple. The limited power of the Nasi and the *Beth Din Ha-Gadol* was now supplemented by the unlimited realm of exegesis.

Just as the designation Beth Hillel often includes Hillel himself, the designation Beth Shammai likewise often includes Shammai himself. This fact is an additional indication as to Shammai's strict position, though the instances in which Shammai is explicitly mentioned already point to his rigorous (or conservative) attitude. In view of all the facts and indications cited, one must reject L. Ginzberg's thesis that it is erroneous to consider Beth Shammai as generally strict, Beth Hillel as lenient.[120]

The fact that social and economic implications often played a role does not refute the existence of strictness and leniency as decisive motives in many cases. The fact that Beth Shammai were conservative and Beth Hillel liberal, a fact which Ginzberg recognizes,[121] naturally suggests that Beth Shammai were more strict than Beth Hillel. Shammai's personal strictness is well documented, even in halakhic matters, see, e.g., Tosefta *Yoma* V(VI),2: "It happened that Shammai the Elder wanted to feed his child [on Yom Kippur] with one hand, but the [sages] prevailed upon him that he fed him with both hands." Mishnah *Sukkah* II,8 states: "Minors are exempt from [the law of] the Sukkah. . . . The daughter-in-law of Shammai the Elder once bore a child; and he broke away some of the roof-plaster and made a Sukkah roofing over the bed for the sake of the child."[122]

Ginzberg stresses the role of intention and asserts that, according to Beth Hillel, an act not accompanied by intention is not to be considered an act, while Beth Shammai hold that deed is more important than thought. He claims that there are at least fifty controversies of this kind and gives a few examples.[123] Tchernowitz points to a few controversies in which just the opposite is true.[124] The fact is that it is the nature of the liberal halakhist to interpret the law more freely, particularly when he has its applicability in mind. This was precisely the reason why Beth Hillel several times departed from the literal meaning of the text of a law to reinterpret it in the light of their time. The method of this reinterpretation varied with circumstances. Occasionally, the intent of the law was used as a means if it served the purpose, although this did not occur as often as Ginzberg would like to have it. Most of Ginzberg's explanations are forced and unacceptable, leaving but a small number of cases where intention may have been the decisive factor. On the other hand, Beth Shammai, being conservative, more often interprets literally, which perforce curtails the use of methods which uproot the literal meaning of the text. For this reason, Beth Shammai, in contradistinction to Hillel, do not make use of legal fiction. Hillel's liberalism is evident in the fact that he introduces practices in vogue in Alexandria. Beth Hillel's consideration for the needs of the time is also obvious when we keep in mind that they abrogated old laws מפני תקון העולם "for the welfare [or betterment] of the world." [125]

Although the traditional notion claiming that Shammai–Beth Shammai are in general rigorous while Hillel–Beth Hillel, on the other hand, are more lenient, is, as we have seen, well established, there are still questions to be answered. Why are Shammai–Beth Shammai rigorous? Why are Hillel–Beth Hillel lenient? Why do Beth Hillel revert occasionally to Beth Shammai's view, but hardly ever vice versa? Why do, in a number of instances, Beth Hillel hold the rigorous views, Beth Shammai, however, the lenient ones?

It is certainly true that the conservative and the liberal sections of the Pharisees, which alternated in the leadership during the period of the *Zugoth*, were represented later by Beth Shammai and Beth Hillel. It is also known that Shammai and his followers were wealthier than the average number of the opposite faction. This is a factor of influence on the unconscious level. Also, a minority party, by its nature, is an opposition party. Some of Beth Shammai's views cannot be explained as being anything but an expression of opposition at all costs. Furthermore, an opposition party does not always have to cope with reality, since the majority view is the Halakhah to be followed even by the minority party. B. *Yev.* 14a even advances a controversy as to whether or not Beth Shammai ever followed their own decisions (see page 115). Already the Tosefta [126] informs us that in spite of the marked divergence between Beth Shammai and Beth Hillel in regard to marriage laws, Shammaites would not in practice refrain from marrying Hillelites and vice versa. Such practices would have been impossible if both schools had adhered rigidly to their own views.

Since the "Sanhedrin" of this period had for decades, only the character of an academy, without power to enforce its decisions, individuals of both Houses occasionally disregarded them and continued to follow practices rejected by the joint meeting of the Houses. Some would not hesitate on occasion to follow practices suggested by the opposition, though contrary to the practice endorsed by their own party. The significance of this point will be discussed later, when we define the party lines.

Let us now turn to the strange phenomenon that in a number of instances Beth Hillel reversed their original opinion, accepting Beth Shammai's view. Beth Shammai, however, hardly ever reversed their stand in favor of Beth Hillel. References:

1) M. *'Eduy.* I,12a.

In this case, involving the *Agunah* problem, Beth Hillel, originally rigorous, later accepted Beth Shammai's lenient view. The divergence is rooted in a different interpretation of a past incident. Beth Hillel limits the law to a case analogous to the incident, whereas Beth Shammai considers the incident as a precedent, applicable to parallel cases. A reversal by Beth Hillel was not difficult in view of their generally liberal tendency.

Tosefta, ibid. I,6b adds an insignificant supplement to Beth Shammai's reasoning.

2) Mishnah, ibid., 12b.

This Mishnah deals with another phase of the same discussion, whether the above woman should receive the *kethuvah* money. Beth

Hillel, originally, refused her the *kethuvah* but were convinced by Beth Shammai's reasoning based on the text of the *kethuvah* document.[127]

3) Mishnah, ibid. 13.

The subject is the plight of the half-slave. Beth Hillel reverse their legally correct but less humane view in favor of Beth Shammai's more humane solution of the problem.

4) Mishnah, ibid. 14. Cf. Mishnah, *Ohaloth* V,3.

In this case of defilement, Beth Hillel reverse their original, more lenient view in favor of Beth Shammai's more cogent logic.

5) Mishnah, *Ohaloth* V,4b.

This Mishnah differs from the passages above in that it does not give the controversy between Beth Shammai and Beth Hillel. First, it advances an anonymous view, then asserts that Beth Hillel reversed their stand in favor of that of Beth Shammai. The two detailed parallel passages, Tosefta, ibid. V,11,12 and a *Baraitha* in *Ḥag.* 22b, neither give the controversy as one conducted between Beth Shammai and Beth Hillel, nor contain the clause "Beth Hillel reversed their stand, etc." According to these sources, the dispute involved a disciple of Beth Shammai and Rabbi Joshua and took place outside of the *Beth Hamidrash* and at a time when Beth Hillel and Beth Shammai no longer existed. We have discussed this matter elsewhere.[128] Later we shall have to elaborate somewhat more on this instance, but for the time being it is sufficient for us to show that this instance is properly omitted in discussing occasions on which Beth Hillel reversed themselves and adopted the view of Beth Shammai.

6) Mishnah *Kelim* IX,2.

In this case of defilement, Beth Hillel, originally lenient, revert to Beth Shammai's strict rule. Commentaries point to the better logic behind Beth Shammai's view as the cause for Beth Hillel's change of mind.

When we sum up the above instances, the following becomes evident: Beth Hillel abandoned their decisions in a few instances and accepted Beth Shammai's rulings when Beth Shammai's views had a more humane character or when Beth Shammai's views were based on superior reasoning.

Yet, how shall we understand the fact that there is no instance related in which Beth Shammai reversed themselves in favor of Beth Hillel?

The absence of such instances in the tradition is no evidence to the effect that such a change never occurred. Yet, even if it did occur, it had no significance. Since the Halakhah was decided by the majority, a change of mind by the minority group, i.e., Beth Shammai, could have no consequences. The Halakhah followed the majority no matter whether the minority changed its stand or not. Therefore, there was no point in recording instances in which Beth Shammai might have reversed themselves. On the other hand, Beth Hillel's reversal was significant for the establishment of the Halakhah. The *semikhah* controversy might be adduced as an instance where Beth Shammai abandoned their original stand in favor of that of Beth Hillel, but this case is essentially different from the above cases because of unusual circumstances.

The next question to be discussed here is why, in a number of instances, do Beth Shammai take a lenient point of view, whereas Beth Hillel are rigorous? Does this mean that there is something wrong about the notion that Beth Shammai are rigorous while Beth Hillel are lenient?

Adolf Schwarz devoted an entire book to this subject.[129] Unfortunately, Schwarz concentrates his acumen on one phase only, on the methodological one, disregarding other aspects almost completely. His conclusion is, therefore, dictated by forcing this one aspect even where it may not apply. He goes so far as to fabricate his own *gezeroth shawoth*, etc., in order to "prove" that a respective leniency of Beth Shammai and strict decision of Beth Hillel is based on methodological grounds. Whereas in a few instances his keen conjectures might reflect the actual reason for the difference between Beth Hillel and Beth Shammai, in no case can such conjecture be considered as a fact. For this reason we deem it necessary to investigate other aspects besides methodology. We have to bear in mind that in practical decisions of Halakhah exegetical considerations were mostly secondary, having no other functions than to justify and endorse certain ways and practices. Exegetical methods were the tools for carrying out legislation in an indirect way, when direct legislation was impossible.

Let us now point to the instances in which Beth Shammai are lenient while Beth Hillel appear to be rigorous.

I

1) M. *'Eduy.* IV,1a; *Beẓah* I,1a:

ביצה שנולדה בי״ט ב״ש אומרים תאכל וב״ה אומרים לא תאכל.

"If an egg was laid on a Festival-day Beth Shammai say: It may be eaten. And Beth Hillel say: It may not be eaten." The subject matter (egg laid on a holiday) is relevant to *Yom Tov*. There are no economic implications.

2) Ibid. 1b:

ב״ש אומרים שאור בכזית וחמץ בככותבת וב״ה אומרים זה וזה בכזית.

"Beth Shammai say: An olive's bulk of leaven and a date's bulk of what is leavened. And Beth Hillel say: An olive's bulk of either." The subject matter (leaven and what is leavened) is pertinent to Passover. There is no apparent economic implication.

3) M. *'Eduy.* IV,2:

השוחט חיה ועוף בי״ט ב״ש אומרים יחפור בדקר ויכסה וב״ה אומרים לא ישחוט אלא א״כ היה לו עפר מוכן.

"If a man slaughtered a wild animal or a bird on a Festival day, Beth Shammai say: He may dig with a mattock and cover up the blood. And Beth Hillel say: He should not slaughter unless he had earth set in readiness." The situation is similar to the above cases. The subject matter (slaughtering of a wild animal or a bird on *Yom Tov* when no material has been readied before *Yom Tov* to cover the blood) is relevant to *Yom Tov*. No economic implications are apparent.

4) Ibid., 3a:

ב״ש אומרים הבקר לעניים הבקר וב״ה אומרים אינו הבקר עד שיובקר אף לעשירים כשמטה.

"Beth Shammai say: If produce is proclaimed 'ownerless' for the benefit of the poor, it is [legally] ownerless [and tithe free]. And

Beth Hillel say: It can only be ownerless if it is made ownerless also for the rich as in the Sabbatical Year."

The subject matter (produce proclaimed ownerless) is relevant to charity. The economic implication is the following: theoretically Beth Shammai is more favorable to the poor; practically, however, there is hardly any difference. Charity, which is made available to both rich and poor, is normally accepted only by the poor.

5) Ibid., 3b:

כל עומרי השדה של קב קב ואחד של ארבעה קבין ושכחו ב"ש
אומרים אינו שכחה וב"ה אומרים שכחה.

"If the sheaves in the field was each of one *qav*'s weight but one was of four *qavs*, if this one was forgotten Beth Shammai say: It may not be considered a Forgotten Sheaf. And Beth Hillel say: It may be considered a Forgotten Sheaf."

The subject matter (forgotten sheaf) is charity. The economic implication is: Beth Shammai's leniency favors the owner of the land; Beth Hillel's stringency promotes the interests of the poor.

6) Ibid., 4 and *Peah* VI,2:

העומר שהוא סמוך לגפה ולגדיש ולבקר ולכלים ושכחו ב"ש אומרים
אינו שכחה וב"ה אומרים שכחה.

"If a sheaf lies near to a wall or to a stack or to the oxen or to the implements, and is forgotten, Beth Shammai say: It may not be deemed a Forgotten Sheaf. And Beth Hillel say: It may be deemed a Forgotten Sheaf."

The situation is the same as above.

7) Ibid., 5a:

כרם רבעי ב"ש אומרים אין לו חומש ואין לו בעור וב"ה אומרים
יש לו (חומש ויש לו) בעור.

"Beth Shammai say: The rules of the [Added] Fifth and of Removal do not apply to [the grapes of] a Fourth Year Vineyard. And Beth Hillel say: They do apply."

The subject matter (added fifth and removal in regard to the grapes of a fourth year vineyard) is charity. The economic implication is as above.

8) Ibid., 5b:

ב"ש אומרים יש לו פרט ויש לו עוללות והעניים פודים לעצמן וב"ה
אומרים כולו לגת.

"Beth Shammai say: The laws of grape-gleanings and of the defective cluster apply, and the poor redeem the grapes for themselves. And Beth Hillel say: The whole yield goes to the winepress."

The subject is (grape-gleanings and defective cluster) charity. The economic implication is: Beth Shammai are more favorable to the poor than Beth Hillel. The matter has *other aspects* as well, such as Qodashim and *Yom Tov.*

9) Ibid., 6a:

חבית של זיתים מגולגלים ב״ש אומרים אינו צריך לנקב וב״ה אומרים
צריך לנקב.

"A jar of pickled olives, according to Beth Shammai, need not be broached. And Beth Hillel say: It must be broached."

The subject is defilement. There are few if any economic implications.

Tosefta II,2 cites an incident in which a Shammaite followed the Hillelite Halakhah.

10) Ibid., 6b. Cf. also Tosefta II,2:

הסך בשמן טהור ונטמא ירד וטבל ב״ש אומרים אע״פ שהוא מנטף טהור
וב״ה אומרים כדי סיכת אבר קטן.

"If a man anointed himself with clean oil and then became unclean, and he went down and immersed himself, Beth Shammai say: Even though he still drips [with oil] it is clean. And Beth Hillel say: [It is unclean so long as there remains] enough to anoint a small member."

The situation is the same as above.

11) Ibid., 6c:

ואם היה שמן טמא מתחלתו ב״ש אומרים כדי סיכת אבר קטן וב״ה
אומרים משקה טופח. רבי יהודה אומר משום ב״ה טופח ומטפיח.

"And if it was unclean oil at the outset, Beth Shammai say: [It remains unclean, even after he has immersed himself, so long as there remains] enough to anoint a small member. And Beth Hillel say: So long as it remains a moist liquid. R. Judah says in the name of Beth Hillel: So long as it is moist enough to moisten something else."

The situation is the same as above.

12) Ibid., 7a:

האשה מתקדשת בדינר ובשוה דינר כדברי ב״ש וב״ה אומרים בפרוטה
ובשוה פרוטה.

"According to Beth Shammai, a woman is betrothed by a *denar* or a *denar's* worth. And Beth Hillel say: By a *peruṭah* or a *peruṭah's* worth."

The subject is marriage (betrothal). The economic implication is that Beth Hillel are more lenient, while Beth Shammai are more stringent.

13) Ibid., 7b:

ב״ש אומרים פוטר הוא את אשתו בגט ישן וב״ה אוסרין.

"Beth Shammai say: A man may divorce his wife with an old bill of divorce. And Beth Hillel forbid it."

The subject is marriage (divorce). The economic implication is difficult to determine. Beth Hillel protect the marriage and the woman's interests better than do Beth Shammai. Beth Shammai is more favorably inclined toward the interests of the man, who economically is usually stronger than the woman.

14) Ibid., 7d:

המגרש את אשתו ולנה עמו בפונדקי ב״ש אומרים אינה צריכה ממנו
גט שני וב״ה אומרים צריכה ממנו גט שני.

"If a man divorced his wife, and she then lodged with him in an inn, Beth Shammai say: She does not need another bill of divorce from him. And Beth Hillel say: She needs another bill of divorce from him."

The subject is marriage (divorce). The situation is as above: Beth Hillel's position protects moral principles more effectively than does that of Beth Shammai.

15) Ibid., 8: = Yev. I,4:

ב״ש מתירין את הצרות לאחים וב״ה אוסרין. חלצו ב״ש פוסלין מן
הכהונה וב״ה מכשירין. נתייבמו ב״ש מכשירין וב״ה פוסלין.

"Beth Shammai permit levirate marriage between the co-wives and the surviving brothers. And Beth Hillel forbid it. If they perform *ḥaliẓah* Beth Shammai declare them ineligible to marry a priest, but Beth Hillel declare them eligible. If they had been taken in levirate marriage, Beth Shammai declare them eligible but Beth Hillel declare them ineligible."

The subject is marriage (levirate). Beth Hillel are basically strict, while Beth Shammai are lenient, though as to the consequences,

Beth Hillel is lenient in a particular case. Beth Hillel's strict position is advantageous to the woman.

16) Ibid., 9. Same as *Yev.* III,5:

שלשה אחים שנים מהם נשואים לשתי אחיות ואחד מופנה מת אחד
מבעלי אחיות ועשה בה מופנה מאמר ואח״כ מת אחיו השני ב״ש אומרים
אשתו עמו והלה תצא משום אחות אשה וב״ה אומרים מוציא את אשתו
בגט וחליצה ואת אשת אחיו בחליצה.

"If there were three brothers, two married to two sisters, and one unmarried, and one of the married brothers died, and the unmarried brother bespoke the widow, and then his second brother died, Beth Shammai say: His [bespoken] wife abides with him and the other is free as being his wife's sister. And Beth Hillel say: He must dismiss his [bespoken] wife both by bill of divorce and by *ḥaliẓah*, and his brother's wife by *ḥaliẓah*."

The subject is marriage (levirate). In this specific case Beth Hillel's strict position weakens the bond of the levirate tie. This is in line with the above observation: weakening of the levirate tie is, in principle, a strengthening of the status of the woman.

17) Ibid., 10a:

המדיר את אשתו מתשמיש המטה ב״ש אומרים שתי שבתות וב״ה
אומרים שבת אחת.

"If a man vowed to have no intercourse with his wife Beth Shammai say: [She must wait] two weeks. And Beth Hillel say: One week."

The subject is marriage (vow, divorce). Beth Shammai's leniency favors the husband; Beth Hillel's "stringency" grants greater protection for the rights of the woman.

18) Ibid., 10b:

המפלת לאור שמנים ואחד ב״ש פוטרין מן הקרבן וב״ה מחייבין.

"If a woman miscarried on the night of the eighty-first day, Beth Shammai declare her exempt from an offering. And Beth Hillel declare her liable."

The subject is sacrifice (subsequent to a miscarriage in a very specific case).

In the economic area, Beth Shammai are lenient. According to Schwarz (op. cit., p. 61), the controversy is the consequence of a difference in phrasing Lev. 12:6.

19) Ibid., 10c:

סדין בציצית ב״ש פוטרין וב״ה מחייבין.

"Beth Shammai declare a linen garment exempt from the law of the Fringe. And Beth Hillel declare it subject to the law."

The subject is ritual (fringes on a sheet סדין בציצית). In economic terms, Beth Shammai's leniency is more advantageous to the rich, who have more sheets than the poor.

20) Ibid., 10d:

כלכלת השבת ב״ש פוטרין וב״ה מחייבין.

"A basket of fruit intended for the Sabbath Beth Shammai declare exempt [from tithes], and Beth Hillel declare it liable."

The subject is tithe. Beth Shammai's leniency favors the owner of the fruit crop.

21) Ibid., 11a. *Nazir* III,6:

מי שנדר נזירות מרובה והשלים נזירותו ואחר כך בא לארץ ב״ש
אומרים נזיר שלושים יום וב״ה אומרים נזיר בתחלה.

"If a man vowed to be a Nazirite for a longer period and he fulfilled his Nazirite-vow and afterward came to the Land [of Israel], Beth Shammai say: He needs to be a Nazirite for thirty days [more]. And Beth Hilllel say: He must be a Nazirite as from the beginning."

The subject is Nazirdom. There is a minor economic implication: Beth Shammai's stand is advantageous to the wine producer (and dealer), but it is doubtful if Beth Shammai had this point in mind. Schwarz (op. cit., p. 64 ff.) attempts to prove that Beth Hillel's opinion was the result of their progressive attitude, whereas that of Beth Shammai is rooted in their conservatism.

22) Ibid., 11b = *Nazir* III,7:

מי שהיו שתי כתי עדים מעידות אותו. אלו מעידים שנדר שתים ואלו
מעידים שנדר חמש ב״ש אומרים נחלקת העדות ואין כאן נזירות וב״ה
אומרים יש בכלל חמש שתים שיהיה נזיר שתים.

"If two pairs of witnesses testified of a man, and the one testified that he had vowed two Nazirite vows, and the other that he had vowed five, Beth Shammai say: Their testimony is at variance, and the Nazirite-vow cannot be held binding. And Beth Hillel say: The two are included within the five, so that he must become a Nazirite for two periods."

The subject is Nazirdom. The situation is as above (except for Schwarz's interpretation).

23) Ibid., 12:

אדם שהוא נתון תחת הסדק ב״ש אומרים אינו מביא את הטומאה
וב״ה אומרים אדם חלול הוא והצד העליון מביא את הטומאה.

"If a man was put there below the split, Beth Shammai say: He does not give passage to the uncleanness. And Beth Hillel say: A man is hollow, and his upper part gives passage to the uncleanness."

The subject is defilement. Even Schwarz admits (ibid., p. 69) the futility of an attempt to find the true reason for the difference between Beth Shammai and Beth Hillel in their text interpretation.

Since Tosefta 'Eduy. II,2a claims that there are twenty-four controversies in which Beth Shammai are lenient while Beth Hillel are rigorous, though the Mishnah lists only twenty-three, attempts have been made to find the twenty-fourth such controversy. Schwarz thinks that the twenty-fourth controversy appears in Tosefta II,2b (ibid. 69 ff.). It is omitted in the Mishnah, he believes, because Rabbi (*Nazir* IV,6) incorporates only the view of Beth Hillel in an anonymous form. Since the main purpose of the Tosefta is to supplement the Mishnah, and II,2b is given in conjunction with II,2a, there can be little doubt, at least in the opinion of the Tosefta compiler, that II,2b is the twenty-fourth controversy in our category. It may have been omitted in the Mishnah, since formally (though not in effect) Beth Shammai are rigorous, whereas Beth Hillel appear to be lenient.

The subject here is Nazirdom.

II

In addition to the above list, individual Tannaites cite controversies of Beth Shammai and Beth Hillel in which the former are lenient and the latter strict.

Rabbi Judah transmits the following controversies:

1) M. 'Eduy. V,1b.

The subject is defilement.

The controversy is not repeated in the Mishnah (as are most of the above controversies), but is cited in the Gemara as a Baraitha in *Shabbath* 77a with the supplement of Tosefta *'Eduy.* II,5.

2) Ibid., 1c.

The subject is ritual law (food, "egg of a *Nevelah*"). In the economic aspect, Beth Shammai are lenient. Talmudic sources give no reason for the difference of opinion.

3) and 4) Ibid. 1d; These are repeated, without the transmitter, in *Niddah* IV,3.

The subject is defilement (gentile woman and Jewish woman afflicted with leprosy).

5) Ibid. 1e (cf. *Shevi'ith* IV,2 and *Sifra* Behar on Lev. 25:6). The subject is fruits of the sabbatical year.

6) Ibid. 1f.

The subject is defilement. Even Schwarz (ibid., p. 82) admits that the difference cannot be based on hermeneutics or other text interpretation.

III

R. Jose transmits the following controversies:

1) M. *'Eduy.* V,2a.

The subject is food law (whether fowl and cheese may be placed on the same table). Both Beth Shammai and Beth Hillel agree that they could not be eaten together. Schwarz (ibid., p. 83) suggests that our controversy is rooted in the question of whether the biblical prohibition of *basar behalav* (meat with milk) includes the meat of fowl or not. Beth Shammai's leniency is the consequence of their opinion maintaining that the biblical prohibition does not include the fowl whereas Beth Hillel hold that it does.

2) Ibid., 2b.

The subject is *Terumah.* Beth Shammai's leniency favors the owner of the crop. According to the version transmitted anonymously in Mishnah *Terumoth* I,4 Beth Shammai and Beth Hillel agree as to the law in principle (*lekhathillah*) and differ merely as to an *ex post facto* situation (*bediavad*) (cf. Tosefta *Terumoth* III,14, p. 29).

3) Ibid., 2c = *Kil.* IV,5.

The subject is *Kil'ayim*. Beth Shammai's stand favors the owner of the crop.

4) Ibid., 2d—cf. *Hallah* I,6.

The subject is *Hallah*. Beth Shammai's position favors the owner of the dough at the expense of the priest.

5) Ibid., 2e.

The subject is defilement.

6) Ibid., 2f.

The subject is proselytism with an aspect of defilement in regard to the Paschal sacrifice. Beth Shammai's leniency favors the proselyte. According to *Pesahim* 92a, the Hillelites' stringency represents a "fence," a *gezerah*. Schwarz (ibid., pp. 89–90), suggests, instead, a *gezerah shawah* of his own creation and considers it as the true reason for Beth Hillel's position. P. *Pes.* VIII,8; 36b advances a difference in the interpretation of Num. 31:19 (not a *gezerah shawah*), as the reason for the controversy.

IV

R. Yishmael (or R. Simon) relates the following controversies:

1) M. *'Eduy.* V,3b; *Yad.* III,5.

The subject is whether *Qoheleth* defiles the hands or not, i.e., whether it is part of the Canon or not. Beth Shammai think it should not belong to the Canon. Even Schwarz (p. 91) admits that here no hermeneutics or any other type of exegesis is involved.

2) Ibid., 3c; *Parah* XII,4.

The subject is defilement.

3) Ibid., 3d; *'Uqzin* III,6.

The subject is defilement. Beth Shammai's position is somewhat advantageous to the owner.

4) Ibid.

The subject is a tithe. Beth Shammai's stand is advantageous to the owner of the crop.

V

R. Eliezer transmits the following controversies:

1) M. *'Eduy.* V,4; *Niddah* IV,3.

The subject is defilement. Schwarz (ibid., pp. 94 ff.) refutes

Geiger's theory given in *He-Chaluz* VI,28 ff. that the reasoning of the Shammaites is similar to that of the Sadducees, Samaritans, and Karaites in the matter.

2) Ibid., V,5.

Beth Shammai are lenient in the matter of *Yibbum*. Tosefta II,9 (458) = *Yev.* V,1 (245) is a parallel to our Mishnah with certain additions: Of particular interest among these is that R. Simon agrees with the Shammaitic view (cf. P. *Yev.* III,1; *Yev.* 28a).

VI

Other exceptions are as follows.

1) Schwarz (op. cit., p. 99) points to a Baraitha in B. *Yoma* 80a (cf. Mishnah VIII,2) which should have been listed among the leniencies of Beth Shammai, etc., but was not. The Gemara eliminated the difficulty by resorting to a forced interpretation.

The subject is ritual (drinking on Yom Kippur).

2) M. *Ket.* VIII,1.

The subject is certain property rights in marriage.

P. T. ad loc. and P. *Peah* VI,2; 19bc consider this case one of the leniencies of Beth Shammai, etc. Why, then, is it not enumerated among the twenty-four cases, asks the Gemara. The Talmud answers: because Beth Shammai's leniency toward the *wife* is, at the same time, a disadvantage to the husband. Subsequently, the Gemara observes that this was also the case elsewhere among the listed cases.

3) Tos. *Zev.* IV,9 (cf. M. *Zev.* IV,1).

This is related by R. Eliezer ben Jacob.

The subject is sacrifice.

Gemara ibid. 38b points out there is also an aspect of leniency on Hillel's side, etc.

4) Baraitha in B. *Bekhor.* 30b.

The subject is acceptance of an *am haarez* as a *haver*.

The Talmud makes an emendation which reverses the situation.

5) M. *Ohaloth* II,3.

The subject is defilement.

It is not at all certain that this controversy is, in fact, one in which Beth Shammai are lenient, etc. This would be the case merely under special circumstances. Tannaitic sources do not claim that this is a case of our category.

6) M. *Ohaloth* II,3.

The subject is defilement.

According to *Ḥul.* 42b the situation as to leniency and strictness is reversed if applied to *ṭerefuth* instead of defilement. So we cannot speak of Beth Shammai's leniency as absolute. Again, no tannaitic source claims that this case belongs in our category.

7) Baraitha in *Ḥul.* 104b.

The subject is a food law (meal with milk).

The Talmud wonders why this case was not enumerated among Beth Shammai's leniencies etc. Schwarz (op. cit., p. 104) shows that there is genuine doubt whether Beth Shammai actually are more lenient, etc. Tannaitic sources do not support the Gemara's suggestion.

8. In B. *'Araḵhin* 27b, the Gemara cites a Baraitha (cf. Mishnah VIII,3). In the course of a discussion, a text manipulation leads to the objection that now there is a case of Beth Shammai's leniency etc. Subsequently the matter is straightened out so that no leniency of Beth Shammai is present. No tannaitic source designates this instance as one belonging to our category.

The subject is Qodashim.

Schwarz (op. cit., pp. 105 ff.) discusses numerous controversies between Beth Shammai and Beth Hillel which some commentators place in our category. He succeeds in showing that these suggestions have no solid basis.

What do the above instances indicate?

The cases in which Beth Shammai are lenient and Beth Hillel are rigorous are limited in number. According to a tannaitic tradition, they are only twenty-four, but the actual list is larger. The reason appears to be the same as in the case of the 613 commandments of the Torah. When Rabbi Simlai transmitted the number of the commandments, he failed to enumerate them.[130] The result was disagreement among the sages as to the way of counting them, since a simple counting would not result in 613. Similarly, there was a tradition that the number of controversies in with Beth Shammai took the lenient position in opposition to Beth Hillel was twenty-four. Yet, obviously, the originator of this tradition failed to specify and transmit the controversies, which resulted in disagreement among the sages of successive generations. The Mishnah redactors first present a list of twenty-three controversies (supplemented in the Tosefta by the twenty-fourth case), transmitting it anonymously, thus making it the "official" (accepted) list. Then they add the traditions of individuals. This is in line with redactorial activities of the time. In this connection, we must raise the following question: What is the reason for the difference in the listing?

In many of the instances listed here, leniency and strictness are a relative matter. A decision or law which favors one of the parties concerned often affects the other party adversely. Consequently, whether a case should be included in our category or not often will depend on the viewpoint of the individual.[131] Therefore, cases which have aspects of both leniency and strictness ought not to be included in the list of exceptions. This holds true particularly for the cases in which Beth Shammai's "leniencies" favor the owner of property to the detriment of a poorer person, cases which constitute approximately one third of the instances listed as leniencies of Beth Shammai. Only very few of Beth Shammai's leniencies show a tendency unfavorable to the wealthy. These may have originated at a later period, when the economic advantage of the (leading) Shammaites vanished.

The tabulation of the controversies considered gives the following picture:

I

Subject Matter	Economic aspect, if any
1. Festival	
2. Festival	
3. Festival	
4. Charity	Theoretically, Beth Shammai favor the poor; practically, little consequence.
5. "Charity" (forgotten sheaf)	Beth Shammai favor the owner of the land.
6. As in 5	As in 5.
7. *Kerem Revai*	As in 6.

91

Subject Matter	Economic aspect, if any
8. "Charity" (grape-gleanings and defective clusters, also an aspect of *Qodashim*)	Beth Shammai more favorable toward the poor.
9. Defilement	
10. Defilement	
11. Defilement	
12. Marriage (betrothal)	In an economic consideration, Beth Hillel more lenient than Beth Shammai.
13. Divorce	Beth Hillel protect marriage and the woman's interests better than Beth Shammai. Let us keep in mind that usually the woman is the weaker partner in economic matters.
14. As in 13	As in 13.
15. Levirate	Beth Hillel's stringency is favorable to the woman.
16. As in 15	As in 15.
17. Divorce, Vow	Beth Shammai favor the husband, i.e., the economically stronger partner.
18. Sacrifice	In an economic consideration, Beth Shammai are lenient.
19. Fringes (*Sadin bezizith*)	In an economic consideration, Beth Shammai are favorable toward the wealthy.
20. Tithe	Beth Shammai favor the owner of the crop.
21. Nazirate	Beth Shammai's position is favorable to the wine producer-dealer.
22. As in 21	As in 21.
23. Defilement	
24. Nazirate	

II (R. Juda's traditions)

1. Defilement	
2. Food — Law	
3. Defilement	Beth Shammai are lenient concerning the economics involved.
4. Defilement	
5. Fruits of the sabbatical year	

Subject Matter	*Economic aspect*, if any
6. Defilement	

III (R. Jose's traditions)

1. Food — Law	
2. *Terumah*	Beth Shammai's position favors the owner of the crop.
3. *Kil'ayim*	As in 2.
4. *Ḥallah*	Beth Shammai's position favors the owner of the dough.
5. Defilement	
6. Proselyte	Beth Shammai's leniency favors the proselyte.

IV (R. Yishmael [or R. Simon]'s traditions)

1. Canonicity of Qoheleth	
2. Defilement	
3. Defilement	In an economic consideration, Beth Shammai's position is somewhat advantageous to the owner.
4. Tithe	Beth Shammai's position is advantageous to the owner of the crop.

V (R. Eliezer's traditions)

1. Defilement	
2. Levirate	

VI (Other "exceptions")

1. Yom Kippur	
2. Property rights in marriage	In economics, Beth Shammai are lenient toward the woman, not the man.
3. Sacrifice	There is also an aspect of leniency on Beth Hillel's side.
4. *'Am ha-areẓ — Ḥaver*	The Talmud reverses the controversy.
5. Defilement	It is quite doubtful whether this controversy belongs in this category.
6. Defilement	The situation as to leniency and strictness is reversed, if controversy refers to *ṭerefuth*.

Subject Matter	*Economic aspect*, if any
7. Food — Law	Highly questionable as to whether Beth Shammai are lenient in the economics of the matter.
8. Qodashim	As in 7.

Why do Beth Shammai and Beth Hillel deviate from their basic positions as to strictness and leniency in certain instances?

Above we pointed out that a true solution of the problem does not lie in laboring the exegesis, and that aspect alone. Whereas in a very few cases, hermeneutics, or exegesis in general, might have played a role, the formal justification of the laws is in most instances secondary and has been advanced merely as a tool in order to make a law acceptable.

Was there a certain area of the law in which Beth Shammai and Beth Hillel reversed their usual basic positions? This possibility must be rejected since the cases include diverse areas of Jewish life and practice: festivals, marriage, food laws, priestly portions, charity, sacrifices, defilement, etc.

We doubt that a satisfactory patent solution will ever be found. Yet we think that some of the exceptions can be explained most plausibly by Beth Shammai's status as an opposition party. It is the nature of the opposition to contradict the opponent whenever possible. When, for example, the majority party proposes a strict ruling, the opposition party, if it puts opposition above consistency, would suggest a lenient ruling and then find some kind of justification. There are many instances in which Beth Shammai and Beth Hillel differ, without the presence of aspects of leniency or strictness or any other known element in their decisions.

In concluding this chapter, let us emphasize that the few instances in which Beth Shammai and Beth Hillel deviate from their usual position as to strictness and leniency afford no basis for establishing any philosophy for the respective schools, or for ascribing the exceptions to one factor only. They are in no way sufficient to shatter the fact that basically Beth Hillel are lenient and Beth Shammai are rigorous.

EXEGETICAL CONTROVERSIES OF BETH SHAMMAI– BETH HILLEL

I. H. Weiss notes that less than ten percent of the 316 Beth Shammai–Beth Hillel controversies are exegetical, i.e., based on differing interpretation of texts.[132] Let us take a close look at these exegetical controversies in order to learn their significance.

1) In Mishnah *Ber.* I,3, Deut. 6:7 is interpreted in different ways. Beth Hillel's opinion is that בשכבך ובקומך "when thou liest down, and when thou risest up" reflects the proper understanding of the text. Beth Shammai's view that these words mean "in a lying and in an upright position, respectively" is one of the possible literal meanings of the passage, but unwarranted in the given context. It could be an interpretation for the sake of mere opposition.

2) M. *Peah* VI,1. The exegesis pertaining to this passage is not given in the Mishnah. The Midrashic association is amoraic. Cf. sages.

3) Ibid. VI,5. No exegesis is given in the Mishnah. In P. Talmud ad loc. two Amoraim (R. Abun and R. Mana) differ as to the exegetical basis of the respective views of Beth Shammai and Beth Hillel.

4),5) Ibid. VII,6, Mishnah *Ma'aser Sheni* V,3. No exegesis is given in the Mishnah. The Midrashic association is amoraic. Cf. P. Talmud 20b ad loc.

6) M. *Shevi'ith* IV,10. No exegesis is given in the Mishnah. Exegetical association is amoraic. Cf. P. Talmud ad loc.

7) Tos. *Terumoth* III,16(30). In a direct controversy, both parties cite *different verses* to prove their point.

8) M. *Shab.* I,5 gives no exegesis. The Tosefta parallel ibid. I, 20–21(111) supplies the exegesis which, however, is not part of the direct controversy. P. Talmud ibid., 3d similar.

9) Baraitha in B. *Shab.* 25a, B. *Men.* 40a gives no exegesis. S. Mishnah *Eduy.* IV, 10. Commentators (Rashi, etc.) refer to the exegesis in B. *Yev.* 4a (*Semukhin*), where, however, our controversy is not mentioned. Since none of the parallels contains exegesis, it is

more than doubtful that Beth Shammai and Beth Hillel based their controversy on an exegesis.

10) Baraitha in B. *Shab.* 135a gives no exegesis. The same holds for Tosefta ibid, XV (XVI) 9 and P. *Yev.* 9a. *Sifra Tazria* I (58b) gives the controversy in connection with an exegesis. However, the exegesis is not advanced by Beth Shammai and Beth Hillel. In fact, there is probably no interrelation between the exegesis and our Beth Shammai–Beth Hillel controversy.

11),12) M. *Bezah* I,1. Two controversies are both without exegesis. The exegetical association is amoraic, see Gemara, ad loc.

13) Baraitha in B. *Yoma* 61b, Tosefta *Neziruth* I,6 (284). No exegesis advanced by Beth Shammai or Beth Hillel.

14) M. *Sukkah* I,1. No exegesis in the Mishnah. Exegesis given in the Gemara, ibid., 9a by *Amoraim*.

15)–17) M. *Yev.* I,4. Three controversies are without exegesis. B. *Yev.* 13b Simon ben Pazzi, an Amora, supplies the exegesis. In P. *Yev.* 3a R. Simon in the name of R. Josse in the name of Nehorai supplies the verse. Other Amoraim join in the discussion, ibid. The parallel in Tosefta *Yev.* I,8 ff. (241) does not give an exegesis either.

18) M. *Yev.* VI,6 gives the verse for Beth Hillel, the Tosefta ad loc. — VIII, 4 (249) — for both. They use different verses.

19) In M. *Git.* IX,10 both Beth Shammai and Beth Hillel are using the same verse. Beth Shammai takes the verse in its most literal sense, while Beth Hillel understands *'erwath davar* as a more general expression. It is quite possible that Beth Hillel is closer to the true meaning of the passage. The word *'erwah* is used already in the Pentateuch in a figurative way (see Gen. 42:9 and 12 לראות את ערות הארץ "to see the nakedness of the land ye are come." The phrase באתם ערות דבר *'erwath davar* does not occur elsewhere). Whenever sexual immoralities are mentioned, which is often the case, other expressions are used.[133]

20) B. *B. Q.* 65b, a Baraitha, is without exegesis. The exegesis is supplied by Amoraim.

21) M. *B. M.* III,12. An exegesis is given by Beth Hillel only. Noteworthy is that not all the Mishnah versions include this exegesis. The Lowe edition, for example, does not have it.

22) Baraitha in B. *Hul.* 88b. Beth Shammai takes Lev. 17:13 literally,

without mentioning the verse explicitly. Beth Hillel, however, understands עפר *afar* in its more general meaning, by referring to Num.
19:17 ולקחו לטמא מעפר שרפת החאטת "And for the unclean they
shall take of the *ashes* of the burning . . ."

23) M. *Ḥul.* XI,2. The verses are not from the Torah but from
Isaiah and Samuel, respectively.

24) M. *Kerithoth* I,6. The Mishnah contains no exegesis, nor does
the Tosefta I,9 parallel. However, in B. Talmud, ibid. 8a, Beth Hillel
gives the exegesis. In *Sifra Tazria* III, as in the Baraitha, Beth Hillel cites the verse, but more fully. The weight of the controversy,
however, rests with the logic of the reasoning based on the law, not
with the wording of the text.

25) M. *Zev.* IV,6. No exegesis is given. This is supplied by *Amoraim* ibid. 37b.

26) Baraitha in B. *Men.* 41b gives no exegesis. Tosafoth, s.v.
Beth Shammai, refer to the exegetical basis of the controversy. This
exegetical basis, ibid. 39b, supporting Beth Shammai is amoraic.
Sifre Num.,[134] and its parallel in Deut.[135] add: The Halakhah is in
accordance with Beth Shammai.

27) M. *Bekhoroth* V,2 gives no exegesis. Tosefta *Bekhor.* III,15, a
different version, adds Akiba's view which corresponds to Beth
Hillel's view in the Mishnah, and this — only this — is with an
exegesis. Gemara ibid., 32b–33a Amoraim advance the exegetical
basis. The Baraitha ibid. agrees with the Tosefta.

What do these "exegetical" controversies reveal?

The number of controversies between Beth Hillel and Beth Shammai which are based on exegetical differences is very small. In fact,
it is much smaller than I. H. Weiss suggests when he considers
about ten percent of the total controversies between Beth Hillel and
Beth Shammai as being of exegetical character. In tannaitic sources,
exegeses are offered merely in 1, 7, 8, 10, 18, 19, 21, 22, 23, and 24.
Of these ten passages, in 8 and 10 the exegeses are not advanced by
Beth Hillel and Beth Shammai themselves, therefore it is doubtful
whether these cases should be considered as exegetical controversies.
Of the remaining eight, in 21 an exegesis is given merely by Beth
Hillel, and even this is not present in all the texts. In 24 it is again
Beth Hillel only who offers an exegesis. In 23 the verses are not

from the Torah, which is at variance with the normal process of halakhic exegesis.

In all the other instances, and they are the vast majority (2, 3, 4, 5, 6, 9, 11, 12, 13, 14, 15, 16, 17, 20, 25, 26 and 27) the exegeses have been advanced at a later period, mostly by Amoraim. It is quite possible that in some cases the Amoraim advance the exegesis on the basis of an old tradition, but this, being a conjecture, cannot be used as evidence.

Most noteworthy is that no one of the exegeses advanced in these controversies involves any of the hermeneutic rules.

It is to be noted that, whereas the exegeses of Beth Hillel and Beth Shammai are about even in number, Hillel himself advances considerably more exegeses than Shammai. As to aggadic exegeses, cf. Bacher's discussion.[136] The significant halakhic exegeses by Hillel are: The famous exegeses in *Pes.* 66 (and parallels) advanced by Hillel in answering the Bene Bathyra; the three exegeses which are given as the reason for Hillel's coming to Palestine;[137] and the one on eating Mazzah, bitter herbs, and meat of the Paschal sacrifice in a certain way.[138] By Shammai, there are two to be mentioned specifically: One referring to times of war;[139] the other deals with a specific aspect of the law about agency.[140] It appears that after the memorable discussion between Hillel and the Bene Bathyra which gave Hillel the opportunity to employ hermeneutic rules, but in which he was rebuffed,[141] these rules played a very small role until the destruction of the Temple. Exegesis in general was not used too frequently either. As to the hermeneutic rules, one of the reasons may be the resistance of some conservative or anti-Hellenistic sages against methods which were in vogue in the first century C.E. in Hellenistic rhetoric, though some of these methods, e.g. the *qal wehomer*, are found in ancient Jewish sources.[142] After the times of Beth Hillel and Beth Shammai, when these rules became part of the culture in general, hermeneutics was used more freely. Almost all the controversies between the schools concern details of older laws, not basically new legislation. For these, reference to Scripture was not as important as it was for new legislation, which became imperative after the destruction of the Temple and needed a source of authority to make it acceptable. Therefore, the vast majority of exegeses, of which the hermeneutic ones are but a fraction, date from the time after 70 c.e. Hillel himself was considerably ahead of his time when he demonstrated and urged the usage of exegesis.[143]

The insignificant role of the hermeneutic rules during the Beth Hillel–Beth Shammai period is indicated by the fact that in Mishnah *Beẓah* I,6, Beth Shammai use the words *gezerah shawah* to mean simply "analogy," without any exegetical connotation. The same holds true for Beth Hillel in the Tosefta parallel *Yom Tov* I,13. Had *gezerah shawah* been in vogue as a hermeneutic rule these words certainly would not have been used to express a simple analogy.

The exegetical controversies between the schools show the same picture as the rest of their controversies. Beth Shammai are more conservative in their exegesis, Beth Hillel, on the whole, more liberal. Beth Shammai cling to the literal meaning of the text, even if this may not be the true meaning of the passage. Beth Hillel, on the other hand, take a passage in its larger context. Cf. particularly I:1, 19, 22.

In instances in which Beth Shammai and Beth Hillel are using different verses in order to support their respective views, the assumption is justified that the exegesis is secondary, and had been advanced later in support of a view existing previously.

While no proof can be adduced, we should not overlook a possibility that could explain the very small role exegesis played during Hillel's and Shammai's time. It is conceivable that Beth Hillel and Beth Shammai concurred in a number of exegeses, which were not preserved except for the Halakhoth derived by these exegeses and transmitted anonymously. As a rule, anonymous Halakhoth represent views agreed upon by certain schools or certain groups of sages.[144]

INTERRELATIONS

Contacts, personal and otherwise (after Hillel and Shammai)

Did Beth Shammai and Beth Hillel have separate schools? If so, did they continue after Hillel and Shammai? Were they mere factions of one school? Did they exist only during the lifetime of the masters? These questions have found contradictory answers based on the same sources. For example, the fact that no heads of Beth Shammai are mentioned after the time of Hillel and Shammai is interpreted by I. H. Weiss as meaning that separate schools existed only at Hillel's and Shammai's time. Afterward, both parties stayed within one school.[145] Halevy, however, infers from the above fact that after Hillel and Shammai, Beth Hillel and Beth Shammai did not continue their existence.[146]

We saw that at Hillel's and Shammai's time matters had been discussed and decided, as they came up, one by one, in joint sessions. Shammai could not have held the office of the *Av Beth Din*, which he did,[147] if his party had not been part of the joint school headed by the Nasi. This does not exclude, however, the possibility that the parties, in addition to the joint academy, had separate schools.

As to the state of affairs after Hillel and Shammai, the following sources are most revealing.

M. *Sukkah* II, 7 gives a direct controversy between Beth Shammai and Beth Hillel. In order to decide the issue in their favor, Beth Hillel cite an incident in which the Shammaite Rabbi Johanan ben Ha-Ḥorani(th) followed the practice approved by Beth Hillel.

מי שהיה ראשו ורובו בסוכה ושולחנו בתוך הבית בית שמאי פוסלין,
ובית הלל מכשירין. אמרו להן בית הלל לבית שמאי: לא כך היה מעשה
שהלכו זקני בית שמאי וזקני בית הלל לבקר את רבי יוחנן בן החורני
ומצאוהו שהיה יושב ראשו ורובו בסוכה ושולחנו בתוך הבית (ולא אמרו
לו דבר)? אמרו להן בית שמאי משם ראיה? אף הם אמרו לו, אם כן
היית נוהג, לא קיימת מצות סוכה מימיך.

If a man's head and the greater part of his body are within the *Sukkah*, but his table is within the house, Beth Shammai declare it invalid, and Beth Hillel declare it valid. Beth Hillel said to Beth Shammai: "Did not the Elders of Beth Shammai and Beth Hillel once go to visit Rabbi Johanan ben Ha-Ḥorani and find him sitting with his head and the greater part of his body within the *Sukkah* while his table was within the house. Beth Shammai answered: "Is there proof from this [incident]? They indeed said to him: If such has been thy practice thou hast never in thy life fulfilled the law of the Sukkah."

This important passage tells us that about the middle of the first century c.e. (R. Johanan ben Haḥorani's time) Beth Shammai and Beth Hillel maintained close contact both within and outside the Sanhedrin. They were not bitter at each other, as shown by the joint social visit. Some time later, when a Halakhah was discussed, Johanan's practice was well remembered; the question was merely whether he had been reprimanded or not. At the time of the discussion Johanan was undoubtedly dead, otherwise he could have been asked to clarify the issue. On the other hand, the fact that the practice was well remembered indicates that the discussion took place not long after the incident.

Whether or not the matter was then decided is not indicated in the text. Yet, since it was a direct controversy, conducted man to man, the probability is that a decision was reached, as was the case in similar instances. A record of the decision was unnecessary from the point of view of the Mishnah redactor, since the principal decision of Javneh eliminated the need for an individual record in normal cases. A record was only needed for the exceptional cases.

Pleasant relations between the members of the houses in the middle of the first century c.e. are attested in Tos. *Sukkah* II,3 (193–194) = *Eduy.* II,2; (457 parallel Baraitha B. *Yev.* 15b). R. Eleazar ben Ẓadok, a Hillelite, studied with the Shammaite R. Johanan ben Haḥoranith. The latter, on the other hand, followed a Hillelite practice.[148] According to the version in B. *Yev.* 15b, he followed Hillel in every instance, but this may be an exaggeration. The case clearly shows that a Shammaite who followed some Hillelite practices did not thereby become a Hillelite. The opposite is just as true.[149]

Tos. *R. H.* IV (II),11 (p. 214) relates an incident in which Ḥoni Haqatan (about middle of the first century c.e.), obviously a Shammaite, follows a Hillelite practice in the presence of the elders of Beth Shammai (and Beth Hillel). When the matter came up in a direct discussion, Beth Hillel referred to this incident. Beth Shammai did not deny the fact but merely claimed exceptional circumstances. Here we have another case in which Shammaites at least tolerated a

Hillelite practice. The passage also indicates that Hillelites and Shammaites attended joint services.

As to the decision of the controversy, the same holds true as in the case above (M. *Sukkah* II,7).

M. *'Orlah* II,12 relates that the Shammaite Yo'ezer Ish Habirah said that while standing at the Eastern Gate (of the Temple enclosure), he asked Rabban Gamaliel the Elder about a ritual matter. The answer he received is given in the previous Mishnah as the view of the sages (i.e., majority opinion) against the view of R. Eliezer.

We see that a Shammaite feels free to consult with the Patriarch, a Hillelite, to learn the proper ruling. This happened, as in the two cases above, about the middle (second third) of the first century C.E. Moreover, we note that the inquiry did not take place in the academy.

Most instances discussed, so far, represent *direct* controversies between the schools. This fact means matters had been discussed within one and the same assembly (unless it was a private discussion, as was the last one cited above). The logical reasoning that the respective views of the parties had to be prepared in their separate schools before being brought before the joint meeting sounds sensible but constitutes no real evidence. Parties opposed to each other are able to raise objections and make counter suggestions without much preparation or even without any preparation.

Considerably more revealing are the *indirect* controversies, though, strangely enough, no attention has been paid to these. Many, if not most, of the controversies without dialogue in tannaitic source literature belong in this category. These controversies, or better, differences, originated at the period close to the destruction of the Temple, when only one joint meeting was held. This one session is most revealing; it is the famous conference concerning the "Eighteen Matters." The fact that in this one conference numerous items came up for settlement proves that no joint meetings had been held for some time; otherwise the matters would have been settled one by one and would not have accumulated. It was obviously at a time when the Sanhedrin could not meet, since this conference was held in a private home under the pretext of a visit.

Where had all the matters that came up in that joint meeting been prepared? There cannot be the least doubt that this was done in the privacy of the respective schools of Beth Shammai and Beth Hillel.

We believe that this shows unequivocally that the Houses had separate schools and were not mere factions of the *"Beth Hamidrash Ha-Gadol,"* the Pharisaic Sanhedrin. These separate schools still existed long after Hillel and Shammai and did not terminate when these "Eighteen Matters" were discussed shortly before the fall of the Temple. I. H. Weiss' argument ex silentio (*Dor.* I. p. 184) that there were no separate schools because no head of Beth Shammai is mentioned after Shammai, is unacceptable.

In further clarifying the role of the "Eighteen Matters," we must inquire as to the significance of the conference at Hananiah ben Hizkiah ben Garon's home for the history of the Halakhah. We turn to the following sources: Babylonian Talmud (incl. Mishnah) *Shab.* 13b ff.—P. *Shab.* I,4; 3c ff.—Tos. *Shab.* I,16 (p. 111).

Each of these sources has various strata, and they are not in complete accord. They have been repeatedly discussed with contradictory results.[150]

The most reliable of them is the oldest datable tannaitic report: that of R. Simon ben Johai in P. *Shab.* 3c. According to this report the result of the conference was the issuance of eighteen prohibitions, *Gezeroth*, intended to separate Jews from gentiles.

These *Gezeroth* were issued a short time before the Jewish War.[151] The initiative was in the hands of Beth Shammai, which displayed great fervor in the matter. They succeeded by a majority vote, which was unusual, since Beth Hillel had been the majority party since Hillel's and Shammai's times. The Talmud itself gives an explanation (P. *Shab.*, loc. cit.): R. Joshua Onaia (of the second and third generation Palestinian Amoraim) cites a Baraitha stating that the Shammaites allowed but six Hillelites to go up to the conference; they prevented the others by the use of force.

Had this been the case, the Hillelites undoubtedly would have repudiated these *Gezeroth* as soon as they could, but they did not do this. In fact, their spiritual successors, the rabbis, emphasized the superiority of these *Gezeroth* over all the other *Gezeroth*. In P. Talmud, ibid. 3d, a statement by Samuel is related advising that while other *Gezeroth* are revocable, the Eighteen *Gezeroth* are not.[152]

When the Gemara (ibid.) points to the fact that the "oil *Gezerah*" had been revoked (150 years later by Judah II), exceptional circumstances are adduced (ibid.).

The probability is that due to the tension between Jews and heathens (Romans and others) at that time, some Hillelites voted with the Shammaites. This is nothing out of order, since we know of many other instances in which individual Shammaites sided with Beth Hillel and vice versa. It is possible, too, that the Hillelites, favoring peaceful relations with the gentiles, did not care to attend the meeting in large numbers.

While the primary purpose of the conference was undoubtedly the issuance of *Gezeroth* against the heathens, all the sources agree that other matters as well were considered. As to these, the sources are not in complete accord. There is a discrepancy, for example, whether there were one or two other categories of Halakhoth on the agenda. According to P. Talmud, ibid. 3c, three categories came up in this conference, each comprising eighteen cases. The first category was the jointly issued *Gezeroth*; the second category of Halakhoth had been decided by vote favoring Beth Shammai; the disputes of the third category had not been resolved. This latter Baraitha allows the conclusion that the Hillelites, being in accidental minority, refused to settle at this time many of the unresolved disagreements.

It is to be noted that not all the *Gezeroth* and other Halakhoth settled at that meeting were new, or even controversial. One of the *Gezeroth* is, for example, the biblical prohibition of intermarriage.[153] This *Gezerah* and some of the others represent a revival and strengthening of old neglected laws.

To evaluate the significance and scope of this conference let us keep in mind the following: 1) It had a limited program. It did not resolve all the pending disagreements. 2) The outcome of the meeting had no effect on the leadership. This remained in the hands of the Hillelite Nasi, a sign of the assembly's limited power. 3) The extensive agenda of the conference proves that for some time no regular joint meetings were held; otherwise no great number of unresolved controversies would have accumulated. 4) When no agreement could be reached, the issue was resolved by vote which was binding on both parties.

THE END OF THE "HOUSES"

B. *'Eruvin* 13b relates:

א″ר אבא אמר שמואל שלש שנים נחלקו ב″ש וב″ה הללו אומרים
הלכה כמותנו והללו אומרים הלכה כמותנו יצאה בת קול ואמרה אלו
ואלו דברי אלהים חיים הן והלכה כב″ה.

To this P. *Yev.* I,6 end; 3b adds some significant details:

... או כדברי בית שמאי כקוליהם וכחומריהן או כדברי בית הלל
כקוליהם וכחומריהן. הדא דתימר עד שלא יצאת בת קול אבל משיצאת
בת קול לעולם הלכה כדברי בית הלל וכל העובר על דברי בית הלל
חייב מיתה. תני יצאתה בת קול ואמרה אילו ואילו דברי אלהים חיים
הם אבל הלכה כב″ה לעולם. באיכן יצאת בת קול. רב ביבי בשם
ר″י אמר ביבנה יצאת בת קול.

Rabbi Abba said in the name of Samuel: Beth Shammai and Beth
Hillel argued for three years. The ones said, "The Halakhah is in
accordance with us," and the others said, "The Halakhah is in accordance with us." Then a *Bath Qol* sounded saying, "These and
these are the words of the living God, but the Halakhah is in
accordance with Beth Hillel."

So far B. *'Eruvin* 13b. The passage in P. *Yev.* I,6; 3b states:
One should either follow Beth Shammai in both their lenient and
their strict rulings; or Beth Hillel in both their lenient and their
strict rulings. This, however, refers to the period prior to the *Bath
Qol*. Yet, after the sounding of the *Bath Qol*, the Halakhah is always in accordance with Beth Hillel, and everyone transgressing
the words of Beth Hillel is guilty of death. . . . Where did the
Bath Qol come forth? Rav Bibi said in the name of Rabbi Johanan: "in Javneh."

This is the most important instance in which the *Bath Qol*, a voice
from heaven, entered the realm of Halakhah.[154]

For our present problem, three points need clarification: 1) When
did the *Bath Qol* make this sweeping verdict? 2) Did the "Houses"
continue their existence after that verdict? 3) What was the extent
of the authority this *Bath Qol* possessed?

1) *Date of the Bath Qol Verdict*

Rabbi Johanan relates that the *Bath Qol* came forth in Javneh.
The repetition of this information several times in the Palestinian
Talmud confirms its accuracy. Rabbi Johanan is known to have pos-

105

sessed data of significance concerning the tannaitic period. Thus it is certain that this event took place (even if we do not accept it in its literal sense) at the time when Javneh was the seat of the *Beth Din Ha-Gadol.* Yet, this body existed over a long period, beginning with the fall of the Temple. The assumption that the conference took place under Gamaliel II, a leader much concerned with preserving Jewish unity, is a conjecture of little value for our purpose, since he held leadership for a long period.[155]

Circumstantial evidence indicates that our *Bath Qol* incident could not have taken place long after the destruction of the Temple. Such evidence is: Only very few controversies of Beth Shammai and Beth Hillel presuppose conditions that existed after 70 c.e.[156] Undoubtedly, nearly all of them were conducted during the existence of the Temple. In fact, the data relevant to the cessation of the Houses, which we consider next, indicate the Houses themselves did not continue as such much after 70 c.e., thus giving us a terminus ad quem for the *Bath Qol* incident.

2) *Time of the Cessation of the Houses*

Among indications that the schools of Shammai and Hillel ended shortly after the destruction of the Temple, the following data are particularly noteworthy:

R. Eliezer and R. Joshua among other sages of the second tannaitic generation (principal activities 90–130 c.e.) disagree on the interpretation of controversies between Beth Shammai and Beth Hillel, indicating that at that time these schools no longer existed. Had they existed, a simple inquiry with the respective schools would have sufficed. We have pointed out elsewhere that interpretation of controversies, particularly those introduced by לא נחלקו... על מה נחלקו "they do not disagree in this . . . but in what do they disagree?" as, for example, in Tosefta *Peah* III,2 (21) (cf. Mishnah, ibid. VI.2) between R. Eliezer and R. Joshua, refer to the controversies of the past.[157]

Most revealing is an incident given in B. *Git.* 81a. Here Dossa ben Horkynos, a Tanna who lived at the end of the first and the beginning of the second century c.e., is identified as belonging to *Doroth Ha-Aḥaronim,* "later generations," in contradistinction to Beth Shammai, who are called *Doroth Ha-Rishonim,* "earlier generations." [158] The implication is obvious. At Dossa's time Beth Shammai existed no longer, otherwise they could not have been designated as "earlier generations."

Another source proves the non-existence of both Beth Shammai and Beth Hillel about the turn of the first century c.e. B. *Yev.* 16a (cf. P. *Yev.* I,6; 3a):

בימי רבי דוסא בן הררכינס התירו צרת הבת לאחין והיה הדבר
קשה לחכמים מפני שחכם גדול היה ועיניו קמו מלבא לבית המדרש
אמרו מי ילך ויודיעו אמר להן רבי יהושע אני אלך ואחריו מי רבי
אלעזר בן עזריה ואחריו מי ר״ע הלכו ועמדו על פתח ביתו... א״ל
רבי אמור לתלמידך אחר וישב אמר לו מי הוא רבי אלעזר בן עזריה
אמר ויש לו בן לעזריה חברנו קרא עליו את המקרא הזה נער הייתי
גם זקנתי ולא ראיתי צדיק נעזב וזרעו מבקש לחם.

In the days of Dossa ben Horkynos the marriage of the co-wife of a deceased man to his brother had been permitted in accordance with Beth Shammai's view. The sages, obviously some time later, felt bad about this decision because they believed that the highly esteemed Dossa was responsible for it. Once they decided to inquire with him about the matter. At that time Dossa was very old. He could not see any more and would not attend the sessions of the Academy. The visitors were: R. Joshua, R. Eleazar ben Azariah, and Rabbi Akiba. Even though Rabbi Eleazar ben Azariah, one of the delegates, was already a recognized sage, Dossa had not heard of him. He knew merely his father, whom he designates as his *ḥaver*, colleague. Upon learning of Azariah's having a son, now a sage before him, he exclaims (Ps. 37:25): "I have been young, and now am old. Yet have I not seen the righteous forsaken, Nor his seed begging bread." Questioned about the above matter, he denies having promoted the cause of the Shammaites. Then he points to his brother, R. Jonathan, a Shammaite, as the man responsible for the decision and cautions them against him.

This passage is significant because it reveals that when men of the second tannaitic generation wished to clarify the circumstances under which a Halakhah had been decided in favor of Beth Shammai, they did not go to Beth Shammai or Beth Hillel, but instead to a very old sage who, according to some tradition, was responsible for the decision. Had the schools of Shammai and Hillel existed at this time, they would have been the logical places for the inquiry.

In Tosefta *Hag.* II,10 (236) Abba Saul, a disciple and contemporary of Johanan ben Zakkai quotes a *qal weḥomer* (an inference a minori or a fortiori) in the name of Beth Hillel at variance with another tradition about the same *qal weḥomer.* This can be taken as an indication that Beth Hillel did not exist any longer at the time of this controversy about the correct wording of Beth Hillel's argument, which took place not long after the destruction of the Temple (Abba Saul's time). We do not overlook the possibility that at a later period of Beth Hillel and Beth Shammai, some controversies of the earlier period became obscure and were subjected to scrutiny. We do not find here, however, a clarification by Beth Hillel but, instead, a secondary controversy is cited regarding the genuine wording used by Beth Hillel. The non-existence of Beth Hillel at this time is thus strongly indicated.

Tos. *Yev.* V,1 (245) (= Tosefta *'Eduy.* II,9) contains a controversy as to Beth Hillel's and Beth Shammai's view in a certain case.[159] One of the men (the oldest) participating in this secondary controversy is Abba Saul. This controversy could hardly have occurred during Beth Hillel's existence, for then their view would not have been so uncertain that diametrically opposite traditions existed about it.

שאלו את ר' יהושע בני צרות מה הן אמר להם למה אתם מכניסין
אותי בין שני הרים גדולים בין בית שמאי ובין בית הילל שיריצו את
ראשי אלא מעיד אני על משפחת בית עלובאי מצביים ועל משפחת בית
קיפא מבית מקושש שהם בני צרות ומהם כהנים גדולים מקריבין לגבי
מזבח.

Here a question had been asked of Rabbi Joshua relative to a dispute between Beth Shammai and Beth Hillel. In answering it, he expresses great veneration for both in a manner that indicates that he did not belong to either. In fact, he refuses to side openly with Beth Hillel, to which House he spiritually belonged, and cites, instead, incidents indicating his stand. Moreover, had the Houses existed at that time, the question certainly would have been put before them, not before R. Joshua.

Tos. *Peah* III,2 (21) relates:

אמר ר' אילעאי שאלתי את ר' יהושע על אלו עמרים נחלקו בית שמאי ובית הלל אמר לי התורה הזאת על העומר סמוך לגפה ולגדיש לבקר ולכלים ושכחו כשבאתי שאלתי את ר' אליעזר אמר לי מודים שאין שכחה על מה נחלקו על העומר שהחזיקו בו להוליכו לעיר וכו'

Here R. Joshua and R. Eliezer had been asked to clarify the respective positions of Beth Shammai and Beth Hillel in a case under discussion. Their answers are contradictory. They possessed different traditions in the matter. Existing schools, no doubt, would have been able to clarify their own views.

P. *Terumoth* III,2; 42a (Tosefta, ibid. III,12, p. 29):

תניי מאימתי תורמין את הענבים... מאימתי מטמאין אותן? בית שמאי אומרים משיוציא את השני ובית הלל אומרים משיוציא את הראשון. א"ר יוסי הלכה כבית שמאי והרבים נהגו כבית הלל... וחכמים אומרים לא כדברי זה ולא כדברי זה אלא, וכו'

Here the sages disagree with both Beth Shammai and Beth Hillel. This may mean that they do not identify themselves with Beth Shammai or with Beth Hillel for the apparent reason that these schools had not existed at the time of the secondary controversy. Yet, it is possible that we are dealing here with post-Hadrianic sages, at whose time the non-existence of schools of Shammai and Hillel is generally admitted.

In this connection, I should like to draw attention to *'Eduyyoth*, the testimonies related in the tractates of Mishnah and Tosefta bearing this name. Shortly after the destruction of the Temple, steps had been initiated to collect teachings of the past in order to preserve them in a systematic way for ready reference. Most of these traditions are teachings of Beth Shammai and Beth Hillel, but the transmitters of the teachings are not the schools, nor their heads or representatives, but rather individuals who claim no affiliation with the schools. What is even more significant, the individual transmitters do not transmit the teachings of one of the schools — which could be taken as an indication of their affiliation with this school — but they transmit almost invariably the traditions of both schools simultaneously. Obviously, the schools belonged to past history at that time, i.e., shortly after the destruction of the Temple.

Not all the passages adduced can be considered as clear-cut evidence for our thesis. Yet even those which are acceptable merely as indications possess certain value, inasmuch as they lend cumulative support to a structure based on other unequivocal source material. We believe that the evidence adduced shows clearly that the men of the second tannaitic generation, after the destruction of the Temple, discuss Beth Shammai and Beth Hillel as schools of the past. Therefore, not long after 70 c.e. the existence of the schools was terminated.

Among other views, Z. Frankel's opinion that the "Houses" continued their existence until the Bar Kokhba uprising deserves serious attention.[160] For evidence, he refers to the chapter on R. Joshua in his *Darke Ha-Mishnah*. However, a careful reading of this chapter leaves the reader unconvinced.[161] The passage Frankel appears to rely on most is B. *Ḥag.* 22b:

תניא א״ר יהושע בושני מדבריכם ב״ש אפשר אשה לשה בעריבה
אשה ועריבה טמאין שבעה ובצק טהור וכו' נטפל לו תלמיד אחד
מתלמידי ב״ש אמר לו אומר לך טעמן של ב״ש אמר לו אמור אמר לו
כלי טמא חוצץ או אינו חוצץ... וזהו טעמן של ב״ש מיד הלך ר' יהושע
ונשתטח על קברי ב״ש אמר נעניתי לכם עצמות ב״ש ומה סתומות
שלכם כך מפורשות על אחת כמה וכמה. אמרו כל ימיו הושחרו שיניו
מפני תעניותיו.

It is taught: R. Joshua said: "I am ashamed of your words, O Beth Shammai." Is it possible that if a woman kneads in a trough, the woman and the trough become unclean for seven days, but the dough remains clean? etc. . . . [Afterward] one of the disciples of Beth Shammai joined him and said to him: "I will tell thee the

110

reason of Beth Shammai." He replied, "Tell then!" He said to him. . . "This is the reason of Beth Shammai." Instantly R. Joshua went and prostrated himself upon the graves of Beth Shammai: "If your unexplained teachings are so [good], how much more so your explained teachings!" It is said that all his days his teeth were black by reason of his fasts.

This incident is not a discussion between Beth Shammai and Beth Hillel, but between Rabbi Joshua, defending a Hillelite view, and a disciple of Beth Shammai, who merely qualifies Beth Shammai's view but does not suggest it. The discussion was held obviously *after* the session of the academy and had a private character. After the qualifying statement of the Shammaite convinced R. Joshua, he went to the *graves* of the Shammaites to make his apology. This is most revealing. Had Beth Shammai existed at that time, R. Joshua certainly would have apologized before them, not on the graves of the deceased Shammaites. The existence of some Shammaites after the termination of Beth Shammai is no puzzle. Termination of the school does not mean the extermination of its members. As individuals they continued to live for some time. They even may have continued as a sectarian school. Yet, they did not exist at the time of this incident as the recognized school of Shammai and the surviving Shammaites ceased to play a traceable role in Judaism.

Termination of the school of Shammai made the designation Beth Hillel, for the remaining school representing the mainstream of Judaism, meaningless. Therefore, this designation was dropped. From now on, the controversies proceed under the names of individual sages, sometimes grouped together, or under the designation "sages."

We elaborated on this point, because Frankel's view still appears to be the predominant one, though other opinions also exist, too. I. Halevy, for example, believes that Beth Shammai and Beth Hillel existed mainly at Hillel's and Shammai's time. This opinion is doomed in view of abundant evidence to the contrary. For example, disputes of paramount importance, such as the "Eighteen Matters" and the three years disputes for supremacy, all took place long after Hillel's and Shammai's death. Halevy's main proof, an argument ex silentio, is quite weak: After Shammai's death no head of Beth Shammai is mentioned, therefore Beth Shammai did not exist any longer (see page 100). On the contrary, one must consider that among the Shammaites mentioned by name, one might have been the head of their school. It is quite understandable that after Beth Shammai had been doomed halakhically by the *Bath Qol*, the sages as successors of the Hillelites did not care to preserve historical data on the rejected school.

Our view regarding the terminus ad quem of the school of Beth Shammai is close to that of I. H. Weiss. Weiss believes that Beth Shammai's existence terminated with the destruction of the Temple. The two controversies between the Houses which do take into account the conditions existing *after* the destruction of the Temple, are subjected to forced interpretation by him.[162]

Further indications pointing to the non-existence of the "Houses" shortly after the destruction of the Temple are the following:

Z. Frankel observed that the range of the subjects discussed by Beth Shammai and Beth Hillel is limited.[163] Most of their controversies concern prayers, festivals, precepts related to the soil of Palestine, marriage and divorce, vows, nazirdom, monetary matters relative to marriage, defilement, purity, and the like. However they do not discuss the priestly service and have only one discussion about a sacrifice and few controversies about monetary matters. They do not discuss matters of the Sanhedrin, judicial error, false witness, penalties by death or flogging. In matters of *nega'im*, "leprosy signs," they are not even mentioned in the sources. On the other hand, all these matters are extensively discussed by Tannaim *after* the destruction of the Temple. What might be the reason for this situation?

Beth Shammai and Beth Hillel obviously concentrated on the Halakhah relevant in their day and within their jurisdiction and sphere of interest. Thus, they took little interest in discussing the details and mechanics of the sacrificial cult, since its administration was in the hands of the priests. Only occasionally did the non-priestly Pharisees enter the realm of the sacrificial cult, e.g., in the case of the *semikhah* controversy,[164] Paschal sacrifice,[165] the burning of the incense on the Day of Atonement,[166] and the water libation on Sukkoth.[167] In these and similar instances, basic issues were involved and the disputes did not arise under the names of Beth Hillel and Beth Shammai.

However, after the destruction of the Temple, the rabbis expanded their interest to all areas of Jewish law, priestly and non-priestly, practical and theoretical. This expansion of interest was induced or, at least, stimulated by the cessation of the priestly functions. Many priests, having lost their professional privileges and class distinction, joined the rabbis, sharing with them their former special interests. Moreover, the rabbis, who now included the priests, believed that their period was but an interim to be followed by the restoration of freedom, Temple, and cult. Therefore, the study of the theoretical laws was considered an essential preparation for their application in the (near) future.

In some areas, the absence of Beth Shammai and Beth Hillel can be attributed to the fact that these areas were not controversial at their time. This may have been the case regarding the matters contained in tractates *Megillah, Ta'anith,* and *'Avodah Zarah.*

3) The Extent of the Authority of our *Bath Qol.* Before suggesting an answer, let us call attention to the following problem. Since the *Bath Qol* possessed the power to decide the issue authoritatively, why did it wait three years before it interfered? What happened during those three years? Why was the issue not decided by vote as had been the case at a number of previous occasions?

The usual procedure of the *Beth Din Ha-Gadol* had been to decide the controversial Halakhoth by vote. However, in the three years' conference obviously a principal decision had been sought. The הללו אומרים הלכה כמותנו והללו אומרים הלכה כמותנו wording "The ones said, 'The Halakhah is in accordance with us,' and the others said, 'The Halakhah is in accordance with us,' " without any reference to particular cases indicates that the issue at stake was exclusive authority in the realm of Halakhah. The conditions after the destruction of the Temple had led the two schools to irreconcilable views regarding the ways of coping with the new situation. But why was this basic issue not decided by vote? It stands to reason that the minority would not submit to a vote, because it would thus be relegated to impotence. Because details of the three year feud have not been transmitted, we only know that the deadlock was abruptly broken by the *Bath Qol.* But did Beth Shammai recognize the *Bath Qol* at another (earlier) occasion when it entered the realm of Halakhah, even though it did not repudiate them.[168] There can be little doubt that they rejected the *Bath Qol* that spelled their doom.

Let us now investigate the extent of authority our *Bath Qol* possessed.

According to the account in the P. Talmud, "The Halakhah is *always* in accordance with Beth Hillel." What does this "always" mean? The obvious meaning is that no exceptions were allowed. The fact, however, is that there were exceptions. While the Babylonian Talmud does not include the word "always," it still wonders about the exceptions, and attempts to explain them.

One of the explanations offered is that the exceptions are in accordance with R. Joshua, who rejected *Bath Qol*.[169] However, he did this, so far as we know, merely in a special case leading to R. Eliezer's banishment, which occurred later than *our Bath Qol*.[170] In our case we hear of no objection by R. Joshua and may safely assume that he raised no objection. It is quite doubtful whether he, a young man at that time, figured in that dispute. On the other hand, it is quite possible that his successful objection to *Bath Qol* in the R. Eliezer case, which led to a basic rejection of *Bath Qol* as a means of making halakhic decisions,[171] weakened even the authority of the *Bath Qol* of the past. Therefore, later sages, living after the "Houses" no longer existed, and viewing the disputes of the past more objectively, without passion or animosity, allowed exceptions in the academy and in personal observance.

The talmudic conjecture that the exceptions were made prior to the sounding of the *Bath Qol* (ibid.) may reflect the truth merely in cases in which the matter had been decided by vote *prior* to our *Bath Qol*. However, all the cases still controversial at the time of the three years' struggle the *Bath Qol* decided in favor of Beth Hillel without exception.

The controversies affected by the *Bath Qol* were mainly the *indirect* controversies, i.e., the differences which arose after the schools no longer held regular joint sessions. This was the case during an indeterminable number of years before the destruction of the Temple.[172] The history of the "Eighteen Matters" and of other Halakhah previously decided in favor of Beth Shammai proves that the *Bath Qol* was not made effective retroactively so as to alter older decisions.

Further clarification and more insight in regard to our problems may be gained by considering the following problem:

Were the differences between Beth Shammai and Beth Hillel practical or merely academic? This issue is already raised in the Talmud. B. *Yev.* 14–16; P. *Yev.* I,6; 3b and parallels transmit a controversy between Rab and Samuel in which the one Amora claimed that both schools followed *the* Halakhah as the one and only valid, binding law, and the other Amora maintained that each school followed *its own* Halakhah.[173] Who was right? A scrutiny of the sources shows that neither of them was fully right or wrong. What actually happened was that the followers of the respective schools practiced the Halakhah of their school as long as the matter in question had not come before the joint session for a decision. The decision of the joint session usually terminated the controversy and the diversified practice. The termination of the *semikhah* controversy is the first significant instance where this can be observed.[174] Tannaitic sources make it quite clear that prior to a decision of a joint session the individual was given the freedom to practice the teachings of his own school though in general the Halakhah was in accordance with Beth Hillel. The case of the "Eighteen Matters" is another instance showing that a decision reached at a joint session was binding upon both Schools.[175]

It is not known how many cases were decided in joint sessions of the Houses. P. *Yev.* I,6; 3b and parallels state in a general way that prior to our *Bath Qol* one was permitted to follow either of the schools. We see that there was a number of cases that had not come before a joint conference for decision. There was an understandable reluctance on the part of the minority to submit every case to a vote. This sometimes leads to quasi-chaotic conditions, for example, in the realm of marriage practices.[176] The obvious purpose of the conference that lasted for three years was to unify the Halakhah. Has the fundamental decision of the *Bath Qol* unified the Halakhah in accordance with Beth Hillel?

We observed elsewhere[177] that halakhic decisions prevailing at a certain period often carried little weight in later periods. After leading sages of a certain period died, or old schools were replaced by new ones and conditions changed, decisions of the past often were reversed or disregarded by new decisions. And this was the case, to a certain degree, in regard to the *Bath Qol* solution of Beth Shammai–Beth Hillel controversies. After the rivalry of the schools had been terminated, their feud became past history, the *Bath Qol* suffered a loss of prestige, and the sages felt free to make changes. To be sure, they did not reverse the principle of Beth Hillel's superiority over Beth Shammai, but they relaxed it. After the destruction of the Temple, the sages of the time, successors of the Hillelites, found existing conditions more conducive to the generally more lenient Halakhah of Beth Hillel. What actually happened was that several sages took the liberty of accepting some shammaitic Halakhoth. Whenever this happened, the *Bath Qol* remained unmentioned. It obviously had lost its prestige.

A few examples follow.

M. *Miqvaoth* IV, 1. R. Meir claims that in the case under discussion a vote had been taken and Beth Shammai won over Beth Hillel. R. Jose, on the other hand, says that the controversy still remains unresolved.[178] The latter view is understood by commentators as a denial that a vote was ever taken in the matter. Yet, did the *Bath Qol* not decide all the unresolved Beth Shammai and Beth Hillel controversies? The obvious conclusion is that just one generation after our *Bath Qol*, it was disregarded by R. Jose. But was he the only one who disregarded this *Bath Qol*? By no means, as is shown by other incidents.

In Tos. *Yev.* I,9, R. Johanan ben Nuri bemoans the unpleasant consequences of a disagreement between Beth Shammai and Beth Hillel. Then he suggests that the matter be settled in a certain way. However, because of unfavorable conditions (probably persecutions), the matter could not be settled.[179] It is obvious here, as in the previous instance, that one generation after the memorable decision, the *Bath Qol* was not heeded, or else no *Taqqanah* would have been deemed necessary.

In Tos. *Pes.* I,7 R. Jose relates that in the controversy under discussion between Beth Shammai and Beth Hillel, R. Akiba made a decision favoring Beth Hillel.[180] The implication is clear: R. Akiba, too, ignored the *Bath Qol*, otherwise his decision would have been superfluous.

M. *B. M.* III,12. Here R. Akiba holds an opinion at variance with the views of both Beth Shammai and Beth Hillel. This means he feels free to disregard the *Bath Qol* as well as loyalty to Beth Hillel to which he spiritually belongs. In B. *B. M.* 43b, Amoraim discuss the Halakhah. Samuel declares that the Halakhah is in accordance with R. Akiba, and so does R. Johanan. Only Raba sides with Beth Hillel.[181] We see that the Amoraim, like the Tannaim, do not hesitate to oppose the old doctrine of Beth Hillel's unconditional halakhic primacy.

In M. *B. B.* IX,9,10 Akiba's disagreement with both Beth Shammai and Beth Hillel furnishes another instance of disregard for the *Bath Qol.*

It is true that already in the time of Beth Hillel and Beth Shammai some sages occasionally disagreed with both schools. However they did so not only before the heavenly decision, but also rarely, under exceptional circumstances. Thus Zechariah ben Abqulos in a certain instance does not follow either Beth Shammai or Beth Hillel.[182] Yet, we have here a case of exaggerated piety, displayed by a man whose unreasonable attitude was severely criticized.[183] Aqabiah ben Mahallalel, another dissident in Beth Hillel's and Beth Shammai's time, was subsequently excommunicated.[184]

In the period following the cessation of the Houses,[185] not merely disregard for Beth Hillel's Halakhah, but also acceptance of Shammaitic views was frequent and entailed no consequences. Moreover, this acceptance of shammaitic views was not limited to the realm of theory, but it included the realm of practice as well. This is attested for all strata from the Nasi down to the common people. Unfortunately, these instances have often been misunderstood.

Examples:

Rabban Gamaliel II, though a patriarch from the House of Hillel, occasionally followed shammaitic views.[186] Does this mean that he was a Shammaite? Some scholars think so. The Talmud itself rejects this thought.[187] While the talmudic reasoning is forced, the fact remains that Gamaliel generally followed Hillelite views, accepting shammaitic opinions only exceptionally. Therefore, there is no justification for calling him a Shammaite.

R. Eliezer, too, occasionally followed Shammaitic views. This, in conjunction with a misinterpretation of his epithet *Shammuti, Shammati,* שמתי, שמותי induced most scholars erroneously to consider him a Shammaite.[188]

Other sages accepting occasionally Shammaitic views are: R. Tarfon,[189] R. Jose,[190] R. Meir.[191] R. Jehudah once related a tradition in the name of Beth Shammai, indicating his agreement.[192]

Tos. *Terumoth* III,12 relates a case in which R. Jehudah states that the Halakhah was in accordance with Beth Shammai. Nonetheless, the people followed the practice suggested by Beth Hillel (cf. P. *Terumoth* III,2; 42a). We hear of no objection to this disregard of the authorized Halakhah.[193]

Mishnah *Demai* VI,6 relates that in a particular case the particularly pious Hillelites would follow the rule of Beth Shammai, one opposed by Beth Hillel. However, they did so *before* our *Bath Qol* came forth.

Occasionally it happened that a person would satisfy a demand of both schools in certain instances. A case in point is in Tosefta *Shevi'ith* IV,21 (67), where we are informed that R. Akiba followed the rulings of both schools in the case under discussion.[194]

The basic primacy of Beth Hillel was not challenged in amoraic times. B. *Ber.* 36b (and parallels) state clearly:

ב"ש במקום ב"ה אינה משנה "Beth Shammai's teaching, when opposed by Beth Hillel, has no validity." Nonetheless, B. *Ber.* 11a (partial parallel P. ibid. I,3,4; 3b) presents a disagreement as to the ex post facto validity of the Shammaitic Halakhah. Rab Jehezkel holds that an act performed in accordance with Beth Shammai's Halakhah has validity ex post facto. Rab Josef denies this, and Rab Nahman bar Jizhak's opinion is that a man acting according to Beth Shammai deserves death.[195]

B. *Ber.* 48b relates that Rabbi Johanan (the greatest Palestinian Amora) declared that, in the case under discussion, the Halakhah was in accordance with Rabban Gamaliel, who decided the controversy in favor of Beth Shammai.[196]

Let us summarize, in brief, this chapter of the history of the Halakhah:

The schools of Shammai and Hillel ceased to exist shortly after the destruction of the Temple. First, Beth Shammai was relegated to impotence. Subsequently, the designation Beth Hillel for the only remaining authoritative school became meaningless and was, therefore, dropped.

The fundamental decision in favor of Beth Hillel was made by a *Bath Qol*, a "Heavenly Voice," at the end of a three years' dispute. The immediate effect of this *Bath Qol* was the doom of Beth Shammai. The *Bath Qol* was not effective retroactively; Halakhoth decided in favor of Beth Shammai prior to this *Bath Qol* remained in force. As time passed, the authority of this *Bath Qol* weakened for the twin reasons of rejection of *Bath Qol* as a means for making a halakhic decision (Aknai incident), and the vanishing of the bitterness of the party struggle which allowed matters of the past to be viewed with more calmness and objectivity. Therefore, a number of sages felt free to abandon some of Beth Hillel's Halakhoth and to accept shammaitic views in theory and in practice. Occasionally, the people too felt free to choose whatever practice they preferred, even one against the decision of the sages.

In later times, a tendency developed toward the revision of earlier Halakhoth. This phenomenon applies also to the Halakhoth of Beth Shammai and Beth Hillel. Accordingly, sages sometimes introduced Halakhoth which were at variance with those suggested by either of the schools, without drawing criticism. At times certain sages even followed the Halakhah of both schools in the same case.

In amoraic times the situation was the same as in that part of the tannaitic period occurring after the bitterness of the party struggle abated. Yet, after the *Bath Qol*, the primacy of Beth Hillel over Beth Shammai as a principle was never challenged, neither in tannaitic nor in amoraic times.

SUMMARY

Our examination of the primary sources dealing with the activities of Hillel and Shammai, and Beth Hillel and Beth Shammai, reveals the following:

1) Beth Hillel and Beth Shammai already existed in Hillel's and Shammai's time. Hillel and Shammai occasionally differed with their own schools. On the other hand, these schools sometimes disagreed with Hillel and Shammai even after their deaths. Thus Hillel and Shammai were not autocratic rulers of their schools, nor were they regarded as infallible. The schools were governed by the principles of democracy. The authority of Hillel and Shammai was based on the recognition of their spiritual stature by their schools and the people.

2) In the course of the existence of these schools certain changes took place. Disregard or neglect of these developments are the most important reasons for discord among scholars as to the role of Hillel, Shammai, and their schools for the making of Rabbinic Judaism. Some of these developments are:

a) For some time both schools convened jointly and constituted the two factions of the *Beth Din Ha-Gadol*, the Pharisaic Sanhedrin. In this *Beth Din Ha-Gadol* pending problems were discussed and decided by vote, if no accord could be reached otherwise. However, as time went on and the discord between these schools widened, they held their regular sessions separately, convening in joint session only periodically to resolve accumulated differences and so maintain the unity of the Jewish people who adhered to their leadership.

b) At Hillel's and Shammai's time, a decision by vote of one single issue could effect a change in the presidency. However, after Hillel's and Shammai's time, the presidency became hereditary in the House of Hillel, so that even the defeat of Beth Hillel in many issues would not result in a change in the presidency. There are indications that the Nasi, though a Hillelite, considered himself the impartial leader of the entire people and enjoyed therefore the trust of at least some Shammaites.

c) While in an earlier period of the schools differences were limited in number and importance, they grew more numerous and weighty as time went on.

3) The fundamental distinction between Beth Shammai and Beth Hillel is well attested in numerous sources notwithstanding efforts of some scholars to disregard the sources or to force them to say what they do not say: Beth Shammai is the conservative faction of

the *Beth Din Ha-Gadol* with an inclination toward stringency while Beth Hillel is the liberal one with a tendency toward leniency. Later, to this basic distinction other differences were added. Beth Shammai changed from a consistently conservative party to an outspoken opposition party. In a number of their decisions we find no other motive than that of opposition to Beth Hillel for the sake of opposition. At the early phase of Beth Shammai, the favorable economic position of its (influential) members inadvertently affected their views and decisions in the sphere of economics. When later their economic superiority vanished, their decisions no longer reflected a tendency favoring the well-to-do. As the tension between Jews and Romans increased, Beth Shammai militated for the introduction of laws aimed against the Romans. This indicates that not long before the Jewish war, ending in 70 c.e., Beth Shammai no longer represented a higher economic class. The wealthy seldom promote unrest and upheaval.

4) The fact that the generally strict Beth Shammai and the generally lenient Beth Hillel reverse their respective positions in some instances has misled some scholars to the conclusion that the notion about the basic stringency of Beth Shammai and the basic leniency of Beth Hillel is a myth. They suggest, instead, theories based on far-fetched conjectures. We showed that not only is the talmudic tradition about the basic stringency of Beth Shammai and leniency of Beth Hillel well established, but also that examination of the supposed exceptions reveals their inadequacy to overthrow it. The generally accepted number of reversed tendencies in their controversies as attested in tannaitic sources is but twenty-four, a small percentage of the total controversies. Moreover, several of these cases are not clear-cut cases of shammaitic leniencies and Hillelite stringencies. A lenient decision in favor of the one party represents a stringency for the other party. According to the Talmud, in financial matters a ruling is lenient if it favors the defendant. That means that such cases, having both an element of stringency and one of leniency, should be subtracted from the list of twenty-four cases. This holds particularly true for the cases in which Beth Shammai's leniency protects the owner of goods against an economically weaker opponent. Only very few of the twenty-four leniencies of Beth Shammai show an unfavorable tendency toward the wealthy. These few leniencies may

be of a later date when Beth Shammai's economic superiority had vanished. There is hardly any case left in which the leniency of Beth Shammai and the stringency of Beth Hillel can be reasonably attributed to exegetical or conceptual differences.

In regard to Bible exegesis, Beth Shammai more often adhere to the literal meaning of the text than do Beth Hillel. Beth Hillel's tendency to modify the law in order to adjust it to the changing conditions and to some extent to the *Zeitgeist* compelled them to interpret the text quite liberally, to make it conform to the needs of the day as they saw it. As the ruling party whose decisions determined the Halakhah for the people, they had to consider the realities of life and the appeal and applicability of the law. Beth Shammai, whose Halakhah was not imposed upon the people, did not need to regard such considerations and could, therefore, stay closer to the literal meaning of the text. Yet, there ensued no open break between the two schools because of their differences in handling the Bible text. Beth Shammai did not utter a basic opposition against the methods of Beth Hillel nor did they ever object to the hermeneutic rules propagated by Hillel and his school. To be sure, at times they differed with Hillel and his school in regard to the applicability of a hermeneutic rule in a case under discussion. Yet, they did not do this more often than in cases where no exegesis at all was utilized in the discussion.

When increasing tension between the two schools threatened to disrupt the unity of normative Judaism, a showdown took place in Javneh shortly after the destruction of the Temple. The lost war had no doubt an adverse effect on the cause of the Shammaites for at least two reasons. First, they advocated measures that contributed, if not led, to the national catastrophe. Then, due to their conservatism, they lacked the flexibility needed to adjust religious expression to the new situation created by the cessation of the centralized Temple cult. After three years of heated debate, a drastic decision was made: the Halakhah is according to Beth Hillel in every case. This decision was made, according to talmudic tradition, by a *Bath Qol*, a heavenly voice. The result was the elimination of Beth Shammai's influence in molding Rabbinic Judaism. Although Beth Shammai may have continued for some time as a peripheral or sectarian school, their views were henceforth ignored by the representatives of mainstream Judaism.

The elimination of Beth Shammai resulted in a change in Beth Hillel's position. No longer a party, a faction of the *Beth Din Ha-Gadol*, Beth Hillel became the *only* representative of the mainstream of Judaism. This made the designation Beth Hillel meaningless and it was, therefore, dropped. Tannaites of the generation after the destruction of the Temple already quote Beth Hillel as a party belonging to the past.

A man of vision, Hillel recognized that Judaism, to live and prosper, had to be consonant with the demands of life. It had to adjust to changing political, economical, and cultural conditions, but at the same time it had to remain true to itself, to its fundamental religious and ethical principles.

He disagreed with the conservative wing of the Pharisees who were slow in adjusting to the needs of the day and the needs of all economic and social classes of the people. The needs of the day included an adjustment to the cultural environment, a most difficult task. This was the crucial area where excessive changes could dejudaize Judaism, as was the case with the Judaism of the thoroughly hellenized Jews of Egypt and elsewhere; too little adjustment, on the other hand, was insufficient to keep pace with the internal need of growth and the cultural progress of the surroundings, and resulted in sectarian or sect-like groups, drifting farther and farther from the mainstream of Judaism.

Hillel's genius was that he, a man thoroughly acquainted with both Jewish and Hellenistic thought, found a synthesis acceptable to the majority of the Jewish people and its representatives in the *Beth Din Ha-Gadol*. He never claimed that he intended to introduce elements of Greek or Roman culture into Judaism, but he did demonstrate the efficacy for Torah study of hermeneutic rules often used by Greek and Roman orators (including jurists) of his day. The very purpose of Hillel's going to Palestine from his native Babylonia, according to the Talmud, was to demonstrate the potency of his text interpretation. While Hillel attempted to project the hermeneutic rules into the limelight and demonstrated their methodological value, he remained firmly within traditional Judaism in regard to the content of his conclusions. He used methods in vogue among non-Jews only to modify Jewish law and practice and thus keep Judaism in touch with ever-changing life. Initially, Hillel met with resistance and the hermeneutic rules were applied but rarely. However, with the progress of time the resistance against the hermeneutic rules vanished.

Rabbinic Judaism commences with Hillel. He successfully demonstrated that legislation is possible even without political backing by changing the form and method of legislation. Instead of direct legislation, which was possible only as long as the government backed the Sanhedrin, Hillel, upon Herod's ascent to power, attempted to project into the limelight indirect legislation, modifications of old laws and practices, primarily by interpretation. It took about a hundred years and men like Akiba to overcome the resistance to making full use of the potentialities inherent in interpretation.

PHARISEES, SADDUCEES, ESSENES

Although it is a recognized fact that the Pharisees are of paramount importance in creating Rabbinic Judaism, a great deal of obscurity surrounds their true character and significance for religion and history. Among the points still cloudy are: What were their origins? When and why did they cease to exist? What were their tenets? What were the motives of their controversies with their adversaries? What were their political roles? Since the role of the Pharisees cannot be defined and appraised properly, unless viewed in the perspective of contemporaneous currents, we shall consider, as far as feasible, the Sadducees and Essenes as well. Of these, the Sadducees are the more important; the Essenes exerted no clearly traceable influence on Rabbinic Judaism.

The most important sources concerning Sadducees and Pharisees are found in Josephus and in talmudic literature. Other sources, including the New Testament and Philo, are of lesser value, since they are either influenced by a polemical tendency against Judaism in general and Pharisaism in particular (as in the New Testament),[197] or because their knowledge of these groups is not based on direct acquaintance with them but on merely approximate information. However, even Josephus and the Talmud, whose knowledge of these groups is intimate, possess tendencies of their own which we must recognize and bear in mind.

Josephus, an historian, tries to give an objective, impartial description of the three parties, Pharisees, Sadducees and Essenes, but does not entirely succeed. It is, of course, impossible to write a perfectly objective history. Also Josephus, as a Roman-Jewish historian, writes in Greek for gentile readers. Therefore he describes the historical role and theological ("philosophical") significance of the parties and disregards the halakhic disputes in which gentile readers would not have been interested.

Josephus does not give the origin of the Pharisees. In his history they appear first during the reign of Jonathan the Hasmonean (161–43 B.C.E.).[198] At this time, they appear as an important group on the contemporary scene, which indicates they must have been in existence for some time.

In characterizing and comparing the three groups, Josephus designates them for the sake of the gentile readers as philosophical schools. He presents their theological differences in detail, while other aspects of differences are given in a more general way. As to the Essenes, he gives a lengthy description of the procedure of admittance to this order and of their way of life. Occasionally he gives information on the social and economic background of the three parties. He describes the political roles of the Sadducees and Pharisees whenever the occasion calls for this.

The characterization of the Pharisees and their position by Josephus is as follows:

In *War* he wrote:

The Pharisees, who are considered the most accurate interpreters of the laws, and hold the position of the leading sect, attribute everything to Fate and to God; they hold that to act rightly or otherwise rests, indeed, for the most part with men, but that in each action Fate co-operates. Every soul, they maintain, is imperishable, but the soul of the good alone passes into another body, while the souls of the wicked suffer eternal punishment.[199]

In *Antiquities* he supplements and modifies the characterization of the Pharisees and says, for instance,

> The Pharisees live frugally and despise delicacies in diet; and they follow the conduct of reason. . . . They also pay respect to their elders. . . . The will of men can act virtuously or viciously. They also believe that souls have an immortal vigor in them, and that under the earth there will be rewards or punishments. . . . The former shall have power to revive and live again; on account of which doctrines, they are able greatly to influence the people; and whatsoever they do about divine worship, prayers and sacrifices, they perform them according to their direction; insomuch that the cities gave great tribute to them on account of their entire virtuous conduct, both in the actions of their lives and their discourses also.[200]

Josephus' characterization of the Pharisees in *Antiquities* is not only more detailed, but also closer to Pharisaic Judaism as described in Rabbinic sources, in which we also find the doctrine of reward and punishment, the emphasis on reverence for the elder, the demand for a frugal way of life, etc.

When attempting an explanation of the modifications in *Antiquities* we have to keep in mind that Josephus wrote *Antiquities* about twenty years after he wrote *War*. During this time he not only had the opportunity to acquaint himself with the content of Pharisaic-Rabbinic Judaism more fully, but several instances suggest that his religious outlook was deepened as well. Henry Guttmann calls attention to incidents which in *War* are explained in a non-theological manner, but which in *Antiquities* receive a theological explanation.[201]

With regard to the observance of traditional practices (oral law), Josephus gives no particulars in *War*. In this regard, he only says that the Pharisees "are considered the most accurate interpreters of the laws." [202] He is more outspoken in *Antiquities*, "The Pharisees had passed on to the people certain regulations handed down by former generations and not recorded in the Laws of Moses, for which reason they are rejected by the Sadducean group, who hold that only those regulations should be considered valid which were written down (in Scripture), and that those which had been handed down by former generations need not be observed. And concerning these matters the two parties came to have controversies and serious differences, the Sadducees having the confidence of the wealthy alone but no following among the populace, while the Pharisees have the support of the masses." [203]

The Sadducean rejection of oral tradition is fundamental in nature.[204] Many of the other differences between Sadducees and Pharisees are rooted herein; this includes theological differences. Josephus asserts that the Sadducees reject the Pharisaic doctrines of immortality, resurrection, reward and punishment, and fate (Providence). They consider these as non-biblical, thus relegating them to the category of oral traditions. Josephus' statements that the differences concerning traditional regulations (practices, Halakhah) led to controversies and serious party differences are most significant. These show that, in applied religion, practices are weightier than beliefs, a point well documented in several instances.

When Josephus states that the Pharisees "are considered the most accurate interpreters of the laws" he speaks as a Pharisaic Jew. Nonetheless, he refrains from making derogatory or polemical remarks about Sadducees as interpreters of the laws.

While Josephus' attitude toward the Pharisees is favorable or, at least, objective when he talks about their activities and beliefs in the realm of religion and law, he becomes quite critical of them when they become involved in politics. He is most outspoken in this matter in *Antiquities*: [205]

There was also a sect of Jewish men priding itself on its adherence to ancestral custom and claiming to observe the laws of which God approves. And by these men, called Pharisees, the women (of the court) were ruled. These men . . . were clearly intent on opposing and harming the king . . . When the whole Jewish people affirmed by an oath that it would be loyal to Caesar and the king's government, these men, over six thousand in number, refused to take this oath . . . And the king put to death those of the Pharisees who were most to blame . . .

Schürer[206] believes "Diese Pharisäerfeindlichen Worte stammen offenbar nicht aus Josephus' Feder, sondern sind von ihm aus Nikolaus Damascenus abgeschrieben (vgl. Derenbourg, p. 123)." This explanation is not satisfactory; since Josephus had intimate personal knowledge of the Pharisees and even stated that he conducted himself according to the rules of the Pharisees,[207] why would he copy anti-Pharisaic utterances from a gentile's chronicle? More plausible is the explanation that Josephus becomes critical of the Pharisees when they interfere in political matters, or whenever their behavior would possibly antagonize the Romans. Josephus, a friend of the Romans, may have felt the urge to express disapproval of the Pharisees' seeming disloyalty to the Roman government and to the Roman vassal Herod before the gentile (Roman) public for whom his book was written. He effected this by a general derogation of the Pharisees. In this connection, we have to keep in mind that Josephus is quite critical of the Pharisees' political activities in influencing Queen Alexandra, but he approves of them at the same time for being a people who are "more religious than others, and seem to interpret the laws more accurately." [208]

Although the Essenes played a relatively small role in the history of Judaism, Josephus describes them in greater detail than the Pharisees and Sadducees.[209] He may have done this in order to impress the gentile reader with a vivid description of the peculiar idealistic system of the Essenes. Theologically, the Essenes are closer to the Pharisees than to the Sadducees. They hold that the soul is immortal and imperishable, and Josephus compares this belief with similar Greek beliefs. Some similarities between Pharisees and Essenes exist also in regard to certain rituals, e.g., saying grace before and after a meal. Regarding the Sabbath, they are "stricter than all Jews in abstaining from work on the seventh day." In many other matters, however, they differ from both Pharisees and Sadducees. Nonetheless, some traces of their influence may be present in Pharisaic-Rabbinic Judaism. The angelology of Talmudic Judaism, for example, may have been influenced (perhaps indirectly) by the angelology of the Essenes.[210] As a matter of principle, Essenes avoid swearing oaths.[211] Some rabbis of the Talmud also oppose the swearing of oaths. They do not try to outlaw it (it is a biblical institution) but occasionally allow a man to replace it with a vow.[212]

The number of the Essenes was small. Philo and Josephus give the number 4000.[213] Their origins are unknown. Scholarly speculations relate them to the Ḥasidim who participated in the Maccabean War.[214] They vanished from the scene of history as inconspicuously as did so many other little sects.

Josephus' description of the three parties deserves credibility. He did not acquire his knowledge about them from secondary sources, but through personal experience. As a result of this experience, he became and remained a follower of the Pharisees.[215] However, in his judgment and evaluation of some historical events, Josephus displays subjectivity, a human weakness of all historians who write about events of their own time or their own people.

Rabbinic sources concur with Josephus to a considerable extent. In contrast to Josephus, however, the rabbis of the Talmud are primarily interested in religious practices; therefore they take pains to preserve the detailed differences in this area. They are brief in describing the theological differences and mention the political roles of the Sadducees and Pharisees only casually.

In regard to theological differences between Sadducees and Pharisees the most outspoken rabbinic source is *ARN*.[216] Here it is stated that Antigonos of Sokho had (among others) two disciples, Zadok and Boethos. When these heard from their master the doctrines of resurrection and reward and punishment in a world-to-come, they said: "Had our forefathers known about these things, they certainly would not have omitted all mention of them. Therefore they broke away. As a consequence, two sects ["families" in version II] came into being, that of the Sadducees and that of the Boethosians."[217]

The veracity of the theological content of this passage is confirmed by Josephus. Significant in *ARN* is the reason given by Zadok and Boethos: "Were these doctrines valid, our forefathers certainly would not have failed to make mention of them." This implies that according to *ARN* introduction of the new doctrines mentioned was the cause for the establishment of the Sadducean and Boethosian parties. The rejection of new non-Pentateuchal laws and doctrines by the Sadducees is likewise confirmed by Josephus. "Our forefathers" in *ARN* most probably refers to the Bible. However the historical content of the *ARN* passage is quite controversial.[218] It is not confirmed in any other source. According to J. Z. Lauterbach, the historical account of *ARN* has to be rejected, because a comparison of the teachings of the Sadducees with those of the Pharisees shows that the Sadducees are closer to the tenets and laws of the Torah than the Pharisees. The conclusion is therefore drawn that the Sadducees were the older group that continued to adhere to the Torah in its literal interpretation, while the Pharisees were separatists who broke away from the old, conservative stream of Judaism. "Liberal separatists" is the term Lauterbach employs to characterize the Pharisees in brief.[219]

The theological differences between Sadducees and Pharisees given in the New Testament agree with Josephus and the Talmud, though not completely. According to Acts 23:8, the Pharisees acknowledge angels and spirits while the Sadducees do not believe in their existence. This difference is not mentioned by Josephus and in the Talmud. Such discrepancies are due to the fact that the New Testament occasionally confuses the Jewish groups and their respective religious positions.[220] For example, in the New Testament Pharisees and Scribes are often mentioned together, a usage which never occurs in talmudic literature.

THE DESIGNATIONS OF
THE PARTIES

The meanings of the names of the parties under discussion are obscure. A brief survey shall suffice here.

Lauterbach believes that the priestly party called the lay teachers פרושים Pharisees, meaning "separatists" in a derogatory sense, when they were excluded from the membership of the Sanhedrin during the reign of John Hyrcanus I.[221]

The first historical incident in which the term פרושים φαρισαῖοι

(Pharisees) is used in the conflict between John Hyrcanus and the "Pharisees" according to both Josephus[222] and the Talmud.[223] Therefore Lauterbach's conjecture that the Pharisees acquired their designation at this time is plausible. However, they did not break away at this time from the Sadducees. The division and antagonism between the high priest and the aristocratic society around him on the one hand, and the lay teachers and masses led by them on the other, had been in existence for many centuries. In the above incident, Pharisees and Sadducees appear as established adversaries of each other. What probably happened was that circumstances occasioned a break between John Hyrcanus and the "Pharisaic" sages, *not* between the Sadducees and these sages. [224] The Talmud states, "The sages of Israel separated in anger," or, "because of [the king's] anger" (Rashi, ad loc.). This means that they separated from the king (and his administration), not from the Sadducees. While "separated" is expressed here by the verb בדל (ויבדלו) not פרש *parash* (the root of "Pharisees"), these verbs are synonymous.

As a result of this withdrawal or separation, the Sadducees, long-standing adversaries of the sages now called פרושים Pharisees, which means "separatists," [225] were entrusted by the king with the duties hitherto performed by the sages. In describing the incident, the Talmud does *not* mention the Sadducees at all. This shows that according to talmudic tradition the Sadducees played no (open) role in this incident.

The exclusion of the sages from their former positions lasted for many years, until their reinstatement by Queen Alexandra (78–69 B.C.E.).[226] During this period the term Pharisees became so well established that it was used even after their reinstatement.

It is questionable whether the term Pharisees originally was a derogatory designation. Actually, it denotes an historical fact. It is possible that the Sadducees used it as a derogatory term, while the Pharisees considered it a term of distinction. In controversies between Sadducees and Pharisees, "Pharisees" has only a functional meaning. It designates the group of sages that subscribe to a certain theology and religious expression, opposed by the Sadducees. This would be analogous to the use of the designation Beth Hillel which

131

is used, as a rule, to identify a group opposed by Beth Shammai, and vice versa.

Bacher's explanation that *parush* is synonymous with *ḥasid*, חסיד "pious," "saintly," [227] may be correct for the post-Hasmonean period, when the original meaning of this word lost its significance. *Bedeutungswandel* of words and terms is a frequent phenomenon. L. Baeck examines the use of *parush, perushim* in tannaitic literature and points out that in this literature *perushim* is occasionally used as an explanation of *qedoshim*.[228] Thus he concurs with Bacher's explanation.[229]

צדוקים *Ẓeduqim*, Sadducees, according to Geiger who is followed by most scholars, is derived from the name Zadok (Ẓadduq), the first high priest of the Solomonic Temple. As a term, it designates an aristocratic society including most high priests.[230] Geiger's explanation is not very plausible. Except for the *ARN* passage, Sadducees is a term used with reference to members of a party that existed during and after the Hasmonean period. However, the Hasmoneans displaced the Zadokite high priestly family and appointed in 152 B.C.E. Jonathan the Hasmonean high priest. Why would the non-Zadokite high priests and their following call themselves Zadokites? [231] Therefore it is more plausible that the Zadokites were named not for the high priest, but for another Zadok, who may have been a disciple of Antigonos of Sokho, as stated in *ARN*. The fact that *ARN* is confirmed by Josephus in matters of reward and punishment, resurrection, the hereafter, and the importance of tradition is a strong indication that it may be accurate also with regard to the personality of Zadok.[232]

The origin and precise character of the party called בייתוסים Boethosians is also obscure. It may be a party originated with Boethos of Alexandria. Simon, his son, was appointed high priest by Herod (in 24 B.C.E.), who married his daughter Mariamne (the second). Later other members of the Boethos family became high priests. The Boethosian party is assumed to be close to the Sadducees, or to a Sadducean group, a plausible assumption.[233] Some scholars believe that "Boethosians" is the talmudic term for Essenes.[234]

The term Essenes may come from the Aramaic חסין, corresponding to the Hebrew חסיד *ḥasid*.[235] Though this is the generally accepted explanation, it cannot be confirmed from talmudic sources in which references to the Essenes are obscure and controversial. It is also noteworthy that the New Testament never mentions the Essenes.[236] Some scholars believe that the Essenes were a peripheral Pharisaic group.[237]

THE POLITICAL ROLE OF THE PHARISEES

Were the Pharisees a religious or a political party? Scholars in the field (and not in the field) have often argued this point, and the argument is not yet over. Ismar Elbogen wrote a noteworthy essay, "Einige neuere Theorien über den Ursprung der Pharisäer und Sadduzäer," [238] in which he discusses, in brief, the respective positions of several scholars on this question. After the publication of this essay, the dispute continued through a series of more recent books and essays.[239]

The various opinions on the matter range from the view that the Pharisees were solely a religious party to the extreme opposite belief that they were only a political party. In between are opinions that the Pharisees combined both religious and political interests to varying degrees.

What do the sources reveal on this matter? According to both Josephus and the Talmud, the Pharisees were primarily religionists who used force or resisted orders of the ruler whenever their religious convictions had been violated. They followed the example of the Ḥasidim, who joined the Maccabees primarily for religious reasons.[240] The following instances may shed light on this point.

1. The cause of the break between John Hyrcanus and the Pharisees was, according to both Josephus and the Talmud, a Pharisee's objection to the king's assumption of the high-priesthood, because this represented a violation of religious law. Some scholars believe that the real reason for the break was something else: John Hyrcanus assumed dictatorial, or quasi-dictatorial, power by dismissing the Sanhedrin, or curtailing its power. This conjecture is based on the fact that an inscription on Hyrcanus' earlier coins was יונתן כהן גדול

וחבר היהודים "Jonathan High Priest and *Ḥever* of the Jews," while the inscriptions on the later coins read יהונתן המלך "King Jonathan" and βασιλέως ’Αλεξάνδρου "King Alexander."[241] Whether *Ḥever* means Community, i.e., the people of the land, or is a synonym for Sanhedrin cannot be decided. What the inscriptions on the coins do seem to prove is only that John Hyrcanus increased his political power and stressed secular interests in his later years. This is also documented by his military endeavors. It is but natural that the religious leaders of the people did not like this change and may have wanted a high priest who was not primarily a king and warrior. Nonetheless, there is no justification for disregarding the testimony of unequivocal sources and substituting conjectures. Josephus and the Talmud give us the incident that triggered the open break. The actions of the king and Sadducean intrigue may have prepared the soil for the incident.

2. Alexander Jannaeus (105–78 B.C.E.) undertook a bloody attack on the people after they pelted him with citrons at the Festival of Tabernacles. According to Josephus this happened while he stood beside the altar to perform a sacrificial act. The reason was the objection of the people to Alexander Jannaeus' being a high priest "because he was descended from captives."[242] The Talmud relates a somewhat similar incident: The people pelted a Sadducee on the Festival of Tabernacles because he violated the (Pharisaic) traditional law of water libation (B. *Sukkah* 48b) by pouring the water on his feet instead of pouring it on the altar. It is believed that the Talmud and Josephus refer to the same incident in spite of the noteworthy discrepancies as to the reason for the pelting and talmudic omission of the culprit's name. It is possible that the combination of both reasons caused the incident. Allon, however, holds that Josephus and the Talmud do not refer to the same incident.[243]

The situation here is similar to the one above. The incident, resulting in a massacre, was caused, or at least triggered, by religious reasons.

3. In another case, the Pharisees refused to swear an oath of allegiance to Herod and to the Romans for religious reasons.[244]

There were, of course, individuals and peripheral groups among the Pharisees who stressed nationalism and advocated the use of force. Such a peripheral group was Josephus' "Fourth sect of Jewish philosophy," founded by Judas the Galilean. He describes them: "These men agree in all other things with the Pharisaic notions; but they have an inviolable attachment to liberty; and say that God is to be their only Ruler and Lord." [245]

While the Pharisees were primarily religionists, religion for them, as in the Bible, was a comprehensive pursuit including interests we consider secular and even nationalistic. Therefore, in spite of the increasingly secular pursuits of the Hasmonean rulers, the Pharisees lived in harmony with them as long as they did not violate their religious convictions, or curtail the leadership rights given them by the early Hasmoneans. The Sanhedrin, vested with legislative power and the direction of religious and civil matters, had Pharisaic membership most of the time. This certainly would not have been the case if the Pharisees and the Hasmoneans had been perennial adversaries, as some scholars believe. G. Allon points out correctly that most of the talmudic references to the Hasmoneans reveal a friendly attitude of the Pharisees and rabbis toward the Hasmoneans. The clashes were the exceptions.[246] Alexander Jannaeus, under whom the most serious clashes between Pharisees and Hasmoneans took place, recommended reconciliation on his death bed and was heeded.[247] The majority of the people followed the Pharisees, and therefore they possessed the potentiality of political power and influence. They used this potentiality rarely, and then, as a rule, only in defense of their religious convictions.

Herod's rule spelled the end of political influence for both the Sadducees and Pharisees. During the Roman occupation of Palestine, none of the Jewish parties nor the puppet kings possessed political power worthy of the name. The Romans made the high priests responsible for the loyalty of the Jewish people as evidenced by the trial of Jesus and other supposed "rebels" against Roman rule. On the other hand, the decisive internal power, i.e., the influence with the Jewish people, remained in the hands of the Pharisees. However the struggle of the parties, which continued after the Roman occupation of the land, was not a struggle for political power but concerned matters of religion, including civil law. In regard to the attitude toward the Roman overlords, Sadducees and Pharisees had no well-defined separate policies.

Since we are not dealing with the general history of Judaism, we shall not discuss any further the political role of the Pharisees nor include the uprisings against Rome, which were endeavors of practically the entire Jewish people, not only the Pharisees.

CONTROVERSIES BETWEEN PHARISEES AND SADDUCEES

Most of the Pharisee-Sadducee controversies may be categorized as 1) disputes rooted in Pharisaic acceptance and Sadducean rejection of oral tradition for all areas of human endeavor, or 2) disputes concerning certain laws of the Torah.

The extensive Pharisaic acceptance of oral law, both in belief and practice, had two purposes: 1) To harmonize Judaism with ever-changing internal and external conditions, and 2) to enrich the religious and, to some extent, also the secular life of the laity by enlarging considerably the realm of practices for them. Thus religious expression, hitherto mainly a priestly privilege, became more extensively a direct concern of the people. The development of the oral law by the Pharisees is the main reason why the masses flocked to them and why they gained control of the religious life of the people.

The Sadducees rejected the oral law of the Pharisees not only because they were conservative, but mainly because they wanted to limit religion and keep it within the boundaries of the Torah, which had entrusted them with leadership. Of course, they would not admit this openly; instead they claimed that the oral law constituted an unnecessary, senseless burden which they did not wish to bear, as seen from a quote in *ARN*, "They [traditionalists] afflict themselves [with the burden of the oral law] in this world." Accordingly, J. Z. Lauterbach's characterization of the Pharisees as "liberal separatists" is somewhat misleading. Instead, we would suggest another two-word characterization: "progressive traditionalists."

The number of the controversies between Sadducees and Pharisees cannot be determined. It varies according to the scholar who is tabulating the incidents. The reason for this is that with regard to many controversies, designated as disputes between Pharisees and Sadducees, doubt exists whether they actually were disputes of these parties. Some controversies had been ascribed erroneously to them even in the ancient sources, and other errors in cataloging the disputes have been made by modern scholars.

The controversies vary in many respects. They embrace all major areas of Jewish law and ritual, including civil law. Some of the disputes are of consequence and others are not.

In certain cases the Pharisees are stricter; in others, the Sadducees are more stringent. In general, the text interpretation of the Sadducees is closer to the literal meaning of the Bible than that of the Pharisees. On the other hand, the assertion that the Pharisees interpret the Torah according to its spirit while the Sadducees according to its letter[248] cannot be accepted. It is true that occasionally the Pharisees, and much more often the rabbis, deviate from the literal meaning of the Torah; but this is generally not for the purpose of interpreting it according to its spirit, but according to the spirit of their time, the *Zeitgeist*.

If we possessed a chronology of the controversies between the Pharisees and the Sadducees, we would know considerably more about their significance for the history of the Halakhah. The earlier controversies that could point to the divergent roads of Sadducees and Pharisees would be of greater significance, while later controversies might be of little importance. Unfortunately, most of their controversies are anonymous and lack other criteria that would enable us to date them.

Among the individual controversies, originally the theological differences were more basic. Origin and true motive of these differences are fogged in obscurity. Did the Sadducees reject the belief in resurrection because they did not recognize the Prophets and the Hagiographa as a source of creed?[249] Did they, moreover, consider the doctrine as a Pharisaic tradition, or as a foreign (Greek) belief, which they refused to incorporate into Judaism? For the ordinary people, the idea of resurrection, followed by reward and punishment, had particular appeal. They believed in God's justice, which they could not always observe on earth. The answer to the problem of theodicy lay in their faith in resurrection, reward of the righteous, and punishment of the wicked.

In addition to its theological importance, belief in resurrection may also have significance for the history of the Halakhah. A. Büchler attempts to show that the biblical methods of execution were considerably revised by the Pharisees because of their notion of resurrection.[250] Thus, for example, חנק "strangulation" is not found in the Torah as a type of death penalty. Nonetheless it is, according to the Talmud, the most frequent method of execution; whenever the Torah does not specify the type of death penalty, the sages ruled that the method was, as a matter of course, strangulation.[251] Prior to this ruling, the death penalty of the Torah was always stoning, unless burning was explicitly ordered.[252] Why was this profound change made? N. Brüll[253] believes that the Pharisees wanted to strengthen the belief in resurrection even for persons who had been given the death penalty and had atoned for their sins by death. To the people, resurrection was more comprehensible if the body was left intact. Strangulation leaves the body more intact than any other form of execution. The same idea underlies (according to Brüll and followers) the changes in the method of burning and stoning. Burning had been changed from a literal burning at the stake to throwing a burning wick (pouring lead) into the mouth of the condemned. Stoning was likewise modified from literal stoning to pushing the culprit from a rock (M. Sanh. VI,4).

In spite of the acumen displayed by Brüll and followers, it is doubtful whether Pharisaic belief in resurrection affected modifications of the forms of biblical executions. Josephus speaks of the tendency of the Pharisees to be lenient in matters of punishment but does not hint of a theological motivation.[254] This tendency, adopted and strengthened by the rabbis of the Talmud, combined with Roman influence, is the probable cause for the changes in the methods of execution. It is doubtful whether these changes had ever been carried out in practice. Rabbi Eleazar ben Zadok (probably middle or second half of the first century C.E.) testifies that he observed an execution by fire. This was performed by burning a condemned daughter of a priest at the stake.[255] Rab Joseph, an Amora, rejects this testimony by saying that the matter was handled by a Sadducean court.[256]

However, none of the tannaitic versions of the case knows of such objection. They reject Eleazar's testimony because he was a minor at the time of the execution and therefore not qualified to testify. Rab Joseph's view, therefore, appears to be a conjecture. The strength of this conjecture lies in the possibility that the sentencing of a priest's daughter was in the hands of a Sadducean priestly court. This does not mean, however, that at that time (about the middle of the first century C.E.) the Pharisees had already altered the form of the burning penalty. Moreover, it is probable that the changes of the methods of execution were not made by the Pharisees, but by their successors, the rabbis. In tannaitic sources the new forms of execution are discussed by Tannaites of the first half of the second century C.E. This indicates that the changes were made at that time and could have had only a theoretical character.[257] They reflect the tendency of the Talmud to interpret the Torah in the light of the culture of their day (the Roman in this case) and according to the humane spiritual atmosphere of the academy.

FALSE WITNESSES

A significant dateable controversy between Pharisees and Sadducees to be discussed next concerns the false witnesses.

This controversy was in full swing at the time of Judah ben Tabbai and Simon ben Shetah, about 100 B.C.E.[258] The apparent bone of contention was the law in Deut. 19:15–21. The Sadducees held that the false witnesses were to be punished only after the falsely accused person had received punishment. If he were merely sentenced but had not yet been punished, the law would not apply. The Pharisees, on the other hand, maintained that the false witnesses were subject to punishment as soon as the falsely accused person had been sentenced, though as yet unpunished. The reason for the divergence, as given in the sources, is the different interpretations of verse 19: "then ye shall do unto him, as he had purposed to do unto his brother." The Pharisees took the words "as he had purposed" more literally, inferring that the purpose, after leading to the sentence sufficed for application of the law, whereas the Sadducees applied the lex talionis, expressed in verse 21, literally.

The stated reasons for the divergence are rooted in the (seeming) conflict of verses 19 and 21. Only one of these verses can be understood literally; the other has to be interpreted so that it would not contradict the passage understood literally. The Sadducees chose to maintain the lex talionis in its literal sense, whereas the Pharisees stressed verse 19, emphasizing the gravity of the evil intent. However, even the Pharisees admit that evil intent alone is not sufficient grounds for punishment; intent must result in the sentencing of the accused person. Thus, the Pharisees themselves do not take the words "as he had purposed" entirely literally.

The sources are not explicit regarding the question whether the Pharisees held that the false witnesses were to be punished only if the accused person had been sentenced, but not yet punished, or that punishment be applied even after sentence had been carried out.

According to a tannaitic view, related by Beribbi, the 'edim zomemim "false witnesses" were not to be punished after the accused person received his penalty.[259] If this were also the Pharisaic interpretation, it would lead to an unreasonable leniency. However, since Beribbi's view is not given in the sources as Pharisaic, scholars believe that it is merely tannaitic, and that the Pharisees would have applied the law even after the sentence had been carried out.[260]

Since we know that the Pharisees were more lenient in matters of punishment than the Sadducees, an apparent exception in our case constitutes a puzzle. The sources give no reason for the exceptional Pharisaic stringency. Whatever modern explanations may be offered, they are only conjectures.

Which interpretation of the law was actually followed in judicial practice? We know of two incidents in which the Pharisaic view was carried out.

One is related in the book of Susanna. Here the false witnesses were executed, though Susanna had merely been sentenced to death and had not yet been executed.[261]

The other incident is related in rabbinic sources.[262] In this incident, according to most versions, Judah ben Tabbai executed a false witness; according to the Mekhilta this was done by Simon ben Shetaḥ in compliance with the Pharisaic interpretation of the law. The other member of the *Zug*, upon hearing of this execution, reprimanded his colleague saying that he shed innocent blood because the law required both witnesses to be convicted of falsehood, but in this incident only the one had been convicted.[263] The error committed was not necessarily a real error. Deut. 19:16 ff. uses the word "witness" in the singular; there is the possibility that originally the law applied even if only one of the witnesses were convicted of falsehood. The accepted interpretation however was that the law applied only if both witnesses were convicted. All the versions agree that the member of the *Zug* who had executed the false witness admitted his error. This means that henceforth the accepted Pharisaic interpretation of "witness" in Deut. 19:16 ff. (and elsewhere) was to be considered in the plural sense (in harmony with Deut. 19:15) in spite of the singular formulation in Scripture. The Saducean interpretation of "witness" was not transmitted.

THE RIGHT OF THE DAUGHTER TO INHERIT HER FATHER'S ESTATE

Who is the legal heir in the following case? A man had a son and a daughter, and the son had a daughter. The son died, while the others remained alive. Then the father died. The Pharisees hold that the granddaughter inherits all the property her father would have inherited. The Sadducees on the other hand, claim that the property should be divided equally between daughter and granddaughter.[264]

The reasoning of the Sadducees, according to the sources (Tosefta version), is the following: If the daughter of my son, who comes by strength of her father who, in turn, comes by my strength, can inherit my property, how much the more can my daughter inherit my property, who comes by my strength. In other words, the daughter who is a closer relative, should have no lesser rights than the granddaughter, who is more distant.

The reasoning of the Pharisees in the same source is the following: The daughter of the deceased son has more rights, since her father had rights of inheritance equal to those of his brothers whereas his sister had no such rights. In other words, the daughter of the deceased son is, in our case, the only one in possession of the right of inheritance, since her father was a legal heir; his sister was not a legal heir of her father, since there had been a brother.

According to the Pharisees, the law of the Torah "If a man die, and have no son, then ye shall cause his inheritance to pass unto his daughter" (Num. 27:8) implies that if there are sons and daughters, only the sons inherit the property. The Pharisees apply this law even after the son died and left a daughter. This daughter, if she had no brothers, is the legal heir to her father who acquired the title to the inheritance while he was alive. According to the Sadducees, the law of the Torah does not apply in our case, since the son never actually inherited his father's property, and therefore the degree of relationship also has to be considered.[265]

Why the Sadducees and Pharisees differ in this case is a matter of conjecture. Many scholars believe that the reason advanced by the Sadducees — importance of the degree of relationship — was not their real reason. Consequently, they advance all kinds of conjectures.[266] From the juridical point of view, the Pharisaic interpretation is superior.[267] The Sadducees' interpretation may have been influenced by a feeling of equity, since they were wealthy and had to deal with this problem in daily life.[268]

According to the accounts in the Babylonian Talmud and *Meg. Ta'anith*, the spokesman arguing against the Sadducees was Johanan ben Zakkai.

Pharisees and Boethosians are mentioned in the Tosefta only. All the other sources name only the Sadducees and do not mention the Pharisees.

142

DAMAGES CAUSED BY SLAVES

The Sadducees say, "We cry out against you, O ye Pharisees," for ye say, "If my ox or my ass have done an injury they are culpable, but if my bondman or my bondwoman have done an injury they are not culpable" — if, in the case of my ox or my ass [about which no commandments are laid upon me] I am responsible for the injury that they do, how much more in the case of my bondman and my bondwoman [about whom certain commandments are laid upon me] must I be responsible for the injury that they do! They said to them, "No — as ye argue concerning my ox or my ass [which have no understanding] would ye likewise argue concerning my bondman or my bondwoman which have understanding? For if I provoke him to anger, he may go and set fire to another's stack of corn; and it is I that must make restitution!" [269]

The problem is not touched upon in the Torah; nonetheless, the Sadducees could not ignore it, since they were the wealthy who owned many slaves. They adhered to the ancient view that slaves were on a level with other kinds of property, and therefore the same laws applied to them. The Pharisees placed the slaves on a different level. The reason is a matter of conjecture. It is possible that the less wealthy, whom the Pharisees had in mind, who happened to own a slave needed more protection in case of damage done by their slaves.

This and the previous case demonstrate that there were instances in daily life, not legislated for in the Torah, in which the Sadducees were compelled to make a decision. A collection made of such decisions may have been the ספר גזרתא *Sefer Gezeratha* of the Sadducees.[270]

THE TAMID SACRIFICE

The Sadducees held that the animals for the Tamid sacrifices might be donated by individuals, while the Pharisees claimed that they had to be purchased with public funds from the Temple treasury.[271] The Talmud states that the Sadducees based their opinion on Num. 28:4, "The one lamb shalt *thou* offer at dusk."

Their opponents quoted (Num. 28:2), "My food which is presented unto me for offerings made by fire . . . shall *ye* observe."

The context of the Torah indicates that the Tamid is a public sacrifice. The question of whether an individual may or may not donate it to the Temple is left open. Since there was a prescribed tax "for the service of the tent of meeting" (Exod. 30:11–16), and this tax continued for the Temple,[272] the public sacrifices were secured with money solicited equally from rich and poor. The Sadducees may have intended to enlarge the scope of their participation in the Temple cult — they were the wealthy and able to make individual donations of sacrificial animals. The Pharisees naturally objected to this.[273] The explanation of the Talmud, based on exegetical differences, is certainly of a later date.

Again, the Talmud does not use the term "Pharisees."

HARVESTING OF THE OMER ON SABBATH

According to Pharisaic ruling, the Omer is always to be harvested the night following the first day of Passover, even if it be on the Sabbath. The Boethosians, however, claim that the Omer must not be harvested on a Sabbath.[274]

The controversy is not rooted in divergent exegesis, since the Torah gives no date for the harvesting of the Omer.[275] Moreover, the harvesting of the Omer is not prescribed in the Torah as a ceremony. Therefore, it is safe to assume that originally it had no ritualistic significance. Obviously the Pharisees developed this insignificant preliminary act which could be performed by laymen and expanded it into an elaborate ceremony for the non-priests. The most important step in the development of this ceremony was the ruling that it was to be performed even on the Sabbath, if this day happens to be the second day of Passover, which is the prescribed day for the harvesting of the Omer. The (Sadducean) priests undoubtedly considered the elaborate ceremony of the harvesting of the Omer a Pharisaic oral law; therefore, they would not accept it, let alone place it on a par with the sacrificial cult which only priests were privileged to perform on a Sabbath. The Pharisees, on the other hand, considered this ceremony as an important step toward their goal of equality with the priests.[276]

Again, neither the term Pharisees nor the term Sadducees appears in the sources.

THE DATE OF *SHAVUOTH*

Lev. 23:15 states "And ye shall count unto you from the morrow after Sabbath, from the day that ye brought the sheaf of the waving; seven weeks shall there be complete."

Boethosians and Pharisees disagreed on the meaning of *sabbath* in this passage. The precise meaning of this word was important for fixing the date of *Shavuoth*. The Pharisees held that *sabbath* here meant the first day of the Passover festival, interpreting *sabbath* as a day of rest, i.e., festival. Therefore, *Shavuoth* fell on the fiftieth day after the first day of Passover. The Boethosians, on the other hand, took *sabbath* as meaning the Sabbath, the seventh day of the week. Consequently, *Shavuoth* fell on the fiftieth day after the Sabbath of Passover, i.e., always on a Sunday.[277]

The interpretations of Lev. 23:15 advanced by the Boethosians and Pharisees respectively are both within the *peshat*, the possible true meaning of the passage. The literal interpretation of *sabbath*, meaning Sabbath, may certainly represent the original meaning. On the other hand, *sabbath* here may actually mean a day of rest, i.e., a festival day (first day of Passover), as it does in Lev. 23:32, where it refers to the Day of Atonement, no matter what day of the week that may be.

Since the passage in Lev. 23:15 unquestionably had only one original meaning, it would be of interest to know what this meaning was, who reinterpreted it, why and when this was done.[278]

The Vulgate takes *sabbath* of our passage literally.[279] The Peshitta renders it "after the last day of Passover," [280] which agrees with the understanding in the *Book of Jubilees* and the Falashas.[281] Samaritans and Karaites take it literally, too.[282] The Karaite interpretation may hark back to Sadducean or Boethosian tradition.[283]

The Pharisaic interpretation of our *sabbath* is also documented in ancient sources. Philo as well as Josephus state that the Omer ceremony was done on the sixteenth of Nisan, in accordance with the Pharisaic interpretation.[284] It is also supported by Targum *Ps. Jonathan*.

Although the ancient sources do not give a clear-cut answer to our question regarding the original meaning of the passage, the Boethosian interpretation is supported by the fact that the Sadducees and the Boethosians, assuming they were a Saducean group, opposed, in principle, deviation from the literal meaning of the text. The Pharisees, on the other hand, were open minded and ready to make changes when deemed necessary. Why the Pharisees may have introduced the change in this case is a matter of conjecture. They may have felt the need for a fixed date for *Shavuoth*, the only festival for which the Torah gives no exact date.[285]

The calendation was (at least most of the time) carried out by the Pharisees according to their views, much to the displeasure of the Sadducees and other groups. In one incident, the latter obviously trying to make Shavuoth occur on a Sunday in accordance with their interpretation, even hired false witnesses in an unsuccessful effort to mislead the Pharisaic sages.[286] In B. *Men.* 65a and *Meg. Ta'anith* (loc. cit.), the Pharisee spokesman, Johanan ben Zakkai,[287] vigorously attacks the Boethosians.

The conjecture that the date of *Shavuoth* was fixed by the Pharisees because of its added historical significance[288] is not too strong. Neither Josephus nor Philo know of such a significance for *Shavuoth*. This is found only in talmudic literature of the second century C.E.[289]

Neither Sadducees nor Pharisees are explicitly mentioned.

WATER LIBATION ON SUKKOTH

This case we discussed incidentally in the chapter on the political role of the Pharisees. Let us review here the case in brief and supplement it with details relevant in this chapter. King and High Priest Alexander Jannaeus was to perform the water libation ceremony, a rite not prescribed in the Torah, but considered very important by the Pharisees because of its significance for the farmer. Alexander Jannaeus, however, despised this ceremony, as did the Sadducees, and by pouring water upon his feet instead of upon the altar, he upset the people. They obviously attributed to this ceremony great significance and effectiveness in securing rain for their crops.

Why did the Sadducees object to the ritual of the water libation? This ceremony is not mentioned in the Torah and belongs, therefore, to the realm of oral law which they rejected in principle.[290] This incident confirms Josephus' contention that the Sadducees had to follow the Pharisaic law even in matters of Temple cult since otherwise the people would not listen to them. It is also noteworthy that the Pharisees do not attempt to find support from the Torah for the ceremony of water libation. Talmudic sources do not mention the Pharisees.

WILLOW BRANCH CEREMONY ON SUKKOTH

The Tosephta relates:

The willow branch ceremony overrides the Sabbath at the end [i.e., if it falls on the seventh day of Sukkoth]. Once it happened that before Sabbath the Boethosians placed big stones over the willow branches. The 'amme ha-areẓ ['people of the land,' followers of the Pharisees] noticed this, removed the stones and brought the willow branches out from under the stones on Sabbath. All this happened because the Boethosians do not admit that the flogging with the willow branches supersedes the Sabbath.[291]

The willow branch ceremony was performed by all the people present in the Temple. Acts of the Temple cult, as a rule, superseded the Sabbath. However, the Boethosians did not concede that this ceremony overrode the Sabbath. Why? Some scholars believe that the Sadducees did not want to raise the laity to the level of the

147

priests, who were privileged to carry out acts of Temple cult on the Sabbath.[292] While this explanation may sound plausible, the real reason may be a principal Sadducean misgiving against this ceremony. The Torah does not speak of a ceremony of beating with willow branches. All the Torah says is: "And ye shall take you on the first day . . . and willows of the brook, and ye shall rejoice before the Lord your God seven days" (Lev. 23:40). This ceremony was developed or adopted by the Pharisees and was considered by the Sadducees as an oral law, which they rejected on principle. The Tosefta explicitly states that "The Willow Branch Ceremony is an *halakhah le-Moshe Mi-Sinai*" (ibid.), an old, traditional law. Abba Saul's interpretation of the scriptural verse (that "willows of the brook" means one for the Lulav and one for the altar" loc. cit.) is not Pharisaic but tannaitic.[293] However, when the Pharisees had control over the Temple, the Sadducees could not prohibit the performance of this ceremony, but tried to prevent it on the Sabbath when, according to the Torah, sacrificial acts were to be performed only by priests.

Why the Pharisees adopted the willow branch ceremony is a matter of conjecture. Sukkoth is called *Ḥag*, the "Feast" par excellence, in tannaitic literature. For the *'amme ha-arez*, mostly farmers, this was the most important festival because of the belief that at this time God rendered the decision concerning rainfall for the coming season.[294] This is generally believed to be the main reason for ceremonies developed for this festival.

We also have to realize that more farmers could come to Jerusalem on Sukkoth than on any of the other Pilgrim festivals, since this festival is celebrated after the final gathering of the crops when a period of leisure begins for the farmer.

Pharisees are not explicitly named in this incident.

THE DAY OF ATONEMENT

The principal ceremonies of the Day of Atonement were functions of the high priest. While the high priests were often Sadducees, they were recognized by the Pharisees, too, as the high priests of the entire Jewish people. Tannaitic sources show that the Pharisees had (at times) decisive influence over the Temple service. They adjured the high priest before the Day of Atonement in order to ascertain that he would perform his duties in accordance with the Pharisaic interpretation of the law.[295] We may cite some particulars that prove the strength of Pharisaic influence. During the night of the Day of Atonement, the sages read before the high priest (or urged him to read) the books of Job, Ezra, Chronicles and Daniel, all from the Hagiographa. This was obviously done in view of the rejection of the Hagiographa by the Sadducees.

One of the hotly debated ceremonies performed by the high priest on the Day of Atonement was a detail concerning the *incense.*

Lev. 16:12–13 asserts, "And he shall take a censer full of coals of fire from off the altar before the Lord, his hands full of sweet incense beaten small, and bring it within the veil. And he shall put the incense upon the fire before the Lord, that the cloud of the incense may cover the ark-cover that is upon the testimony, that he die not."

The Pharisees understood this to mean that the high priest should carry the censer with the burning coals in his right hand, and the incense in his left hand while on his way to enter the Holy of Holies. After entering the Holy of Holies, he should place the incense upon the burning coals. The Sadducees, on the other hand, demanded that the incense be placed upon the burning coals outside of the Holy of Holies and only then could the high priest enter the holy chamber.[296]

The Pharisaic view is in harmony with the obvious meaning of the text, but the Sadducean interpretation of the same does not violate its possible meaning either. Why the Pharisees and Sadducees differ in this case is a matter of conjecture. Lauterbach devoted a long essay to this problem.[297] He believes, in brief, that the Sadducean high priests, who performed this ceremony, were afraid that they would die if they entered the Holy of Holies before the incense was put on the coal because of the verse in Exodus "for man shall not see me and live" (33:20). They were afraid that they might look at the Deity (inadvertently) if they were to enter the holy chamber before the incense had been kindled. The Pharisees, on the other hand, believed that the *Shekhinah* was present everywhere: therefore there was no cause for worry about "seeing God." The Scripture was to be followed in its literal and obvious meaning; superstition was to be disregarded.

In spite of Lauterbach's great acumen and keen analysis of the sources, his conclusion leaves some questions unanswered. Why would the Sadducees believe that a punctilious observance of a law could lead to death, while a violation of it would assure safety? Moreover, the high priest had to perform his duty in accordance with the Pharisaic interpretation of the law, and the Sadducean interpretation remained theory, save for exceptional instances. Therefore, the Sadducean interpretation could not save the high priest, and the performance of the ritual in accordance with the Pharisaic interpretation never hurt him.

We only know of one case in which the ceremony was performed in accordance with the Sadducean interpretation of the law. In this case the high priest in doing so was reprimanded by his father, "Even though we are Sadducees, we are afraid of the Pharisees." [298]

In light of these questions, Ralph Marcus' conjecture that the Sadducees' desire to place the incense upon the coals before entering the holy chamber was motivated by an interest to demonstrate this service in public, deserves attention.[299]

However, more likely is the possibility that the Pharisees insisted on the observance of their interpretation in order to diminish the visible role of the high priest, usually suspect of Sadducean leanings.

Except for B. *Yoma* 19b, all the other sources citing our controversy do not use the word "Pharisees," but "*Hakhamim*," sages.

THE RED HEIFER

According to the Sadducees, the Red Heifer (Num. 19) was to be burnt by a priest who, if he were defiled, had to take a bath and wait until sunset before officiating. However their Pharisaic opponents claimed that the priest had to perform the act of burning after the bath and must not wait until sunset.[300]

This controversy was probably based on an exegetical disagreement between Sadducees and Pharisees. Its significance lies in the fact that the Pharisees possessed the power to compel the high priest who, as indicated in the Mishnah,[301] performed the burning ritual, to act in accordance with their decision. They defiled the priest on purpose in order to test whether he would act in accordance with the Pharisaic law or not.

An incident related in the Tosefta[302] is most significant. A Sadducean high priest acted in accordance with the Sadducean law. When Johanan ben Zakkai learned about it, he defiled him, ordered him to take a bath, which he did, and then nipped his ear to make him unfit for priestly functions.

This incident shows that the Pharisees at times had full control over religious life, even over the sacrificial cult, much to the irritation of the Sadducees. Even the high priests had to conform to their wishes at Johanan ben Zakkai's time. The word "Pharisee" is not used here.

DEFILEMENT OF THE HANDS BY TOUCHING HOLY BOOKS

The Pharisees ruled that Holy Books defiled the hands, but not secular books, while the Sadducees rejected this law. The question why the Sadducees rejected this law is easily answered. They rejected oral law in principle and saw no reason to make an exception in this instance. The real problem is why the Pharisees introduced this new law. Pharisees and Sadducees themselves discuss this issue.[303]

First, the Sadducees point out that the Pharisaic law is illogical. Why should the Holy Books defile the hands, while secular (or heretical) books should not? Johanan ben Zakkai defends the Pharisaic position by pointing out ironically that there was a better reason to complain about the Pharisees maintaining that the bones of a donkey were clean,[304] while the bones of Johanan, the high priest, were unclean. This contention, based on a law of the Torah,[305] could not be rejected by the Sadducees. The Sadducees replied that the reason for this is to prevent a man from making spoons of the bones of his parents. Johanan ben Zakkai retorts that the same holds true for the Holy Scripts; they cause defilement because they are so beloved; but secular books, since they are not beloved, do not defile the hands.

According to Johanan ben Zakkai's statement, the purpose of the law was to protect the Holy Books. The question now is in what way could such a law protect the Holy Books? According to Johanan ben Zakkai,[306] people might use them as covers for their cattle. This implies that since they were now declared ritually unclean, people would refrain from using them for such purposes.

According to this explanation, defilement can serve a higher purpose and protect something that is precious. This is not the only instance where defilement serves such a purpose. M. *Ḥul.* IX,2, informs us that the skin of humans that was finished as leather defiles, while the leather of other creatures does not.[307] The Talmud points out that this is not a law of the Torah, but it was made lest people make covers from the skins of their parents.[308]

Some scholars do not think that Johanan ben Zakkai gave the Sadducees the true reason, and suggest other reasons, e.g., that the defilement of Holy Books was a measure against the Sadducees. Its purpose was to prevent the Saducean priests from eating the *Terumah* (heave offering) before nightfall whenever they touched the Holy Books.[309] The Pharisees, therefore, intended to penalize the priests for using the Holy Books. This does not seem to be plausible. (Moreover, the farmer could choose the priest to whom he gave the *Terumah* and could give it therefore, to non-Saducean priests just as well.) Tchernowitz points out that in antiquity, the concepts of holiness and defilement were closely related, and says in conclusion: "The Sadducees say that holiness sanctifies, while the Pharisees hold that holiness defiles." [310]

We have to keep in mind that the oral law considerably increased the scope of defilement for priests and laymen alike. It ordained, for example, that every Jew had to wash his hands before eating secular food, even when he had not touched anything that might have defiled him.[311] The fact that the largest order of Mishnah (Seder

Țohoroth) is that which deals with the laws of defilement demonstrates the importance of these laws in the eyes of the sages, Pharisees, and rabbis of the Talmud alike. While it is a fact that the Pharisees disliked the Sadducees, many of whom were priests, we do not see the need of any conjecture, based on this fact, as long as the sources are explicit and make good sense. We believe, therefore, that Johanan ben Zakkai's words are more trustworthy than any conjecture,[312] and that he meant what he said. In this controversy both Pharisees and Sadducees are explicitly mentioned.

NIẒẒOQ

"The Sadducees say, 'We complain about you, Pharisees, for you declare clean the *niẓẓoq*.' The Pharisees reply, 'We complain against you, Sadducees, for you declare clean a channel of water that flows from a grave yard.' "[313]

The word *niẓẓoq* is considered by some modern scholars to be obscure and in need of interpretation. The traditional interpretation is that if a liquid is poured from a ritually clean vessel into an unclean vessel, whatever is left in the clean vessel remains clean. The *niẓẓoq*, meaning "stream of liquid," does not constitute a real connection, which would lead to the defilement of the liquid left in the clean vessel.

This interpretation is plausible in view of Mishnah *Makhshirin* V,9: "Any *niẓẓoq* is clean, except a stream of thick honey or batter. The School of Shammai say, 'Also one of porridge made from grits or beans, since it shrinks backwards.' " It is obvious that *niẓẓoq* here means a stream of liquid. A heavy, slow-flowing stream of liquid is unclean, because it shrinks backwards whenever the stream is broken, projecting thereby the defilement of liquid of the lower vessel into the upper vessel. However, this is not the case if the liquid is not heavy.[314]

Many scholars are dissatisfied with this interpretation and suggest various conjectures, more or less fanciful.[315]

If we accept the traditional interpretation, as done by L. Ginzberg and others, the reason that the Sadducees declared the *nizzoq* unclean is that they considered the stream of liquid as a connecting link between the two vessels, by which the unclean vessel could defile the clean one. The Pharisees rejected this view and believed that the uncleanliness did not go against the running stream to the upper vessel. Adhering literally to the Torah law that the touch of the unclean thing (or person) defiles the clean object, the Sadducees considered liquids connected by a stream while being poured as touching. The Pharisees did not call this touching.

The case of the water canal is different, the Sadducees may have replied to the Pharisees, because of the explicit statement of Lev. 11:36: "... a fountain or a cistern wherein is a gathering of water shall be clean."

Pharisees and Sadducees are explicitly mentioned here.

THE IMMERSION OF
THE *MENORAH*

It once happened that the *Menorah* was immersed. Hereupon the Sadducees exclaimed, "Come and see, the Pharisees immerse the orb of the moon"[316] (according to another version, "the orb of the sun").[317] This incident presupposes a controversy which the sources have not preserved. It is quite obvious that the immersion, i.e., purification of the *Menorah*, the candelabrum of the Temple, was an oral law introduced by the Pharisees and, therefore, rejected by the Sadducees. The reason for introducing this law is not transmitted. According to one conjecture, the purification of the *Menorah* was a measure against a priestly privilege. After every festival, the vessels of the Temple were purified because of the fear that the pilgrims (non-priests) might have touched them.[318] Because the *Menorah* was touched by the priests only, they held that it remained clean and needed no immersion. According to a Baraitha, a special warning had been issued against touching the Table and the *Menorah*.[319]

According to another conjecture, the reason for the Sadducean objection was that defilement of metal was not a biblical law but an ordinance of Simon ben Shetaḥ,[320] i.e., an oral law.[321] The weakness of this conjecture is that we do not hear of Sadducean objections against the immersion of the other metal utensils of the Temple.

It is possible that the real reason for the Sadducean objection was that the *Menorah* was not a vessel in the ordinary sense of the word — the ordinary vessels of the Temple served the purpose of preparing or receiving sacrificial food and liquid — but the *Menorah* resembled the sun or moon in dispensing light. Therefore it was not susceptible to defilement, and its immersion would be ridiculous.

Other controversies which might be included if this were an exhaustive study of Pharisees and Sadducees have been omitted because they add little to that which the controversies considered already show. Furthermore, their authenticity is questionable in many instances.[322]

Among the disputes probably erroneously ascribed to the Sadducees and Pharisees are those listed in the "Gemara" of *Megillath Ta'anith*. These the rabbis may have inserted into the original *Megillath Ta'anith* in order to combat the Karaites.[323] The principal argument against the authenticity of the cases listed in the "Gemara" of *Megillath Ta'anith* is that the talmudic discussion of the cases in question — among them the lex talionis — does not state that these problems were debated by the Pharisees and Sadducees.

In addition to the three historical incidents — John Hyrcanus' break with the Pharisees, Alexander Jannaeus' persecution of the Pharisees, and the incident related in the *ARN* account — we have noted fourteen controversies between Pharisees and Sadducees (including Boethosians) on the following topics:

1) Theology
2) False witnesses
3) The right of the daughter to inherit her father's estate
4) Damages caused by slaves
5) The Tamid sacrifice
6) Harvesting the Omer on Sabbath

7) Date of Shavuoth
8) Water libation on Sukkoth
9) Willow branch ceremony on Sukkoth
10) The Day of Atonement
11) The Red Heifer
12) Defilement of the hands by touching Holy Books
13) *Nizzoq*
14) Immersion of the *Menorah*

Study of various aspects of these disputes may prove revealing.

Chronological aspects

Less than half of the above controversies included names of persons who can be dated. Yet, even the participation of known persons does not mean that the controversy in which they participated had originated during their lifetime. A good illustration for this is the controversy on the date of Pentecost. According to rabbinic sources, the spokesman of the Pharisees in this discussion was Johanan ben Zakkai. This could mean that the controversy originated in his time. However, older sources show that this difference is considerably more ancient. This was certainly the case in other instances, too.

Naming of personalities

Besides the chronological aspect, the naming of persons in the controversies has additional significance. It shows that the spokesmen of the Pharisees were leading personalities: Antigonos of Sokho, Judah ben Tabbai, and Johanan ben Zakkai. Johanan ben Zakkai acted as the spokesman of the Pharisees, so far as ascertainable, prior to the destruction of the Temple, while he was *Av Beth Din*. Why did not the Nasi himself lead the struggle against the Sadducees, as one would expect? He certainly considered himself as the head of the entire nation and may not have wanted to antagonize a section of it. Besides, socially he stood closer to the Sadducees than to the Pharisees.

Exegesis

Whenever a controversy is rooted in or associated with an exegesis, both Pharisees and Sadducees interpreted the text in a rationalistic manner, avoiding dialectical, homiletical, allegorical or mystical interpretations. Usually, but not always, the Sadducees adhere more strictly to the literal meaning of the text than the Pharisees. In the fourteen controversies considered above, hermeneutic rules were not used, at least not explicitly. Of the fourteen controversies, 2, 5, 7 and 10 in particular have exegetical aspects, but the exegesis in the first three of these cases was probably added later. Exegetical aspects not preserved in the sources may also have played a part in such issues as 11 and 13.

Social aspects

The Pharisees strove to inject more democracy into Jewish life. Lauterbach thinks that this reflects the influence of the democratic Greek colonies in Palestine, in which the priests were the servants of the people.[324] Among the Jews, however, the priests were the rulers. Readiness to make changes in the light of developments from within and without, a characteristic Pharisee trait, explains their endeavor to emulate the Greek democracies. We also have to keep in mind that striving for equality is a powerful human drive, present whenever an alert lower social stratum lives with a higher social class.

Stringency and leniency; Conservatism and Liberalism

Stringency and leniency constituted no issue with the two groups. In certain instances the Pharisees are more strict, in others the Sadducees, depending on the respective philosophies of the groups, or on other reasons.

The Sadducees were conservative in strictly adhering to the Torah and rejecting changes. On the other hand, the Pharisees were not liberal in the sense this word is used today in referring to "Liberal Judaism." They were liberal in the sense of being progressive but without being lenient save for exceptional instances. They tried to adjust religion to changing conditions, not by discarding laws of the Torah, but generally by adding to them a body of oral laws.

Oral tradition

The principal distinction of consequences between the Sadducees and the Pharisees is the large scale development of the oral law by the Pharisees and its rejection by the Sadducees. The Sadducees were opposed to the oral law for more than one reason. The oral laws, introduced in response to the spiritual or material needs of the day, found genuine appeal among the people, enhancing the prestige and popularity of the lay teachers, who therefore became the de facto leaders of the people. This is confirmed by both Josephus and talmudic sources. Further, we have to keep in mind that some of the oral laws had the purpose of raising the laymen to the level of the priests, which the latter vehemently opposed.

In spite of the fact that the Sadducees rejected oral law on principle, they found instances in daily life which needed settlement, since the written Torah had failed to legislate for them. Such a case was the right of the daughter to inherit. In this and other cases, the Sadducees tried to solve the problem on the basis of their particular needs, which had become more pressing than the desire to stay as close as possible to the related laws of the Torah.

Use of the designations Sadducees and Pharisees

The way talmudic sources use the designations Sadducees and Pharisees is puzzling. In regard to the Sadducees, we have some variant texts that read "Boethosians," generally assumed to be a Sadducean group, or a group close to the Sadducees. Some scholars, however, believe this to be a group distinct from the Sadducees. Should the latter be true, the variant readings are the result of errors in transmission. There are, however, instances in which all texts read "Boethosians" or "Sadducees," respectively. In 4, 6, and 7, all the texts read Boethosians; in 2, 8, 10, 11, and 13 all the texts read Sadducees. This clearly indicates that Sadducees and Boethosians were two distinct groups. In the *ARN* passage cited they are listed next to each other meaning that they were two separate groups. At the same time, *ARN* ascribes the same basic beliefs (or disbeliefs) to both groups, indicating that they were close to each other and constituted a common front against the Pharisees. The affinity of Sadducees and Boethosians is also indicated by the confusion of these groups in rabbinic sources.

More perplexing is the use of the designation "Pharisees" in talmudic sources. Particularly enigmatic is the fact that most of the controversies between Sadducees or Boethosians and Pharisees *do not mention the Pharisees by name.* Of the fourteen controversies considered above, the following do not mention the Pharisees: 2, Mishnah and Baraitha read "*Ḥakhamim,*" *Sifre* version is anonymous. Eight has *kol ha-am* in all talmudic texts (Mishnah, Tosefta, Baraitha). Nine has *'amme ha-arez*. In 11, Johanan ben Zakkai opposes the Sadducees in the Tosefta. The Mishnah here is anonymous. In 7 some versions have Johanan ben Zakkai, others have *Ḥakhamim.* Six is anonymous in both, Mishnah and Tosefta. Five is anonymous. In 10, the B. Talmud has "Pharisees," but the other sources read *Ḥakhamim* instead. In 3, Pharisees are named only in the Tosefta. In the other versions, Johanan ben Zakkai opposes the Sadducees, e.g., in *Megillath Ta'anith* and its parallel in the B. Talmud. The P. Talmud version is anonymous.

In the *ARN* passage, the Pharisees are only mentioned in version I, but not in II. In the historical incident of *Qid.* 66a, Pharisees and *Ḥakhamim* are synonyms. In the incident of water libation (8) the Pharisees are not mentioned, neither in the Talmud nor in Josephus. Josephus does not mention the Sadducees, either. According to Josephus, this was a clash between Alexander Jannaeus and the Jewish people.

Sadducees or Boethosians *and* Pharisees are mentioned only in 1, *ARN* I. In 3 and 10, Pharisees are named in only *one* version. In 4, 12, 13, 14 the Pharisees are named in the various versions. Thus the Pharisees are named in six passages only, and in two of these they are designated as Pharisees in just one of several versions!

On the other hand, in the historical incidents in *Qid.* 66a and *Soṭah* 22b, the Sadducees are not mentioned, only the Pharisees.

If we consider the fact that in the majority of passages in which

159

the Sadducees are explicitly named, the Pharisees are not mentioned, and vice versa, the question is to be raised: are the unnamed opponents in those passages really the Sadducees and Pharisees, respectively? If so, why are they not named?

A partial explanation may be found in the term "Pharisee," if it actually meant "separatists" in a derogatory sense, when used by the Sadducees. This would explain why the Pharisees avoid the use of this term. However, we find a number of instances in which this term is used not by the Sadducees and not even in connection with the Sadducees. The answer we shall find when we consider the post-classical Pharisees.

The classical period of the Pharisees and Sadducees ended with the destruction of the Temple in 70 c.e. After this date, there was no high priest, nor a wealthy class of distinguished priests. Further, most of the wealthy Sadducean socialites lost their wealth during the war, leaving no basis on which to continue the Sadducean party as a party of the wealthy social elite. This, however, did not spell the end of the Sadducees. They continued their separate existence by upholding and fostering the religious ideas and practices of their predecessors. We find references to Sadducees who lived after the destruction of the Temple in talmudic literature, though in a number of passages, mainly in aggadic ones, "Sadducees" is used as a synonym for מין *min*, heretic or Judeo-Christian (cf. variant readings especially in manuscripts, e.g., the Munich MS. of the Talmud).

M. *Niddah* IV,2 is a discussion of the second century c.e. The topic is the religious status of the Sadducean woman of that time. According to the first (anonymous) opinion, they are like the Samaritans, if they follow the Sadducean law, but they are like the Israelites if they follow the practice of Rabbinic Judaism. However R. Jose holds they are like the Israelites, unless they separate themselves and follow the Sadducean practice. Thus in the second century the Sadducees were no longer afraid to live in accordance with their own laws, which had been the case prior to the destruction of the Temple, though R. Jose's view implies that, generally, they would follow the instructions of the non-Sadducean sages.[325]

In an amoraic passage, Rab Judah relates in the name of Samuel (first half of the third century c.e.) that a court is not liable for an erroneous decision, unless it concerns a matter in which the Sadducees disagree with the sages.[326] That means that the criterion for a serious error on the part of a court is a decision at variance with a rabbinic law which is opposed by the Sadducees. While the liability entails a sin offering, the rule given by Samuel allows the inference that he has the Sadducees of his time in mind and does not mean to give a rule merely for the past (or future). As time progressed the Sadducees moved further and further from the mainstream of Judaism until they became an heretical or quasi-heretical sect.

We do not know when the Sadducees vanished from the scene of history. The last talmudic reference to them certainly does not coincide with their extinction. Therefore, the claim that the karaitic movement represents a continuation (or a revival) of Sadducaism cannot be brushed aside lightly.

PHARISAISM IN TRANSITION

Although much has been written on the origin and history of the Pharisees, on their teachings and their importance for the evolution of normative Judaism and early Christianity, less attention has been given to developments *within* Pharisaic Judaism, to the transition from Pharisaic to Rabbinic Judaism, the relationship between rabbis and Pharisees, and the seemingly inconsistent attitude of the Talmud toward the Pharisees. The Pharisees are generally considered as belonging to one main group and to several peripheral branches such as Apocalyptic Pharisees, political extremists (e.g. "Fourth Philosophy" Pharisees), unaffiliated Pharisees, and others. According to some scholars even the Essenes were Pharisees.[327] The consensus of most scholars is that the main group has a single theology and a fairly unified attitude toward the law from the beginning to the end — a period of hundreds of years. The basic unity of the mainstream is not impaired by its division into conservative and liberal wings, a division that existed before the establishment of

161

the Great Sanhedrin and continued throughout the existence of the schools of Shammai and Hillel.

Among the problems that have not found satisfactory solution thus far is the decline of the Pharisees and their vanishing from the scene of history. When and why did the Pharisees leave the scene of history? Or did the Pharisees and Pharisaism continue through the talmudic period? Were the rabbis of the Talmud Pharisees?

If we examine the talmudic literature we can see that the Pharisees were not only not identical with the rabbis but that the latter often severely criticized the Pharisees. Talmudic references to the Pharisees include references to Pharisees of the past and statements about contemporaneous Pharisees. Derogatory statements are directed against the latter, particularly against the Pharisees of the amoraic period (200–500 C.E.) but to some extent also against those of the tannaitic period after the destruction of the Temple in 70 C.E. The implication of this is that the later Pharisees were not an integral or respectable part of Talmudic Judaism, let alone identical with it, as is so often assumed in scholarly treatises. In tannaitic sources the word "Pharisees" is used to denote various groups. It may refer to the *Ḥakhamim*, sages, rabbis; it may simply designate pious people; or it may label groups of extreme pietists whose harsh religious practices were considered improper. Occasionally it refers to hypocrites.

In brief, talmudic sources refer to Pharisees both in a laudatory and in a derogatory sense. How can this be explained?

Generally, this is explained by pointing out that every group has extremists, inferior members, and opportunists who join for other than idealistic reasons. The derogatory remarks of the Talmud refer to these types among the Pharisees, the scholars say.[328] While, at first, this may sound plausible, it does not explain passages in which derogatory statements are clearly directed against the *majority* of the Pharisees or against Pharisees in general.

The answer to the puzzle is that when the Temple was destroyed, the progressive wing of the Pharisees (Beth Hillel) prevailed and became the mainstream of Judaism while some peripheral groups perpetuated themselves, remaining on the sidelines of history. Considering themselves as *the* true representatives of Judaism, the Hillelites dropped the limiting designation "Beth Hillel," as we have shown elsewhere.[329] The designation "Pharisees" was now used by the Talmud for the dissident peripheral groups, mostly exaggerating pietists who no doubt opposed the changes necessitated by the destruction of the Temple. While Rabbinic Judaism of the post-Temple period was well aware of its Pharisaic roots and conceded that there were genuinely pious men among the Pharisees of their own day too, the tension between the progressive Rabbinic Judaism and the reactionary Pharisees resulted in derogatory remarks by some rabbis against these non-conforming Pharisees, as was also the case in other instances of tension, e.g., in cases of conflicts between the *haverim* and the *'amme ha-arez*.[330]

This split between reactionary Pharisees and progressive ones, which widened to the extent that the progressives did not even consider themselves as Pharisees, may even antedate somewhat the destruction of the Temple. Johanan ben Zakkai, the great Jewish leader before and after 70 c.e., defends the Pharisees speaking in the third person.[331] This may mean that, while strongly opposed to the Sadducees, he does not consider himself a Pharisee, but merely defends them against the common adversary. However, it is also possible that the third person formulation is of later date and represents an editorial change undertaken lest Johanan ben Zakkai be considered a Pharisee. It is noteworthy that talmudic sources, which often mention presidents (or vice-presidents) of the Sanhedrin, designate none of them as Pharisees, although this is done by Josephus and the New Testament[332] that refer to these leaders only a few times. This indicates that the rabbis of the Talmud purposely avoided designating the revered men of the past as Pharisees and employed this term only where it was unavoidable, as for example in the controversies between Sadducees and Pharisees.

The following derogatory statements made by the rabbis of the Talmud about the Pharisees are the basis of our observations:

1) M. *Soṭah* III,4:

הוא (רבי יהושע) היח אומר חסיד שוטה ורשע ערום ואשה פרושה
ומכות פרושין הרי אלו מבלי עולם.

"R. Joshua says: A foolish saint and a cunning knave and a Pharisaic woman and the wounds of the Pharisees: these wear out [destroy] the world."

R. Joshua was a leading sage during the Patriarchate of Gamaliel II, i.e., at the end of the first and the beginning of the second centuries c.e. His official position was that of *Av Beth Din*, vice president at Gamaliel's academy, the highest office beside the Patriarchate. He acted as the deputy of the Patriarch and carried out his policies.

Why does R. Joshua, a responsible leader, make such a statement against the Pharisees? Even more significant is that he does not seem to limit his condemnation to a non-representative minority of the Pharisees.

The wording of the Mishnah and its context show that his statement refers only to the Pharisees of *his own time*, whom he condemns entirely. Why? There can be no other reason except that the Pharisees of his time constituted a group distinct from Rabbinic Judaism.

Whereas the general meaning of Joshua's words is unequivocal, their precise meaning is somewhat obscure.

Why, for example, does he mention specifically the Pharisaic woman?

There is a case in the Talmud which sheds light upon our passage. B. *Pes.* 49b, discussing the antagonism that existed between the rabbis and the *'amme ha-arez*, "the people of the land" includes the assertion that the wives of the *'amme ha-arez* hated the rabbis more than the *'amme ha-arez* themselves. This reveals that the women were more ardent and outspoken in their antagonism than men, and were therefore worthy of specific mention. Similarly, we may safely assume that Pharisaic women were more hateful and antagonistic to the rabbis than their husbands.

What does *makkoth perushim* "wounds of the Pharisees" mean? The Babylonian Talmud[333] cites a Baraitha listing the seven categories of the Pharisees, but does not elaborate on the concept "wounds of the Pharisees." This expression had obviously no present-day relevance for the Babylonian Amoraim.

The Palestinian Talmud[334] elaborates on *makkoth perushim* and defines it as an act of hypocrisy. First, it says that *makkoth perushim* characterizes a person who advises orphans cunningly to deprive the widow of the support due her. Subsequently, two acts of hypocrisy are cited to illustrate the meaning of *makkoth perushim*. The first incident occurred in the amoraic period and was called *makkoth perushim* by Rabbi Eleazar (Amora). The second incident[335] occurred at the end of the tannaitic period and was designated as *makkoth perushim* by Judah the Prince.[336] We see that the term *makkoth perushim* was used, though obviously to a limited extent, during the second and third centuries in Palestine as a connotation for the hypocrisy of that day. This certainly could not have been the case had the Pharisees as a whole been considered by the Palestinian rabbis of the Talmud as the mainstream of Judaism or even a respectable wing of Judaism. The Pharisees they knew must have been a group antagonistic to the mainstream of Rabbinic Judaism, which in turn considered the Pharisees of their time a sect or quasi-sect.

In this connection Tosefta B. *Ber.* III,25 may be of significance כולל של מינים בשל פרושין "he includes the reference to the *minim* in the benediction of the *perushim*." If *perushim* here means Pharisees, then Pharisees would be included in the category of heretical or quasi-heretical Jews. This appears so absurd to scholars that they suggest פרושין(ם) *perushim* here is a different term and does not denote Pharisees.[337]

In the light of what we observed above, *perushim* may well mean Pharisees in this context; and this term was employed at a time when the antagonism between the rabbis and the Pharisees had grown strong.

Further indication as to the character of the Pharisees in later times may be found in Justin Martyr's "Dialogue with Trypho" where Justin lists the Baptist Pharisees (Hemero Baptists טובלי שחר?) among the heretical Jewish sects.[338] If Justin's information is correct, this would mean that Jews of the second century c.e. considered at least one group of the Pharisees of their time a heretical sect, just as they considered the Sadducees to be heretical (ibid.).

2) The seven categories of the Pharisees.

The sources are P. *Soṭah* V,5; 20c, P. *Ber.* IX,7; 14b, a somewhat different version in B. *Soṭah* 22b, a markedly different and obviously corrupted version in *ARN.*[339]

The Baraitha cited in the Palestinian Talmud appears to have the best text. It reads:

שבעה פרושין הן. פרוש שכמי. פרוש ניקפי. פרוש קיזי פרוש מכייה.
פרוש אדע חובתי ואעשנה. פרוש יראה. פרוש אהבה: פרוש שכמי. טעין
מצותיה על כתפיה: פרוש ניקפי. אקיף לי ואנא עבד מצוה: פרוש קיזיי.
עביד חדא חובה וחדא מצוה ומקזז חדא עם חדא: פרוש מנכייה. מאן
דית לי מה אנא מנכי עביד מצוה: פרוש אדע חובתי ואעשנה. איידי
חובתא עבדית דנעביד מצוה דכוותה: פרוש יראה כאיוב: פרוש אהבה
כאברהם:

There are seven kinds of Pharisees: 1. The shoulder Pharisee. 2.
The wait-a-while Pharisee. 3. The balance Pharisee. 4. The deducting Pharisee. 5. The "I want to know my guilt and shall compensate for it" Pharisee. 6. The fearing Pharisee. 7. The loving Pharisee.

The meaning of some of these designations is obscure. The Palestinian Talmud, in its amoraic stratum, explain them thus:

1) The "shoulder Pharisee" is the one who carries his good deeds
on his shoulders, i.e., displays them ostentatiously. 2) The "wait-a-
while Pharisee" is the one who says: wait for me and I shall do a
good deed. 3) The "balance Pharisee" is the one who commits a sin
and does a good deed and balances them against one another. 4) The
"deducting Pharisee" is the one who says: from that little I have,
I shall take out some and perform a good deed. 5) The "I want to
know my guilt and shall compensate for it" Pharisee is the one who
says: Tell me the sin I have committed so that I can do a corresponding *mizwah*. 6) The "fearing Pharisee" is the one like Job. 7) The
"loving Pharisee" is the one like Abraham. Among the variants in
B. *Soṭah* 22b the following should be noted. In place of 4) "the deducting Pharisee," B. reads "the pestle Pharisee" and the Gemara explains this as meaning a person who bends his head in mock
humility. However, the similarity of the words מנכייה and מדוכיא
indicates that originally we had here the same word and one of them
(if not both) was transmitted in a corrupt version.

The explanations in the Babylonian and Palestinian Talmudim
differ quite markedly. It stands to reason that in Palestine the meaning of this Baraitha, a Palestinian source, was better known than it
was in Babylonia. The basic difference is that while the Babylonian
Talmud understands the Baraitha as a derogation of everyone in all
seven categories, the Palestinian Talmud holds that the "loving

Pharisee," one like Abraham, is a praise for an upright and pious man. The difference may be rooted in the erroneous premise held by the Babylonian Amoraim that the Baraitha considers all the Pharisees as blemished. Consequently, they search for the blemish in the last two categories as well. The Palestinian Talmud, whose teachers knew the Pharisees of their time — they lived in their midst — expressed a realistic attitude. While blaming most members of the sect-like Pharisees of their time, the rabbis of the Palestinian Talmud admitted that there were also some genuinely pious men among them.

What is the date of this Baraitha? It is anonymous, making an exact dating impossible. It could not have been authored by a Pharisee. A Pharisee would certainly not admit that only one of their seven groups was genuinely pious. Since it is transmitted in various talmudic sources with no objection voiced against it, it was undoubtedly uttered by some rabbi at a time when Pharisaic and Rabbinic Judaism were clearly separated, i.e., after the destruction of the Temple.

Does our Baraitha speak of the Pharisees in the technical sense of the word? The context shows clearly that the rabbis of the Talmud understood *perushim* of our Baraitha as meaning "Pharisees." Not only do they cite the Baraitha to illustrate the "wounds of the Pharisees" of the Mishnah, but they also cite in connection with our Baraitha (B. *Soṭah* 22b) a historical incident in which *perushim* unequivocally designates "Pharisees."

3) There is the following talmudic passage where derogatory statements have reference only to exceptions among the Pharisees. However, the reference is to the Pharisees of the past:

B. *Soṭah* 22b:

אמר לה ינאי מלכא לדביתיה אל תתיראי מן הפרושין ולא ממי שינו פרושין אלא מן הצבועין שדומין לפרושין שמעשיהן כמעשה זמרי ומבקשין שכר פנחס.

King Jannai said to his wife: Don't be afraid of the Pharisees, nor of the non-Pharisees, but only of the "dyed" ones who appear like the Pharisees: whose deeds are like the deeds of Zimri, but who demand the reward of Pinhas.

167

According to this passage, there were among the Pharisees insincere individuals as early as the time of Alexander Jannaeus.[340] However, we must keep in mind that the passage above is a relatively late source recounting an early event. Josephus' account, which is older and more detailed, does not speak of two kinds of Pharisees.[341] The rabbinic sources, on the other hand, do not concur with the claim of Josephus[342] that the Pharisees retracted their unfavorable opinion of Alexander Jannaeus. Whether the reference to the "dyed" Pharisees is historically true or represents a later addition of the non-Pharisaic rabbis relating the incident, is immaterial. In any large group we find individuals who join for other than idealistic reasons.

Besides the Talmud, the writings of Josephus are the most important source of our knowledge about the Pharisees. Does Josephus concur with the talmudic sources in dividing the Pharisees into two or more categories: a progressive group representing the mainstream of the Pharisees and peripheral groups, among them a group of exaggerating pietists? We do not find that Josephus divided the Pharisees into such categories. A division such as made by the Talmud into earlier, or classical Pharisees (until the destruction of the Temple) and later quasi-sectarian Pharisees would hardly be included in Josephus' writings since he did not continue his history beyond the destruction of the Temple. Nonetheless, Josephus' attitude toward the Pharisees was not always favorable as shown above.

There are a few passages in which *perushim* may mean "separatists," not Pharisees. Yet, even in these passages the undertone "Pharisees" may well have been on the mind of the critics. Such passages are:

1) Tosefta *Soṭah* XV,11,12 (see also *B. B.* 60b):

משחרב בית המקדש רבו פרושים בישראל ולא היו אוכלין בשר
ולא היו שותין יין ניטפל להן ר' יהושע אמר להם בניי מפני מה אין
אתם אוכלין בשר אמרו לו נאכל בשר שבכל יום היה תמיד קרב על
גבי המזבח ועכשיו בטל וכו'

After the destruction of the Temple the *perushim* increased in Israel, and they would not eat meat and would not drink wine. R. Joshua approached them and said to them: My sons, why don't you eat meat? They replied: Should we eat meat, when the Tamid was offered on the altar every day and it has been stopped. . . ?

A possible meaning of *perushim* here is "separatists." But in what sense were they "separatists"? They were separatists by displaying an exaggerated piety, which R. Joshua considered improper. The "Seven categories of the Pharisees" were also displaying exaggerated forms of piety which, according to the Talmud, R. Joshua had in mind when he spoke about the "wounds of the Pharisees." Pharisees of the second century c.e. were considered by the rabbis as separatists in the sense that they were extremists and dissenters. It is questionable whether the rabbis drew a clear line between confessed Pharisees and other separatists of their time.

Rabban Gamaliel II was well aware of the danger of disintegration for his people. He saw the inroads Christianity had made at the expense of the Jewish people. Like the responsible leader of his people that he was, he took steps whenever signs of heresy or serious dissent were present. He did not merely introduce *birkath haminim*, the benediction against heretics (and other serious offenders of Judaism), but watched most carefully even over his closest associates for signs of serious dissent. He did not even spare Rabbi Joshua, his *Av Beth Din*, deputy head of the *Beth Din Ha-Gadol*, when the latter differed with him in matters of calendation or other important issues.[343] He also excommunicated R. Eliezer the Great, his own brother-in-law, when he believed that the latter was not quite in accord with Rabbinic Judaism.[344] We also know that Rabbi Joshua assisted R. Gamaliel in trying similarly to preserve the unity of the Jewish people. In the dispute resulting in R. Eliezer's excommunication, R. Joshua led the fight against R. Eliezer.[345] When R. Hananja, Joshua's nephew, showed signs of Christian influence, Joshua sent him to Babylonia to save him from possible heresy.[346] In another instance Joshua engaged a disciple of the Shammaites outside of the Academy in a discussion trying to persuade him to accept the Hillelite position in a specific instance.[347] R. Joshua is the man who spoke so emphatically about "the wounds of the Pharisees" and the Pharisaic women. Now he engaged *perushim* in a discussion — it was not an academic discussion — in order to persuade them to give up their exaggerated way of piety: refraining from drinking wine and eating meat as an expression of their mourning for Jerusalem. Noteworthy is the use of the words ניטפל להן "he joined them,"

169

here meaning "he approached them." These are the very same words used by the Talmud (Baraitha) when R. Joshua engaged the disciple of the Shammaite in a dispute. The discussion was not held in the academy (נּיטפל is not used in connection with a dispute within the academy), allowing the inference that these *perushim* were men who separated themselves from Rabbinic Judaism and may have been a Pharisaic group. Interesting is the fact that these *perushim* utilized for their expression of sorrow customs known to be followed by the Essenes, even before the destruction of the Temple. Whether Essene influence was responsible for the ascetic behavior of these *perushim*, is difficult to determine.

2) B. *Pes.* 70b:

תניא יהודה בן דורתאי פירש הוא ודורתאי בנו והלך וישב לו בדרום
אמר אם יבוא אליהו ויאמר להם לישראל מפני מה לא חגגתם חגיגה
בשבת מה הן אומרים לו תמהני על שני גדולי הדור שמעיה ואבטליון
שהן חכמים גדולים ודרשנין גדולים ולא אמרו להן לישראל חגיגה דוחה
את השבת... א"'ר אשי ואנן טעמא דפרושים ניקו וניפרוש? וכו'

Juda, son of Dortai *perash*, i.e., separated himself [from the sages], he and his son Dortai and he went and settled in the South. He said: If Elijah should come and say to Israel, "Why did you not sacrifice the *Ḥagigah* on the Sabbath?" what can they answer him? I am astonished at the two greatest men of their generation, Shemaiah and Avtalion, who were great sages and great interpreters, yet who have not told Israel that the *Ḥagigah* overrides the Sabbath. . . . Rab Ashi said: "Should we interpret [i.e., consider] the reasoning of the *perushim*?"

This Juda was apparently a disciple of Shemaiah and Avtalion, which makes him a contemporary of Hillel. The problem referred to in our passage is similar to that of *Pes.* 66a, except that it does not concern the *Pesaḥ*, but the *Ḥagigah* sacrifice. Juda claims that Shemaiah and Avtalion never said that the *Ḥagigah* supersedes the Sabbath. This implies that he questioned the validity of the opposing view, since it was not based on the tradition of the *Zugoth*. On the other hand, he speaks of the possibility that the opposition was right; but he adds that even in such a case there would be no harm done in not sacrificing the *Ḥagigah* on the Sabbath. The lack of an authoritative tradition is sufficient excuse for omitting this sacrifice on a Sabbath. It is interesting that the impact of the dispute was so strong that Juda and his son left the scene of the controversy, undoubtedly Jerusalem, and settled in the South. The wording פירש פרושים, may be significant. When Rab Ashi said, "Should we interpret the reasoning of the *perushim*?" it is quite possible that he had the Pharisees in mind in conformity with the later usage of *perushim* when this term was used only to designate a group of exaggerating (or hypocritical) pietists.[348]

While the rabbis of the second century c.e. and later did not consider themselves as Pharisees and criticized them for their exaggerated piety, they were not condemnatory in regard to those of the earlier part of the tannaitic period. They did not use the same harsh language in criticizing the Pharisees as they used in criticizing the *'amme ha-arez*, the unaffiliated who displayed laxity in some areas of religious law, and who failed to pledge allegiance to the law as interpreted by the rabbis. There is also a difference between law and casual criticism. The latter was often harsh, revealing the feelings toward the opposing groups, whereas the law intended to dispense justice even for the opposition and refrained from expressing subjective criticism.

We find no anti-Pharisaic legislation, but there are a few anti-*'am ha-arez* laws. The few anti-*'am ha-arez* laws that exist were based on objective criteria. Since the *'amme ha-arez* were lax in some areas of ritual purity and in matters of the tithe, etc., the rabbis felt the necessity of introducing corrective measures. No such measures were deemed necessary (or effective) in regard to the Pharisees.

The attitude of the rabbis toward the Pharisees of the Temple period was friendly, for they were well aware that these Pharisees were their predecessors. Most significant in this respect is the account in *Qid.* 66a (a Baraitha) for which there is a parallel in *Ant.* XIII. x.5,6.

In the talmudic account of this incident, *Ḥakhamim*, sages and Pharisees are used as synonyms while Josephus uses throughout "Pharisees." [349] This fact is significant because it shows that the rabbis of the Talmud considered the Pharisees of the past to be "the sages of Israel," a term used for the sages of classical Rabbinic Judaism.

171

The equation Pharisees = sages (in the past), implied in this talmudic passage is, historically speaking, not quite accurate. Josephus describes the Pharisees as the most accurate interpreters of the law[350] who had great influence with the masses. This obviously means that the Pharisees were a class of teachers, but *not* the masses. On the other hand, their number at Herod's time, according to Josephus, was about 6000,[351] which number appears to be too large if all the Pharisees were teachers. New Testament accounts shed light on this issue by often referring to "scribes and Pharisees," for example in Matt. 15:1; 23:2; Mark, 7:5; Luke, 5:30, etc.; and in Acts 23:9 to "the scribes that were of the Pharisees." This means that the Pharisees were a group composed of both learned men *and* laymen, adhering to a certain theology, a system of law and ritual and exerting a leading influence on the masses.[352] Further clarification of the distinction between Pharisees and sages prior to the destruction of the Temple is found in a Baraitha, B. *Niddah* 33b, where the following incident is related: Once, while talking to the high priest, the spittle of a Sadducee fell upon the garment of the high priest. This upset the high priest because of a possible defilement. Immediately he enquired of the wife of this Sadducee about her observance of the laws of (menstrual) defilement. She replied that the wives of the Sadducees, fearing the Pharisees, show their blood stains to the *sages* in order to be declared clean or unclean. Consequently the high priest was not defiled by the spittle of her husband since she, by complying with the proper Pharisaic law, did not render her husband and his spittle ritually unclean.

In this passage Pharisees and sages appear to be two different categories but components of the same larger Pharisaic group: 1) The sages among whose tasks was the decision of matters pertaining to religion. 2) Pharisees who were not themselves sages, but possessed the power and zeal to force the Sadducees to comply with the Halakhah of the Pharisaic sages.

Friendly relationship between the Pharisees and the masses prevailed perhaps primarily because the Pharisees emerged from the masses and remained, to a certain extent, part of them. Significant in this respect is an incident in which the 'amme ha-arez actively complied with the Pharisaic law, opposed to the Boethosians, that the flogging with the willow branches on the Festival of Tabernacles supersedes the Sabbath. In another incident, the people supported a Pharisaic view by militant action. We refer to their pelting King and High Priest Alexander Jannaeus with citrons (*ethrogim*) when he violated the Pharisaic water libation ceremony of the Sukkoth festival by pouring the water upon his feet instead of upon the altar.

The situation changed after the destruction of the Temple. The Sadducees lost their importance making unnecessary further joint endeavors against them by Pharisees and the "people of the land." On the other hand, with the passage of time the gap widened between the learned class and the masses, the *'amme ha-arez*, who were mostly but not always uneducated people.[353]

Successors to the mainstream of the Pharisees were now the *haverim*, including the rabbis, while the designation "Pharisees" remained in usage for peripheral Pharisaic groups. That Pharisees and *haverim* were not identical is evidenced by their respective relations to the masses, the *'amme ha-arez*. Pharisees lived in full harmony with the *'amme ha-arez* [354] as we have seen while between *haverim* and *'amme ha-arez* considerable tension persisted.

The requirement of a pledge for becoming a *haver* constituted an official barrier between the two groups.[355] More antagonism developed on the part of the *'amme ha-arez* due to the introduction of certain laws and rules concerning the *'am ha-arez*, no matter how justified these laws were.[356]

The transition from Pharisees to *haverim* was not a sudden one. A few matters concerning the *haver* had been discussed already by the schools of Hillel and Shammai[357] whose existence terminated shortly after the destruction of the Temple.[358]

It is to be noted that the *haver* played an important role only in tannaitic times as indicated by the numerous rules about him in Tos. *Demai*, II and III, and in Baraithoth, particularly in B. *Bekhor.* 30b. His importance already had diminished by the end of the tannaitic period as indicated by the fact that Mishnah contains but few references to the *haver*.[359] In amoraic times *haver* or *havra*, its Aramaic equivalent, are relatively seldom used in a technical sense, the reason being that most of the laws introduced against the *'amme ha-arez* became obsolete or less important in later talmudic times

173

which reduced the enmity between them and the learned class. The primary meaning of the term 'am ha-arez became ignorant, uncultured people.

In a few tannaitic passages parush and 'am ha-arez are contrasted to each other in a way similar to the more frequent contrasting of haver and 'am ha-arez. These passages may date from the transition period. Examples: B. Shab. 13a (Baraitha): לא יאכל זב פרוש עם זב עם הארץ "A Pharisee that has a flux may not eat with an 'am ha-arez that has a flux." M. Ḥag. II,7: בגדי עם הארץ מדרס לפרושין "For the Pharisees the clothes of the 'am ha-arez count as suffering midras—uncleanliness." R. Ḥananel explains[360] that "Pharisees" here is synonymous with "ḥaverim." He would have been more accurate had he said that the Pharisees here correspond to the ḥaverim, who succeeded them.

Rashi[361] explains that "Pharisees" here refers to those eating Ḥullin (secular food) in cleanliness. Therefore, according to Rashi, the word "Pharisee" was no longer a term designating teachers and leaders as before — (these are now the rabbis and ḥaverim) — but a designation for the ritualistic pietists, who had not yet seceded from Rabbinic Judaism.

Our investigation of the attitude of the Talmud toward the Pharisees shows the following:

The Talmud makes a clear distinction between Pharisees that lived before the destruction of the Temple and those that lived afterward.[362] Its attitude toward the former is friendly; toward the latter, however, it is just the opposite. The reason thereof is that talmudic Judaism evolved from the mainstream of Pharisaic Judaism whereas several peripheral Pharisaic groups continued their separate sect-like existence for centuries. Since "Pharisees" remained the designation of these groups while the leaders of the mainstream were now the ḥaverim including and particularly the rabbis, the word "Pharisees," because of its obnoxious contemporary sound, had been avoided with reference to the (good) Pharisees of the past whenever possible. Thus, e.g., the Talmud never designates a Jewish leader of the past a Pharisee, as is done by Josephus and the New Testament. The Talmud, referring to the past, uses the term Pharisee only when it is unavoidable, as in the discussions between Sadducees and Pharisees.

Classical Pharisaism and Rabbinic Judaism are not identical but they are congenial. As the historical and spiritual successor of Pharisaic Judaism, Rabbinic Judaism continues to interpret Judaism meaningfully. However, Rabbinic Judaism possesses characteristics of its own, the most significant being the vast development of the law and the relative neglect of theology. This shift of emphasis began already before the destruction of the Temple — note the controversies between the two leading schools of Hillel and Shammai — and continued steadily throughout the ages.

Enlightening in this respect is an incident related by Qirqisani stating that he asked Jacob ben Ephraim of Palestine, "You [Rabbanites] draw near the Isunians [followers of Abu Isa Al-Isfahani] and intermarry with them, though you yourself know that they ascribe prophecy to men who did not possess it," i.e., to Jesus, Mohammed, and Abu Isa. Jacob ben Ephraim replied, "[We do so because] they do not differ with us with regard to the festivals. . . ."[363]

After citing Jacob ben Ephraim's reply, Louis Ginzberg observes that Jacob's words are characteristic not merely for the end of the first millennium but are just as valid for earlier centuries and suggests that even Judeo-Christianity was considered a legitimate part of Judaism as long as it did not differ from it with respect to the attitude toward the law.[364] While the full validity of this view may be questioned, the paramount importance of the law for Rabbinic Judaism, including the period of transition from Pharisaic to Rabbinic Judaism, remains a well-established fact. Noteworthy in this connection is, in spite of a midrashic setting, a statement of R. Johanan, Amora of the third century C.E. (B. *Shab.* 118b and parallels), "Everyone who keeps the Sabbath according to the Halakhah, even if he worship idols like the generation of Enosh, is forgiven."

LEADERSHIP AFTER HILLEL

The known sources give insufficient information for dating accurately the office tenures of the *Nesi'im*, the Princes. One of the most important pieces of chronological information about this matter is the talmudic and midrashic account that Hillel became Nasi one hundred years before the destruction of the Temple and officiated for forty years.[365] Accepting the historicity of this account, Graetz gives Hillel a tenure of forty years, i.e., from 30 B.C.E. to 10 C.E. Then he divides the remaining sixty years evenly allotting the three succeeding Princes, Simon I, Gamaliel I, and Simon II, twenty years each.[366]

Such unrealistic dating is unacceptable even as conjecture. A sound conjecture must be based on whatever pertinent indications are present in the sources. Thus, e.g., the fact that nothing (or almost nothing) is transmitted either in the name of or about Simon I, while a considerable amount of tradition is transmitted in regard to Gamaliel I, convincingly indicates that the latter must have held leadership much longer than Simon I.

Further, since Johanan ben Zakkai, who officiated still after the destruction of the Temple was among the disciples of Hillel in the literal sense of the word, Hillel's leadership probably ended later than given in the Talmud. Again the talmudic numbers 100 and 40 are not to be taken literally. Taking into consideration the traditions about the individual *Nesi'im*, the following conjectural dates may be more realistic than those suggested by Graetz (and some other scholars):

Hillel I	between 30 and 20 B.C.E. to between 10 and 20 C.E.[367]
Simon I	between 10 and 20–25 C.E.
Gamaliel I	25–55 C.E.
Simon II	55–70, or close to 70 C.E.
Johanan ben Zakkai	70–85 C.E.
Gamaliel II	85–135, or close to 135 C.E.
Simon III	140–175 C.E.
Judah I	175–217 C.E.

SIMON BEN HILLEL

*E*xcept for his name — see B. *Shab.* 15a — nothing (or almost nothing)[368] is known about Simon, son of Hillel. The reason for this is unknown. While we may safely assume that he accomplished nothing important enough to be transmitted to later generations, a more weighty reason for the silence about him was probably the brevity of his career as the head of the Sanhedrin.[369] The baseless conjectures of some scholars that Simon I never existed and that Gamaliel I was the son and direct successor of Hillel are not acceptable.[370]

GAMALIEL I

*T*he date of Gamaliel's presidency is controversial. Graetz' dating is 30–50[371] while I. Halevy claims that Gamaliel I came to power shortly after 10 c.e. and officiated until close to the destruction of the Temple in 70 c.e.[372] We have previously put forth the reason for our dating: about 25–55 c.e.

Gamaliel I is the first Nasi to be called רבן *Rabban*, "Our Master." Z. Frankel believes that he was given this title because he apparently presided over the Sanhedrin alone, without an *Av Beth Din*.[373] While it is certain that Gamaliel I officiated without an *Av Beth Din* of the opposition leader type present in the *Zugoth*, the same holds true with regard to Simon I, yet we do not find that he was called *Rabban*. *Rabban* may have been a title recognizing Gamaliel I as the legitimate leader of the Jewish people. However, we must not rule out Roman influence, which is apparent throughout the talmudic (especially early talmudic) period. Roman officials of any standing were, as a matter of course, bearers of titles. The Aramaic form *Rabban* suggests that this was not a title coined in the Sanhedrin or academy. Had it originated in the academy a Hebrew

177

word would have been chosen, as was the case with all the other titles alloted to the distinguished members of the Sanhedrin or *Beth Din*, such as: אב בית דין, חכם, מופלא ,נשיא Nasi, *Av Beth Din, Mufla, Ḥakham*. The *Rabban* title was probably coined outside of the academy by the people who commonly spoke Aramaic and was subsequently accepted by the learned members of Sanhedrin.

Gamaliel I is never designated as a member of a *Zug*, neither is Simon I. This shows that the *Zugoth* came to an end with Hillel and Shammai. The later *Nesi'im*, Princes, were the leaders of the entire Jewish people, not just party or majority leaders as were the *Zugoth*. They enjoyed special privileges with regard to partaking in Greek and Roman cultural endeavors because of their contacts with Roman officials.[374] That the Princes after Hillel did not have to step down when the Hillelites were outvoted by the Shammaites indicates that the Nasi after Hillel stood above the parties. Another indication to the same effect is an incident in which Gamaliel I, while standing at the Eastern Gate, answered a question put before him by the Shammaite Joezer Ish Habirah (M. *'Orlah* II,12). Such cases indicate that at least some Shammaites considered the Nasi a nonpartisan leader. The wealth accumulated by the originally poor patriarchal family drew them in some respects closer to the Shammaites, making them more acceptable to the latter.

The reference to the Eastern Gate in connection with Gamaliel I is significant. After the Sanhedrin was forced to abandon its seat in the *Lishkath Ha-Gazith* of the Temple, it went into "exile" and convened in the *Ḥanuth*. The emigration from the *Lishkath Ha-Gazith* to the *Ḥanuth* took place under Gamaliel I, according to A. Büchler, between 40 and 50 c.e.[375] We find him both, in the *Lishkath Ha-Gazith* and in the *Ḥanuth*. In addition to the above passage from M. *'Orlah* II,12, the following passages should be considered:

M. *Peah* II.6 relates an incident in which R. Simon of Mizpah and Gamaliel went to the *Lishkath Ha-Gazith* and inquired there about a halakhic matter.[376] The passage, however, does not reveal whether Gamaliel was Nasi at that time. Yet, he was certainly the Nasi when he sent out letters while sitting together with the sages on the "Steps of the Temple Mount," asking the Jews in one case to surrender the tithes, and in another, declaring a leap year (Tos. *Sanhedrin* II,6 and parallels). The "Steps of the Temple Mount" which are also mentioned elsewhere (cf. Tosefta *Shab.* XIII [XIV], 2) as a place of Gamaliel's activities cannot simply mean "steps," but rather designates a meeting place.[377] A. Büchler tries to show that this place is identical with the *Hanuth*, mentioned in B. *R. H.* 31a and is probably identical with the stores at the Eastern Gate of the outer wall of the Temple Mount.

Gamaliel's halakhic activity consisted mostly of the issuing of *Taqqanoth*, a prerogative of the Nasi. His *Taqqanoth* are characterized by a liberal and realistic tendency. Examples:

In M. *R. H.* II,5, Gamaliel issues a *Taqqanah* in behalf of the witnesses of the new moon who happened to come to the designated court yard in Jerusalem (called Beth Ya'azeq) on a Sabbath. This *Taqqanah* permits them to walk two thousand cubits in every direction; the old Halakhah had allowed them merely four cubits. The same leniency was allotted to a midwife and to people who came from out of town to rescue (people) from fire, armed gangs, the river, or debris.

Gamaliel's *Taqqanoth* regarding family life are chiefly concerned with the improvement of women's rights.

In M. *Git.* IV,2, Gamaliel ordained that a bill of divorce could not be invalidated by proxy before a court in a place other than the divorcee's own town, once it was already on the way to being handed to her. The reason for this *Taqqanah* is that the news of the annulment by proxy might reach her too late, i.e., after she remarried, resulting in marital calamity.

Another *Taqqanah* of Gamaliel with a similar purpose (i.e., preventing marital calamity) requires all the names of both man and wife to be entered in the bill of divorce (ibid.).

R. Gamaliel ordained that a widow may collect her *kethuvah* after the pronouncement of a vow instead of an oath (ibid. IV,3).

He ordained that the witnesses to a divorce must sign the bill of divorce (ibid.).

R. Gamaliel permits the remarriage of a woman on the testimony of only one person who claims to be a witness to the death of her husband, though normally two eyewitnesses would be required.

179

In all but the last of these cases regarding family life, the reason given is מפני תקון העולם "the general good."

There are instances in which doubt exists whether the R. Gamaliel mentioned is Gamaliel I or II. For example, R. Gamaliel the Elder is mentioned in M. *Yev.* XVI,7. According to Z. Frankel[378] the reference should be to R. Gamaliel II.

Few Halakhoth are related in the name of Gamaliel I. Except for cases involving ritual purity (B. *Ber.* 38a, Tos. *Parah* XI), his Halakhoth and decisions are mostly lenient (cf. M. *'Orlah* II,12; B. *Pes.* 74a, 88b; B. *Bekhor.* 38a; Tos. *A. Z.* III). The reason for the paucity of his Halakhoth may be the fact that the Halakhoth of his time were generally communicated in the name of the schools of Hillel and Shammai, respectively.

Tolerant toward Christians, Gamaliel was only an ordinary member of the Sanhedrin that tried Peter and John, not its president. They were tried by a Sanhedrin headed by the high priest, not by the Pharisaic Sanhedrin. In Acts 5:34, Gamaliel, who pleads against the execution of Peter and John, is called "a Pharisee, a doctor of the Law." The fact that his name is not mentioned at the trial of Jesus allows no safe inference. He may have been present without playing a significant role and was, therefore, not specifically mentioned. Also, he may have been unimportant in the eyes of the high priest at that time and therefore not invited to join his Sanhedrin. Even more obscure is the reason for his absence at Jacobus' trial, unless we assume that this trial was held before an exclusively Sadducean Sanhedrin.[379] His absence at Paul's trial close to the year 60 might mean that he was already dead.[380] It is more probable, however, that this trial was held by an exclusively Sadducean court, for otherwise Simon, son and successor of Gamaliel, would probably have been present.

Onkelos, author of the Targum on the Pentateuch, was a friend of Gamaliel (Tos. *Shab.* VII,18 and parallels; Tos. *Miqva'oth* VI,3). We have to keep this in mind when we try to solve the puzzle why Gamaliel ordered the Targum of Job to be buried (or concealed) under a wall (Tos. *Shab.* XIII [XIV],2 and parallels). It stands to reason that Gamaliel consulted with this Targum expert on the matter. It is doubtful that more was involved in the incident although more is often assumed.

In view of Gamaliel's friendly attitude toward dissidents (Judeo-Christians) and gentiles, I. H. Weiss, Graetz, and others ascribe the introduction of measures promoting good will between Jews and gentiles to him.[381] Such measures are: "They do not try to prevent the poor among the gentiles from gathering Gleanings, the Forgotten Sheaf and *Peah* — in the interest of peace" (M. *Giṭ.* V,8 and parallels); "Gentiles may be encouraged [when tending their fields] in the Seventh Year, but not Israelites. Greetings may be offered to gentiles in the interest of peace" (ibid. 9); and "In a town that is inhabited by Jews and gentiles, the trustees collect [for charity] from Jews and gentiles in the interest of peace. We must support the poor among the gentiles in the interest of peace. We must eulogize the deceased of the gentiles, comfort the mourners of the gentiles, and bury the dead of the gentiles in the interest of peace" (Tosefta *Giṭ.* V(III),4,5 and parallels, see especially B. *Giṭ.* 59b, 61 ff; P. *Giṭ.* V end).

Graetz[382] ascribes the above measures to R. Gamaliel I, claiming "hohe Wahrscheinlichkeit" for them. He includes in this category of measures "in the interests of peace" some that have no reference to the gentiles.[383] As a further conjecture, he considers the possibility that the ruling about the seven Noachian Commandments likewise originate with Gamaliel I.[384]

The weakness of Graetz' conjecture is that if Gamaliel I really had been the originator of these anonymous measures, why do all the sources conceal the fact? The answer might be that most of the laws and practices introduced at this period sailed under the flags of Beth Shammai and Beth Hillel, respectively. Joint measures of both schools need no reference to the schools, and the above measures may belong in the category of joint action.[385]

High esteem for R. Gamaliel I is expressed in M. *Soṭah* IX,15 (and parallels): "When Rabban Gamaliel the Elder died, the glory of the Torah ceased; and purity and abstinence (*perishuth*) died." A more complete version of this passage is found in B. *Meg.* 21a (a Baraitha): "From the days of Moses up to Rabban Gamaliel, the Torah was studied only standing. When Rabban Gamaliel died, illness descended upon the world, and they studied sitting. That is why we have learnt: 'When Rabban Gamaliel died, the glory of the Torah ceased.' " [386]

SIMON BEN GAMALIEL I

*T*he halakhic activity of Simon II appears to have been limited in comparison with that of his father Gamaliel. He played an eminent role during the war against the Romans in the years prior to the destruction of the Temple as related by Josephus (*Life* 38):

> Meanwhile . . . John, son of Levi . . . dispatched his brother . . . to Jerusalem, to Simon, son of Gamaliel, to entreat him to induce the national assembly of Jerusalem to deprive me of the command of Galilee. . . . This Simon was a native of Jerusalem, of a very illustrious family, and of the sect of the Pharisees, who have the reputation of being unrivalled experts in their country's laws. A man highly gifted with intelligence and judgment, he could by sheer genius retrieve an unfortunate situation in affairs of state.

We do not want to discuss the political aspects of his career, his alleged hesitation before joining the uprising, his real or perhaps nominal leadership of the people, or the conjectures of his dying as a martyr or murder victim. More important for us is the fact that Josephus calls Simon a Pharisee, and that the Pharisees excelled others in the accurate knowledge of the laws. Although he cooperated politically with Jishmael, the high priest, in matters of law, we find him in close cooperation with Johanan ben Zakkai.

Most important evidence of his religious leadership is his letter in matters of tithes, etc., sent out jointly with Johanan ben Zakkai. His father had issued similar dispatches during his presidency.

His liberal spirit emerges in an ordinance that copes with a situation realistically, though it contravenes the law of the Torah. In order to counteract the skyrocketing price of doves used for sacrifices, he declared that under certain conditions, a smaller number of sacrifices (than prescribed in the Torah) would be sufficient. This measure resulted in a sudden decrease in the price of doves.[387]

The same spirit is expressed in a general ruling: "No [prohibitive] measure must be imposed on the community unless the majority of the community is able to bear it." [388] This rule, directed against unduly burdensome measures, is transmitted in the names of R. Simon, son of Gamaliel, and R. Eleazar, son of Zadok (B. A. Z. 36a and parallels). It is assumed, perhaps erroneously, that Simon here is Simon II.[389] We find in the Tosefta (Sanh. II,13 [418]) a statement which is basically similar to the above rule and may represent its original form "R. Simon, son of Gamaliel, and R. Eleazar, son of Zadok, said: They may not intercalate the year nor act in matters pertaining to the needs of the congregation except conditionally, so that the majority of the congregation accept them." [390]

In his time, tension between Pharisees and Sadducees was considerable. Simon, while a Pharisee, certainly considered himself to be the leader of the entire people including the Sadducees and therefore may have refrained from disputations with them. This chore was carried out by Johanan ben Zakkai, his Av Beth Din.

There is only one incident transmitted in which Simon II was halakhically involved with Sadducees. (M. 'Eruvin VI,2). The obvious meaning of the passage is that Simon's attitude toward the Sadducee was positive, that is, he considered him a (full) Israelite even though the Sadducee did not recognize the 'Eruv, a rabbinic institution.[391] However, the passage is obscure and allows no safe inference.[392]

No specific Halakhoth are transmitted in Simon's name. The reason may be the same as in the case of his father, Gamaliel. There is also the possibility that he did not consider himself competent enough to dwell independently on halakhic matters. The indications to this effect are: He issued a letter on matters of tithes in concert with Johanan ben Zakkai (his father did not add another name to his requests about tithes, etc.); he issued another ruling together with Eleazar, son of Zadok; he states (Avoth I,17): "All my days have I grown up among the sages, and I have found naught better for a man than silence; and not the expounding of the Law is the chief thing but the doing of it; and he that multiplies words occasions sin." A man of silence is not likely to devote himself to an extensive halakhic endeavor. Bacher observed[393] that no Midrash had been transmitted in his name. This is quite understandable in view of his adage "not the expounding of the Law is the chief thing." Expounding of the law, however, is the basis of halakhic endeavor.

In several instances Simon II, Simon III, and others are confused in the sources. Although we shall not try to untangle them here, some cases may be mentioned.

M. *Ket.* V,5, "These are the works which the wife must perform for her husband. . . . R. Simon ben Gamaliel says: Even if a man put his wife under a vow to do no work he should divorce her and give her her *ḳethuvah*, for idleness leads to lowness of spirit." That is, Simon ben Gamaliel opposes the wife as a mere luxury item for the sake of her own mental well-being.[394]

B. *A. Z.* 20a relates an incident: "R. Simon ben Gamaliel was on the steps of the Temple Mount and saw a very beautiful gentile woman and exclaimed 'How manifold are Thy works, O Lord'" (Ps. 104:24). However P. *Ber.* IX,2 and P. *A. Z.* I,9 read "Rabban Gamaliel" instead of "Rabban Simon ben Gamaliel."

B. *A. Z.* 32a. R. Simon, son of Gamaliel relates in the name of Joshua son of Kaposai that drinking from the (wine) skins of the idol worshippers is prohibited. Tosafoth, ibid. s.v. אבל tries to prove that the reference should be to Gamaliel the Elder instead.

In the same Tosafoth, the claim is made that the passage in *Soṭah*, end—"R. Simon ben Gamaliel said: 'There were a thousand children in the house of my father, etc.'" has reference to Simon, son of Gamaliel I. This, however, is very questionable.[395]

III

TANNAITIC PERIOD

JOHANAN BEN ZAKKAI

*J*ohanan ben Zakkai was a leader of normative Judaism for many years before and after the destruction of the Temple in 70 c.e. The significance of his leadership during these years is well attested in the sources and discussed in many articles and books. Nonetheless, a number of issues relative to his personality, activities, and accomplishments still need clarification.

Was he a direct disciple of Hillel? Did his important role commence during the presidency of Gamaliel I or that of his son Simon? Was he involved in the internal political struggle during the war against the Romans? Why was *he* the Pharisee spokesman against the Sadducees instead of Simon, the Nasi? Was he Nasi after the destruction of the Temple? Why did he issue ordinances after the destruction of the Temple for the continuation of some Temple ceremonies in places outside Jerusalem, while opposing the continuation of the sacrificial cult? What is the significance of his *Taqqanoth*? When and why did his leadership come to an end?

The numerous activities of Johanan ben Zakkai are indicative of a long life. According to *Sifre Berakhah*,[1] Johanan ben Zakkai lived for 120 years. While this life span of Moses ascribed to various persons is not to be taken literally, it is an indication that Johanan lived very long and therefore could have been a disciple of Hillel as stated in talmudic sources. Although some scholars claim he was merely a spiritual disciple of Hillel,[2] there is no compelling reason to discredit the explicit sources or to interpret them figuratively. See, for example, B. *Pes.* 3b, "Two disciples were sitting before Hillel, one of them Johanan ben Zakkai."[3] According to another talmudic tradition "Hillel had 80 disciples. . . . The youngest of them all was Johanan ben Zakkai."[4]

What was Johanan ben Zakkai's position or status before the destruction of the Temple? He was second only to Simon, son of Gamaliel I, the Nasi. He and the Nasi jointly sent out epistles to the various communities in matters of tithes ("taxes"), etc. Although it is uncertain whether he held the title *Av Beth Din*, he appears to have commanded more authority than any former or subsequent *Av Beth Din*.

M. *Soṭah* IX,9 relates that Johanan ben Zakkai suspended the application of the *Soṭah* law, a biblical precept (Num. 5:11–31). This must have been done before the destruction of the Temple because the *Soṭah* procedure included the requirement of a *Minḥah* sacrifice (see Num. loc. cit.). After the destruction of the Temple, no suspension of the law would have been necessary, since sacrifices had terminated at that time. The interpretation of Tos. *Soṭah* XIV,1,2, to the effect that Johanan ben Zakkai merely related the change, but did not introduce it, seems less reliable than the clear statement of the Mishnah.[5]

Johanan ben Zakkai's leadership before the fall of the Temple is also evidenced by his role as defender of the Pharisees against the Sadducees in the disputations held prior to the destruction of the Temple.

The most conclusive evidence of Johanan ben Zakkai's great power prior to the destruction of the Temple is the incident involving a high priest, whom he forced to conform to the Pharisaic interpretation of the law (see Tosefta *Parah* III,8).

He also sat as a judge, undoubtedly as the head of the court, in capital cases, as is evident in M. *Sanh.* V,2, "Ben Zakkai once tested the evidence even to the inquiring about the stalks of figs." This passage also indicates that he was most reluctant to sentence a man to death — a characteristic of Pharisees and rabbis alike.

An (aggadic) passage — *ARN* I, ch. VI. — shows that Johanan ben Zakkai was a leading sage, probably *the* leading sage of his time in Jerusalem: "Johanan ben Zakkai was sitting and lecturing in Jerusalem, and all the great men of Israel were sitting before him."

It is not known when Johanan ben Zakkai rose to prominence. In M. *Sukkah* II,5, we find him in the company of Gamaliel. This may have been Gamaliel I (but more probably it was Gamaliel II).

The fact that Johanan ben Zakkai accomplished more before the destruction of the Temple than did Simon II allows the inference that he may have begun his significant work already under Gamaliel I and might have been his assistant (or *Av Beth Din*). On the other hand, it may merely mean that he devoted more time and effort to halakhic and theological endeavors than did Simon, who was occupied with administrative and political involvements.

After the destruction of the Temple, Johanan ben Zakkai became *the* leader of the Jewish people, while Gamaliel, son of Simon, could not take the place of his father. Why was Johanan ben Zakkai chosen to succeed Simon II?

This choice was wise for political reasons. Johanan did not approve of the uprising against Rome. On the contrary, that he favored peaceful relations with other nations is well attested.

Mekhilta, Jethro, XI (p. 244; Lauterbach, p. 290): "R. Johanan ben Zakkai says: Behold it says, 'Thou shalt build [the altar] of whole stones' (Deut. 27:6). They are to be stones that establish peace. Behold, you reason a fortiori [using a *qal wehomer*]: The stones for the altar do not see nor hear nor speak. Yet because they serve to establish peace between Israel and their Father in heaven the Holy One, blessed be He, said: 'Thou shalt lift up no iron tool upon them' (ibid. v. 5). How much more then should he who establishes *peace* between man and his fellowman, between husband and wife, between city and city, *between nation and nation, between government and government,* between family and family [be protected], so that no harm should come to him."

In the discourse in B. *B. B.* 10b all the interpretations reveal hostility toward the gentiles, i.e., the Romans, with the exception of Johanan's interpretation which reflects a friendly attitude: "Just as the sin offering atones for Israel, so righteousness atones for the nations of the world," Johanan declares.

189

A more weighty reason for the choice of Johanan ben Zakkai as the post-war leader of the Jewish people may have been the fact that he exercised leadership in matters concerning religion already under the presidency of Simon II.[6] Thus Johanan was in every respect, politically and otherwise, the man best suited for the leadership of the Jewish people after the national catastrophe.

Did Johanan exercise his leadership as Nasi? Not every scholar believes that he was a Nasi.[7] However, the facts that he held the title "Rabban" and issued *Taqqanoth*, both prerogatives of the Nasi, carry decisive weight to the effect that he was the Nasi (or perhaps acting Nasi) of the post-war years.[8]

Johanan chose Javneh to succeed Jerusalem as the seat of the new religious leadership of the Jewish people. The reason for the choice of Javneh is a controversial issue. Many scholars believe that Johanan chose Javneh because there was already a school before the fall of the Temple. This opinion is based on B. *Giṭ.* 65b, which states that Johanan asked of Vespasian the favor of granting him תן לי יבנה וחכמיה "Javneh and its sages." This is interpreted to mean that there was an academy in Javneh prior to the destruction of the Temple. However, parallel versions of the account do not have the words "Give me Javneh and its sages."[9] While choice of Javneh by Johanan, whether there was a school before or not, is well documented and generally accepted as a fact,[10] G. Allon disagrees and suggests that Johanan ben Zakkai was sent there by the Romans forcibly, as a sort of political deportation.[11] This conjecture has no solid basis in the sources and must be rejected in view of the unequivocal sources to the contrary.

Johanan ben Zakkai's most important task in Javneh was to adjust Jewish religious life, hitherto Temple-centered, to existing conditions. Needless to say, he, a man of old age at the time, could not complete the task; yet he did introduce measures which constituted an important link in the transition.

The following are some of his more important measures:

M. *R. H.* IV,1:

When Rosh Ha-Shanah fell on a Sabbath, the *shofar* was blown in the Sanctuary but not in the provinces. After the Temple was destroyed Rabban Johanan ben Zakkai ordained that it be blown in any place where there is a court. Rabbi Eliezer said: R. Johanan ben Zakkai ordained it so only in Javneh. They replied to him, "It is all the same whether it was Javneh or any other place wherein was a court."

The scope of this *Taqqanah* depends on several uncertain factors: Who was in possession of the correct facts, R. Eliezer, a disciple of Johanan ben Zakkai, or his opponents? Further, what was the function of the *shofar* in Jerusalem? Was it connected with the sacrificial cult; or did it merely accompany the proclamation of the new year, as it was used in connection with the proclamation of the Jubilee year? [12]

No matter what the answer, the *Taqqanah* represented an innovation, transferring privileges of the Temple (or of Jerusalem) to other places. The opposition of the Bene Bathyra to this *Taqqanah* in Gemara ibid. 29b, a Baraitha: "It happened that Rosh Ha-Shanah fell on the Sabbath. The people assembled, and Johanan ben Zakkai suggested to the Bene Bathyra that the *shofar* be sounded. The Bene Bathyra rejoined that the matter should be discussed first. Johanan insisted that first the *shofar* be blown. After this was done, he refused to discuss the matter any further." He obviously possessed the authority to close the matter and reject the opposition of the Bene Bathyra, who were evidently leading figures, perhaps similar to the Bene Bathyra of Hillel's time.[13]

M. R. H. IV,3 records that after the destruction of the Temple, Johanan ben Zakkai ordained that the Lulav be carried in the provinces seven days, as was the custom in the Temple, whereas in the provinces they formerly carried it for one day only. The reason given for this is "in memory of the Temple."

According to a report in R. H. 31b., Johanan ben Zakkai suspended the law concerning כרם רבעי *kerem revi'i*, fruits of the fourth year, which formerly had to be taken to Jerusalem. According to M. *Ma'aser Sheni*, V,2, the suspension of this laws was conditional so that upon the restoration of the Temple, the *kerem revi'i* practice would be resumed. This stipulation is to be understood as a concession Johanan was compelled to make to opponents of the measure.[14]

In matters of calendation, Johanan ben Zakkai likewise introduced measures that show his appreciation of reality. B. *R. H.* 21b, a Baraitha (see also Mishnah, ibid.) informs us that in former times the witnesses to the new moon were permitted to transgress the Sabbath (by traveling on that day to report their observation of the new moon) for all the months. After the destruction of the Temple, Johanan ben Zakkai restricted this permission to the months of Nisan and Tishri. The reason for this measure is that since we no longer have a sacrificial cult, the permission regarding the other months lost its justification.

In M. *R. H.* IV,4, Johanan restores an old practice. Originally, the witnesses to the new moon were admitted all day long. Once it happened that the witnesses came late in the day, thus confusing the Levites in their singing. Subsequently, a *Taqqanah* was introduced that the witnesses be received only until *minḥah* time. After the destruction of the Temple, this *Taqqanah* had lost its meaning and Johanan ben Zakkai therefore annulled it.

A further *Taqqanah* (ibid.) introduced by Johanan ben Zakkai which is independent of the affairs of the Temple provides that the witnesses to the new moon should always go to the place of the assembly, no matter where the head of the court may be at that time. Certainly this is a very practical measure implying that the head of the court or the Nasi was not always at the "assembly," or *Beth Din Ha-Gadol*, when the witnesses of the new moon were expected to appear. Such an incident recorded in B. *Sanhedrin* 11a relates that a year was intercalated in the absence of Rabban Gamaliel, who went to Syria at that time to secure *reshuth*, some kind of permit or authorization, on condition that he would later confirm the action.

B. *R. H.* 31b, a Baraitha, relates that Johanan ben Zakkai ordained that the priests must not go up to the stage with their sandals for the recital of the priestly benediction. Although the reason for this *Taqqanah* is uncertain (cf. B. *Soṭah* 40a), the *Taqqanah* prohibits the priest from doing what was hitherto not proscribed.

The same passage relates that a proselyte who embraced Judaism after the destruction of the Temple had to set aside a certain amount of money for a bird sacrifice required of him when the Temple would be rebuilt. Johanan ben Zakkai abolished this practice "because of stumbling," i.e., it may lead to using this money for a secular purpose.

Johanan ben Zakkai ordained that the חדש *ḥadash*, the new crop, be prohibited all day of the Omer swinging. Therefore, he made this law entirely independent not only of the sacrificial act but also of the time of such act (M. *R. H.* IV,3; M. *Men.* X,5; Tosefta, ibid. X,25,26).

Johanan ben Zakkai's roles before and after the destruction of the Temple are consistent. Before the destruction, he fought the Sadducees in general and the high priest, who conformed to Sadducean interpretation of the law, in particular. His measure against the Sadducean high priest reveals animosity, even if we do not take literally the report that he injured the high priest in order to disqualify him. After the destruction of the Temple, he continued his fight against the priests (*kohanim*) from whose midst many of the Sadduceans (including the high priests) came, and who may have tried to continue to exercise former privileges. A group of them continued for some time as a Sadducean sect, but played no further role.

We saw that Johanan ben Zakkai considered it his duty to appraise the new situation realistically and to make corresponding adjustments in matters of religious practices. One important area of adjustments was that of *priestly privileges*. Since the main function of the priests — the Temple service — had disappeared, there was no justification for continuing their privileges. A formal justification for a continuation of these privileges would have been the hope that the Temple would soon be rebuilt and that the priests would then naturally resume their functions. We have evidence that attempts were made to continue the sacrificial cult even after the destruction of the Temple (see especially M. Guttmann, *Erez Jisrael Be-Midrash Ve-Talmud*, pp. 88 ff). Johanan ben Zakkai, Nasi of the period following the destruction of the Temple, would have been the authority to ordain (or at least to permit) the continuation of the sacrificial cult outside of the Temple. Yet he did not do this. Further, he obviously did not consider likely the revival of the sacrificial cult in the near future.[15]

Already before the fall of the Temple, he terminated a priestly function, the execution of the *Soṭah* law, claiming that circumstances

RABBINIC JUDAISM IN THE MAKING

which had made this law meaningful no longer existed. After the destruction of the Temple, he should have acted similarly and suspended all priestly privileges and laws connected with the Temple. Instead, he retained some of the practices connected with the Temple and Jerusalem and rejected others. Where is the dividing line?

He retained some of the Temple practices such as carrying the Lulav for seven days and blowing the Shofar on a Sabbath (of Rosh Ha-Shanah) as *non-priestly* ceremonies. Thus he enriched the functions and services of the courts and synagogues outside of Jerusalem through lay participation. Yet, he allowed no practices of the Temple and the Temple period to be continued as *priestly* functions in the provinces, unless these had been in vogue before 70 c.e., as was undoubtedly the case with the priestly benediction. He was obviously unable to annul the priestly privileges in vogue throughout the land, as, e.g., the *Terumah*, *Ḥallah*, etc.

In M. *Sheq.* I,4, Ben Bokhri testified in Javneh that a priest who pays the *sheqel*, does not hereby sin. Johanan ben Zakkai, retorts: On the contrary, any priest who does *not* pay the *sheqel*, sins, but the priests were interpreting a biblical verse to their advantage[16] in order to save their money. This is certainly not a flattering opinion of the priests.

In M. *'Eduy.* VIII,3, Rabban (Simon) ben Gamaliel II relates that Johanan ben Zakkai ordained that no court session could be held to clear the widow of a questionable priest (i.e., who may not be a priest because of certain doubts as to his lineage), because the priests would accept only a negative ruling in the matter. That means Johanan ben Zakkai believed that the priests would ignore a court decision in their marital matters, if it suited them.

In M. *Ket.* XIII, 1 and 2, Ḥanan and the "sons of high priests" disagree in two matters of support, and Johanan ben Zakkai sides with Ḥanan against the sons of the high priests. Whether he had objective reasons to oppose the sons of the high priests or was (perhaps unconsciously) influenced by his dislike for the priests, cannot be determined.

In *ARN* I, Ch. 12 (p. 56), we see that Johanan ben Zakkai uses strong language in arguing with a high priest over a matter of defilement.[17]

194

Most of Johanan ben Zakkai's halakhic activity, so far as is identifiable, consists in his *Taqqanoth* and discussions with the Sadducees. He may have originated many Halakhoth which were included in the Halakhoth of Beth Hillel and are, therefore, unidentifiable as his. Some of his explicit Halakhoth not yet mentioned are the following:

A detailed Halakhah regarding a matter of defilement is recorded in M. *Kelim* II,2.

In a case of defilement, he exclaims, "Woe is me if I speak of them, and woe is me if I speak not of them." This means that whatever he would say in the matter could be misconstrued. The implication of the above dictum is that any decision by Johanan would carry weight (ibid. XVII,16).

In Tos. *Ḥag.* III,36, Rabbi Tarfon cites a Halakhah he received from Johanan ben Zakkai[18] in order to justify his practice in a matter of *Terumah* (heave offering). Nonetheless, since the people talked in a derogatory manner about his practice, Tarfon resolves not to take any further advantage of Johanan ben Zakkai's lenient Halakhah.

Tos. *Soṭah* VI,13 relates an incident in which R. Joshua exclaims that Johanan ben Zakkai predicted that in a matter of defilement a lenient solution would be found (which did not come true).

In Tos. *Ahiluth* XVI,8, Johanan ben Zakkai's disciples ask him a question in a matter of defilement. After rendering a strict decision, he is reminded that once he rendered an applicable lenient decision which he then confirms.

Tos. *Parah* IV,7 relates a similar incident in connection with another matter connected with defilement.

Tos. *Parah* X(IX),2 records that Johanan ben Zakkai, asked to decide a matter of defilement while the Temple yet stood, rendered a lenient decision.

In Tos. *Yadayim* II,16, an *isnad*, chain of tradition, is cited (and the statement made that the vote should therefore be disregarded) which starts with Johanan ben Zakkai and ends with *Halakhah Lemosheh Mi-Sinai* (as the starting point). The subject is tithe of Jews living in Ammon and Moab.

Johanan ben Zakkai also had areas of interest outside of the realm of the law. He displayed interest in mysticism and (homiletical) theology.

In Tos. *Ḥagigah* II,2, Rabbi Eleazar ben Arakh, a distinguished disciple of Johanan ben Zakkai, asked his master to expound some of the mysteries of Ezekiel's Chariot, a favorite topic of ancient Jewish mysticism. Although he complied, after initial hesitancy, Johanan's exposition is not transmitted.

In Tos. *B. Q.* VII,2, when Johanan ben Zakkai's disciples ask him about the perplexing fact that, according to the Torah, the punishment of the thief is heavier than that of the robber, he gives a theological explanation: the robber, by committing his crime in the open, equates God and man; the thief, however, regards God lower than man.

Five of Johanan's theological-homiletical interpretations of biblical incidents then follow in the text (ibid. 3–6).

B. *Sukkah* 28a and *ARN* I, ch. 14, relate the wide range of Johanan's knowledge, which included mathematics (for calendation), mysticism, homiletics, etc. These passages, unhistorical in part, reflect deep reverence for Johanan ben Zakkai and paint an idealistic picture of him.

M. *Avoth* II,8 (*ARN* I, 14 and II, 29 [p. 58]) tells us that Johanan ben Zakkai had five disciples: Eliezer ben Hyrcanus, Joshua ben Hananjah, Jose the Priest, Simon ben Nethanel, and Eleazar ben Arakh. That this statement is not to be taken literally, but has reference to outstanding students who were particularly close to him, is indicated in the following sources:

B. *Pes.* 26a (P. *A. Z.* III,43b) relates that Johanan ben Zakkai was sitting in the "shade of the Temple" (i.e., near the Temple) and lecturing. This he did undoubtedly before more than five or six men.

Of all his disciples, Johanan ben Zakkai considered Eleazar ben Arakh to be the best (M. *Avoth* and *ARN*, loc. cit.). This disciple, however, would not follow his master to Javneh and fell into obscurity, while the others, who went to Javneh, flourished (*ARN*, ibid.).[19]

Conspicuously absent from Johanan's list of disciples is Gamaliel, son of Simon II. Some scholars take this as a proof of tension between Johanan ben Zakkai and the House of the Patriarch.[20] However, in view of the fact that only five of Johanan's closest disciples are enumerated, we have to disagree with these scholars. Johanan had many more students, some of them quite outstanding. Thus we learn from a casual remark that Akiba was also one of Johanan's disciples (Tos. *Soṭah* VI,13).

An unequivocal reference to the effect that Gamaliel was a disciple of Johanan ben Zakkai is found in a colloquy in B. *B. B.* 10b (a Baraitha): "Johanan ben Zakkai said to his students: What is the meaning of 'Righteousness exalteth the nation, but sin is a reproach to any people'?" One of the respondents is Gamaliel.[21]

Occasionally we find Johanan ben Zakkai in the company of Gamaliel but not in a teacher-disciple relationship. Thus in M. *Sukkah* II,4,5 an occurrence is related in which both Johanan ben Zakkai and Gamaliel jointly follow the same religious practice.

Other disciples of Johanan ben Zakkai not mentioned in the *Avoth* account but named in B. *B. B.* 10b are Rabbi Eliezer of Modi'-in and Rabbi Nehunja ben Haqanah. Of the *Avoth* list, only two names are here included: R. Eliezer and R. Joshua. How is this to be explained? It is quite natural that not all the students present responded. However it is safe to assume that Eleazar ben Arakh, Johanan's most outstanding disciple (in Johanan's opinion), certainly would have responded had he been present.

A plausible explanation is that the *Avoth* list gives Johanan's select disciples who had studied with him in Jerusalem prior to the destruction of the Temple. However, the B. *B. B.* discourse took place *after* the destruction of the Temple, certainly in Javneh, with disciples present who played a significant role in the development of Rabbinic Judaism. The three men of the *Avoth* account who are now absent, Jose the Priest, Simon ben Nethanel, and Eleazar ben Arakh played only minor roles in the history of the Halakhah. They may have objected to the changes made in the realm of religious practices after the destruction of the Temple and withdrawn from the mainstream of Rabbinic Judaism. They may have joined the group of orthodox Pharisees who refused to go along with the reforms necessitated by the destruction of the central sanctuary. In the conclusion of this discussion let us add but one more disciple of Johanan not listed in the *Avoth* account, the renowned Tanna Haninah ben Dosa (B. *Ber.* 34b).

How long did Johanan ben Zakkai continue as the leader of the Jewish people? Why did Gamaliel replace him? Why did Johanan retire to his private school at Beror Ḥail? The answers to all these questions can be given only tentatively since conclusive source material pertaining to these questions does not exist.

The belief of some scholars that Johanan ben Zakkai's nasidom lasted but a very few years[22] is unlikely in view of his considerable activity after the destruction of the Temple. The wrath of the Romans needed some time to cool off before Gamaliel could risk taking over the leadership. About fifteen years is a more plausible conjecture for the length of Johanan's presidency.

More enigmatic is the reason for Johanan's relinquishing of the leadership. Old age may have been one of the reasons, but not necessarily the only reason since he afterward continued his teaching activities in Beror Ḥail. A conjecture deserving attention is that Johanan was merely acting Nasi until Gamaliel was able to take over the nasidom.[23] Conjectures that Johanan was forced out of his leadership by Gamaliel and his circle have no basis in the sources.[24] We believe that the following circumstances contributed to Johanan's retirement from the presidency:

Johanan's strong stand on certain issues created many adversaries. The opposition of the Sadducees whom he fought so vehemently meant little after the fall of the Temple, but the antagonism of the priests in general carried more weight.[25] His unfriendly attitude toward the wealthy — see *ARN* II, ch. 31 (p. 34) — undoubtedly turned this group against him.

In view of the Roman oppression and exploitation that increased after the war, Johanan's conciliatory attitude toward Rome was detrimental to his popularity. The general attitude of the Jewish people toward the Romans remained hostile. Further, the people hoped for an early restoration of the Temple with all its sacrifices, a hope which Johanan ben Zakkai obviously did not share.[26]

Noteworthy in this respect is the following account:

Once Johanan ben Zakkai and R. Joshua revisited the ruins of the Temple. R. Joshua expressed his deep sorrow about the loss of the

Temple because it had the important function of effecting atonement. Johanan comforted him saying that he should not feel bad about it since we have another way of atoning which is just as good, namely גמילות חסדים deeds of loving-kindness, and cited Hosea 6:6, "For I desire mercy, and not sacrifice." [27]

The loss of the Temple resulting in a sudden termination of pilgrimage and sacrificial cult, created a vacuum in the religious life of the people. The need for a substitute that would replace the old cult with new forms of religious expression was keenly felt. Johanan (and other sages) objected to the most obvious step in this direction, i.e., to the continuation of the sacrificial cult in places outside of Jerusalem. In this, his antagonism to the priestly caste may have played a role, at least unconsciously. Johanan's measures aiming to enrich religious life to fill the vacuum, though important, were of a limited scope. Some of these were a transfer of certain ceremonies formerly performed only in the Temple to places outside of the Temple. The use of the Lulav for seven days, instead of one day and the sounding of the *shofar* on Rosh Ha-Shanah that fell on a Sabbath (in Javneh), which may be but a revival of an old practice, belong in this category. Most of his other *Taqqanoth* constitute minor adjustments, particularly in matters of calendation. However, Johanan failed to introduce forms of religious expression on the major scale necessary to replace the Temple cult. Though he thought otherwise, loving-kindness would not take the place of the sacrificial cult because it could not satisfy the desire of the people for expressing their religious feelings in rituals. Johanan ben Zakkai, a man who לא אמר דבר שלא שמע מפי רבו מעולם "Never said a word which he did not hear from his teacher" (B. *Sukkah* 28a) was not a suitable leader to undertake substantial adjustments on a large scale. Although in view of the adjustments he did make, the authenticity or accuracy of this statement is questionable.

Therefore, it was probably the combination of several circumstances — the need for more cultic expression, no further necessity of having a "pro-Roman" leader (a man advocating peace with the Romans), Johanan's old age, Gamaliel's maturity, and the passing of the danger of punishment by the Romans — that led to Johanan's

199

retirement and Gamaliel's ascent to the nasidom as the rightful heir of noble descent which Johanan could not claim for himself.[28]

However, after resigning his nasidom, Johanan ben Zakkai did not retire altogether. He went to Beror Ḥail where he presided over an academy of his own, perhaps already before his retirement from the nasidom. This must have been an academy of note since talmudic sources, when giving examples for excellent "courts" (schools), mention the court of Johanan ben Zakkai in Beror Ḥail among them,[29] but not his former courts in Jerusalem or Javneh. We do not know how many of his disciples followed him to Beror Ḥail. Some of his former disciples who stayed in Javneh visited him in Beror Ḥail, e.g., Joshua.[30] After his death, his students went to Javneh and entered Gamaliel's academy.[31]

The greatness of Johanan ben Zakkai's personality is reflected in numerous legends surrounding his life and death.[32]

GAMALIEL II

Gamaliel II succeeded Johanan ben Zakkai as Nasi probably between 80 and 90 c.e. The most often accepted date is 80 c.e., although there is no indication in the sources that this is correct. It is more likely that Gamaliel took over the reins of the Nasi not long after the death of Titus in 81 c.e., or perhaps (officially and openly) after the dynasty of Vespasian became extinct with the death of his son Domitian in 96 c.e. for which the family of Simon II was non grata because of its participation in the uprising against Rome.

We find that Gamaliel officiated in Javneh and in Lud. In view of this it is generally believed that the *Beth Din Ha-Gadol* moved during his presidency from Javneh to Lud, but a close examination of the sources does not confirm this belief. What the sources tell us is that Gamaliel lived in Lud where he had a *Beth Ha-Midrash*, an academy where his disciples studied with him.[33] However, the *Beth*

Din Ha-Gadol, which succeeded the Sanhedrin, and was located in Javneh for many years, was *not* the *Beth Ha-Midrash* of the Nasi.

B. *R. H.* 31ab — which gives us all the changes of the location of the Sanhedrin, including the *Beth Din Ha-Gadol*, does not mention Lud, meaning that according to R. Johanan (Amora), a most reliable transmitter of events of the past, Lud was not at any time a seat of the *Beth Din Ha-Gadol*. Apart from its obvious historical significance, this passage in combination with the reference to Gamaliel's academy in Lud reveals that Gamaliel, in addition to his presidency of the *Beth Din Ha-Gadol* in Javneh, maintained a private academy in Lud where he probably resided most of the time. This indicates that the situation may have been the same at Johanan ben Zakkai's time, i.e., that he maintained a private academy in Beror Ḥail even during his leadership in Javneh, which made his retirement to Beror Ḥail much easier.

A further implication of the two-fold presidency of the Nasi is that, in contradistinction to the Sanhedrin of old, the *Beth Din Ha-Gadol* held no daily sessions. This is also evident from the fact that not only the Nasi but also other distinguished members of the *Beth Din Ha-Gadol* maintained private academies in places outside of Javneh and assembled in Javneh only periodically. Such was easily possible since these sages did not live in distant towns. Lud, for instance, is but approximately ten miles from Javneh, Beror Ḥail about twice this distance.

A seeming contradiction to our view just discussed is found in B. *Sanh.* 32b (Baraitha),

ת״ר צדק צדק תרדף הלך אחר חכמים לישיבה אחר ר' אליעזר
ללוד אחר רבן יוחנן בן זכאי לברור חיל אחר ר' יהושע לפקיעין אחר
רבן גמליאל ליבנה אחר רבי עקיבא לבני ברק אחר רבי מתיא לרומי
אחר רבי חנניא בן תרדיון לסיכני אחר ר' יוסי לציפורי אחר רבי יהודה
בן בתירה לנציבין אחר (רבה חנינא בן אחי) רבי יהושע לגולה אחר
רבי לבית שערים אחר חכמים ללשכת הגזית.

"Justice, justice shalt thou follow" (Deut. 16:20):
Go after the sages to the *Yeshivah*; after Rabban Johanan ben Zakkai to Beror Ḥail, after R. Eliezer to Lud, after Rabbi Joshua to Peqiʻin, after Rabban Gamaliel to Javneh, after Rabbi

Akiba to Bene Berak, after R. Matja to Rome, after R. Hananiah ben Teradion to Sikni, after R. Jose to Sepphoris, after R. Judah ben Bathyra to Nezibin, after R. Hananiah, nephew of R. Joshua to the Exile (Babylonia), after Rabbi (Judah the Prince) to Beth Shearim, after the Sages to the Hall of the Hewn Stone.

This Baraitha does not give Lud as Gamaliel's seat of his *Yeshivah* but Javneh, whereas for Johanan ben Zakkai it gives Beror Ḥail but not Javneh. Why does it not mention in both instances either Javneh or the respective private academies? Does this mean that Johanan ben Zakkai was not Nasi in Javneh or that Gamaliel had no academy in Lud? In view of abundant sources to the contrary this cannot be the meaning of the Baraitha. One possible solution is that the author of the Baraitha was aware of the great achievements of Gamaliel in Javneh in contrast to his less important teaching career in Lud and therefore he mentioned Javneh as the seat of Gamaliel's academy, whereas on the other hand he thought that Johanan ben Zakkai's career in Beror Ḥail was more important than his teaching role in Javneh. It is also possible that the author of the Baraitha did not want to repeat the same name choosing, therefore, to mention Javneh with regard to Gamaliel and Beror Ḥail with reference to Johanan ben Zakkai. Considering the chronological disorder in this Baraitha we cannot rule out the possibility of other inaccuracies that might account for the inconsistency regarding the names of the towns mentioned in it.

The sources do not reveal the circumstances of Gamaliel's ascent to nasidom. The combination of circumstances that worked against Johanan ben Zakkai's continued leadership worked for Gamaliel's ascent to leadership. The first step making Gamaliel's nasidom possible is credited to Johanan ben Zakkai who pleaded with Vespasian to spare the family of Gamaliel (B. *Giṭ.* 68a). Of the various reasons for the change in leadership, the most important may have been the need for a man ready to introduce new religious practices on a large scale to replace the sacrificial cult.

After the spadework done by Johanan ben Zakkai it was up to Gamaliel II to carry out the transition from the centralized sacrificial cult to a decentralized but disciplined non-sacrificial system of religious expression.

He soon realized that a decentralized mode of observance could lead to chaos and disintegration if not directed and supervised effectively by central authority. The central authority of his day was the Nasi in conjunction with the *Beth Din Ha-Gadol* of Javneh.

While the issues of the day were freely discussed in this *Beth Din*, Gamaliel would not tolerate serious dissent on the part of the leading sages. He feared that such dissent would spread the sectarianism which flourished in his day and threatened the very survival of Judaism. He was particularly sensitive to serious dissent on the part of the leading sages because their dissent was more likely to divide the unity of Judaism and the Jewish people. In this light we have to understand Gamaliel's strong measures. He excommunicated Rabbi Eliezer, son of Hyrcanus (his own brother-in-law), after the memorable Akhnai incident,[34] and he humiliated Rabbi Joshua, his *Av Beth Din* (M. *R. H.* II,8,9; B. *Ber.* 27b–28a). He did not even spare Akiba who was excommunicated by him according to an opinion in the P. Talmud (P. *R. H.* I,5; 57b) though there is also a view to the contrary. It is to be noted that all these men constituted Gamaliel's "inner cabinet."

Gamaliel concentrated his efforts in behalf of the re-orientation of Jewish life in two areas: 1) The Jewish calendar. 2) Prayers.

The Jewish calendar

Gamaliel was well aware that a single calendar for all of the Jewish people was a conditio sine qua non for their unity. For this reason he devoted much work to matters of calendation. Both Geonim and Karaites ascribe basic achievements to Gamaliel in matters of calendric calculations.[35] Gamaliel's stressing of the importance of calendation, his knowledge of the field and deep concern in instances of dissent are documented in many talmudic passages. For example, M. *R. H.* II,8 informs us that Gamaliel possessed "pictures of the shape of the moon on a tablet and on the wall of his upper chamber. These he used to show to the laymen (witnesses) and say, 'Didst thou see it on this wise or on that?'" This shows that Gamaliel possessed knowledge in astronomy which he applied for calendric purposes. It is quite possible that his knowledge was so substantial that the testimony of the witnesses became a mere formality with him. Nonetheless he considered the testimony of the witnesses to the appearance of the new moon so essential that he set no limit to the number of witnesses allowed to desecrate the Sabbath by traveling on it in order to testify before the *Beth Din* even though, according to the law, two witnesses are sufficient.

Gamaliel's deep concern in instances of serious dissent in matters of calendation is evident in the following cases:

Rabbi Joshua's calendation which set a date for Yom Kippur at variance with that of Gamaliel was a real threat to the unity of Judaism. Joshua's reluctant obedience to Gamaliel's strict order for him to appear before him with staff and money bag on the Day of Atonement according to Joshua's reckoning averted this threat (M. *R. H.* II,9).

Rabbi Akiba's interference with a large group of witnesses to the new moon on a Sabbath drew serious reprimand from Gamaliel (M. *R. H.* I,6). (Cf. B. *R. H.* 22a, a Baraitha, where R. Judah denies that the man in question was Akiba. Yet it is safe to assume that the Mishnah gives the correct name.) According to a report in the P. Talmud, this incident led to Akiba's excommunication.

Gamaliel had the assistance of a "committee" (*Beth Din*) of seven in carrying out the process of intercalating the year (B. *Sanhedrin* 11a). In case the Nasi was absent, the committee had the authority to intercalate the year with the proviso that the Nasi, upon his return, would endorse the action. In such a case recorded in M. *'Eduy.* VII,7 (and parallels) Gamaliel was in Syria while the conditional intercalation took place.

Prayers

While Gamaliel's successful endeavors in matters of calendation were instrumental in preserving the unity of Judaism, they did not fill the vacuum caused by the cessation of the sacrificial cult. Gamaliel filled this void first and foremost by developing the prayer service and moving it into the foreground of Jewish religious life, thus making it the equivalent of and replacement for the lost sacrificial cult. To be sure many, if not most, of the prayers Gamaliel dealt with had existed before the fall of the Temple. However, they were mostly of private or local character and had imprecise, variable texts. No well-defined, regular prayer services had been made mandatory,[36] whatever existed was of secondary importance in comparison with the sacrificial cult.

Gamaliel's endeavor to strengthen the prayer ritual is most evident in his efforts concerning the *Amidah*, the "Eighteen Benedictions."

While other prayers, too, existed (e.g., the *Shema* with its benedictions, grace after the meal, *Kiddush*, benedictions for various occasions, etc.), the *Amidah* is called *Tefillah*, "prayer" par excellence. Gamaliel's most important step in the matter was the making of the *Amidah* mandatory three times daily. In doing so he had the full cooperation of the sages with reference to the morning and afternoon *Tefillah*, but not with reference to the evening *Tefillah*. His opponent here was R. Joshua whom he humiliated by making him stand on his feet throughout a session of the academy which led to an uproar of the sages deposing Gamaliel,[37] though he was soon re-instated.

Another step of Gamaliel's in raising the importance of the *Amidah* was making it mandatory for both public *and* private services (M. *Ber.* IV,3). The emphasis in both instances is on the word "mandatory" since the *Tefillah* has been recited by some people three times daily publicly as well as privately before Gamaliel's endeavors but on a more or less voluntary basis, and was peripheral compared to the sacrificial cult.[38]

The final important step toward making the *Tefillah* a main pillar of Jewish services was the establishment of its contents. The first three and final three benedictions of this prayer had already been quite well established before the destruction of the Temple in 70 c.e. (cf. Tosefta *R. H.* IV (II), 11; p. 213). This is evident from the fact that an argument of Beth Hillel and Beth Shammai (certainly conducted before the destruction of the Temple) presupposes an accord in regard to the first and last three benedictions of the *Tefillah*, for only the sections constituting the middle portion are discussed.

Gamaliel asked Simon Ha-Paqqoli to "arrange" the "Eighteen Benedictions." [39] The exact nature of this arranging is not known. The "Eighteen Benedictions" are very old, dating back according to the Talmud to the times of the "Men of the Great Synod," or even to the Prophets (P. *Ber.* II,4;4d; B. *Ber.* 33a). While these datings are certainly not factual, they still mean that the arrangement of Simon Ha-Paqqoli was executed within an existing framework of eighteen benedictions. Did he fix the text of the *Tefillah*? Texts of the *Tefillah* found in the Genizah give variant wordings,[40] which implies that Simon did not fix throughout the wording of the *Tefillah*. Consequently, the work he did was probably fixing the content of the benedictions and perhaps also their sequence. The talmudic Baraitha B. *Ber.* 28b also tells us that Gamaliel asked who of the sages could compose לתקן a benediction concerning the מינים *minim*, most probably Judeo-Christians in this case (cf. Tos. *Ber.* III,25; P. *Ber.* IV,8a). Gamaliel did this in view of the serious threat which the Judeo-Christians constituted to Rabbinic Judaism, a threat increased by the profound influence of Paulinistic Christianity which developed between 90 and 100 subsequent to the dissemination of the Paulinistic letters.[41]

The introduction of *Birkath Ha-Minim* is an evidence for the limited power Gamaliel possessed. He obviously possessed no power to punish sectarian Jews; otherwise he certainly would have done more about the serious threat presented by them than merely introducing a prayer against them. This is a further indication that the Nasi received no recognition by the Romans as the leader of the Jewish people. Whatever authority he exercised was based on voluntary recognition by the followers of Rabbinic Judaism. Whatever disciplinary measures he employed — mainly excommunication — were only effective against adherents of Rabbinic Judaism.

Bible

The concern of Gamaliel and of other responsible sages for protecting and strengthening true Judaism compelled him to pay attention to biblical literature. The issue was not the establishment of a correct text,[42] nor a final canonization of the Bible, but rather the chief interest was in dealing with extraneous literature, particularly Gospels and (other) heretical literature. The main issue with regard to these books, however, was not whether they were sacred or not — as Moore presumes.[43] Since they are anti-Jewish, their acceptability was out of question. The problem was whether they should be destroyed "as is," or whether God's name written in them should be spared.[44]

The process of canonization was slow. In Gamaliel's time, it had been in progress but had not been concluded. The books discussed in his time were Shir Ha-Shirim and Qoheleth (M. *Yadayim* III,5). Discussions concerning Qoheleth and Esther were still held generations after Gamaliel's time (Tosefta, ibid. II,14, B. *Meg.* 7a). In the discussions about the sanctity of certain books, Gamaliel himself does not participate. While an argumentum ex silentio is not strong, it is quite certain that Gamaliel's name would not have been omitted if he had taken a stand in the matter. Yet, as we saw in the case of the *Tefillah*, we have to keep in mind that Gamaliel assigned certain tasks to his "experts," and he may have relied on experts in this case as well. His absence is also understandable if the respective discussions were held immediately after his demotion (cf. Mishnah, ibid.).

Very significant is the statement in Tos. *Yadayim* II,13 that Ben Sira and all the books written from now on "do not defile the hands," i.e., possess no sanctity. This declaration, obviously undisputed, barred the canonization of all later books automatically. This, however, obviously did not suffice to eliminate the influence of extracanonical books. So R. Akiba, certainly expressing the sentiment of other rabbis as well, declared that the reader of "extraneous books" had no portion in the world-to-come (M. *Sanh.* X,1). The nature of these extraneous books is not precisely known. B. *Sanh.* 100b (Baraitha) says these are the books of the "Sadducees" (a reading probably chosen because of censorship; the implication may be directed toward the *minim*, understood as Christians, though it may refer as well to any sectarian). The P. Talmud, ibid. X,1; 28a, understands it as referring to books like Ben Sira and Ben La'anah; however, reading books of Homeros or books written from that point on is as reading a letter (i.e., not prohibited). The Mishnah probably had both types of literature in mind, the books of the Christians and the

207

apocrypha, since both include books that may have had an undesired influence upon followers of Rabbinic Judaism.

The prohibition was not limited to extra-canonical books, but was extended to translations of biblical books as well. Whereas other sages permit written vernacular translations of all the biblical books, Gamaliel permits the Greek translation only.[45]

When Gamaliel once read the Targum of Job, he was told that his grandfather, Gamaliel I, had the Targum of Job destroyed, whereupon Gamaliel placed this Targum in a *Genizah* (B. *Shab.* 115a). This act shows that he realized this Targum was prohibited and must not be read or even kept in the house.

The reading of the legitimate Bible was curtailed, too. M. *Shab.* XVI,1 informs us that reading of the Hagiographa on Sabbath was prohibited, lest people neglect the *Beth Hamidrash*. The *Beth Hamidrash* was the place where people were taught the rabbinic interpretation of Judaism. This was especially so on the Sabbath, the day of rest, when everybody could come and listen to the discourses of the preachers and teachers. Lest people concentrate entirely on the Bible and stay away from the *Beth Hamidrash*, the rabbis ruled that Hagiographa, the most pleasant readings of the Bible, could not be read on a Sabbath.[46]

The destruction of the Temple constituted a serious threat to classical Judaism. Even before the destruction, Christianity had made considerable inroads at the expense of normative Judaism. Utilizing the destruction of the Temple for apologetical purposes, Christian leaders heralded it as punishment to the Jews for killing Jesus and as evidence for the annulment of the Torah.[47]

Rabbinic Judaism naturally rejected these charges, more so for internal theological reasons than for external apologetical considerations. While there are several more or less aggadic reasons for the destruction of the Temple transmitted in talmudic literature,[48] the predominant theological explanation was that the destruction of the Temple served as punishment for sins. Gamaliel is the foremost sage to suggest this explanation.[49]

The notion that with the destruction of the Temple not merely the sacrificial cult, but the rest of the Torah also had lost its validity, was rejected by the rabbis in theory as well as in practice. *Mekhilta* Yethro, II (p. 201)[50] relates: "Three things were given conditionally: The Land of Israel, the Sanctuary, and the Kingdom of the House of David. But the Torah and the Covenant with Aaron were given without a condition, etc." This means, that the validity of the Torah will never terminate, since it was given without condition.

The rabbis considered the destruction of the Temple and the cessation of its cult as a temporary calamity and often used the words, "Soon the Sanctuary will be rebuilt." While this statement is apparently an amoraic one, it is cited to qualify old laws, among them an institution of Johanan ben Zakkai (B. *Sukkah* 41a).

Above we discussed the reasons why the sacrificial cult was not continued after the destruction of the Temple in places outside of Jerusalem at Johanan ben Zakkai's time. We noted Johanan ben Zakkai's dislike for high priests and priests in general. He was the champion of the (Pharisaic) laity and as such was not interested in the continuance of priestly privileges. However, Gamaliel II apparently did not consider the priests as an opposition party that had to be restrained. Why did he not ordain or permit the resumption of the sacrificial cult outside of Jerusalem?

He was probably unable or unwilling to reverse a trend against worshipping God by animal sacrifices apparent in Christianity and other groups of the time. This was, of course, not openly admitted. The official reason was based on exegesis.

While the *Nesi'im* and the rabbis did not introduce a decentralized cult, they saw to it that some other forms of Temple cult and priestly laws were continued throughout the land. According to Num. 18:21, "And unto the children of Levi, behold, I have given all the tithe in Israel for an inheritance, in return for their service which they serve, etc," the Levites were to receive the tithes as the pay for their service in the Temple. The clear implication is that if they do not perform their Temple service, they are not entitled to the tithes. However, the rabbis ruled that the tithes (and various *matnoth kehunnah*, priestly dues) should be given[51] even after the destruction of the Temple (*Sifre Qorah* 119, p. 146). That the qualification for this ruling is an exegetical one must be considered as a mere formality. Some of the real considerations may have been hope for a speedy restoration of the Temple, emphasis on the validity of the Torah laws even after the fall of the Temple, desire to keep the people aware of their duties to their fellowmen and prevention of a vacuum in religious life. Naturally, there was also opposition to the continuance of giving dues to the priests. We cite, for example, P. *Sheq.* VIII,4; 51b where it is stated in a Baraitha that among others, no *Terumah* (heave offering for the priests) nor tithes are to be levied in this time (i.e., after the destruction of the Temple).[52] (The version in B. *A. Z.* 13a omits the reference to heave offerings and tithes.)

The *'amme ha-arez*, mostly farmers, were not particularly eager to give tithes. The Nasi and his administration obviously possessed no power to control the people. All they could do was to declare their produce *Demai*,[53] under suspicion of being untithed, and to ask the purchaser of such grain to tithe it.[54]

Among other laws connected with the Temple and offerings, many laws concerning defilement were carried over and observed after the destruction of the Temple. Thus, for example, the laws concerning the defilement of the priests were originally to be applied in the Temple or in view of their service in the Temple and in connection with eating "holy" food. These laws should have been suspended after the fall of the Sanctuary, but such was not the case. The reasons noted above may be valid here, too. The purification of the leper by the priest also required a sacrifice (Lev. 14). However, we find that this act was performed, though probably only in exceptional instances, even after the year 70 c.e. (Tos. *Nega'im* VIII,2 [628]; *Sifra*, Mezora *Nega'im* I,13). These passages inform us that R. Tarfon purified (ritually) three lepers. This precedent is considered in the sources as evidence that the purification of the leper may be performed after the fall of the Temple.

Among other laws logically to be observed only while the Temple existed, but continued afterwards for some time, are: The tithe of the cattle and sheep (M. *Sheq.* VIII,8; M. *Bekhor.* IX,1); second tithe (M. *'Eduy.* VIII,6); giving first born animals to the priests (M. *Sheq.* VIII,8).

Gamaliel issued a number of *Taqqanoth*, mostly in conjunction with "his Beth Din." This *Beth Din* may refer to the *Beth Din Ha-Gadol*, or to a smaller body, his "executive committee," or possibly to his academy in Lud. Most of his *Taqqanoth* have limited scope.

Some of his *Taqqanoth* follow:

In Tos. *Kil.* IV,1 (78), Gamaliel and his *Beth Din* ordained that grape vines be planted four cubits from the fence "separating grain plantations from grape vines." Previously a fence without a separating strip of land sufficed to satisfy the biblical law in Deut. 22:9, "Thou shalt not sow thy vineyard with two kinds of seed."

In Tos. *Shevi'ith* VI,27(70), Gamaliel and his *Beth Din* ordain a lenient practice in making olive oil in the sabbatical year (a variant reading has Simon ben Gamaliel instead of Gamaliel).

In B. *M. Q.* 3b, Gamaliel and his *Beth Din* nullified a strict practice in a matter regarding the sabbatical year. The words used here are ר״ג ובית דינו נמנו "R. Gamaliel and his court voted." This may be taken as indication that the *Taqqanoth* issued by Gamaliel and his *Beth Din* were likewise the result of a majority vote.

In B. *Git.* 36a, Gamaliel reports that a תקנה גדולה, an important ordinance, had been issued (i.e., by the *Beth Din*) to the effect that witnesses to a bill of divorce must sign their names on the bill "because of the general welfare." The report does not state that Gamaliel joined the *Beth Din* in making this *Taqqanah*; however his participation or consent would be practically a certainty. His name might have been included had a third party, rather than Gamaliel himself, made the reference to the *Taqqanah*.

Most of Gamaliel's halakhic activity did not consist of the issuance of ordinances, but was mainly the discussion of laws with his colleagues on equal terms, with the majority opinion prevailing. Significant in this respect is the following incident in which Akiba points out to Gamaliel that his view in a matter involving benedictions over fruits is of no avail against majority opinion: (B. *Ber.* 37a,b) Akiba says . . . "You said yourself that when an individual opposes the majority, the Halakhah is in accordance with the majority." In P. *B. Q.* IV,3; 4b, an incident is related in which the Romans sent two officials to study with Gamaliel. These officials, while praising most of the teachings of Judaism, disapproved of some Halakhoth unfriendly to gentiles. Whereupon Gamaliel issued a *Gezerah* (prohibition) regarding property robbed from gentiles "because of profanation of the Name." The Talmud does not say that Gamaliel issued this prohibition in conjunction with his *Beth Din*, implying that he possessed the authority to act independently, although all previous instances appeared to prove just the opposite.

What may be the reason for this discrepancy? If we do not assume an error or an omission in the transmission of the text, we may assume that, in dealing with problems of gentiles, the Nasi commanded more liberty to act independently than he did in other matters. Because he was responsible for dealing with gentile authorities, the Nasi also possessed certain privileges with regard to secular education and culture.

Once a Halakhah was determined by the majority, Gamaliel saw to it that it was observed. We saw how he used his authority against his close associates, forcing them to submission or excommunicating them. Occasionally, he even objected to strict personal observance of others, though sometimes he himself acted thus in his own household. For example, Tosefta *Demai* V,24 (p. 56) relates that Akiba, while on a trip with some of his colleagues, strictly observed a law of tithing for himself. When Gamaliel objected, Akiba defended himself by saying that he had not established a Halakhah. This significant incident shows that the practice of great men, though of a personal nature, may originate a Halakhah.

Occasionally Gamaliel levied a fine against a transgressor of a Halakhah. In B. *Ḥul.* 87, Gamaliel ordered a man to pay ten gold coins to another man for whom the first man had performed a rite contrary to the law.

While shortly after the destruction of the Temple, the rule had been established that the Halakhah would follow Beth Hillel, not Beth Shammai, Gamaliel (as well as some other sages) did not hesitate at times to deviate from this rule. In a few instances, he followed Shammai, which led some scholars to the belief that he was a Shammaite. We discussed this problem elsewhere[55] and pointed out the fallacy of basing theories on exceptions and of considering some sages as Shammaites when Beth Shammai no longer existed.

Gamaliel (and others) sometimes differed with both Beth Shammai *and* Beth Hillel. (Cf. M. *Tohoroth* IX,1 where Gamaliel differs with both Houses, and the sages agree with him!) Such instances usually mean that Beth Hillel no longer existed at this time.[56] The topic here is the time of defilement of the olives.

Another case in which Gamaliel differs with both Beth Shammai *and* Beth Hillel is found in M. *Sukkah* III,9 and involves his performing the act of shaking the Lulav in a most lenient way, although he did not voice a lenient Halakhah. Gamaliel called upon experts in other matters of Halakhah in the same way that he had called upon them in the case of the Eighteen Benedictions. See, for example, Tosefta *Kil.* III,5 (p. 77). Here a case was put before Gamaliel for a decision in matters of כלאי הכרם diverse kinds in a vineyard. He tells the questioners to ask an expert in the laws concerning "vineyard," Jose ben Golai, who then answered their question.

Gamaliel took a serious view even toward ridiculous positions (*Derekh Erez Rabbah* I). R. Jose ben Taddai once used the *qal wehomer*, the method of reasoning a fortiori, in a ridiculous manner by concluding that a man is not permitted to marry the daughter of a married woman. After showing the absurdity of Jose ben Taddai's reasoning, Gamaliel excommunicated him.

In matters of Halakhah, Gamaliel had no decided tendency as to leniency or stringency, though if we take all his views into consideration, he was more often lenient. His decisions were often influenced by practical considerations. We saw that a part of his effort in the realm of Halakhah was aimed at creating good will between Jews and gentiles.

In M. *R. H.* IV,9, Gamaliel, in contradistinction to others, held that the reader, by reciting the prayers in the service, fulfills the obligation of praying not merely for himself but for the community as well. B. *R. H.* 34b–35a cites a Baraitha in which Gamaliel is asked: If the praying of the reader suffices, why do the individuals also pray? He replies: In order to give the reader time to arrange his prayer. According to a tradition cited ibid., Gamaliel only excused the people working in the fields from reciting the prayers. If this tradition reflects the truth, economic considerations would have influenced Gamaliel. However, this tradition is in conflict with Gamaliel's own words and may be but an attempt to reconcile Gamaliel's view with the general practice.

In M. *Peah* VI,5–6, which deals with a matter of forgotten sheaves, Gamaliel favors the land owner while the sages favor the poor.

In marital matters, Gamaliel's decisions often favor the woman, a tendency of the wealthy. We cite the following examples:

M. *Kethuvoth* I,6–9 lists four cases about women in "trouble." In the first two cases, the topic of the dispute is the loss of virginity. Although the use of symbolic language makes the third case obscure, the source of the trouble in it is either extra-marital intercourse or the suspicion of it. The fourth case deals with the question of the fatherhood of an embryo conceived outside of wedlock. In all these instances, Gamaliel and Eliezer (his wealthy brother-in-law) accept the woman's side of the dispute in opposition to Joshua.

In M. *Kethuvoth* VIII,1, Gamaliel sides with Beth Shammai by stating that a woman has the right to sell property she acquired after her betrothal, but prior to her marriage. He also holds that such sale is valid even if executed after the marriage was performed.

When a husband once complained before Gamaliel that he did not find his bride to be a virgin, Gamaliel explained to him that his observation might have been erroneous (B. *Kethuvoth* 10a).

When a case came before Gamaliel involving a bill of divorce signed by gentile witnesses, Gamaliel declared the bill of divorce to be valid (M. *Git.* I,5). A contrary decision might have rendered a woman divorced by such a bill an *agunah*, thus denying her the right to remarry.

Economic consideration often affected the Halakhah. M. *B. Q.* VII,7 states that the raising of goats and lambs in the land of Israel, except for certain desert areas, is prohibited.[57] According to B. *Q.* 80a, Gamaliel permitted the raising of goats and sheep. The Talmud tries to harmonize his view here with the prohibition of the Mishnah. While such harmonization is artificial, the Tosefta and other Baraitha sources indicate that his permissiveness was not unlimited. He obviously did not consider the raising of such animals to be as harmful as did the rabbis, who became so extreme in their opposition to these shepherds that they treated them as gentiles in some respects.[58] In addition to the original list of men disqualified to act as witnesses (given in M. *Sanh*. III,3–5) the rabbis later included among others, the shepherds (Tosefta *Sanh*. V,5, p. 423 and parallels in B. *Sanh*. 25b and P. *Sanh*. III,21a.) The rabbis also declared that it was difficult for the shepherds to gain repentance (B. *B. Q.* 94b).

In this respect, it is significant that Rabbi Eliezer among others, upon being questioned about raising of small animals (goats and sheep), gave an evasive answer.[59] The Tosefta then remarks that he did not answer the question directly because he never said a thing concerning which he possessed no tradition. The implication is clear: raising of goats and sheep constituted a new problem at the time of Eliezer and Gamaliel, i.e., shortly after the destruction of the Temple. Why did this problem come up at this particular time?

The main reason is the termination of the sacrificial cult, particularly of the Paschal sacrifice. The large animal husbandry in Palestine at the time of the Temple was necessary to provide a large yearly supply of yearling goats and lambs required for the Paschal sacrifice, and also numerous older animals for the other sacrifices. Suddenly, the demand dropped, particularly for the one-year-old animals, which were now allowed to grow older. The natural consequence was an increase in large herds of sheep and goats that needed food and caused considerable damage to agriculture. This naturally infuriated the farmers, and the rabbis sought to help them through their stand against the stock breeders.

There may have been a trend away from farming because of heavy taxes on farmers, or better profits in breeding, etc. Cf. Tos. *'Arakhin* V,6, which says that one must not sell a field in order to buy various other items, among them cattle and small animals (p. 549).[60]

But why did Gamaliel not join the other sages in this matter? He, as the Nasi, may have refused to antagonize a part of his people. He was also Nasi of the shepherds. Also noteworthy is Gamaliel's endeavor to have the celebration with the Paschal lamb in Jerusalem continued throughout the land in a fashion similar to the celebration at the time of the Temple.[61] Since he held this opinion, he could not oppose breeders of animals needed for the *Seder*. Gamaliel's view favoring a whole roasted kid (or lamb) as the Paschal meal (M. *Beẓah* II,7; cf. Tosefta, ibid. II,15) was rejected by the sages (ibid.); therefore, they had no reason to spare the breeders of these animals.

While Gamaliel did not succeed in making the existing custom[62] of having a roasted whole kid for the Seder a law, his contribution to the establishment of the Seder ritual is noteworthy. See particularly M. *Pesaḥim* X,5:

רבן גמליאל היה אומר כל שלא אמר שלשה דברים אלו בפסח לא
יצא ידי חובתו ואלו הן: פסח מצה ומרור. פסח על שום שפסח המקום
על בתי אבותינו במצרים, וכו'

> Rabban Gamaliel used to say, Whosoever has not said [explained] these three things at Passover has not fulfilled his obligation. And these are they: Paschal sacrifice, unleavened bread, and bitter herbs. "Paschal sacrifice" — because God passed over the houses of our fathers in Egypt; "unleavened bread" — because our fathers were redeemed from Egypt; "bitter herbs" — because the Egyptians embittered the lives of our fathers in Egypt.

The Gamaliel of this passage is certainly Gamaliel II,[63] not Gamaliel I as some scholars believe.[64]

Parallel versions to our Mishnah include biblical references. Such versions are, for example, the text of the Passover Haggadah and old Genizah fragments.

The above statement of Gamaliel, though simple on the surface, is difficult in more than one respect, such as:

To what kind of obligation does Gamaliel refer? A noteworthy conjecture is that of E. D. Goldschmidt stating that Gamaliel refers to Exod. 13:8 והגדת לבנך "And thou shalt tell thy son." [65] However, if this is what Gamaliel had in mind the wording expected would be לא קיים מצות והגדת לבנך "He has not fulfilled the commandment of 'And thou shalt tell they son.'" Therefore, we believe that Gamaliel, in making the above statement, wanted to emphasize the importance of explaining the essential Passover rituals, and had no specific biblical law in mind commanding the expounding of these rituals. Thus, in effect, he established a law that influenced the spiritual and liturgical expansion of the Passover ritual. Gamaliel, at least, once spent a whole Seder night with his colleagues (not with children) in Lud discussing the matters concerning Passover,[66] as did (probably later) Akiba in Bene Berak.

Some scholars believe that Gamaliel, who was so much concerned about Christian (and other sectarian) influences, intended to counteract the belief that the Seder commemorates the Last Supper by making the expounding of the true reasons for the Passover ceremonies a requirement.[67]

The destruction of the Temple might have resulted in the complete loss of the Passover night ritual since the center of this ritual was the Passover sacrifice. With this sacrifice abolished, Maẓẓah and bitter herbs, which accompany this sacrifice and are secondary to it (Num. 9:11, "they shall eat it [the Paschal sacrifice] with unleavened bread and bitter herbs") could have been abandoned as well. It was the genius of the rabbis, and particularly of Gamaliel, that saved the Seder and compensated for the lack of the sacrifice by shifting the emphasis to spiritual aspects of the Exodus, thus making the Seder meaningful throughout the ages. Had Gamaliel done nothing else for Judaism but this, he would have been one of the pillars of Rabbinic Judaism.

Gamaliel's Journeys

Beside performing his presidential duties and lecturing at the academy in Javneh and his school in Lud, Gamaliel spent much time on journeys in Palestine and abroad as did other Princes, particularly those succeeding him. We cite the following instances of Gamaliel's journeys:

In M. *'Eruvin* X,10, Gamaliel and the Elders came to Tiberias and forbade a lenient practice regarding the use of a certain bolt for shutting a door on a Sabbath. Thus R. Eliezer relates the incident. R. Joshua's tradition reverses matters.

This incident demonstrates that Gamaliel and the Elders supervised and corrected religious practices of their people.

Tos. *Terumoth* II,13 (p. 28) relates an incident that occurred in Akzib in reference to matters of כרם רבעי grapes of the fourth year, bought from a gentile in Syria. For decision the matter was put

217

before Gamaliel "who was travelling from place to place." The actual content of his decision is a matter of controversy.

In B. 'Eruvin 64b (a Baraitha), Gamaliel accompanied by R. Ilai, rode on a donkey from Akko to Kezib. On the road, Gamaliel gave some instructions with halakhic implications. In Kezib, a man approached Gamaliel with a request to annul his vow. Since Gamaliel had drunk wine shortly before this request, he traveled three more miles until he arrived at the "Ladder of Tyre," whereupon he annulled the vow. His action was considered as having the following implications: 1) Drinking of a *revi'ith* wine intoxicates; 2) An intoxicated person may not render a halakhic decision; 3) Travel dissipates the effects of alcohol; 4) A vow may not be annulled while riding, walking or standing, but only while sitting. This is another incident demonstrating that the example of a great man may be considered as a precedent for Halakhah.

Among other places Gamaliel visited were: Jericho, Kefar Otnai, Narvad, Ashkelon — towns that had predominantly non-Jewish populations.

He journeyed several times to Rome usually in the company of Joshua, Akiba, and Eleazar ben Azariah.

In B. *Makkoth* 24ab, Gamaliel, Eleazar ben Azariah, Joshua and Akiba traveled together (cf. *Midrash Tannaim*, p. 37). The purpose of this trip is not revealed.

In P. *Sanh.* VII,13, Eliezer, Joshua, and Gamaliel are together. They were surprised to find Jews in an (unidentified) town. They prayed that the childless son of their host would become a father. The prayer was effective, and the son born became a sage, Rabbi Judah ben Bathyra. The actual purpose of the trip is unknown.

In *Devarim Rabbah* II,15, "our sages happened to be in Rome, R. Eliezer, R. Joshua and Rabban Gamaliel." The occasion of the trip obviously was an evil decree ("within thirty days there must be no Jew in the entire World") which they successfully averted. The incident is given legendary form, which represents a later embellishment of the historical nucleus. The incident is significant because it points to the importance of at least some of the trips to Rome undertaken by Gamaliel and his associates.

In *Shemoth Rabbah* 39, Gamaliel, Joshua, Eleazar ben Azariah and Akiba went to Rome and preached there. While there, they also had a dispute with a *min* (probably Judeo-Christian).

This incident reveals that Gamaliel and other leaders of Rabbinic Judaism were concerned over sectarian influence and sought to counteract it. To some extent, these trips parallel the journeys of the Apostles and may have been undertaken as a counter measure.

In B. *A. Z.* 54b, Gamaliel had a dispute while in Rome with an idol-worshipping philosopher over God's power and the quality of idols as living gods. No associates of Gamaliel are mentioned in this case.

We find other cases in which Gamaliel traveled alone. Such a case is M. *'Eduy.* VII,7.

Although the purpose of these travels is seldom revealed, the instances in which the purpose of the trips is known permit the conclusion that most, if not all of them, were "business trips" of importance. Some of them were of political nature, as is especially obvious with regard to the trips to Rome. Others were undertaken to strengthen the bonds with the Jews in the Diaspora and the towns under Hellenistic influence. They often combined both purposes. Due to the busy schedule of the Patriarchs, they often sent sages as their representatives on such trips. These שליחים *sheliḥim*, apostles, performed important tasks. They saw to it that the religious life in distant Jewish communities was in harmony with Judaism as interpreted by the *Beth Din Ha-Gadol* to prevent chaos and sectarianism. Sages were also dispatched to various communities to solicit money for the academy in Javneh and other religious purposes.[68]

Gamaliel (and the other Patriarchs) seldom traveled alone. Gamaliel's most frequent travel companions were R. Joshua, his *Av Beth Din*, R. Eleazar ben Azariah, who shared honors with him in the academy of Javneh, and R. Akiba, who performed some official functions, such as intercalating the year for (or communicating such information to) the Jews in Babylonia. These men obviously ranked highest among the members of the *Beth Din Ha-Gadol*; they constituted the "executive committee" under Gamaliel's presidency.

According to the Talmud, Gamaliel II was still alive during the Bar Kokhba war. When the Romans sought to kill him, he went into hiding.[69] Nonetheless Graetz (followed by other scholars)

219

claims that Gamaliel died about 117 c.e. and emends the sources so that they uphold his claim.[70] He also maintains that Simon, Gamaliel's son, became Patriarch about 140.[71] The identity of the man in charge of the Patriarchate during the interim is controversial.

According to Graetz during the interim R. Joshua, the *Av Beth Din*, was the acting Patriarch.[72]

I. Halevy, followed by J. S. Zuri, holds that after Gamaliel's death Eleazar ben Azariah became the Patriarch. He also claims that Gamaliel died thirty-five years after the fall of the Temple, in 105 c.e.[73] This would give Eleazar ben Azariah a presidency of thirty-five years after Gamaliel's death. However, the Talmud never says that Eleazar ben Azariah was Patriarch after Gamaliel's death, nor that it was R. Joshua, and we can see no reason why such a long presidency should be totally without mention in the entire talmudic literature. In our opinion neither Graetz's nor Halevy's conjectures deserve credence. The explicit talmudic sources are certainly more reliable. Gamaliel, who married more than once, reached an old age, therefore there could not have been a long interim between his death and the beginning of Simon's Patriarchate. The man most likely to have been the acting Patriarch during these years was Akiba. Some of the indications to this effect are the following: Akiba, even while held in prison by the Romans, was in charge of the calendation, a prerogative of the Nasi and Sanhedrin.[74] Like Gamaliel II, Akiba too traveled to many places and countries, apart from those journeys made with Gamaliel.[75] During his visit to the various countries Akiba did some teaching, intercalating of years and performance of other tasks as well. In giving opinions, Akiba, like Gamaliel, hardly ever quotes other Tannaim. The authority of the great Patriarchs made a frequent reference to other sages unnecessary. After the last uprising, Akiba's activities, which resulted in his imprisonment, may have included duties of the Patriarch.

Whether Akiba held the office of an acting Patriarch during the interim between Gamaliel's death and Simon's presidency, is of little importance. Essential is his accomplishment for the history of Rabbinic Judaism. In this respect, he ranks with the outstanding patriarchs. The oral law, which moved into the limelight of Judaism after the destruction of the Temple, grew into a vast bulk of learning and practices. As time progressed, this vast uncoordinated bulk became quite chaotic and threatened to destroy itself. The man who came to the rescue of the law was Akiba, as we shall see later.

ELEAZAR BEN AZARIAH

*A*fter Gamaliel II was demoted, Eleazar ben Azariah was elected in his place. Whether Gamaliel was stripped of all his power, losing both the presidency of the Sanhedrin and his office as Nasi, is a controversial issue. Proponents of the opinion that Gamaliel lost merely the presidency of the academy but not his Nasi office point to the fact that neither the account in the Babylonian Talmud (*Ber.* 27b–28a) nor the one in the P. Talmud (P. *Ber.* IV,1; 7d) state explicitly that Gamaliel lost his Nasi office or that Eleazar ben Azariah succeeded him in this office. The B. Talmud merely says תא ונעבריה "Let us depose him" (i.e., Gamaliel); and with reference to Eleazar ben Azariah the term ריש מתיבתא "head of the academy" is used. The P. Talmud states that ומינו את ר"א בן עזריה בישיבה "They appointted [or: ordained] Eleazar ben Azariah [as member and head] of the academy," and: לא הורידו אותו מגדולתו אלא מינו אותו אב בית דין "They did not demote him from his high office, but appointed him *Av Beth Din.*" In addition they claim that the members of the academy had no right to depose the Nasi since he was endorsed by the Roman authorities.[76] It should also be noted that Eleazar ben Azariah is never called Nasi or referred to as *Rabban*, a title borne by the Princes.

While at first sight these considerations seem to carry decisive weight, a scrutiny of their premises and relevant sources show that they are unacceptable. For example, the assumption that Gamaliel lost merely the presidency of the academy but not the office of the Nasi is based on the premise that these two offices could be separated. However, this conjectural premise is unacceptable since there is no case on record where such was done.

The view that the Nasi could not be deposed because he was endorsed by the Roman authorities is likewise erroneous. The truth is that the Nasi possessed no official status in the eyes of the Roman authorities, who did not endorse, but merely tolerated him.[77]

Most illuminating in this matter is an incident related in B. *Horayoth* 13b, in which R. Meir and R. Nathan conspire in order to effect the fall of Simon, son of Gamaliel II.

A further proof of Eleazar ben Azariah's appointment to nasidom is the talmudic statement (B. *Ber.* loc. cit.) that one of the reasons for selecting Eleazar ben Azariah to replace Gamaliel was that he was wealthy and able to "serve" (pay) the emperor when needed. There should be no doubt that this was a function of the Nasi and not that of a mere head of the academy.[78] Furthermore, after the re-instatement of Gamaliel, Eleazar ben Azariah was appointed *Av Beth Din*, an office second only to that of the Nasi. This is an indication that hitherto his office was that of the Nasi.[79]

Eleazar ben Azariah was Nasi for a very short time only. This explains the absence of references to his title "Rabban" or to his office as Nasi. This also explains why he could not accomplish much during his presidency. Another factor in this respect may have been his youth. According to the B. Talmud (loc. cit.) he was sixteen years old when he was appointed Nasi. The accuracy of this given age (as is so often the case with dates in ancient literature) is questionable. They merely mean that he was a young scholar at this time.

While Eleazar ben Azariah may not have accomplished much personally during his presidency, his ascent to nasidom had significant consequences. The very day he accepted his high office (after consulting with his wife who tried to dissuade him), the doorman of the academy was removed and everybody who so desired was free to enter the hitherto restricted *Beth Ha-Midrash*. This gave many men an opportunity to come and relate their traditions or to bring their own halakhic problems before the members of the academy. Most of the traditions introduced by the words בו ביום "on that day" refer to the traditions brought up in the academy on the day Eleazar ben Azariah ascended to the presidency. Particularly important of these are the "testimonies" related in tractate *'Eduyyoth* which, according to the Talmud (B. *Ber.* loc. cit.) were given on this day.[80]

Probably the most significant decision made under Eleazar ben Azariah's presidency was that the Song of Songs and Qoheleth were to be included in the Canon, as stated in M. *Yadayim* III,5, ". . . R. Simon ben Azzai said: I have heard a tradition from the seventy-two elders on the day when they appointed R. Eleazar ben Azariah [member and] head of the academy that the Song of Songs and Ecclesiastes render the hands unclean [i.e., are Holy Books]. . . ."[81]

In spite of his demotion, Gamaliel continued to attend the sessions of the academy and soon apologized to R. Joshua. All this resulted in his early reinstatement, terminating Eleazar ben Azariah's presidency shortly after it commenced. However, Eleazar ben Azariah was not completely demoted but, besides being appointed *Av Beth Din*, he was privileged to lead the academy sessions one Sabbath (week) while Gamaliel was to preside two Sabbaths (or weeks).[82] He also accompanied Gamaliel on many of his trips, and excelled throughout his career not merely as a halakhist but also as an aggadist.[83]

AKIBA

One of the obscurities of the tannaitic period is based on the reasonable assumption that between the death (or retirement) of Gamaliel II and the commencement of the nasidom of his son Simon there was an interim of several years during which period the leadership was in the hands of an acting Nasi. Since the sources do not give the name of this personage, scholars make various conjectures; we feel that probability favors Akiba. However, Akiba's leadership as acting Nasi, even if it were an established fact, still would be of secondary importance in comparison with his accomplishment for the history of Rabbinic Judaism, for in this respect he ranks with the outstanding Patriarchs.

Let us clarify this by pointing to pertinent data explicit or implicit in the relevant sources.

As the oral law moved into the limelight of Judaism after the destruction of the Temple, it grew into a vast uncoordinated bulk of learning and practices, which with time became quite chaotic and threatened to destroy itself. The man who came to the rescue of the law was Akiba, as the sources demonstrate.

Sifre to Deut. 48[84] ranks Akiba with Shaphan and Ezra as a person who snatched the Torah from oblivion. Tradition credits Shaphan with exerting a marked influence upon King Josiah at the time the Torah was restored by Josiah to its pristine status as law book, while the merits of Ezra are so well known as to need no explication.

Assuredly there must be some warrant underlying a remark so momentous. For the encomium bestowed upon Shaphan, the basis is a tradition which interprets II Kings 22 to Shaphan's honor in the way just mentioned. But such interpretations carry little historical significance. The praise accorded Ezra, on the other hand, rests upon the solid foundation of reliable accounts both in the Bible and in subsequent lore. Nonetheless, it is with regard to Akiba that the author of the passage in *Sifre* must have possessed the amplest information, since he and Akiba were almost contemporaries. Of course, a precise knowledge of events and a correct appraisal of those same events need not necessarily go hand in hand, and we shall keep this fact in mind as we ferret out the grounds for this high praise of Akiba. In what sense, then, we ask, did Akiba save the Torah from oblivion?

Foremost among considerations which might occur to one would be Akiba's courageous activity as a teacher despite Roman interdict immediately after the insurrection of Bar Kokhba. Yet not only Akiba but also Judah ben Baba and many others defied Rome.[85] We must therefore seek further for our explanation.

Happily our context, here as elsewhere, indicates the direction. And what does that context indicate?

In the same chapter to *Sifre* to Deut., a few lines further down, oblivion is construed to mean: confusion or chaos in matters of practice.[86] Significant also is the warning, in the same chapter,[87] against studying only one section of the Torah and neglecting the others.

Thus, possessing at least a hint as to the direction we have to take, we must ask: What did Akiba do to save the Torah from oblivion?[88] What, to the benefit of Jewish tradition, were his outstanding achievements? What distinguished him from all the other scholars of his period?[89]

The sources which seem to hold essential importance for our problem are the following:

ARN II[90] describes the methods of three authorities. R. Tarphon taught everything in one lecture — Bible, Mishnah, Midrash, Hala- khoth, and Aggadoth — whenever a student came to him requesting instruction. With reference to R. Eleazar ben Azariah, the notice states that, whenever a student called, the student would ask about Bible, Midrash, Mishnah, Halakhah, and Haggadah, and would receive all the answers in one sitting. Akiba acted differently. After gathering all that he could find, Akiba would then classify the materials and arrange them in proper order, that is, each in its separate compartment. Akiba's work therefore is characterized as *Oẓar Balus*, "a packed warehouse," the goods of which are well arranged, in contrast to the "heap of stones or nuts" and the "spice-peddler's basket" that respectively characterize the efforts of R. Tarphon and R. Eleazar ben Azariah.[91] Akiba's special merit, according to this source, was that he separated the fruits of Jewish learning and arranged them according to their species. He did not, like the other sages, mix the different kinds. The phrase ועשה כל התורה טבעות טבעות cannot, in our context, mean anything except: He arranged the entire Torah (i.e., traditional materials) in separate divisions according to its several species.[92]

P. *Sheq.* V,1; 48c reads:

אמר ר' יונה כתיב לכן אחלק לו ברבים ואת עצומים יחלק שלל זה
ר"ע שהתקין (סדר =) מדרש הלכות והגדות.

"Said Rabbi Jonah, it is written [Isa. 53:12] 'Therefore will I divide him a portion among the great, and he shall divide the spoil with the mighty.' This is Rabbi Akiba who *arranged* Midrash, Halakhoth and Aggadoth."

This means that in the opinion of R. Jonah, a Palestinian Amora, the high praise of Isa. 53:12 befits Akiba because he arranged the above categories of the oral law.

Meḵhilta of R. Ishmael, Mishpatim I relates:[93]

רבי עקיבא אומר, ואלה המשפטים למה נאמר... ערכם לפניהם
כשלחן ערוך, וכו'

Rabbi Akiba said: Why is it said [Exod. 21:1] "And these are the laws. . . ." [The answer is] *arrange* them before them [the students] like a set table, etc.

In this passage Akiba requires a systematic arrangement of the laws for the benefit of the students.[94]

Tos. *Zavim* I,5 relates:

כשהיה ר' עקיבא מסדר הלכות לתלמידים אמר כל מי ששמע טעם
על חברו יבוא ויאמר... אמר לפניו ר' שמעון... הואיל ו... חזר ר' עקיבא
להיות שונה כדברי ר' שמעון.

When R. Akiba *arranged* Halakhoth for the students he said: "Whoever knows a reason in regard to [the view of] his friend, shall come and say it. . . ." Rabbi Simon said before him . . . subsequently Rabbi Akiba "learned" [= accepted the version] in accordance with R. Simon.[95]

B. *Sanh.* 86a informs us:

דאמר ר' יוחנן סתם מתני' ר' מאיר סתם תוספתא ר' נחמיה סתם
ספרא ר' יהודה סתם ספרי ר' שמעון וכולהו אליבא דר' עקיבא.

Rabbi Johanan said:
"*Mishnah*, if not specified, is the Mishnah of R. Meir; *Tosefta*, if not specified, is the Tosefta of R. Nehemiah; *Sifra*, if not specified, is that of R. Judah; *Sifre*, if not specified, is that of R. Simon; and all these [works] are [i.e., were compiled or redacted] in accordance with [the instructions of] R. Akiba."

We showed elsewhere that the usual "literal" translation of this statement of R. Johanan is erroneous. Thus, for example, Rabbi Johanan, in searching for the author of a Mishnah, never cites his own dictum סתם מתניתין ר' מאיר usually translated "An anonymous view of our Mishnah is that of R. Meir," and never applies it. Had he meant what this "literal" translation says, he would have made ample use of it.[96] We also showed that this "literal" meaning is refuted by the fact that the majority of the anonymous views of our Mishnah do not reflect the views of R. Meir.[97]

Thus not only is R. Johanan's dictum in line with the aforementioned statements which praise Akiba for organizing the oral tradition, but it goes a step farther and proves that Akiba's plan of organizing the tradition was actually carried out, or at least completed by his students.

That Akiba himself did not complete the arrangement of the tradition in special literary works is indicated by the fact that the sources merely state that he arranged the traditions but do not speak of his completed works. Although the nature of his משניות גדולות "great Mishnajoth" [98] is uncertain, this expression probably means "important teachings" and does not refer to a work or collection.[99]

The enthusiastic statement in *Sifre* Deut. 48, praising Akiba for having saved the Torah from oblivion, is, though exaggerated,[100] true in two respects.

First, by sifting and arranging systematically the traditions Akiba saved the significant species of these traditions from oblivion. This Midrash (*Sifre* Deut. 48), contained in a collection that came mainly from Akiba's school, reflects the spirit of Akiba who maintained that all of the species of oral tradition are of equal importance and must be cultivated. The fact that our passage which demands the same care for all branches of tradition, and the other which praises Akiba as the preserver of the Torah, are recorded in the same chapter is hardly a mere coincidence.

But Akiba saved the Torah also in another respect. He saved it as the basis for the life and the future of his people. R. Simon ben Johai, a disciple of Akiba, commenting on Amos 8:12 ישוטטו לבקש את דבר ה' ולא ימצאו. "They shall run to and fro to seek the word of the Lord, and shall not find it," explains that oblivion means chaos in matters of Halakhah. Noteworthy is the fact that this Midrash is contained in the paragraph following the statement that Akiba saved the Torah from oblivion. Simon's utterance has special significance for, as B. *Shab.* 138b shows, he intends to comment on a Baraitha, ibid.,[101] and to correct it. This significant Baraitha, given in a more complete version in Tos. *'Eduy.* I,1, relates the fear of the sages after the destruction of the Temple in 70 c.e. that the Torah might be forgotten. To prevent this, they decided to collect the Halakhoth. Their method was to collect them author by author, indicating that they were concerned with saving all the material and not the preparing of a well-arranged code, although the method of arranging the material according to subjects was known.[102] Simon saw the vast amount of the collected material as something that only caused confusion and chaos and afforded no solid basis for life. Therefore he understood "oblivion" as the uselessness of collected traditions for the life of the people.

Akiba, Simon's teacher, saw both: What the sages saw in the vineyard of Javneh and what Simon saw two generations later, and he acted accordingly. He arranged the entire oral tradition, of which the Halakhah was of particular importance as the basis of Jewish life. However, a systematic arrangement of the Halakhah according to subject matter alone could not terminate all the confusion. Of greater practical value was the evaluation and classification of the Halakhoth in separate works according to their importance for Jewish life. Accordingly, the Mishnah, designed as a code of practice, was of primary importance, while the Tosefta, supplementing and often clarifying the Mishnah, was of secondary importance. Of further significance in this direction was Akiba's endeavor to establish the correct version of traditions and to reduce the number of divergent practices and views by giving in most cases only one opinion.[103]

Akiba did not content himself with rescuing the Torah and tradition merely by arranging for their judicial systematization. He keenly realized that the law had to be flexible if it was to serve its purpose of keeping Judaism livable and meaningful. Although he shared this insight with other sages of his generation, none other did nearly as much as he did to promote flexibility. Under his spiritual leadership the sages of his generation projected text interpretation into the limelight of halakhic activity, thus succeeding where Hillel had failed a century before. During this century, text interpretation played a minor role as a means of developing the Halakhah. Akiba's generation expanded Hillel's system of hermeneutic rules as suggested by Rabbi Ishmael.[104] Akiba himself substituted one of these rules by another, more potent one.[105] Most potent and consequential is Akiba's rule that every seemingly "superfluous" text element of the Torah, such as את (sign of the accusative and preposition "with") has a specific meaning which he was always able to point out, even when his teacher, Nahum of Gimzo, whose ideas in this matter Akiba developed, was unable to do so. As a result, Akiba became the foremost champion of *eisegesis*, while other scholars tried to stay (somewhat) closer to the actual meaning of the text, as did R. Yishmael who maintained דברה תורה כלשון בני אדם "The Torah speaks the language of the people," [106] i.e., seemingly superfluous text elements need not have a specific meaning. From the scientific point of view Ishmael was right, but Akiba's method was more useful and mostly prevailed.

Akiba's Halakhoth are several times contrasted with the משנה ראשונה the "old law," [107] meaning that he introduced new laws to replace corresponding old laws.

Akiba's Halakhoth take the realities of life into consideration. Examples: In a case of food laws (*kashruth*), Akiba renders a lenient decision while Johanan ben Nuri is strict. Akiba reproaches Johanan by saying, "How long will you waste the money of Israel?" This means that a strict decision rendering the controversial food (meat) non-kosher would result in a financial loss to the owner which, in Akiba's opinion, must be considered. However, he did not convince Johanan who replied, "How long will you feed Israel prohibited meat?" (B. *Kerithoth* 40a). Akiba is also lenient, as are some other sages, when the observance of a law and human life are in conflict with each other (B. *Yoma* 85ab).

Dignity of man is, in Akiba's opinion, of paramount importance, and supersedes even religious custom. Accordingly he declares עשה שבתך חול ואל תצטרך לבריות "Rather make your Sabbath like a week day [by foregoing the prescribed festival meals], than accepting charity [to finance these meals]" (B. *Shab.* 118a).

Somewhat enigmatic is Akiba's view that a man may divorce his wife if he finds another woman that is prettier than she (or: if he finds that another woman is prettier than she) (M. *Giṭ.* IX,9). Akiba, while ascribing this meaning to Deut. 24:1, "if she find no favor in his eyes" — an obvious *eisegesis* — may have had a psychological

229

reason in mind, i.e., the plight of the unloved woman in a polygamous society.

In the manner of the Nasi and the leading sages of the time, Akiba likewise maintained a *Beth Ha-Midrash*, a private academy, near Javneh, seat of the Sanhedrin. This academy, located in Bene Berak (B. *Sanh.* 32b and parallels) had a great reputation and may have been the leading private academy of the time. However, Akiba did not limit his teaching to the academy halls but also lectured publicly, even during the Hadrianic ban on teaching, and continued to instruct and lead his people even after imprisonment by the Romans on a charge of publicly defying the ban (B. *Ber.* 61b and parallels). Some of the sages were permitted to visit him in the prison (B. *'Eruvin* 21b; B. *Pes.* 112a, etc.), and they communicated his teachings and decisions to the sages throughout the land. Only his death as a martyr terminated his activities as the teacher and leader of his people. M. *Sotah* IX,15 informs us משמת ר' עקיבא בטל כבוד התורה "When Rabbi Akiba died the glory of the Torah ceased." The corresponding Mishnah in the Palestinian Talmud משמת ר' עקיבא פסקו הדרשנים "When Rabbi Akiba died the interpreters ceased" probably indicates what the "glory of the Torah" here means: its elaborate interpretation as undertaken by Rabbi Akiba.

Akiba concentrated his entire strength on the saving of his people mainly by saving and teaching the Torah, including the oral law. His effort did not fail for he contributed essentially to the preservation of the Torah and of the Jewish people.

SIMON BEN GAMALIEL II

*A*kiba's contribution to the rescue and molding of Judaism did not end with the organization of traditional materials and the promotion of text interpretation as a principal means of modifying and enriching the realm of Halakhah, but instead his contribution increased through the work of his disciples, the principal torchbearers of Judaism after the unsuccessful Bar Kokhba uprising.

After Hadrian's death in 138 c.e., the anti-Jewish laws were annulled by Antoninus Pius. Subsequently the rabbinical leaders (most of them disciples of Akiba) convened in Usha, a town in Galilee. Simon, son of Gamaliel II, is not mentioned among the rabbis who convened in Usha.[108] No reason is given for this in the sources. He may have been very cautious and wanted more time to pass until taking over the leadership of his people.

Before Simon ben Gamaliel II appeared on the scene and resumed his duties as the Nasi, the Synod of Usha assumed the duties usually within the authority of the Nasi and issued several enactments, called אושא תקנות the *Taqqanoth* of Usha. These enactments, necessitated by the prevailing conditions after the lost war and the period of persecutions, are the following:

1) Parents must support their children as long as they are minors. 2) If the father deeds all his property to his children, they must support their parents from this property. 3) One who spends freely (by giving too much money for charity, etc.) may not spend more than one fifth of his property. 4) A father must be patient with his son (while teaching him) until he is twelve years old, but after that he should apply strict measures. (He should chastise him and refrain from supporting him if he does not want to study.) 5) Should a wife sell her property while her husband is alive and then die, he may take the property from the purchaser.[109] 6) The *Terumah* must be burned in six cases of doubtful defilement.[110] 7) Tithing and "removal" of the *ethrog* depends on the time of its harvesting (i.e., *ethrog* of the sixth year that ripened in the seventh year is exempt from tithing but requires "removal" since it was harvested in the sabbatical year. On the other hand, *ethrog* of the seventh year that ripened in the eighth year requires tithing but is exempt from the "removal" because it was harvested after the sabbatical year).[111]

Some of these ordinances are significant because they reveal unhealthy after-effects of the war. There were parents who would not support their children and had to be forced to do so. On the other hand, children who were given their parents' property had to be in-

231

structed to support their parents. Another enactment prevented unreasonable spending for charity and for other matters. An excessive
spending would impoverish the family of the spender, making them
a public charge. All these enactments (including the one concerning
the *kethuvah*) show that the bonds of family responsibilities loos-
ened during the war and had to be strengthened. Not all of these
enactments were new. Nos. five and six represent a strengthening of
neglected practices.

Whether all these enactments were issued by the Synod of Usha
is uncertain. The sources merely say that these enactments had been
decided upon in Usha. However, Usha was not merely the locale of
the famous Synod, but also the seat of the academy ("Sanhedrin")
after the Bar Kokhba uprising. Therefore, some of the enactments
could have been issued by the "Sanhedrin" of Usha that was established in Usha some time after the Synod. The strongest indication
that at least most of the above enactments were issued by the Synod
of Usha is the statement in *Shir. R.* II,5, "They [the sages]gathered
and studied and did everything that was necessary" (i.e., at the
Synod of Usha). Perhaps more important than the enactments was
the message of the seven leaders of the Synod to the rabbis of Galilee, inviting them to the Synod and announcing "Those who have
already studied, come and teach. Those who have not yet studied,
come and be taught." Studying was considered the basic requirement
for maintaining and strengthening Judaism (ibid.). Another source
tells us that the seven surviving disciples of Akiba filled the entire
land of Israel with Torah (*Gen. R.* 61:3). There may be more enactments of Usha but the sources are not clear on this.[112]

According to R. Johanan, the Sanhedrin went into exile: . . . .
from Javneh to Usha, from Usha to Javneh, from Javneh to Usha,
from Usha to Shefar-Am, etc. (B. *R. H.* 31ab). The wording "went
into exile" means that the Sanhedrin (or central academy) changed
its seat time and again under the force of circumstances. After the
Bar Kokhba war, due to Judea's desolation, a town in Galilee had to
be selected as the new seat of the academy. The most hospitable recep-
tion of the participants by the people of Usha at the occasion of the
Synod may have persuaded the sages to make Usha the seat of the
reestablished academy. However, on one occasion the seven named

232

disciples of Akiba assembled not in Usha, but in Biq'ath Rimmon (Beth Rimmon), in Galilee and intercalated the year there,[113] thus performing a function of the Nasi and the Sanhedrin. This may indicate that for a short time the *Beth Din Ha-Gadol* convened in Biq'ath Rimmon. As in the time of Gamaliel II, now too the calendation became a crucial issue, one that threatened to disrupt the unity of Rabbinic Judaism.

Hananiah, the nephew of R. Joshua, regulated the calendar during the Hadrianic persecutions in Babylonia, where he was sent by his uncle Joshua because he seemed to be susceptible to Christian influence.[114] After the Hadrianic persecutions in Palestine ended, two sages were sent to Hananiah from Palestine requesting that he desist from the regulation of the calendar and leave it to the sages of the land of Israel. First he refused to comply with this request, but after a threat of excommunication he yielded and cancelled his last act of calendation.[115] Thus the unity of Rabbinic Judaism had been saved once more.

Henceforth the Palestinian leadership regulated the calendar without interference as evident from cases of calendation related in the Talmud. A case of such calendation occurring at Simon's time is revealed incidentally in a dispute about a liturgical issue. In this case the *Beth Din* of Usha sanctified the New Year, which implies that the calendar was regulated there.[116]

According to the above liturgical dispute, Simon ben Gamaliel II attended the worship services both days of Rosh Ha-Shanah and confirmed Akiba's view which was followed the second day of Rosh Ha-Shanah by saying, "This was the practice in Javneh." The reference to Javneh is certainly a reference to the pre-Bar-Kokhba Javneh as Rashi (ad loc.) states. This needs to be pointed out because according to some sources the central academy ("Sanhedrin") moved from Usha to Javneh for reasons unknown.[117] It could have been a move dictated by nostalgic feelings. The second period of Javneh, if historical at all, could have been but a short one since merely two sources refer to it. According to one of these the sages who convened in the Vineyard of Javneh were Rabbi Judah, Rabbi Eleazar ben Jose, and Rabbi Simon.[118] In another passage, among the congregants in the Vineyard of Javneh are named R. Judah, R. Jose, and R. Eliezer the son of R. Jose the Galilean.[119] However, the accuracy or historicity of this account is questionable since the words spoken there are, on the whole, those uttered at the Synod of Usha.[120]

After a possible short interruption, the academy continued to function in Usha for an indeterminable number of years under Simon ben Gamaliel's presidency. His precaution not to take over the leadership of his people right after Hadrian's death was justified in view of the watchful attitude of the Romans even after Antoninus Pius (138–161) annulled the Hadrianic decrees against the Jews. The Romans had spies who watched the conversations of the Jews and informed the Roman authorities. At one occasion, Judah, Jose, and Simon were discussing the accomplishments of the Romans, while Judah, a son of proselytes, was with them. The latter, a spy, informed the Roman authorities about the conversation of the named sages. As a result, Simon was to be killed (but managed to escape), Jose was exiled to Sepphoris, and Judah, who praised the accomplishments of the Romans, was to be "elevated" (rewarded).[121]

In another incident, the Romans entrusted two proselytes with spying on Gamaliel II in Usha.[122] In this case no calamity resulted. The historical implication of this case is noteworthy. If the text is accurate, it would mean that Gamaliel II officiated in Usha, at least for a short time. Since no other ancient source corroborates this, the probability is that the patriarch referred to is Simon ben Gamaliel, though Rashi states that Gamaliel officiated in Usha as well as in Javneh.[123] Should the text of our *Sifre* and Rashi's tradition be right, the statement that the Sanhedrin moved from Javneh to Usha and from Usha to Javneh could refer to Gamaliel II's Sanhedrin.[124]

The academy of Usha created a new office, that of the *Hakham*. His functions are not defined in the sources. Under Simon ben Gamaliel's presidency, R. Nathan, son of the Babylonian Exilarch, was the *Av Beth Din* and R. Meir was the *Hakham*.[125] Thus the *Hakham* obviously ranked third.

Simon ben Gamaliel was not the greatest sage of his time, and he knew it. He often quotes his own contemporaries, admits having learned from them,[126] praises them in most laudatory terms,[127] and acts in accordance with their halakhic decisions.[128] In ordinary relations with his people, he displays signs of great humility.[129]

Simon ben Gamaliel's acts of recognition of and admiration for the sages resulted in a weakening of his personal authority, and he realized this. For example, the members of the academy rose not merely when he entered, but when the *Av Beth Din* and the *Ḥakham* entered as well. Simon ben Gamaliel, in order to bolster his own authority, introduced a new procedure. All those present were to rise only for him and would not sit down before instructed to do so. However, when the *Av Beth Din* entered only two rows were to rise, one on each side and were to remain standing until he was seated. For the *Ḥakham* only one of these rose and remained standing until he was seated.[130] R. Nathan and R. Meir, taken by surprise, planned vengeance. The plan, suggested by R. Meir, was that Simon ben Gamaliel be asked to discuss the laws of defilement about *uqẓin* 'stalks' of fruits and plants. They knew that the Nasi was unprepared to do this and, after pointing to his ignorance, they expected that the academy would dismiss him. Subsequently, Nathan would become the Nasi and Meir the *Av Beth Din* — so they thought. However, the plan failed because a sage faithful to Simon ben Gamaliel indicated to him that *uqẓin* would be discussed in the academy by studying about it aloud near the residence of the Nasi, who took the hint and studied this section of the law. Next day, when the Nasi was asked to discuss *uqẓin*, he was able to do so. He also knew the purpose of the question and expelled Nathan and Meir from the academy. They continued asking questions by sending notes from the outside. The sages of the academy were able to answer some of them. Those they could not answer were answered by Nathan and Meir in written notes which they threw inside the academy. R. Jose intervened for Nathan and Meir by saying "The Torah is outside and we are inside." Hereupon Simon ben Gamaliel permitted them to re-enter, but penalized them by ordering that their names should not be mentioned when their views are quoted, but that Meir should be quoted as "others" (say), and Nathan as "some say" רבי מאיר אחרים ר' נתן יש אומרים. Later R. Nathan asked the Nasi for forgiveness, R. Meir did not.[131]

This incident is significant, because it shows that the academy ("Sanhedrin," or *Beth Din Ha-Gadol*) could dismiss a Nasi and appoint another person in his place. This would not be possible if the office of the Nasi were independent of the academy, or were an office endorsed by the Roman authorities. The situation was probably the same at the time of Gamaliel II's demotion.

In exercising his duties as Nasi, Simon ben Gamaliel pursued a course of democracy, realism, and flexibility.

Simon ben Gamaliel points out that in former times the witnesses who signed the *kethuvah* were either priests. Levites or Israelites of unblemished descent.[132] This implies that matters changed under his presidency. While he was not necessarily the initiator of the change, his pointing to it indicates that it had his consent and support. From that time on the signers of a *kethuvah* did not have to belong to a pedigreed group.

Simon ben Gamaliel proclaimed the principle that הכל כמנהג המדינה the custom of a place is binding.[133] This is an important legislative measure. Declaring a custom as binding gives it in large measure the character of a law.[134]

Simon ben Gamaliel holds that a man who gave his property away to deprive his unworthy sons from inheriting it is praiseworthy.[135] This shows that he had no scruples about disregarding biblical law (law of inheritance) if circumstances warranted such a measure. But he would not permit the setting aside of a law of the Torah without compelling reason.[136] Another example: "You may transgress the Sabbath for a newborn baby [to save his life], but not for King David when he is dead," he declared.[137]

Simon ben Gamaliel strengthened the authority of the courts.[138]

One statement by Simon ben Gamaliel is, at first glance, puzzling: "Wherever the sages cast their [evil] eye, the consequence is poverty or death.[139] However, if we keep in mind his unagreeable experiences with some of the sages, this dictum is understandable.

The only foreign language in which the Bible may be written, according to Simon ben Gamaliel, was Greek.[140] This indicates that he did not oppose Greek culture. In fact he studied Greek himself as did other Patriarchs and many other Pharisaic and Rabbinic Jews.[141]

As to the financial settlements pertaining to marriage, he strengthened the position of the woman.[142]

A sensible rule related in the name of Simon ben Gamaliel is "No [restrictive] measure must be imposed on the community unless the majority of the community is able to bear it." [143] This rule is generally attributed to Simon ben Gamaliel I. Since the rulings of the Patriarchs were issued in response to need, this ruling was unquestionably directed against the endeavors of some extremists.

Rabbi Judah, son and successor of Simon ben Gamaliel, is often involved in halakhic discussions with his father. This shows that Judah, born about 135 C.E.,[144] was a mature scholar during his father's lifetime and also proves that Simon was Patriarch for a long period, perhaps until 170 or 175. The obscure statement in M. *Sotah* IX,15, "When Rabban Simon ben Gamaliel died the 'locust' [145] came and troubles grew many," allows no safe inference as to the time of his death.

JUDAH I

*J*udah I succeeded his father Simon at about 170–75 C.E. and held leadership until his death at about 217 C.E.[146] Since Judah was a mature scholar during the lifetime of his father — tannaitic sources preserved many halakhic disputes between father and son — a date earlier than 170 as the terminus a quo for Judah's ascent to leadership is unlikely.

The period of Judah's leadership, while lacking spectacular events, such as the Bar Kokhba uprising, is one of the landmarks in Jewish history. With Judah's death, the tannaitic period ends, followed by three profound changes: 1) The center of Jewish life, spiritual and material, shifted from Palestine to Babylonia. 2) The Mishnah of Judah I became the focal point and basic text in the academies of Palestine as well as of Babylonia. 3) The language of the academies was changed from Hebrew to Aramaic.

Roman oppression and acts of persecution were frequent and heavy at Judah's time.[147] Rabbi Ḥiyya, a close associate of Judah, states: "God knew that Israel could not bear the persecution of the

237

Romans, therefore he exiled them to Babylon."[148] Though Rashi believes that this has reference to the time of the destruction of the Temple (ibid.), circumstances indicate that Ḥiyya had primarily his own time in mind.[149] He himself was among those who emigrated to Babylonia and stayed there for many years.[150] Several accounts about R. Ḥiyya, some of which concern his relation to Judah, serve as a key to the understanding of certain consequential occurrences of Judah's time. One of these accounts is B. *Sukkah* 20a:

דאמר ריש לקיש... שבתחלה כשנשתכחה תורה מישראל עלה עזרא
מבבל ויסדה חזרה ונשתכחה עלה הלל הבבלי ויסדה חזרה ונשתכחה
עלו רבי חייא ובניו ויסדוה.

> Resh Laqish said . . . When the Torah was forgotten in Israel, Ezra came from Babylonia and established it . . . Then Hillel the Babylonian came and established it . . . Then Ḥiyya and his sons came [from Babylonia] and established it.

In this passage, Ḥiyya ranks with Ezra and Hillel in regard to importance for the "establishment" of the Torah. "Establishment" with reference to Ḥiyya means that during the years of his stay in Babylonia the (oral) Torah was forgotten in Palestine. Even Judah the Patriarch forgot the oral law, it seems. B. *Ned.* 41a relates that Judah studied thirteen אפי (ways, methods, more probably: categories) of Halakhah. Seven of these he taught R. Ḥiyya. Then Judah fell sick (and forgot everything), subsequently R. Ḥiyya returned to him the knowledge of the seven categories he (Judah) had taught him.[151] "Sickness" is here either not to be taken literally or it represents an error. Had it been literally true, Palestinian scholars could have taught him upon recovery, since he had many disciples besides Ḥiyya.

In this connection, it is interesting to note the method of saving the Torah from oblivion which Ḥiyya suggests:[152]

> R. Ḥiyya said, "I take steps that the Torah shall not be forgotten in Israel: I bring flax seed, sow it, and weave nets [from the flax]. Then I catch stags with whose flesh I feed orphans and from whose skins I prepare scrolls, and then go to a town where there are no teachers of children, and write out the five Books of the Torah for five children, and teach another six children the six Orders of the Mishnah, and then tell each one: Teach your section

to your colleagues." Therefore did Rabbi exclaim, "How great are the deeds of Ḥiyya!"

Some scholars, e.g., W. Bacher,[153] believe that Ḥiyya actually saved the Torah by applying the method he described, and this is why Judah exclaims "How great are the deeds of Ḥiyya."

While Ḥiyya is ranked with Ezra and Hillel because of his achievement in behalf of saving the Torah, Judah is compared with Daniel, Hananyah, Mishael, and Azaryah in the Chaldean period, with Mordekhai and Esther in the Persian period, and with the Hasmoneans in the Greek period.[154] This means Judah is credited with saving Judaism and the Jewish people of his time. Statements of this kind are not to be taken too literally, yet as a rule they are to a certain extent true. Accordingly, Judah contributed essentially to the preservation of Judaism and Jewry of his time.

The best known accomplishment of Judah was the redaction of the Mishnah. Was it this that the Talmud had in mind when it compared Judah to the great saviors of the past? In order to answer this question, we have to scrutinize the significance of Judah's Mishnah.

What circumstances led Judah to the redaction of his Mishnah? Why did his Mishnah become the basic Mishnah, though other editions had also been composed? [155] What was the impact of Judah's Mishnah upon Judaism?

The sources do not spell out clearly the reason or reasons for Judah's endeavor in creating the Mishnah. Nonetheless, a satisfactory answer can be found by comparing the Mishnah with other tannaitic literature, by considering the implications of some casual, but relevant utterances, and by considering the paramount importance of Judah's Mishnah in the schools of Palestine and Babylonia.

A wise man such as Judah certainly learned from the historical circumstances of his time. He foresaw the possibility of another break in the continuity of school activities and wanted therefore to forestall a repetition of the loss resulting from such breaks. This, therefore, may have been at least one of his reasons for compiling a Mishnah collection. Such a Mishnah could serve its purpose best if committed to writing. While the question whether the Mishnah of Judah was committed to writing at the time of its redaction is controversial,[156] internal evidence indicates that it existed in written form either at Judah's time or shortly after his death. The Tosefta, compiled not long after the redaction of the Mishnah — probably in the first half of the third century c.e. — obviously presupposes a written Mishnah.[157]

Why did Judah's Mishnah, in contrast to other Mishnah collections, such as those of R. Meir, Eleazar ben Shamua, Jose, Ḥiyya, Hoshayah, Bar Kapparah, and others, not merely gain prominence, but supplant all the other Mishnah collections?

The principal reason was undoubtedly the fact that Judah's Mishnah was basically different from the other collections. The other Mishnah collections were works of individual sages who considered exclusively or predominantly the views and traditions of their own respective schools.[158] One of the purposes of Judah was obviously to create a Mishnah that was acceptable to the various local academies which directed and regulated Jewish life in their own respective districts and thus to work toward the unification of Jewish life.

Was Judah's intention in composing the Mishnah to make a compilation of existing traditions, or to create a code of laws? A comparison with kindred literature, particularly the Tosefta, shows that Judah's intention was to create a code of more important laws and to include also some basic traditions and beliefs. For this reason, he reduced greatly the contents of his *Vorlagen*[159] by the following redactorial steps: omission or abbreviation of numerous details such as definitions, exegeses, examples, generalizations, reasons for certain laws, and actual cases, omission of the historical background of a number of Halakhoth, and shortening of many background stories or reports. The Mishnah often reduces the number of different opinions uttered in a controversy, and also shortens the retained parts of the controversies, mostly giving just the views but not the arguments, or, if given, abbreviating the arguments. Most significant are the numerous instances in which the Mishnah omits the entire controversy and gives but one view in an anonymous form, or where the Mishnah omits the author or transmitter of a law.[160]

All these editorial activities prove that the intention of the redactor(s) of the Mishnah was not to create a mere collection of traditions, but essentially and primarily to create a basic but not too detailed code. It has been the normal way of legislative procedure at all times that, when the view of an individual or school is made a law, the name of the individual or school is omitted in the codes. Instances in which the names of the authors (or transmitters) of laws are recorded in the codes are less frequent. In a number of cases the authors of laws were certainly unknown to the redactor of the Mishnah. However, we are considering now merely those instances where the *Vorlagen* include the names of men who held a certain viewpoint with regard to a law. Whether they were the actual originators of this viewpoint or merely transmitters is not even important — our Mishnah omits their names.

More conclusive in this respect are relevant explicit statements of the Talmud, for example:

אמר רבי חייא בר אבא א״ר יוחנן, ראה רבי דבריו של ר״מ באותו
ואת בנו ושנאו בלשון חכמים ודרבי שמעון בכסוי הדם ושנאו בלשון
חכמים.

In one case, Rabbi approved the view of R. Meir and recorded it as that of the sages, in another case he approved of R. Simon's view and recorded it as that of the sages.[161] Recording a view as that of the sages means accepting it as the law, and corresponds precisely to the anonymous formulation of the law.[162] The author of the statement under discussion is Rabbi Johanan Bar Nappaḥa, the greatest Palestinian Amora and a disciple of Judah I in his younger years. In matters of authorship,[163] he is a reliable spokesman.

How did Judah go about redacting his Mishnah? While some statements, such as "Behold, who redacted the Mishnah? Rabbi." [164] or "He who arranged the Mishnah" [165] may be understood as meaning that he did this work alone, there is abundant proof to the contrary. Instances in which the law was decided by majority vote of Judah and his Court are on record. A few cases here will suffice.

1) "Rabbi summoned a Court, and they voted that if the land was in the possession of the *Sicaricon* for twelve months whoever buys it first acquires it, but has to give to the former owners one fourth of the land or [and] one fourth of the money, etc." [166]

2) "It once happened that Rabbi and R. Ishmael, son of R. Jose

241

and R. Eliezer Ha-Qappar tarried in the store of Pazzi in Lud, and Pinḥas ben Jair was sitting before them. They said to him: What about Ashkelon? [in respect to certain aspects of Jewish law restricted to the land of Israel]. . . . They said to him: If this is so come and let us vote about it to exempt it from tithes [i.e., Ashkelon should be considered as foreign soil in regard to tithes]. R. Jishmael son of R. Jose did not vote with them. When he left, Rabbi said to him: Why did you not vote with us? He replied: Regarding a matter which I formerly declared unclean, I changed my mind and declared it clean. Therefore I did not want [to vote for leniency] in regard to the tithes too, being afraid of the *Beth Din Ha-Gadol* lest they bash my head." [167]

3) "Rabbi and his Court voted on Qeni and declared it clean." [168] That means, a place bearing the name Qeni was in matters of defilement not to be considered as part of the land of Israel.

4) Rabbi and his Court permitted the purchase of greens immediately after the sabbatical year.[169]

The instances which show explicitly that a law incorporated in our Mishnah was decided by the majority vote of Judah's court are, on the one hand, quite revealing, while, on the other hand, they leave many questions unanswered.

They reveal that the court Judah summoned is not identical with the *Beth Din Ha-Gadol.* Passage 2 shows clearly that Judah's Court was a small body which we may call a committee. The fact that one of its members refrained from voting because he was afraid of the *Beth Din Ha-Gadol,* may or may not mean that the final decision was in its hands. In any case, it indicates that it reviewed and criticized the actions of the committee members.

A controversial issue is the question whether every law included in the Mishnah was passed by Judah's *Beth Din* (or also required the endorsement of the *Beth Din Ha-Gadol*), or whether this was the procedure for exceptions only. Ch. Tchernowitz believes that a decision by vote was needed only for the issuance of *Taqqanoth* and *Gezeroth,* but not for the redaction of the Mishnah. It is true that the anonymous Halakhoth of the Mishnah generally represent the views of the majority, although no formal vote was taken. Judah often accepted the view of an individual, but in such cases he added his own consent to make it a quasi-majority opinion.[170]

In contrast to Tchernowitz, other scholars believe that the redaction of the Mishnah was done throughout by Judah in conjunction with his *Beth Din*.[171]

Apart from the passages where Judah (Rabbi) is named in connection with passing a law by vote, there are many other instances of legislation by voting on simple Halakhoth and not on *Taqqanoth* and *Gezeroth*. Zuri believes that in most cases where the expression רבותינו "our masters" is used, a halakhic decision by vote is implied.[172]

In our opinion the decisive question is not whether or not a formal vote was taken in every instance but that, as a rule, the majority opinion was accepted as the Halakhah. Illustrative in this respect is Tos. *Ahiluth* XVIII,16 (617) where it is stated that Caesarea, which hitherto had been considered with regard to certain halakhic matters as part of Jewish Palestine, was exempted by the sages from these laws without a vote. This indicates that when there was an obvious majority, no formal vote was required for the establishment of a new law. However, in judicial matters "voice vote" was not as a rule sufficient. According to the Tosefta, if there was no traditional law in a case before the court, the court decided the case by vote, thus establishing a precedent, a case law.[173]

The view that the Mishnah was not written as a code at all, but that it is merely a collection of laws and other traditions since it contains not anonymous laws exclusively but also many controversies, opinions of individuals, and non-halakhic passages, is erroneous. True, it is not a modern code, or a code issued by an authority possessing political power able to enforce its dicta. Judah's authority was essentially a spiritual one and he had to proceed, therefore, cautiously and wisely. Needing the cooperation of the leading sages and the established schools, he had to include many names, views and traditions of prominent schools and sages, thus making his Mishnah acceptable to the various schools and scholars as an impartial compilation of basic law and tradition. The best proof of the fact that Judah did not intend to make a mere collection of traditions, or to write a personal Mishnah, is the fact that most of Judah's own views are not included in his Mishnah, neither in anonymous form nor explicitly.[174] This tells us unequivocally that Judah in redacting the Mishnah accepted the majority view even if it opposed his own. An explicit case to this effect is found in Tosefta Ḥag. I,1 stating that "The sages decided the issue in favor of R. Judah [son of Ilai]" against Rabbi. The Mishnah (ibid. I,1) took cognizance of this decision and gives R. Judah (ben Ilai's) view, disregarding Judah (the Prince).[175] How open-minded Judah was is evidenced by the occasional admission (unusual among scholars) that the view of his opponents is superior to his own.[176]

A mere collection of a limited amount of traditions, as some believe the Mishnah was, could never have become *the* basic concern of all the academies in Palestine as well as in Babylonia.

We referred to some of the circumstances that Judah may have had in mind when he undertook the task of redacting the Mishnah, such as the persecutions, the political unrest of his time, and his intention to work toward unification of Jewish life and thought, and centralization of Jewish religious leadership. Besides all this, however, we have to keep in mind that the Jews of Palestine did not live behind Chinese walls, but had daily contacts, material and spiritual, with the non-Jewish peoples of the land. It is a well-known fact that the Princes (and some other rabbis) maintained close contact with the culture of their surroundings.[177] Therefore, it is not impossible that external influence was among the factors that prompted Judah, perhaps subconsciously, to create his Mishnah. We have to keep in mind that Judah's time was also the period in which Christianity consolidated its early traditions by sifting and compiling them. Therefore, it may be more than a coincidence that Judah's redaction of the Mishnah is paralleled, to a certain extent, by a corresponding endeavor of St. Irenaeus, ca. 140–200 C.E., i.e., an exact contemporary of Judah I. St. Irenaeus presented Christianity for the first time in a systematic form, and this was about the same time Judah edited his Mishnah.[178]

The compilation of Judah's Mishnah was decisive not merely for the history of the Halakhah, but likewise for the history of Judaism in various respects. The most important consequence of the general acceptance of the Mishnah was that it contributed essentially toward the unification of Jewish life and thought by serving as a guide and basis for all subsequent activities of the academies. In proceeding in the direction shown by the Mishnah redactors, the academies were able to make substantial gains toward the unification of the Halakhah. The main reason for this was that after the close of the tannaitic epoch the various schools which Judah had to consider in compiling his Mishnah existed no longer. Consequently, the academies could proceed unhampered towards the creation of a unified Halakhah.[179]

The acceptance of Judah's Mishnah had other consequences too, not all of them foreseen or desired by Judah and his colleagues. One of the important consequences of the acceptance of Judah's Mishnah was that the Mishnah collections of the district-academies lost their significance and were later supplanted by Judah's Mishnah. Instead of writing new Mishnah collections, the schools concentrated on the interpretation and halakhic clarification of Judah's Mishnah. Quite instructive in this respect is P. *Horayoth* III,5; 48c "Always pursue the study of the Mishnah, more so than that of the 'Talmud' [discussion of tannaitic materials]. This, however, was right only before Rabbi had included [in his Mishnah] most of the Mishnah collections.[180] But after Rabbi had incorporated most of the Mishnah collections, pursue the Talmud more than the Mishnah."[181]

The consequences of the edition of the Mishnah which were unforeseen and undesired from the viewpoint of its editors were the following:

1) With the basic book of tannaitic law and learning in their hand, the Babylonian academies were no longer dependent on the Palestinian schools. This fact, in combination with the unfavorable political climate in Palestine, resulted in a shift of the center of Jewish learning from Palestine to Babylonia.

2) Since Judah's Mishnah was adopted as *the* basic text and law book of Rabbinic Judaism, the academies now concentrated on the interpretation and clarification of this book. As the language of interpreting the biblical books was the vernacular, i.e., Aramaic (Targum), so was the language of the Mishnah interpretation the vernacular, i.e., Aramaic. This must have been most undesirable for Judah, a fanatic concerning the Hebrew language, in whose home

even the maidservants spoke Hebrew.[182] Judah himself once re-
marked "Why speak Aramaic לשון סורסי [lit. Syriac] in the land
of Israel. One should use either Hebrew or Greek." [183]

Considering the decisive impact of the Mishnah upon Jewish life
and thought, and its influence toward unity, we may safely assume
that it was mainly because of his Mishnah that Judah was considered as one of the saviors of Judaism, ranking (with some exaggeration) with the Hasmoneans.

In another source Judah is compared to Moses:[184] "From the days
of Moses to the days of Rabbi we do not find Torah and greatness
[leadership] [185] in one place [person]."

The statements recognizing Judah's greatness and his decisive
contribution to the preservation of Rabbinic Judaism, which we have
discussed so far, were made by Amoraim, who were primarily interested in Judah's accomplishments that contributed toward the
preservation of Judaism throughout the ages. However, to understand fully Judah's role in the development of Judaism, his activities
of immediate consequence in his own time must be considered, too.
These activities may be divided in two principal categories: 1)
Measures aimed at strengthening the bonds of Rabbinic Judaism
in order to prevent sect-breeding schools and groups or other sources
of chaos. 2) Measures aimed at adjusting the Halakhah to the needs
of the time.

1) In regard to the first category, Judah undertook steps to concentrate more power in his own hands. The most important measure
in this respect concerned the ordination.

Prior to Judah's innovation, any rabbi could ordain his disciples.
This fact and subsequent changes are related in P. *Sanh.* I,2; 19a:
"Rabbi Ba said: First, every [rabbi] ordained his disciples. For ex-
ample, Rabban Johanan ben Zakkai ordained Rabbi [E]liezer and
R. Joshua. R. Joshua ordained R. Akiba. Rabbi Akiba ordained
R. Meir and R. Simon. . . . Later, they bestowed honor to this
House [the Nasi, i.e., Judah Ha-Nasi] and said: The ordination by
a *Beth Din* without the consent of the Nasi has no validity but the
ordination of the Nasi without the consent of the *Beth Din* does
have validity. Later an ordinance was made that the *Beth Din*

could not ordain without the consent of the Nasi and that the Nasi must not ordain without the consent of the *Beth Din*." [186]

Whereas the period of the first two phases of the ordination in this passage was clearly that of Judah, the time of the third phase cannot be determined. It is certain merely that the period in question was one after Judah's death, probably the third century.

The source just cited does not include all the changes made at Judah's time regarding the ordination. Other sources inform us that Judah executed the ordination alone, and do not mention that he sought the consent of the *Beth Din*. They also state that he ordained but two men every year.[187] Also he himself retained the right to revoke the ordination if the ordained man proved to be unsatisfactory. By thus concentrating more power in his hand, he was able to curb dissent and disunity to a considerable extent.

Ordaining only two men a year for the entire Jewish community compelled him to be extremely selective and this may have accounted, at least in part, for the fact that he did not ordain some of the greatest sages of his time, such as Mar Samuel (who was to become head of the academy in Nehardea in Babylonia [Persia] and an outstanding authority on Jewish Law), and Ḥaninah bar Ḥamah. Krochmal believes that Judah used his power of ordination as a whip and he would not ordain a man who contradicted or corrected him. Thus, for example, when Ḥaninah once corrected Judah's reading of a biblical word, Judah implied to him that he would not ordain him as a rabbi.[188] Although we saw above that Judah often yielded to the opinion of others without showing the least resentment, the correction of a reading before the academy must have deeply embarrassed him. However, this may not even have been the main reason (ibid.).[189] In his later years, Judah realized that he went too far in restricting the number of ordinands to two in a year and instructed his son and successor on his deathbed to discontinue this practice and to ordain everybody (qualified) without delay. He also told him to ordain first Ḥaninah, son of Ḥamah (ibid.), thus correcting his former mistake.[190]

Related to the problem of ordination is a regulation issued at Judah's time that a student must not render an halakhic decision, particularly not in the locale of his teacher.[191] This *Gezerah* may

247

have been issued at an earlier time during Judah's presidency, when the old procedure that the teacher ordained his pupils had not yet been altered.

Both the extent and limitations of Judah's authority are well illustrated in an incident related in B. *Horayoth* 11b: Judah asked R. Ḥiyya whether he would have to bring (under the prescribed conditions) the שעיר goat sacrifice required of the Nasi (ruler, king). Ḥiyya replied in the negative, since Judah had a צרה his rival and equal — the Exilarch — in Babylonia, i.e., he was not the sole ruler of the Jews, which is a precondition of the biblical law in question.[192]

This passage reveals two significant factors. On the one hand, it shows that Judah was not merely head of an academy or the *Beth Din Ha-Gadol* but, since he was compared to the Exilarch, he was considered to be the head of the Jewish people (in Palestine).[193] On the other hand, it makes it quite clear that Judah possessed no authority over the Babylonian Jewish community. His lack of authority in Babylonia is evident also in an incident in which nobody listened to his vehement protest against a lenient practice in Babylonia, and he possessed no power to prohibit the matter.[194] While the Babylonian Jewry in Judah's lifetime was independent of the Palestinian leadership, still it is considerably to Judah's credit that Babylonian Jewry did not develop a separate, independent brand of Judaism. Judah's Mishnah became the unifying force of the two great branches of Rabbinic Judaism, thus accomplishing after his death a feat he was unable to realize in his lifetime.

2) The following are among the measures of Judah designed to adjust the Halakhah to the needs and realities of his time.

Measures pertaining to the laws related to agriculture

Judah's measures in this area were dictated by the need of the time. The heavy burden of taxes imposed by the Romans upon the Jews [195] compelled Judah to liberalize the laws of agricultural dues and restrictions of the Torah.

For instance, Judah freed several Palestinian towns, which came under gentile economic domination, from certain agricultural duties and observances, such as: Beth Shan, Beth Guvrin, Kefar Zemaḥ, Caesarea.[196]

In carrying out these measures, Judah sometimes had to contend with resistance and criticism. Thus, when he freed Beth Shan from tithes on the basis of a testimony stating that R. Meir ate there untithed vegetables, his brothers and relatives strongly objected. His defense is very significant:[197]

> R. Joshua ben Zeruz, the son of R. Meir's father-in-law, testified before Rabbi that R. Meir ate a leaf of a herb in Beth Shan [Scythopolis, in Galilee] [without tithing it]. On this testimony Rabbi permitted [eating without tithing in] the entire territory of Beth Shan. Thereupon his brothers and other relatives [lit. 'his father's family'] joined in protest against him and said, "The place where [eating without tithing] was prohibited by your parents and grandparents will you regard as free?" Rabbi, thereupon, expounded to them the following verse, "And he [Hezekiah] broke in pieces the copper serpent that Moses had made; for unto those days the children of Israel did offer to it; and it was called Nehushtan [II Kings 18:4]." Now is it at all likely that Asa did not destroy it? Or that Jehoshafat did not destroy it? Surely Asa and Jehoshafat destroyed every form of idolatry in the world! It must therefore be that his ancestors left something undone whereby he [Hezekiah] might distinguish himself; so in my case, my ancestors left room for me to distinguish myself.

This answer is an important key to the understanding of Judah's theology which guided him and contributed so much to his success in preserving Judaism. It tells us, in effect, that it is an essential characteristic of our religion that it be not final in all of its details. It is designed this way in order to give later generations the opportunity to make contributions of their own.

Judah wanted to abrogate the sabbatical year altogether. He did not go through with his plan because Pinḥas ben Ja'ir, whom he consulted in the matter, would not consent.[198] However, he succeeded in introducing some leniencies concerning the sabbatical year:

Judah permitted the importation of vegetables from abroad in the sabbatical year,[199] which was hitherto prohibited as a "fence" of the law.

Judah permitted the buying of vegetables (greens) immediately after the sabbatical year.[200] He did this when he was told that two radishes, brought before him between Rosh Ha-Shanah and Yom Ha-Kippurim following a sabbatical year, grew from seeds planted *after* New Year.[201] The possibility of such quick growth is more than questionable, and Judah, owner of much land yielding large crops,[202] certainly knew that this was not possible. Yet, he wanted to lessen the burden of the sabbatical year whenever he saw a way of doing so.

Judah permitted, in contrast to other sages, the export of produce, etc. from Palestinian districts bordering Syria to neighboring districts in Syria.[203]

Measures pertaining to sabbath, the festivals, and fasts

Judah declared two leniencies with regard to walking to certain places מגדל, חמתא, גדר on a Sabbath.[204]

Judah permits the going out on a Sabbath with false teeth — he does not consider this as a likely cause of a transgression of the law prohibiting carrying objects on a Sabbath — while the sages prohibit it.[205] In this instance, Judah may have taken human nature, i.e., vanity of man, into consideration.

Judah is lenient in a certain case of the *'Eruv*, while the sages are strict.[206] He is lenient in regard to the moving of certain stones on a Sabbath, considering these (according to an explanation) as resembling chairs.[207] He is in agreement with R. Simon in limiting the scope of the מוקצה *muqzeh* prohibition for the Sabbath.[208]

Judah wanted to abolish the fast of the 9th of Av, but the sages prevented this by withholding their consent. According to another (later) account, Judah merely wanted to cancel a 9th of Av fast that happened to fall on a Sabbath.[209] S. Krauss connects Judah's attempt to abrogate the fast of the 9th of Av with Judah's Messianic ideas.[210]

Lenient in other instances of fasts also, Judah limited the number of fasts for lack of rain to thirteen "because one must not place too heavy a burden upon a congregation." [211] The qualification for this ruling is most significant, for it guided Judah on many occasions and is one of the reasons for his success.[212] Judah bathed on the fast of the 17th of Tammuz.²¹³ He was lenient also regarding the beginning of a fast.²¹⁴

Judah once said the Sabbath prayers while it was still day (Friday afternoon), and then went to the bathhouse, though for him it was already Sabbath. Later Amoraim claim, without proof, that Judah did not take a bath at this occasion.²¹⁵ Moreover, once on a cloudy day people recited the prayers of מוצאי שבת (prayers to be said after the Sabbath) while it was still Sabbath. Afterward the sun appeared in the sky. Judah then was asked what should now be done (i.e., whether the people should repeat the respective prayers at the proper time). He replied that since they had already prayed (though at the wrong time), this was sufficient. He did not want to burden the people with the repetition of the prayers.²¹⁶

Judah also did some planting on Purim which was considered objectionable by other sages. (See n. 213.)

Measures pertaining to the calendar

In this matter Judah introduced or, at least, completed a significant change. Before this change, the beginning of the month had been communicated to the Jewish people in Palestine and Babylonia through fire signals.²¹⁷ Due to interference by a certain category of people — the terms used in the sources vary: צדוקים Sadducees כותים Samaritans מינים minim, sectarians, or Christians — who made fire signals at the wrong time (either to confuse the Jews, or to express their own decision), Judah completely abolished the fire signals. In their place he introduced (or expanded) the ruling that messengers be sent out to the Jewish communities to convey to them the news about the beginning of the new month.²¹⁸

The consequence of this innovation was the introduction of the יום טוב שני של גליות "second day of the holy day of the Diaspora." Since the messengers were often unable to reach all the places of the Diaspora before the festival of the respective month, an additional day had to be observed as a holiday to be sure that the proper day had been celebrated.²¹⁹

Judah also introduced some leniencies regarding calendation, such as the following:

He permitted a murderer either to testify about the new moon (*Qorban Ha-Edah*, ad loc.) or to serve as a messenger (*Peneh Mosheh*, ad loc.).

He admitted עד מפי עד indirect testimony in regard to the new moon.

He permitted messengers to leave for their respective destination the evening before the official proclamation of the new moon if the time of the new moon was evident.[220]

Decisions revealing a tendency to strengthen the legal status of women and to further marriages

Judah was lenient in certain cases of betrothal, except when enmity within the family might have resulted from such leniency.[221] Judah thus proved himself to possess good psychological insight, as he promoted the cause of family peace.

Judah's stand in certain instances protected the woman from becoming an עגונה *'agunah*, thus becoming unable to remarry,[222] and in other cases Judah protected the women by not permitting stipulations to be entered in the bill of divorce.[223]

Judah (following Simon ben Johai's view) permitted a proselytess who had been converted to Judaism while less than three years old to marry a priest.[224]

Judah permitted a girl raped by a dog to marry a priest.[225]

Some decisions in other miscellaneous areas in which a tendency of welfare or realistic approach is evident

In a case of snake bite, Judah permitted the bitten person to eat food recommended as part of the cure though it was *untithed*, whereas Eleazar, son of Simon, did not permit this.[226] Judah did not want to endanger the life of the stricken man by delaying the healing procedure by the observance of rituals.

Judah ruled that if two sons in a family died after the circumcision, the third son must not be circumcised, whereas Simon, son of Gamaliel (Judah's father) required the circumcision of the third son, too. However, there is a Baraitha which reverses Judah's view. Ac-

252

cording to the Talmud, there was a change of opinion in this matter on the part of Judah.[227] The question is, which was his final opinion? Judging from Judah's basic tendency in matters of life and welfare, the conclusion that his lenient decision was the final one is the plausible one. (B. *Yev.* 65b. P. *Yev.* VI,6 does not give names.)

Judah realized, as did other sages, that the priests should not drink wine after the destruction of the Temple. Drunken priests are not allowed to serve in the Temple of Jerusalem (see Lev. 10:9). A sudden restoration of the Temple could not lead to a prompt resumption of the prescribed cult if the priests were drunk. Yet, knowing the priests would not observe such a prohibition, he did not prohibit them wine. Accordingly, the Talmud observes that the priests rely on Judah when they drink wine in our day.[228] Judah was realistic when he did not want to make a prohibition which would not have been observed anyway. His stand in this matter also shows that he did not believe in a sudden restoration of the Temple.

On one occasion, Judah refused to introduce a prohibition that would have been justified, if he had taken a certain occurrence as a precedent. "Shall we prohibit all the butchershops because of this fool who acted improperly?" he declares.[229] He did not want to introduce a prohibition because of one reprehensible incident. He certainly realized that such a prohibition would not have worked.

The measures and decisions of Judah, just cited, show Judah's endeavor to harmonize religion with life, thus keeping religion meaningful in his day. Livability, not leniency as it may appear on the surface, was his real motive when he made the above decisions. Thus, for example, his measure changing or endorsing the method of communicating the new moon from fire signals to the dispatching of messengers was just the opposite of a leniency. Apart from creating the need for an expensive host of messengers, it led to the introduction of additional days to the holidays throughout the Diaspora: To Passover, to Shavuoth, to Sukkoth and Shemini Azereth. The addition of a day to Rosh Ha-Shanah, which applied also to Palestine, had another reason.[230]

In instances not requiring special considerations, Judah's decisions reveal no definite tendency toward either leniency or stringency. They are decided by him on the specific merit of the respective case, as he sees it.[231] Occasionally he changes his former view and introduces a new Halakhah.

Whatever we said in this chapter applies to Halakhoth and measures original with Judah, and to those which he accepted (but which originated with other sages). However, in regard to controversial Halakhoth originating with other sages, he often suggested a compromise, accepting the view of both controversialists, each one under a specific set of circumstances.[232] This was one of his methods aimed at the unification of the Halakhah and the promoting of the acceptability of his Mishnah by the various academies and opposing sages. Valid evidence for Judah's sound judgment and foresight was the fulfillment of his expectations. Judah's activities terminated the significance of the private academies of his day. The heads and teachers of these academies raised no disciples who served as steady transmitters of the teachings of their masters as was the rule with regard to the sages of previous tannaitic generations[233] or as later happened during the amoraic period.

Judah's great accomplishments, coupled with his personal qualities, earned him a recognition not allotted to any of the other *Nesi'im* before or after him. Thus he is the only prince with the epithet קדוש the Holy.[234] The meaning of the epithet "holy" is not quite clear. Some scholars believe it is an adaptation of *Divus*, an epithet of the Roman emperors, while others hold that Judah's holiness had reference to his self-sacrificing labor for the national ideals of his people. He was the martyr of a lost cause, a persecuted man, as were Akiba, Meir, Jose, and others.[235] However, neither of these explanations finds real support in the sources. More conservative conjectures connect the epithet "holy" with Judah's saintly way of life, with his stature as a man of deep religiosity and high morality.[236] It is quite possible that *qadosh* is merely an attribute of high veneration without a specific denotation. This then would be comparable to the veneration allotted to him by Ḥiyya when he calls Judah "the Anointed" (משיח Messiah) of God.[237]

The same may hold true regarding the friendship between Judah and the Roman emperor Antoninus. This friendship, and all the

254

stories about it, may well be fictitious and perhaps should be taken as expressions of high regard and admiration for Judah.[238]

In spite of all his great achievements, recognition, and veneration, Judah admitted the superior right of Huna, the contemporary Exilarch of Babylonia, to the leadership of the Jewish people.[239]

Judah continued to emphasize the paramount importance of study even to the hour of his death. In this hour he demanded that thirty days after his death, the academy resume its sessions.[240]

In Judah's time the transfer of the center of Jewish learning, leadership and administration in Palestine from Judah to Galilee was completed and was firmly established there. It was to stay there for centuries to come. The last phase of this move was the transfer of the site of calendation (of intercalating the year עבור השנה) from Lud to Galilee due to a disastrous occurrence: "It once happened that 24 קרונות qeronoth ['wagons,' probably wagons with rabbis] of the house of Rabbi went to Lud to intercalate the year, but an evil eye fell upon them and all of them died at the same time. In that hour they moved it [intercalation of the year] from Judah and established it in Galilee." [241]

Where did Judah live? It is certain that he lived in Beth She'arim,[242] where he headed his academy, and in Sepphoris, where he spent the last seventeen years of his life for reasons of health.[243] According to a Talmud passage he lived also in Tiberias.[244] However, the accuracy of this account is questioned by some scholars.[245]

Like his predecessors, Judah, too, traveled to many places to promote the cause of Judaism. Among these were: לוד Lud[246] עכו Akko[247] לודקייא Ludaqyia[248] דיספורה Diaspora,[249] perhaps also בני ברק Bene Berak.[250] On these trips he was, as a rule, accompanied by R. Jose, son of Judah ben Ilai.

A later addition to our Mishnah enlightens us in very few words about the root of Judah's greatness: "When Rabbi died, humility and the shunning of sin ceased." [251]

Notes

I

SOFERIC PERIOD

[1] See H. H. Schaeder, *Esra der Schreiber*, p. 62.

[2] See Schaeder, pp. 45 ff. For history of the term סופרא *safra*, including Akkadian and Kanaanite parallels, cf. ibid. pp. 39 ff.

[3] Cf. J. Z. Lauterbach, *Rabbinic Essays*, p. 100; Schaeder, p. 71.

[4] *Taqqanah* is an enactment or institution promulgated by the leaders or the leading body of pre-Rabbinic and Rabbinic Judaism. The purpose of the *Taqqanah* was to supplement or modify the law in accordance with changing conditions, to provide for new situations, to improve religious and civil life and to harmonize it with the prevailing ways of life, both cultural and material. There are several types of *Taqqanoth*, depending on origin, structure, purpose, and significance.

Somewhat similar to but not identical with the *Taqqanah* is the *Gezerah*, an enactment of prohibitive nature. Its purpose is either to prohibit a practice or a custom in vogue, or to strengthen neglected laws.

Z. Frankel (*Darkhe*, pp. 27 ff.) divides the sages included in the tannaitic writings into two categories: 1) Sages who promulgated *Taqqanoth* and *Gezeroth*; 2) Sages who concentrated on Halakhoth (for various meanings of the term Halakhah, its history and significance, see M. Guttmann, *Zur Einleitung in die Halacha*). The sages of the first category end with Hillel and Shammai, those of the second category are the Tannaites beginning with the disciples of Hillel and Shammai.

While the originators and transmitters of the Halakhoth are often named, the promulgators of the *Taqqanoth* and *Gezeroth* of the early period are mostly unnamed. Later *Taqqanoth* are often associated with biblical passages while most earlier ones are not. The reasons hereof will be dealt with later. Some further literature: I. H. Weiss, *Dor*, II,53 ff.; Tchernowitz, *Toledoth*, I,174 ff.

[5] B. B. Q. 82b wonders why this law is listed as a *Taqqanah* of Ezra although

it is given in the Torah (Lev. 15:16). Then an explanation is given stating that דאורייתא הוא לתרומה וקדשים אתא הוא תיקן אפילו לדברי תורה the Torah requires the immersion of the man suffering from a pollution only for eating from *Terumah* and from the sacrifices, whereas Ezra ordained the immersion even for the study of the Torah.

[6] See Schaeder, pp. 55 ff. He points out that the talmudic tradition ascribing to Ezra the introduction of the Aramaic script was accepted even by the students of the early Church, such as Origen on Ps. 2:2; Hieronymus, Prol. Galeatus; see Wellhausen in Bleek, *Einleitung in das AT* (1886), pp. 508, 582.

[7] See A. Cowley, *Aramaic Papyri of the Fifth Century* b.c., No. 30, pp. 108 ff. V. Tcherikover, *Hellenistic Civilization and the Jews*, pp. 58, 120–21 points out that the "theocracy" in Palestine developed gradually. The transfer of authority from the satrap or vice-satrap to the high priest was completed only in the period of Alexander. "In the Persian period, not the priests, but the 'nobles' [*horim*] and the 'rulers' [*s'ganim*], who are frequently referred to in Nehemiah, ruled the people." Cf. also E. Bickerman, *Der Gott der Makkabäer*, p. 57. He maintains that the high priests became very powerful in Judea only in the third century b.c.e. Cf. also Rowley, *JQR* 36:183 ff., disputed ibid. by S. Zeitlin.

[8] See A. Kuenen, *Gesammelte Abhandlungen*, pp. 125, 161.

[9] See *ARN*, II, Ch. 1, p. 2.

[10] See Leopold Löw, *Gesammelte Schriften*, I,399 ff. (reprint from בן חנניה).

[11] Ch. Tchernowitz, *Toledoth*, III, pp. 74 ff. discusses various attempts at a harmonization of the conflicting sources. J. L. Maimon in *Isaac Herzog Memorial Volume* (Jerusalem, 1963), pp. 565 ff., makes the conjecture that the first group of men about to return to Palestine began to organize a leading body, headed by Zerubbabel and Joshua, the high priest. First, this body was small (it may have had nine or twelve men), but was already then called *Kenesseth Ha-Gedolah*. At the time of Ezra and Nehemiah the membership was eighty-five and was later increased to one hundred and twenty.

[12] Examples: *Ber. Rabba* 6:5 (p. 328); *Shemoth Rabba. Ki Tissa* 41:1; *Ruth Rabba* 4:5.

[13] The Men of the Great Assembly are often referred to in aggadic passages; see a list of such passages in L. Finkelstein, הפרושים ואנשי כנסת הגדולה pp. 45 ff.

[14] Lauterbach's explanation of "Soferim" in his *Essays*, p. 28 (The Sadducees and Pharisees), "because they occupied themselves with the *Sefer* Torah" has the real meaning of Soferim in sight, though the etymology suggested is not necessarily correct.

[15] Lauterbach, op. cit., pp. 27, 28.

[16] Weiss, *Dor*, I,55.

[17] Krochmall מורה נבוכי הזמן pp. 62 ff. holds that Soferim was basically the designation for the members of the Assembly at Ezra's time but had been continued although the Great Assembly was discontinued. Cf. also Ch. Tchernowitz, op. cit., IV, 29 ff.

[18] See, for example, Mishnah *'Orlah*, III,9 with reference to a certain kind of *kil'ayim*; Mishnah *Yev.* II,4 regarding the secondary grades of forbidden

degrees; ibid. IX,3 for further details on the same subject; *Sifra, Shemini* VIII regarding liquids causing defilement; *Sifre Numbers 73* concerning blowing of the Shofar.

[19] *Ant.* XII.ii.5.

[20] Cf. W. Bacher, *Traditionen und Tradenten*, pp. 47 f.

[21] Cf. Z. Frankel, *Darkhe*, p. 10, and H. Englander, *The Men in the Great Synagogue*, pp. 145 ff.

[22] See also R. T. Herford, *The Pharisees*, pp. 22–23.

[23] See discussion of this point in Tchernowitz, op. cit., III,58 ff. See also H. Englander, pp. 147–48.

[24] Cf. B. *Men.* 109b; Tosefta *Sotah* XIII,7 (p. 319); B. *Sotah* 33a.

[25] B. *Yoma* 39b:

Our Rabbis taught: In the year in which Simon the Righteous died, he foretold them that he would die. They said: Whence do you know that? He replied: On every Day of Atonement an old man, dressed in white, would join me, entering [the Holy of Holies] and leaving it with me, but today I was joined by an old man, dressed in black wrapped in black, who entered, but did not leave, with me. After the festival [Sukkoth] he was sick for seven days and died.

[26] The context does not allow us to read into the passage a controversy against the Sadducees; cf. Tchernowitz, op. cit., IV,139 f.

[27] Cf. B. *Ned.* 9b,10; P. *Nazir* I,5; 51c.

[28] *Traditionen und Tradenten*, p. 48.

[29] See S. Zeitlin, *JQR* 32:179, n. 130.

[30] L. Finkelstein, הפרושים ואנשי כנסת הגדולה, p. 48, believes that the *Gerousia* was changed into a *Sanhedrin* and admitted non-aristocratic laymen whereas the *Gerousia* had only priests and aristocrats as members.

[31] See Hoenig, op. cit., p. 151, and notes on pp. 11 ff. and 148 ff.

[32] H. Zucker, *Studien zur jüdischen Selbstverwaltung im Altertum*, discusses the term *Gerousia* in the light of its usage in Greek literature.

[33] See, e.g., Z. Lauterbach, *Essays*, p. 105. G. Allon, *Toledoth*, I,116.

[34] Cf. Zeitlin, *Megillat Ta'anit As a Source for Jewish Chronology*, p. 6.

[35] Cf. Josephus, *War* VII.x.1.

[36] See Zeitlin, *JQR* 32, loc. cit.

II

PHARISAIC-EARLY TANNAITIC PERIOD

[1] See D. Hoffmann, *Der oberste Gerichtshof*, p. 38; A. Geiger, *Urschrift*, pp. 121 ff.

[2] See Pauly-Wissowa, s.v. Συνέδριον.

[3] See references in Zucker, op. cit., p. 54, n. 1.

[4] Cf. E. Schürer, *Geschichte*, II,238 ff.

[5] See S. Zeitlin, *JQR* 36 (October 1945).

[6] See H. Wolfson in *JQR* 36:303, where he points out that the "elders" in the Bible were also counselors: I Kings 12:6–8; Ezek. 7:26; Ezra 10:8. They served as judges, too: Deut. 22:15–19; 25:7–9; Job 32:9. This remained so after the biblical period. For this reason *synedrion* acquired the meaning "court of justice." *Synedrion* is used in this new meaning already in pre-tannaitic Jewish literature written in Greek.

[7] A. Büchler, *Das Synedrion.*

[8] See J. Z. Lauterbach, *JE* 11:41 ff.

[9] See, for example, L. Zunz, *Gottesdienstliche Vortäge*, pp. 37 ff.

[10] See T. Mommsen, *Römische Geschichte*, V, Ch. 11. Cf. particularly pp. 511–12. See also Mommsen, *Römisches Staatsrecht*, III, 715–64.

[11] Hoenig's conjecture: *The Great Sanhedrin*, p. 272, note 19.

[12] Cf. E. J. Bickermann, *JQR* 37:387 ff.

[13] B. *Shab.* 15a; B. *Sanh.* 41a; B. *A. Z.* 8b; P. *Sanh.* I,1; 18a. Ibid., VII,2; 24b.

[14]

על הוראת ב״ד הגדול שבירושלם חייבים מיתה ואין חייבים מיתה על הוראת ב״ד שביבנה.

[15] See extended version with supplements in Tos. *Ḥag.* II,9; Tos. *Sanh.* VII,1; B. *Sanh.* 88b and an additional supplement in Tos. *Sanh.* XIV,12.

[16] ומגיהין אותו מספר עזרה על פי ב״ד של ע״א

[17]

ומגיהין אותו בבית דין של כהנים ובבית דין של לוים ובבית דין של ישראל

[18] See A. Guttmann, *Mischna*, pp. 147 ff.

[19] Patriarch Judah I was, according to talmudic and midrashic sources a scion of King David and was well aware of this (see pp. 266 n. 114, 296 n. 239).

[20] See Büchler, op. cit., pp. 69 ff.; Zucker, op. cit., p. 107 ff.

[21] M. *Pe'ah* II,6, "It once happened that R. Simon of Mizpah [thus] sowed and came before Rabban Gamaliel; and they went up to the Chamber of Hewn Stone [Sanhedrin] to inquire, etc."

[22] M. *'Eduy.* VII,4, "R. Zadok testified that if flowing water was led through [a channel made from] foliage of nuts, it remains proper [for certain ritual purposes]. Such a case happened to Ohaliyyah, and when the case came before the sages in the Chamber of Hewn Stone they pronounced it proper."

[23] See *Megillath Ta'anith*, ed. Hans Lichtenstein, pp. 342–43:

בעשרין ותמניא לטבת יתיבת כנשתא על דינא. מפני שהיו הצדוקין יושבין בסנהדרין ינאי המלך ושלמינון המלכה יושבת אצלו ולא אחד מישראל יושב עמהם חוץ משמעון בן שטח והיו שואלין תשובות והלכות ולא היו יודעין להביא ראיה מן התורה. אמר להם שמעון בן שטח כל מי שהוא יודע להביא ראיה מן התורה כשר לישב בסנהדרין. פעם אחת נפל דבר של מעשה ביניהם ולא היו יודעים להביא ראיה מן התורה אלא אחד שהיה מפטפט כנגדו ואומר תן לי זמן ולמחר אשוב. נתן לו זמן הלך וישב לו בינו לבין עצמו ואינו יכול להביא ראיה מן התורה. למחר נתבייש לבא ולישב בסנהדרין והעמיד שמעון בן שטח אחד מן התלמידים והושיבו במקומו. אמר להם אין פוחתין בסנהדרין משבעים ואחד וכך עשה להם (בכל יום ויום) עד שנסתלקו כלם וישבה סנהדרין של ישראל...

On the 28th of Teveth the Assembly [Sanhedrin] sat in judgment. Because the Sadducees sat in the Sanhedrin [and so did] King Jannaeus, and Queen Shalminon sat with him; but not one Israelite [=Pharisee] sat with them except Simon ben Sheṭaḥ. Some people sought answers and halakhoth but they [the members of the Sanhedrin] were unable to bring proof from the Torah. Simon|ben Sheṭaḥ said to them, "Everyone who is able to bring proof|from the Torah is qualified to sit in the Sanhedrin." Once a case came before them and they were unable to bring evidence from the Torah, except for one man who babbled and said to him, "Give me time and I shall reply to-morrow." He gave him time. He [the Sadducee] went and sat down for himself, but was unable to bring proof from the Torah. The following day he felt ashamed to come and sit in the Sanhedrin. Then Simon ben Sheṭaḥ appointed one of the [Pharisaic] disciples and seated him in his place. He [Simon] said to them, "The Sanhedrin can have no fewer than 71 members." Thus he did to them [day after day] until all [Sadducees] departed and an Israelite Sanhedrin was seated, etc.

Cf. Discussion of this passage, ibid., pp. 297–98.

[24] See Tos. *Sanh.* VIII,1

כל סנהדרין שיש בה שנים יודעין לדבר וכולן ראויין לשמוע ראויה לעשות
סנהדרי. שלשה בינונית, ארבעה חכמה.

[25] Cf. Tosefta *Sheqalim*, III,27.

[26] See, e.g., Hoenig, op. cit., pp. 62 ff.

[27] B. *Sanh.* 3b and parallels: אין בית דין שקול

[28] See Exod. 20:25; I Kings 5:31; 6:36, etc.

[29] For example, Schürer, *Geschichte*, II,264.

[30] See *Dictionary of Antiquities*, p. 1020.

[31] See B. *Shab.* 15a; B. *Sanh.* 41a; B. *A. Z.* 8b.

[32] See Derenbourg, *Essai*, pp. 465 ff. S. Krauss thinks that the *Ḥanuth* was the Chamber of the Sons of Ḥanan, see Jer. 35:4. See *REJ* 63:66 f.

[33] See Josephus, *War*, I,viii,5; *Ant.* XIV,v,3; Cf. B. Kanael, "The Partition of Judaea by Gabinius," *Isr. Exp. Journal* 7 (1957): 98–106. Josephus uses the term συνέδρια only in the *Ant.* version while in *War* he employs instead the term συνόδους. Thus he uses these words as synonyms.

[34] See also D. Hoffmann, *Der Oberste Gerichtshof*, p. 38, n. 1.

[35] See S. Krauss, *Lehnwörter*.

[36] See I. H. Weiss, *Dor*, I, Ch. 12.

[37] L. Zunz, *Gottesdienstliche Vorträge*, p. 37.

[38] Bacher, *Traditionen und Tradenten*, p. 50.

[39] Graetz, *Geschichte*, II,369.

[40] Z. Frankel, *Darkhe*, p. 30. Cf. Geiger, op. cit., p. 64.

[41] See *Magazin*, pp. 125 ff., where D. Hoffmann proposes that the unmentioned transmitters of the Torah were Zadok and Boethos, disciples of Antigonos of Soko, who officiated, at the latest between 270–230 B.C.E. The way Zadok and Boethos transmitted the teachings of their master resulted in the emergence of the sects erroneously named after them Sadduceans and Boethosians. For this reason, the names of Zadok and Boethos were omitted. This reminds us of the case of Elisha ben Abuya whose name remained unmen-

tioned after his aberration, and was designated merely as *Aḥer* "an other person."

42 The reason for his leaving the Sanhedrin and his later activities are obscure. See particularly J. Rosenthal. "The Identity of Menaḥem" (Hebrew), *Sinai* 56 and 57 (1965).

43 See more detailed version in B. *Beẓah* 19, 20 and P. *Ḥag.* II,3; 78a.

44 Cf. literature in L. Ginzberg, *Significance of the Halachah*, p. 248, n. 14.

45 See Frankel, op. cit., pp. 43, 44; Ginzberg, מקומה של ההלכה בחכמת ישראל pp. 18 f. believes that the controversy of the Zugoth dealt with the question whether עולות *Oloth* and שלמי חובה *Shalme Ḥovah* sacrifices needed *semiḳhah* at all. According to talmudic sources it is controversial whether this was the real issue. (See particularly B. *Beẓah* and P. *Ḥag.*, loc. cit.)

46 See Frankel, op. cit., p. 44, n. 6, citing from *Philon Fragmenta*, p. 646, ed. Mangey.

47 Ginzberg, loc. cit. suggests complex and weighty implications of the *semiḳhah* issue. It is unlikely that the sages of the second century B.C.E. reasoned the same way and considered Ginzberg's points.

48 Cf. Büchler, *Das Synedrion*, pp. 179, 180.

49 57 B.C.E. *Ant.* XIV,v,4.

50 See G. Allon, ספר קלוזנר (Tel Aviv, 1937), p. 164.

51 See Frankel, op. cit., p. 31.

52 Weiss, op. cit., I,105.

53 L. Ginzberg, *Commentary*, IV,44 makes the conjecture that Jose ben Joezer of 'Eduyyoth VIII,4 is not the Jose of the first Zug but a contemporary of Gamaliel II, as is also Aqaviah ben Mahallalel of 'Eduyyoth V,6, since all the men testifying in 'Eduyyoth are sages of Javneh. A further conjecture of his is that Jose ben Joezer of M. *Ḥag.* II,7 is likewise Jose II. However, the word "testify" does not necessarily refer to direct testimony. It is more probable that a sage of Javneh quoted Jose's testimony than that there was another Jose ben Joezer of Zeredah (or another Aqaviah ben Mahallalel) whose existence is nowhere confirmed. Therefore, Ginzberg's conjectures are not acceptable.

54 Ibid.

55 L. Ginzberg, *Significance*, p. 5 (Hebrew).

56 Tchernowitz, op. cit., IV,155 ff.

57 Op. cit., pp. 34, 35.

58 See Tchernowitz, op. cit., IV,170 f.

59 Ibid., p. 171.

60 Op. cit., I,132.

61 Frankel, ibid., points to the corrupt version in *ARN* II, 10.

62 Op. cit., p. 33 f.

63 See *Ket.*, end of chapter 8 in both Talmudim; Tos. *Ket.* 12:1 (274).

64 P. T. ibid. gives Simon ben Shetah's *Taqqanah* ordering compulsory schooling of children.

65 See Frankel, op. cit., p. 35.

66 See M. Guttmann, מפתח התלמוד I,86 ff.

[67] Cf. Büchler, op. cit., pp. 188 f.

[68] M. *Sanh.* VI,4: ". . . R. Eliezer said to them: Did not Simon ben Sheṭaḥ hang women in Ashkelon? They [the sages] answered: He hanged eighty women, whereas two ought not to be judged in the one day."

[69] See, for example, Büchler, op. cit., p. 189, n. 170, where he proposes that the witches fled from Judea to Ashkelon and were put to death with the permission of the non-Jewish authorities there. The method of execution may have been determined by the courts in Ashkelon, and Simon ben Sheṭaḥ was merely asked whether he approved of it.

[70] Therefore Tchernowitz' interpretation, op. cit., I,175, is not acceptable.

[71] See M. *Ta'anith* III,8; B. *Talmud*, ibid., 19a; P. *Talmud*, ibid., IV,1; 67a; P. M. Q., III,81d; Cf. also Tos. *Ta'anith* III,1 (218), where no names are given.

[72] Cf. Graetz, op. cit., III,2, n. 1. C, pp. 567 ff. "Antisadducäische Gedektage." See supra, n. 23.

[73] See Hans Lichtenstein, *Die Fastenrolle*, pp. 297, 298, 342, 343, giving the various views regarding the significance of the event of the 28th of Teveth referred to in *Megillath Ta'anith*.

[74] Graetz, op. cit., III,2, n. 16 points out that none of the sources, except the aggadic ones, states unequivocally that Shemaiah and Avtalion were proselytes. He logically proposes that it would have been most improbable for both Nasi *and Av Beth Din* to be proselytes in the same administration. Yet, he admits the possibility that one of them could have been a proselyte; and later tradition extended this amazing fact to the other member of the *Zug* as well. I. H. Weiss, op. cit., I,148 f., n. 1 attempts to refute Graetz and to uphold the tradition about the proselyte status of both Shemaiah and Avtalion. His reasoning, however, is forced.

[75] Cf. Graetz, loc. cit. This is followed, among others, by Tchernowitz, op. cit., IV,210 ff.; see ibid., p. 211, n. 7 for supporting literature.

[76] See Weiss, loc. cit.

[77] While Graetz believes he was Antigonos, see *MGWJ*, 1:119, Tchernowitz thinks it may have been either Hyrcanus or Aristobul, probably the latter; see Graetz, *Geschichte*, IV,210.

[78] Cf. Büchler, op. cit., pp. 178 ff. See further details in P. *Soṭah* II,5; 18b; B. *Soṭah* 18b, a parallel passage, does not cite the incident of Shemaiah and Avtalion.

[79] See Graetz, *Geschichte*, III,2, n. 16.

[80] See parallel version in Tosefta, ibid., I,3 (454 f.).

[81] See A. Guttmann, "The Problem of the Anonymous Mishna," *HUCA* 16: 137 ff.

[82] Rab Ashi tries to interpret the word הודו as not having the meaning קבלו "accepted," i.e., the sages did not accept their view.

[83] *War*, I.x.6.

[84] *Ant.* XIV.ix.3–5.

[85] See Graetz, *Geschichte* III,2, n. 16.

[86] In B. *Qid.* 43a Shammai quotes this principle in the name of the Prophet Haggai.

[87] For literature on the question of who was Samaias see in Ralph Marcus' ed. of Josephus, *Jewish Antiquities*, Appendix K.

[88] Some scholars believe that the court trying Herod was the Sanhedrin of the high priest. See, for example, J. S. Kennard Jr., "The Jewish Provincial Assembly," *Zeitschrift für die neutestamentliche Wissenschaft* 53 (1962): 41. Kennard calls this court "Ethnic Assembly." This view finds support in the fact that Josephus, who relates Herod's trial twice, does not designate this body as the Pharisaic Sanhedrin. However, this opinion is contradicted by the fact that the Talmud, apparently relating the same trial, never takes cognizance of the Sanhedrin of the high priest. This difficulty can be resolved, for example, by assuming that at the time of this incident no separate high-priestly Sanhedrin existed as yet, or that the trial court was composed of members of both the Pharisaic and high-priestly Sanhedrins.

[89] Talmudic sources dealing with this and the other matters of Johanan related in our Mishnah: Tos. *Soṭah* XIII,9,10 (pp. 319–20). P. *Ma'aser Sheni* V,4; 56d. P. *Soṭah* IX,11; 24a. B. *Soṭah* 48a.

[90] B. *Yev.* 86ab.

[91] See Z. Frankel, op. cit., pp. 32 f.

[92] I. H. Weiss, op. cit., II,28 f. suggests that high priest Johanan, in prohibiting the stunning of sacrificial animals, was combatting Greek influence.

[93] *Ant.* XIII.x.7. Johanan also heard a *Bath Qol*. See Tos. *Soṭah* XIII,5 (p. 319); B. *Soṭah* 33a; P. *Soṭah* IX,13; 24b.

[94] See Z. Frankel, op. cit., p. 41.

[95] Cf. I. H. Weiss, op. cit., I,108 f. He attempts to identify the Court of the Hasmoneans with certain groups mentioned in Josephus, *Ant.* XIII.v. and in I *Macc.* 14:27.

[96] Cf. I. H. Weiss, op. cit., I,110.

[97] Op. cit., p. 40.

[98] Mentioned in M. *Ta'anith* III,8; Josephus, *Ant.* XIV.xxi.2.

[99] See Frankel, op. cit. p. 42. See also A. Guttmann, *HUCA* 23, Part I, 455 f.

[100] See Kaatz, "Hillel und die Bne Batyra," in *Jeschurun* 9 (1922): 247 ff.

[101] See conjectures regarding origin, name, official standing, etc., of the Bene Bathyra: Z. Frankel, in *MGWJ* 1:115 ff.

[102] R. Marcus, in *JBL*, September 1954 lists five categories of Pharisees: A. Right wing — Shammaites. B. Middle — Hillelites. C. Left wing —Apocalyptic Pharisees. D. Unclassified — *'Am Ha-arez*. This is not a complete list. For example, he does not take cognizance of post-classical Pharisees.

[103] We shall not deal here with biographical details irrelevant to the history of Jewish tradition.

[104] A. Schwarz, *Die Erleichterungen der Shammaiten und die Erschwerungen der Hilleliten.*

[105] A. Guttmann, in *HUCA Jubilee Volume 1*: 453 ff.

[106] See I. Halevy, *Dorot Harischonim*, pp. 548 ff.

[107] See, for example, B. *Pes.* 66a.

[108] See A. Guttmann, loc. cit.

[109] See A. Schwarz, op. cit., ad loc., opposing Z. Frankel.

[110] Some Mishnah versions have Beth Shammai instead of Shammai. Tosefta *Ma'aser Sheni* II,1 gives a controversy between R. Meir and R. Judah regarding the correct version of our controversy between Beth Shammai and Beth Hillel. Shammai is not mentioned here.

[111] In offering this explanation, we accept the version since this is the best attested one.

[112] Op. cit., I,c,555 ff.

[113] Loc. cit.

[114] In recent talmudic literature Hillel's and Shammai's economic status, the tendency of their Halakhah regarding the various social and economic classes were re-examined resulting in a reversal of the hitherto accepted view in the matter. The older view claims that Hillel was poor, he and his school belonged to a lower social and economic class, and therefore favored this class in their halakhic views. The latest prominent scholar upholding this view was L. Ginzberg; see מקומה של ההלכה בחכמת ישראל p. 21 — English translation, "Significance of the Halachah for Jewish History" in *On Jewish Law and Lore*, pp. 77 ff.

Opinions to the contrary find increasing credence making it necessary to re-examine the matter. Among the followers of the latter view are David S. Shapiro, *Bitzaron* 8 (46) (1943): 302 ff; Ch. Tchernowitz, *Toledoth*, IV, 289 f.

In order to clarify the issue we shall examine first the pertinent sources.

B. *Yoma* 35b, a Baraitha, describes Hillel as a family man who spent a part of his very meager earnings for study purposes ("tuition"). While the passage has some embellishments, its basic historicity should not be doubted. It would be absurd to assume that the Baraitha, an early talmudic source, was ignorant of significant facts concerning an almost contemporaneous leading personality, or that it willfully reversed the truth.

Another talmudic passage, B. *Soṭah* 21a, also concurs with the above Baraitha. According to this passage (which includes aggadic embellishment), Hillel refused to join with his brother Shebna in business and preferred to study in poverty (see Rashi).

More important than these passages concerning Hillel is a passage about Beth Hillel and Beth Shammai. *ARN* I, 3, (ed. Schechter, pp. 14–15) states:

והעמידו תלמידים הרבה שבית שמאי אומרים אל ישנה אדם אלא למי
שהוא חכם ועניו ובן אבות ועשיר ובית הלל אומרים לכל אדם ישנה שהרבה
פושעים היו בהם בישראל ונתקרבו לתלמוד תורה ויצאו מהם צדיקים חסידים
וכשרים.

"And raise many disciples" (M. *Avoth*, 1:1). Beth Shammai say: One should teach only those who are bright, humble, of noble descent and wealthy. However Beth Hillel say one should teach everybody for there were many sinners in Israel who were brought to the study of the Torah, and from them came forth righteous, pious, and upright people.

This passage unequivocally shows that Beth Shammai favored the people of noble descent and the wealthy in suggesting that only they ought to be given instruction. This favoritism naturally did not stop at the instruction. It would be absurd to assume that in the area of halakhic endeavor Beth

Shammai reversed their attitude and showed favoritism toward the low classes and the poor. The writers who assume such reversal come to their conclusion by ignoring certain historical developments, and by citing exceptional incidents as the proof for their theory. The most important factors ignored by the above scholars are: The economic superiority of a class is not permanent, but is subject to change, particularly at times of exploitation by an occupational garrison as was that of Rome. Some scholars also erroneously call every or almost every rabbi after 70 c.e. a Hillelite, ignoring the fact that shortly after the destruction of the Temple Beth Hillel and Beth Shammai existed no longer. Thus citing later rabbis and equating them with the Hillelites and Shammaites of the past for "proof" is inappropriate.

The argument that Hillel must have leaned toward the socially prominent (mostly the wealthy) because he was a scion of King David is weak since the historicity of his Davidic descent is more than questionable. Hillel himself and his descendents prior to Judah I, The Prince, never claimed that they were descendants from David. Nonetheless, there were scholars, among them I. H. Weiss (*Dor*, I,155), who accepted the historicity of Hillel's Davidic descent. They supposed that political wisdom was the cause for not publicizing his royal descent.

P. *Ta'aniyyoth* IV,2; 68a (and its parallel in *Ber. Rabbah* 98:8, ed. Theodor-Albeck, pp. 306, 1258 f.) is the only source that explicitly states that "Hillel descended from David":

א״ר לוי מגילת יוחסין מצאו בירושלים וכתוב בה הלל מן דדוד. בן יצף מן דאסף. בן ציצית הכסת מן דאבנר. בן קובסין מן דאחאב. בן כלבע שבוע מן דכלב, וכו׳

Rabbi Levi (Amora, third century c.e.) said, "A scroll of genealogies was found in Jerusalem and in it was written: Hillel descended from David."

This passage, taken as a whole, is aggadic as evident from the popular etymologies given in it.

This account and others, ascribing Davidic ancestry to several personalities such as the Hasmoneans, Herodians, Hillel, Judah I, the Exilarchs, and others, are not to be taken as records of history but as expressions of great veneration. See especially Israel Lévi, "L'Origine Davidique de Hillel," *REJ* 31: 202 ff; 33:143 f. A detailed and recent treatment of the subject is found in Jacob Liver, *The House of David*, pp. 28–41 (Hebrew). Cf. also J. Neusner, *A History of the Jews in Babylonia*, I,175–76.

[115] Cf. S. Zeitlin, *JQR* 37:341 ff.

[116] See A. Guttmann, ibid., pp. 456 ff.

[117] B. *Pes.* 66a and parallels; cf. *HUCA*, ibid., pp. 453 ff.

[118] See Tosefta *Sanh.* VII,11 (427); *Sifra*, Introduction (end); *ARN* II, Ch. 37 (p. 110).

[119] See H. L. Strack, *Introduction*, pp. 93 and 285; D. Daube, *HUCA*, 22 (1949): 239 ff.

[120] See Ginzberg מקומה של ההלכה בחכמת ישראל *Significance of the Halachah*, pp. 102 ff.

[121] See op. cit., pp. 14 ff.

[122] Cf. also A. Kaminka פרצופו המוסרי של שמאי in *Bitzaron* (1940), No. 9.

[123] Ginzberg, loc. cit.

[124] Op. cit., IV,307 f.

[125] See Tchernowitz, op. cit., p. 304.

[126] *Yev.* I,10 (p. 241).

[127] Additional details in the Tosefta, ibid. are insignificant.

[128] *HUCA* 20:372 f.

[129] A. Schwarz, op. cit.

[130] See B. *Maḳ.* 23b–24a.

[131] See p. 69.

[132] I. H. Weiss, op. cit., I,179.

[133] Examples: ערוה, נאפים, זנות, זמה

[134] *Shelaḥ* 115 (p. 124).

[135] *Ki Teze* 234.

[136] W. Bacher, *Agada der Tannaiten*, I, Ch. 1. For aggadic exegetical discussions between Beth Shammai and Beth Hillel, see ibid., Ch. 2.

[137] P. *Pes.* VI,1; 33a. Tos. *Negaʿim* I,16 (619).

[138] B. *Pes.* 115a.

[139] See B. *Shab.* 19a. P. *Shab.* I,8 and parallel P. M. Q. II,4;4b, where the exegesis is given anonymously.

[140] B. *Qid.* 43a.

[141] B. *Pes.* 66a and parallels.

[142] Gen. 44:8; Exod. 6:12; Num. 12:14; Deut. 31:27.

[143] See pp. 74–75.

[144] Cf. A. Guttmann, "The Problem of the Anonymous Mishna," in *HUCA*, 16:137 ff.

[145] See I. H. Weiss, op. cit., I,184–85.

[146] See I. Halevy, op. cit., I,552 ff. and 602.

[147] Mishnah *Ḥag.* II,2.

[148]

א' ר' אלע' בר' צדוק כשהייתי למד תורה אצל ר' יוחנן בן החרנית וראיתיו שאוכל פתו חריבה שהיו שני בצורת... כדברי בית הילל... שאף על פי שמתלמידי בית שמאי היה לא היה נוהג אלא כדברי בית הלל.

[149] See A. Guttmann, "Hillelites and Shammaites — a Clarification," in *HUCA* 28:115 ff.

[150] Cf. especially Graetz, op. cit., III, n. 26; I. Halevy, op. cit., 580 ff.

[151] See Graetz, loc. cit.; S. Zeitlin, "The Eighteen Measures," *Bitzaron* 50 (1964): 2 ff.

[152]

ר' יונתן בעי ולא כן תניין שאין ב"ד יכול לבטל את דברי ב"ד חבירו אלא אם כן גדול ממנו בחכמה ובמנין. אתא רב אבון בשם שמואל לא שנו אלא חוץ לשמונה עשרה. הא בתוך שמונה עשרה אפילו גדול אינו מבטל מפני שעמדה להן בנפשותיהן.

153 Cf. however P. Talmud, ibid. claiming that the biblical prohibition of intermarriage refers merely to the seven Canaanite peoples.

154 For definition and history of the *Bath Qol*, see L. Blau, *JE* 2:588-92; for the significance of *Bath Qol* in the realm of the Halakhah, see A. Guttmann, *HUCA* 20 (1947): 363 ff. We are referring here to the role of the *Bath Qol* historically as understood by the talmudic sages and will not discuss the phenomenon as such. This belongs primarily in the realm of theology.

155 Generally assumed from about 80 c.e. to his death shortly before 117 c.e., or perhaps until the Bar Kokhba war, as some scholars believe. See *HUCA* 25 (1954): 246 ff.

156 M. *Ma'aser Sheni* V,7:

מי שהיו לו פירות בזמן הזה והגיע שעת הביעור ב״ש אומרים... וב״ה
אומרים...

Baraitha in B. *Men.* 63a:

ב״ש אומרים האומר הרי עלי מרחשת יהא מונח עד שיבא אליהו וב״ה
אומרים כלי היה במקדש ומרחשת שמה...

157 See A. Guttmann, *Mischna*, pp. 138 ff.

158

אמר רבב״ח א״ר יוחנן משום רבי יהודה בר אילעי בא וראה שלא כדורות
הראשונים דורות האחרונים דורות הראשונים ב״ש דורות האחרונים רבי
דוסא דתניא...

159

ארבעה אחים... ר׳ אלעזר אומר בית שמאי אומרים יקיימו ובית הלל
אומרים יוציאו ר׳ שמעון אומר יקיימו אבא שאול אומר קול היה לבית הלל
בדבר זה

160 *Darkhe*, pp. 45-46.
161 See details in *HUCA* 20:371 ff.
162 Op. cit., pp. 183 ff.
163 Op. cit., p. 55.
164 M. *Ḥag.* II,2,3 and parallels.
165 B. *Pes.* 66a and parallels.
166 Tos. *Yoma*, I,8 (181) and parallels.
167 M. *Sukkah* I,9 and parallels.
168 Tos. *Neziruth* I,1 (283) (also in B. *Yev.* 112a, reading
אין משיאין על פי אין מעידין על) for

בית שמאי אומרים אין מעידין על בת קול ובית הלל אומרין מעידין על
בת קול

"Beth Shammai hold that no testimony based on *Bath Qol* be admitted; Beth Hillel, however, admit it."

M. *Yev.* XVI,6 and Tosefta, ibid. XIV,7 (259) state anonymously ומשיאין על בת קול "(Re)marriage is to be permitted on the basis of a *Bath Qol*." This means, that Beth Hillel's view was accepted as Halakhah and *Bath Qol* was admitted as legal evidence of the death of a man so his widow could remarry.

169 B. *Ber.* 52a and parallels.

[170] See P. *M. Q.* II,1; 81cd. B. *B. M.* 59ab.

[171] See *HUCA* 20:383 ff.

[172] See pp. 102–3.

[173] ... דרב אומר לא עשו ב"ש כדבריהם ושמואל אמר עשו ועשו...

[174] Tos. *Ḥag.* II,11 (236) and parallels.

[175] Cf. P. *Shab.* 3c ff., I,4; B. *Shab.* 13b ff.; Tosefta *Shab.* I,16 (111).

[176] See Tos. *Yev.* I,13 (242) and parallels

... אם לקיים דברי בי בית שמאי הוולד ממזר כדברי בית הילל אם לקיים
דברי בית הילל הוולד פגום כדברי בית שמאי

[177] *Dezisionsmotive im Talmud*, pp. 6 ff.

[178]
אר"מ נמנו וובו ב"ש על ב"ה... אמר רבי יוסי עדיין מחלוקת במקומה
עומדת

[179]
אמר ר' יוחנן בן נורי... בואו ונתקן שיהא צרות חולצות ולא מתייבמות
ולא הספיקו לתקן את הדבר עד שנטרפה השעה

[180]
בראשונה היו אומרין... אילו דברי בית שמאי... הכריע ר' עקיבא לסייע
דברי בית הילל

[181]
אמר שמואל הלכה כר' עקיבא... אמר ר' יוחנן הלכה כדברי עקיבא
ורבא אמר הלכה כבית הלל

[182] Tos. *Shab.* XVI(XVII), 6 (135)
זכריה בן אבקולס לא היה נוהג לא כדברי בית שמאי ולא כדברי בית
הלל אלא...

אמר ר' יוסי עינוותנותו של בן אבקולס היא שרפה את ההיכל [183] Ibid.

[184] M. *'Eduy.* V,6.

[185] The second generation Tannaites considerd Beth Hillel as a school of
past history, as shown by a number of passages cited. Cf. also *HUCA* 20:370 f.

[186] Examples in: Mishnah *Beẓah* II,6 = *'Eduy.* III,10, three instances. See
also B. *Ber.* 43b and 53a. B. *Yev.* 15a.

[187] B. *Yev.* 15a. ותסברא רבן גמליאל מתלמידי ב"ש הוא

[188] See "Hillelites and Shammaites — a Clarification," *HUCA* 28:115 ff.

[189] M. *Ber.* I,3.

[190] Tosefta *Kelim,* B. B. I,12 (591).

[191] Tosefta *Niddah* IX,9 (651).

[192] Tosefta *Miqva'oth* V,3 (657).

[193]
אמר ר' יהודה הלכה כדברי בית שמאי אלא שנהגו הרבים כדברי בית
הלל

[194]
ומעשה בר' עקיבא שליקט אתרוג באחד בשבט ונהג בו כדברי בית שמאי
וכדברי בית הילל ר' יוסי בר' יהודה או' כדברי רבן גמליאל וכדברי ר'
אליעזר

See also B. *R. H.* 14ab.

195

תני רב יחזקאל עשה כדברי ב״ש עשה כדברי ב״ה עשה רב יוסף אמר
עשה כדברי ב״ש לא עשה ולא כלום... רב נחמן בר יצחק אמר עשה כדברי
בית שמאי חייב מיתה.

196

ת״ר הביאו לפניו שמן והדס ב״ש אומרים מברך על השמן וכו׳ וב״ה
אומרים מברך על ההדס וכו׳ אמר ר״ג אני מכריע (לצד ב״ש: רש״י) וכו׳
א״ר יוחנן הלכה כדברי המכריע

[197] R. T. Herford, *The Pharisees*, p. 199 points out the limited value of the N.T. accounts in this area.

[198] *Ant.* XIII.v.9.

[199] *War* II,viii,14.

[200] *Ant.* XVIII.i.3.

[201] H. Guttmann, *Darstellung der jüdischen Religion bei Flavius Josephus,* pp. 36 f.

[202] *War*, loc. cit.

[203] *Ant.* XVIII.x.6.

[204] See E. Schürer, *Geschichte*, II,484.

[205] *Ant.* XVII.ii.4. W.

[206] *Geschichte*, II,450, n. 1.

[207] *Life* I,2.

[208] *War* I.v.2. For Josephus' complex personality see particularly H. S. T. Thackeray, *Josephus the Man and the Historian*.

[209] *War* II.viii.2–13.

[210] Cf. *War* ibid., p. 377, n. 6, conjecture by Reinach.

[211] Ibid., 6.

[212] Cf., e.g., Tos. *Sanh.* V,1 (422–23).

[213] Philo, *Quod omnis probus liber*, XII,75; *Ant.* XVIII.i.5.

[214] See Geiger, *Urschrift*, p. 103, followed among others by S. Zeitlin, *JQR* 45: (1954), 83 ff.

[215] *Life* I,2.

[216] *ARN* I, Ch. 5; *ARN* II, Ch. 10, ed. Schechter, p. 26.

217

נוסחא א: אנטיגנוס איש סוכו היו לו שני תלמידים שהיו שונין בדבריו...
אלו היו יודעין אבותינו שיש עולם אחר ויש תחיית המתים לא היו אומרים
כך. עמדו ופרשו מן התורה ונפרצו מהם שתי פרצות צדוקים וביתוסים.
צדוקים על שם צדוק ביתוסים על שם ביתוס. והיו משתמשין בכלי כסף
וכלי זהב כל ימיהם. שלא היתה דעתן גסה עליהם אלא צדוקים אומרים
מסורת הוא ביד פרושים שהן מצערין עצמן בעולם הזה ובעולם הבא אין
להם כלום.

[218] E. Baneth defends the historicity of the *ARN* account in his dissertation, *Ursprung der Saddoḳäer* (also in *Magazin* 9:3 ff.). Eduard Meyer, *Ursprung und Anfänge des Christentums*, II,290 f., while disputing some details of *ARN*, agrees with it on an essential point. He maintains that Zadok, for whom the Sadducees are named, is the name of the founder or an outstanding teacher of the Sadducean party.

[219] *Essays*, pp. 87 ff.

[220] Cf. Lauterbach, *Essays*, p. 93, nn. 8,9.

[221] Ibid., pp. 109–10; see ibid., other etymologies.

[222] *Ant.* XIII.x.5.

[223] *Qid.* 66a.

[224] J. Wellhausen, *Die Pharisäer und Sadducäer*, p. 90 points out that in our incident (as elsewhere) Josephus gives an anachronistic explanation in maintaining that it was caused by the antagonism between Sadducees and Pharisees. Wellhausen, in rejecting this antagonism as the cause of the incident, (inadvertently) agrees with the Talmud.

[225] Cf. R. Marcus, "The Pharisees in the Light of Modern Scholarship," *Journal of Religion* 32 (July 1952): 153.

[226] *Ant.* XIII.xvi.2; *War* I.v.2.

[227] *Traditionen und Tradenten*, p. 50, n. 4.

[228] Baeck, *Aus drei Jahrtausenden*; "Die Pharisäer," pp. 188 ff. Cf. also S. Baron, *A Social and Religious History of the Jews*, II,342, n. 43.

[229] See discussion of the term "Pharisees": R. Marcus, loc. cit., pp. 153 ff.

[230] A. Geiger, *Urschrift*, pp. 104 ff.

[231] Schürer, *Geschichte*, II,487 ff. gives a weak explanation.

[232] *Ant.* XV.ix.3.

[233] See Geiger, *Urschrift*, p. 102, followed by most scholars, e.g., Strack and Billerbeck, op. cit., p. 341; Lauterbach, op. cit., p. 142, n. 49; L. Ginzberg, "Boethunians," *J.E.*, and *Eine unbekannte jüdische Sekte*, p. 196.

[234] Azariah de Rossi, *Me'or 'Enayim, Imre Binah*, III, pp. 78–79.

[235] Geiger, *Urschrift*, p. 103 suggests that the Essenes were the successors to the Ḥasidim mentioned in the *Books of the Maccabees* (I,7,13; II,14,6).

[236] See Schürer, *Geschichte*, II,651 off.

[237] See A. Geiger, *Nachgelassene Schriften* II, 23, "die Essäer bloss mystische Pharisäer." L. Ginzberg, "Eine unbekannte jüdische Sekte," *MGWJ* 57 (1913): 298: "Die Essener . . . keine Haeretiker, sondern Hyperpharisäer." R. Marcus, "Pharisees, Essenes and Gnostics," *JBL* (1954), p. 161 states that the Essenes and the Qumran-Damascus covenanters are gnosticizing Pharisees.

[238] *Jewish Studies in Memory of Israel Abrahams*, pp. 135–48.

[239] Cf. particularly: Ralph Marcus, *A Selected Bibliography (1920–1945) of the Jews in the Hellenistic-Roman Period* (New York, 1947), pp. 135–37 in *PAAJR* 16; "The Pharisees in the Light of Modern Scholarship," *Journal of Religion* 32 (July, 1952); G. Allon in *Zion*, N. S. 4.

[240] Cf. II Macc. (Pharisaic author) 13,14.

[241] See M. A. Levy, *Geschichte der jüdischen Münzen*, pp. 55 ff. See also E. L. Sukenik, "A Hoard of Coins of John Hyrcanus," *JQR* 38 (1947). A. Reifenberg, *Ancient Jewish Coins* (Jerusalem, 1963).

[242] *Ant.* XIII.xiii.5.

[243] Allon, loc. cit., p. 311.

[244] *Ant.* XV.x.4; *Ant.* XVII.ii.4.

[245] *Ant.* XVIII.i.6.

[246] Zion, loc. cit., pp. 311–312.

[247] *Ant.* XIII.xiii.5.

[248] Lauterbach, op. cit., p. 107.
[249] Cf. Dan. 12:2; Isa. 26:19.
[250] *MGWJ* 50:539–62, 664–706.
[251] B. *Sanh.* 52b.
[252] Büchler, ibid., p. 664.
[253] *Beth Talmud* IV,7 ff.
[254] *Ant.* XIII.x.6.
[255] M. *Sanh.* VII,2; Tos., ibid. IX,11; P. Talmud, ibid., VII,24b; B. Talmud, ibid. 52b.
[256] B. *Sanh.* 52b.
[257] See M. *Sanh.* VII and parallels, particularly Tos. ibid. IX–XI and talmudic *Baraithoth*.
[258] M. *Maḳ.* I,6; B. Talmud, ibid. 5b and parallels.
[259] B. *Maḳ.* 5b.
[260] Cf. Geiger, *Urschrift*, p. 140; I. H. Weiss, op. cit., I,138, followed by others, e.g., Zeitlin, *Horeb* 3–4:83; Finkelstein, *The Pharisees*, pp. 142 ff.
[261] *Susanna*, 41 ff.
[262] See p. 45.
[263] B. *Maḳ.* 5b:

אמ' ר' יהודה בן טבאי אראה בנחמה אם לא הרגתי עד זומם בשביל
לעקור מליבן של ביתוסין שהיו אומ' עד שיהרג הנידון א' לו שמעון בן שטח
אראה בנחמה אם לא שפכתה דם נקי שהרי אמרה תורה על פי שנים עדים
או על פי שלשה עדים יומת המת מה עדים שנים אף זוממין שנים באותה שעה
קיבל עליו יהודה בן טבאי שלא יהא מורה הלכה אלא על פי שמעון בן שטח.

Said R. Judah, the son of Tabbai: "May I not see consolation if I did not put to death a false witness in order to root out the view of the Boethosians, who said that the false witness could not be put to death until after the [innocently] sentenced man had been put to death." Simon, the son of Shetaḥ, said to him: "May I not see consolation, if you have not shed innocent blood! For the Torah said: At the testimony of two witnesses or three witnesses shall he that is to die be put to death (Deut. 17:6). Just as there are two witnesses, so there must be two false witnesses." At that time Judah, the son of Tabbai, took upon himself that he would never make a legal decision except in agreement with Simon, the son of Shetaḥ.

[264] Tos. *Yadayim* II,20 (p. 684); B. *B. B.* 115b; P. Talmud, ibid. VIII,1; 16a. See also *Megillath Ta'anith*, Ch. 5, ed. Lichtenstein in *HUCA* 8–9:334.
[265] Cf. L. Ginzberg, *Ginze Schechter*, II, *Kitbe Hageonim*, p. 470.
[266] Finkelstein, op. cit., pp. 138 ff. and notes give a brief review of several conjectures.
[267] See Tchernowitz, op. cit., II, 327 f.
[268] According to Geiger, *Urschrift*, pp. 142 ff., the Sadducean position is rooted in a case that occurred in Herod's family. This conjecture is not plausible.
[269] M. *Yadayim* IV,7.
[270] Cf. Lauterbach, op. cit., pp. 34 ff. Cf. also M. Joel, *Blicke in die Religionsgeschichte*, I,58 ff.

271 B. *Men.* 65a.

272 See Tractate *Sheqalim.*

273 Cf. Tchernowitz, op. cit., II,260 ff.

274 M. *Men.* X,3; Tos., ibid. X,23 (p. 528).

275 See Lev. 23:10.

276 Cf. Zeitlin, ibid., pp. 68 f.

277 Tos. *R. H.* I,15 (p. 210); P. *R. H.* II,1; Cf. also M. *Ḥag.* II,4.

278 The question of the original meaning of the passage is discussed extensively by D. Hoffman, *Das Buch Leviticus: Die Zeit der Omer-Schwingung des Wochenfestes,* pp. 159 ff.

279 *ab altero die sabbati.*

280 ه خٰلو ﻟٰٰﻌﻪﻟ ﻟٰﺴٰﺎﻟ

281 See *HTR* 16:41; *Tarbiz* 7:129, 378, 387. Cf. Finkelstein, op. cit., pp. 667 ff.

282 A. Geiger, *Nachgelassene Schriften,* III,294 f. For Karaites cf. Bashjazi, *Shabuoth* I ff (quite detailed).

283 Geiger, loc. cit: Poznanski in *Gedenkbuch zur Erinnerung an David Kaufmann,* p. 173, opposed by L. Ginzberg, op. cit., p. 478.

284 Philo, *De Specialibus Legibus* II,21,176, ed. Cohn-Wendland, V, p. 129, *De Decalogo,* 30, 160, IV, p. 304. Josephus, *Ant.* III.x.5.

285 Cf. Finkelstein, ibid., pp. 115 f.

286 Tos. *R. H.* I,15 (p. 210); P. ibid., II,1; 57d.

287 B. *Men.* 65ab:

... שהיו בייתוסין אומרים עצרת אחר השבת ניטפל להם רבן יוחנן בן
זכאי ואמר להם שוטים מנין לכם... אמר לו שוטה ולא תהא תורה שלמה
שלנו כשיחה בטילה שלכם וכו'

For the Boethosians held that the Feast of Weeks must always be on the day after Sabbath. But R. Johanan ben Zakkai approached them saying, "Fools that you are! whence do you derive it? . . ." He [Johanan ben Zakkai] retorted: "You fool, should not our perfect Torah be as [important] as your senseless talk?" etc.

288 Finkelstein, ibid.

289 Cf. *Mekhilta, Beshallaḥ, Vayassa,* Ch. 1; ibid., *Jethro, Baḥodesh,* Ch. 3; B. *Shab.* 8ab; Targum *Ps. Jonathan,* Exod. 19:16.

290 It may be of foreign origin, cf. Robertson Smith, *The Religion of the Semites,* p. 231 ff.

291 Tos. *Sukkah* III,1 (p. 195).

292 Cf. Zeitlin, *Horeb* (1936–37), pp. 69 ff.

293 Cf. talmudic versions: B. *Sukkah* 43b; P. *Sukkah* IV,1; 54b.

294 M. *R. H.* I,2; Tosefta, ibid., I,12 (p. 210).

295 M. *Yoma* I,5.

296 See Tos. *Yom Ha-Kippurim* I,8 (p. 181); See also *Yoma* 19a; P. *Yoma* I,5; 39ab; Sifra, *Aḥare Moth,* III (Weiss, 81b).

297 *HUCA* 4:185 ff; *Essays,* pp. 51 ff.

298 B. *Yoma* 19b. The Tosefta version, loc. cit., of the incident reads "Boethosians" for "Sadducees" and "Ḥakhamim" for "Pharisees."

299 *Journal of Religion* 32 (1952): 153 ff.
300 M. *Parah* III,7; Tos. ibid., III,8 (p. 632).
301 Ibid., III,5.
302 Ibid.
303 M. *Yadayim* IV,6; Tosefta ibid., II,19 (p. 684).
304 Cf. B. *Ḥul.* 77b.
305 Num. 19:16.
306 Tosefta, loc. cit.
307 M. *Ḥul.* IX,2; Tosefta ibid. VIII,15 (p. 510).
308 B. *Ḥul.* 122a.
309 Cf. Zeitlin, *Horeb*, ibid., pp. 75 ff.
310 Tchernowitz, op. cit., II,284–86.
311 M. *Ḥag.* II,5.
312 The emendation (or text ?) of Elijah of Wilna, ad loc., "lest he use them as a cover for the *Terumah*" violates the logic of the context and is to be rejected.
313 M. *Yadajim* IV,7.
314 Cf. L. Ginzberg, *Eine unbekannte jüdische Sekte*, p. 77.
315 Finkelstein, op. cit., p. 637 presents a summary of a number of conjectures. See also Tchernowitz, op. cit., II,287 ff. Zeitlin, op. cit., pp. 73 ff.
316 Tos. *Ḥag.* III,35 (p. 238).
317 P. *Ḥag.* III,8; 79d.
318 See M. *Ḥag.* II,7,8.
319 B. *Ḥag.* 26b. Cf. Zeitlin, ibid.
320 P. *Ket.* VIII,11; 32c.
321 Finkelstein, op. cit., pp. 128 ff.
322 Various lists of controversies are given, e.g., in Geiger, op. cit., pp. 127–49; S. Zeitlin, *The Sadducees and Pharisees* (Hebrew) in *Horeb* (1936); L. Finkelstein, *The Pharisees*, I,101–59, 281–85; II, 637 ff.
323 Cf. Brann, *MGWJ* (1876), p. 410, followed by Zeitlin in *Horeb*, loc. cit., pp. 86–87.
324 Lauterbach, op. cit., p. 103.
325 Cf. Z. L. Lauterbach, *Essays*, pp. 244–46, who refutes A. Büchler's contention (*JQR* [1913], p. 446) that in the beginning of the second century c.e. the Sadducees existed no more, by showing that they existed even later in the tannaitic period.
326 B. *Horayoth* 4a.
327 See n. 237.
328 See, for example, R. T. Herford, *The Pharisees*, pp. 118 ff.; Montefiore-Lowe, *A Rabbinic Anthology*, pp. 487 ff. Some scholars believe that in these passages *perushim* does not mean "Pharisees" but "separatists." See, e.g., S. Zeitlin *JQR* 43 (1953): 299.
329 See A. Guttmann, *HUCA* 20 (1947): 371 ff.
330 See B. *Pes.* 49ab for the most antagonistic remarks against the *'am ha-areẓ.*
331 M. *Yadayim*, IV,6.
332 Josephus, *Ant.* XV.i.1 "Pollio (Avtalion) the Pharisee and Sameas his

disciple." *Life* 38 "Simon [son of Gamaliel I] was . . . of the sect of the Pharisees." Acts 5:34 Gamaliel I is called "a Pharisee, a doctor of the Law."
[333] B. *Soṭah* 22b; see also ibid. 22a, a Baraitha with reference to Pharisaic women.
[334] P. *Soṭah* III,4; 19a.
[335] P. *Soṭah*, loc. cit.; also quoted in P. *Peah* VIII,8; 21a:

ומכת פרושים זה שהוא נותן עצה ליתומים להבריח מזונות מן האלמנה.
כההדא ארמלתא דר' שובתי הוות מבזבזה בנכסייא. אתון יתמייא ורבון לר'
אלעזר. אמר לון ומה נעביד לכון ואתון שטיין נפק כתובה. אמר לון נימר
לכון מימר עיבדון גרמיכון מזבנין והיא טבעה פורנה ומובדא מזונה. עבדין
כן ברומשא אתת וקרבת גבי ר' אלעזר אמר זו מכת פרושין נגעו בה. יבוא
עלי אם נתכוונתי לכך.

חד תלמיד מדרבי היו לו מאתים זוז חסר דינר והוה ר' יליף זכי עימיה
חדא לתלת שנין מעשר מסכינין. חד זמן עבדין ביה תלמידי עין ביש ומלון
ליה. אתא בעי מיזכי עימיה היך מה דהוה יליף. א"ל ר' אית לי שיעורא.
אמר זה מכת פרושים נגעו בו. רמז לתלמידיו ואעלוניה לקפילין וחסרוניה
חד קרט. וזכיה עימיה היך דהוה יליף:

And the wound [or "plague"] of the Pharisees. This refers to a person who advises the orphans to deprive the widow of the support due to her.

Subsequently two incidents are related to illustrate the "wound of the Pharisees." Both are acts of hypocrisy.

1) The widow of Rabbi Shobtai spent money for her sustenance quite lavishly, thus reducing the estate that ultimately would go to the orphans. The orphans complained about this to Rabbi Eleazar. He replied to them that the only thing that could be done would be to pay her the *kethuvah* (this would terminate her right to support from the estate of her deceased husband). A person who heard about this conversation advised the orphans to pretend that they were selling the estate (in order to induce her to ask for her *kethuvah*. As soon as a widow asks for her *kethuvah*, she loses the right of support from the estate). When she realized the deceit, she went and complained to Rabbi Eleazar. R. Eleazar replied that the advice given her was a "Pharisaic plague," and denied emphatically that he, in discussing the matter with the orphans, intended to advise them to deceive her.

2) A student of Rabbi Judah the Prince had 199 *denars*. Rabbi Judah used to give him the tithe of the poor once every three years. (A person having less than 200 *denars* is entitled to this tithe.) It happened once that the other students added (in secret) a *denar* to the poor student's 199 *denars* in order to make him ineligible for the acceptance of charity funds. When Judah was about to give him the usual charity grant, the would be recipient informed him (with regrets) that he was not eligible for the grant because now he had 200 *denars*. Judah, realizing what had happened, declared the act of the students to be a "wound of the Pharisees," and hinted to them that they correct the matter. This they did, and the victimized student received a share from the tithe of the poor.

[336] See A. Guttmann, "The Patriarch Judah I," *HUCA*, 25 (1954): 239 ff.
[337] See, e.g., Perles, in *OLZ* 16 (1913): 68 ff., col. 173–74. See also Levy, *Wb.*, IV,142 stating that better readings for פרושים *perushim* here are:

פושעים "sinners" (P. *Ta'anith* II; 65b) and רשעים "wicked ones" (P. *Ber.* II;5a).

338 See Justin Martyr, *Dialogue with Trypho* p. 276.

339 See *ARN* I, ed. Schechter, Ch. 37, p. 55. See particularly note 4; see also version II in Ch. 45, p. 124, which is closer to the version of the P. Talmud.

340 "Jannai" stands here for Alexander Jannaeus. See Josephus, *Ant.* XIII. v.9.

341 *Ant.* XIII.xv.5.

342 Ibid. XIII.xvi.1.

343 See M. *R. H.* II,8,9; B. *Ber.* 27b–28a; P. *Ber.* IV,1; 7cd; P. *Ta'aniyyoth* IV,1; 67d; B. *Bekhor.* 36a.

344 See B. *B. M.* 59b P. *M. Q.* III,1; 81cd. Cf. A. Guttmann, in *HUCA* 20 loc. cit.

345 See *HUCA* 20 loc. cit.

346 *Qoheleth Rabbah* I,8:4.

347 *HUCA* 20 ibid.

348 R. Hananel, ad loc., obviously takes *perushim* as meaning Pharisees. Why did Judah ben Dortai and his son settle in the South? Did he join the Qumran sect located there? Does the fact that his wife obviously did not accompany him have any significance? The sources indicate no answer to these questions.

349 The Talmud does not relate the incident quite accurately and completely. For Hyrcanus, Jannaeus is substituted. It omits the reason for the king's wrath, i.e., that the Pharisees punished the slanderer of the king with flogging only, which is the proper punishment for the slanderer of a lay person, not for the slanderer of a king (see Josephus, loc. cit.). It does not mention that the man who provoked the king against the Pharisees was a Sadducee.

350 *War* II,viii,14.

351 *Ant.* XVII.ii.4, referring to Herod's time.

352 See, however, G. Allon, in *Zion* (July 1938), pp. 301 ff., especially note 8a (cf. also literature cited ibid.), forcing the Josephus passage *Ant.* XVII.ii.4 to mean that the 6000 Pharisees refusing the oath were but exceptions. He does this in order to defend the thought that the Pharisees were the majority of the Jewish people, not just their teachers, as assumed by some scholars, particularly by those stressing the N.T. accounts, in which "Pharisees" apparently designates a select group of people, not the masses. While the N.T. terminology regarding the terms "Pharisees, Scribes, Elders, Rabbis" is in need of clarification, both Josephus and the Talmud employ, in agreement with the N.T. usage, the term "Pharisees" mostly with reference to a select group of the Jewish people. The disagreement among scholars is rooted, at least to a certain extent, in equating by some of them the Pharisees with Pharisaic Judaism (Jewry). However, Pharisaic Judaism does not mean that all the Jews subscribing to this Judaism are Pharisees, just as not all the followers of Rabbinic Judaism are rabbis.

353 For detailed discussion of the *'am ha-arez* see particularly A. Büchler,

Der galiläische 'Am-ha'Areṣ. Cf. also S. Zeitlin, "The 'Am Haareẓ," in *JQR* 23 (1932–1933).

[354] See also Josephus, *War* II.viii.14, "The Pharisees . . . cultivate harmonious relations with the community."

[355] M. *Demai*, II,2,3; Tosefta, ibid., II,2,3 (p. 47). See also B. *Beḵhor.* 30–31.

[356] See particularly the Baraithoth in B. *Beḵhor.* 30b and Tos. *Demai*, II, III.

[357] See Tos. *Demai*, II,12. M. *Demai*, VI,6. P. *Demai* VI,5; 25c. Neither of these passages includes the term *'am ha-areẓ.*

[358] See A. Guttmann, 20:270 ff.

[359] See Kassowsky, *Mishnah Concordance*, I, 648.

[360] B. *Ḥag.* 19b.

[361] B. *Ḥul.* 35a.

[362] An implication of our observation is that it would be a mistake to equate the charges of the N.T. against the Pharisees which are not limited to peripheral groups with the charges made in the Talmud against such groups as was done, among others, by Ralph Marcus in the *Journal of Religion* (July 1952), p. 163. Samuel Sandmel, in contradistinction to Marcus, correctly points to the fundamental difference between the limited criticism of the Pharisees in Jewish sources and the unlimited one in the N.T. See S. Sandmel, *A Jewish Understanding of the New Testament*, pp. 24–25.

[363] See Qirqisani, *Kitab al-'anwar*, Ch. 11 (ed. Nemoy, I,51–52), discussed by S. Poznanski, in the article "Jacob ben Ephraim," *Kaufmann Memorial Volume* (1900). See also L. Nemoy, *Karaite Anthology*, pp. 51, 334; *HUCA* 7 (1930): 328.

[364] See *MGWJ* 57 (1913): 153 ff.

[365] B. *Shab.* 15a informs us that Hillel commenced his presidency one hundred years before the destruction of the Temple. *Sifre Deut.* 357 states that he officiated for forty years.

[366] Graetz, *Geschichte*, IV, n. 22, p. 445.

[367] I. Elbogen accepts the date 20 B.C.E.–25–30 C.E. See EJ 8:42.

[368] See L. Ginzberg's conjecture ascribing a saying in *Avoth* I,17 to Simon, son of Hillel: *Commentary* IV, p. 38.

[369] Cf. Halevy, op. cit., I,c,707.

[370] See references in Mielziner, *Introduction*, p. 286 in a note by J. Bloch, which includes the erroneous statement that the passage in B. *Shab.* 15a gives Simon's name in a prayer. L. Ginzberg, op. cit., IV,38 and 44 rightfully objects to the conjecture that Simon I never existed.

[371] Graetz, *Geschichte*, pp. 445 ff.

[372] Ibid.

[373] Frankel, *Darḵhe*, p. 58.

[374] See Tosefta *Soṭah* XV,8 (p. 322); Tos. *A. Z.* III,5 (463).

[375] A. Büchler, *Das Synedrion*, p. 191.

[376]

מעשה שזרע ר' שמעון איש המצפה לפני רבן גמליאל ועלה ללשכת הגזית
ושאלו אמר נחום הלבלר... הלכה למשה מסיני וכו'

277

It once happened that R. Simon of Mizpah [thus] sowed [and then came] before Rabban Gamaliel; and they went up to the Chamber of Hewn Stone to inquire, etc.

377 See Büchler, ibid., pp. 124 ff.

378 Op. cit., p. 57, n. 8.

379 See H. Zucker, *Studien zur jüdischen Selbstverwaltung im Altertum*.

380 Cf. Zucker, op. cit., p. 126:2.

381 See, e.g., I. H. Weiss, op. cit., I,189.

382 Op. cit., 3.I, 351.

383 Ibid.

384 Ibid., pp. 351 ff. The seven Noachide Laws: Tos. *A. Z.* VIII[IX], 4 ff. (473–474) and parallels.

385 Anonymity of a ruling usually means that it was recognized as *the* law, *the* accepted practice. See A. Guttmann, "The Problem of the Anonymous Mishna," *HUCA* 16:137 ff.

386 The change from standing to sitting position while studying is discussed and accepted by M. Auerbach as a historical fact. See *JQR* 52, No. 2 (October 1961). The reasons for the change given by Auerbach are highly conjectural; his conclusions are, therefore, unacceptable.

387 M. *Kerithoth* I,7:

Once in Jerusalem a pair of doves cost a golden *denar*. Rabban Simon ben Gamaliel said: "By this Temple, I shall not sleep this night before they cost but [silver] *denars*." He went into the court and taught: If a woman suffered five miscarriages that were not in doubt or five issues that were not in doubt, she need bring but one offering, and she may then eat of the animal offerings; and she is not bound to offer the other offering. The same day the price of a pair of doves stood at a quarter [silver] *denar* each.

388 אין גוזרין גזירה על הצבור אא״כ רוב צבור יכולין לעמוד בה

389 See I. H. Weiss, op. cit., I,191.

390

רבן שמעון בן גמליאל ור׳ אלעזר בר צדוק אומרין אין מעברין את השנה
ואין עושין כל צרכי צבור אלא על תנאי כדי שיקבלו רוב צבור עליהן.

391 Cf. I. H. Weiss, ibid.

392 Cf. B. *'Eruvin* 68b–69a.

393 אגדות התנאים. (Jerusalem, Berlin, 1922), I,10.

394 Cf. *Tosafoth*, ibid., 61b s.v. הלכה stating that this Simon was not the later one, i.e., the son of Gamaliel II. Tosafoth's suggestion is supported by the fact that the Palestinian Mishnah, ed. Lowe, reads in the Mishnah cited "Eliezer ben Jakob" (a contemporary of Simon II) instead of "Eliezer" (i.e., son of Hyracanos), a later Tanna.

395 Cf. A. Hyman, תולדות תנאים ואמוראים III, 1163 for a listing of pros and cons without a definite opinion.

III

TANNAITIC PERIOD

[1] See *Sifre Deut.* No. 357 (7), p. 429.

[2] See e.g., G. Allon, *Toledoth*, I,54. Cf. also Derenbourg, *Essai*, p. 276.

[3] An alternate tradition is cited there as well.

[4] See B. *Sukkah* 28a; B. *B. B.* 134a. P. *Ned.* V,6 offers a different version. See also *ARN* I, Ch. 14 (p. 57 II); *ARN* II, Ch. 28 (p. 57); *Soferim* 16,8, etc. See also M. *Avoth* II,8, "R. Johanan ben Zakkai received [the Torah] from Hillel and Shammai."

[5] J. N. Epstein מבואות לספרות התנאים p. 400 (cf. also pp. 41–42) claims that the clause in M. *Sotah* IX,9 רבן יוחנן בן זכאי הפסיקן is a later stratum, added from a later Mishnah. It represents an untrue allegation because Tosefta *Sotah* XIV,1 does not have it. Accordingly, the practice of the *Sotah* procedure, though ceased in Johanan's days, was not terminated by his action. This explanation of Epstein shows that he is unaware of the fundamental literary character of the Tosefta, namely, that the Tosefta supplements the Mishnah and repeats from it only as much as necessary to make the additions intelligible in the given context. (See A. Guttmann, *Mischna*.) Epstein also misconstrues the context of the Tosefta. He claims that all the statements of the Tosefta, 1–9, beginning with משרבו, are by Johanan ben Zakkai. If this were the case, then the parallels in the Talmud where these cases are separated, would have to give Johanan's name in each instance. However, this is not the case. Therefore Johanan's role as a mere transmitter of a change can be ascribed to him, with some justification (though not with certainty since he still could have been responsible for a change which he transmits as a fact) only in Tosefta *Sotah* XIV,1, the only case (*'eglah 'arufah*, which is not under discussion) transmitted by him explicitly.

[6] The conjecture that Johanan ben Zakkai pushed Gamaliel aside in order to take over the leadership (Allon, op. cit., p. 64) has no basis in the sources. (Literature on both sides, Allon, ibid.)

[7] For example: Z. Frankel, op. cit., p. 65; Halevy, op. cit., I,5,52. Although Johanan ben Zakkai is never called explicitly Nasi, his performing the duties of this office has led most scholars to believe that he was. Among the scholars who claim that Johanan ben Zakkai was not a Nasi is Z. Frankel, *Darkhe*, p. 65, who bases his opinion on the fact that the texts of the Mishnah and Baraitha call him "rabbi," not "Rabban." This arguement, however, is quite weak, since there are texts in which he is called "Rabban." More decisive is the fact that he issued *Taqqanoth*, a prerogative of the Nasi. This fact Frankel tries to reject by advancing conjectures. These are: Before the Jewish-Roman war Simon, the Nasi, was too busy with political matters and entrusted, therefore, Johanan ben Zakkai with the performance of duties usually within the authority of the Nasi, among them the issuance of *Taqqanoth*. After the destruction of the Temple he became the leader of the Jewish people but not its Nasi. Because of the sorrow and confusion no Nasi was appointed imme-

diately after the destruction of the Temple. Whether or not Johanan ben Zakkai bore the title Nasi is in the opinion of most scholars of secondary importance. Decisive is the fact that he performed the duties of the Nasi.

[8] For example: Graetz, *Geschichte*, IV,14; Weiss, op. cit., II,34; Krochmal,
מורה נבוכי הזמן ed. Rawidowicz, p. 105; Allon in ספר קלוזנר p. 154.

[9] See *ARN* I, Ch. 2, p. 23; *ARN* II, Ch. 6, p. 19; *Ekhah Rabbah* I,35.

[10] See M. Stein's view in *Zion* (January 1938), pp. 118 ff., pointing out
the special political status of Javneh since Herod's time as the basis of Johanan's choice.

[11] See op. cit., pp. 59 ff.

[12] See Allon, op. cit., pp. 67 ff.

[13] See M. Guttmann אוץ ישראל במדרש ותלמוד p. 101.

[14] See M. Guttmann, loc. cit.

[15] See A. Guttmann, "The End of the Jewish Sacrificial Cult," *HUCA* 38
(1967): 137 ff.

[16]
... העיד בן בוכרי ביבנה כל כהן ששוקל אינו חוטא. אמר לו רבי יוחנן
בן זכאי לא כי אלא כל כהן שאינו שוקל דוטא. אלא שהכהנים דורשים
מקרא זה לעצמן, וכו'

[17] In version II we read "Joshua" instead of "Johanan ben Zakkai."

[18] Another version reads "Rabban Gamaliel." See variants in Zuckermandel's
Tosefta, ad loc.

[19] According to *Qoheleth Rabba* VII, Eleazar ben Arakh left his colleagues
for his new destination after Johanan ben Zakkai's death.

[20] Cf. A. Geiger, *Zeitschrift*, VI.

[21] However, the version in *Pesiqta de Rav Kahana* 12:2 omits him.

[22] See, e.g., Frankel, op. cit., pp. 65–66. The length of Johanan's presidency
varies, depending on the scholar dealing with the problem. The range is between two and fifteen years, i.e., it terminated between 72 and 85 c.e. See list
of opinions in J. Neusner, *Rabban Yohanan*, p. 172, n. 1.

[23] See M. Kleinmann, ספר קלוזנר p. 459.

[24] See, e.g., Allon, *Studies*, 267 ff.

[25] Cf. Allon, op. cit., pp. 255 ff.

[26] See M. Guttmann, op. cit., pp. 99 ff.

[27] *ARN* I, p. 21:
פעם אחת היה רבן יוחנן בן זכאי יוצא מירושלים והיה ר' יהושע הולך
אחריו וראה בית המקדש חרב אמר ר' יהושע אוי לנו על זה שהוא חרב
מקום שמכפרים בו עונותיהם של ישראל. א״ל בני אל ירע לך יש לנו כפרה
אחת שהיא כמותה ואיזה זה גמילות חסדים שנאמר כי חסד חפצתי ולא זבח
(הושע ו')

[28] Johanan ben Zakkai probably was not a priest. See particularly B. *Men.*
21b, Tosafoth (bottom). See literature pro and con on this topic in Mantel,
Studies in the History of the Sanhedrin, p. 31, n. 179.

[29] B. *Sanh.* 32b; *Sifre Deut.* 144 (ed. Horovitz-Finkelstein, p. 200).

[30] Tosefta *Ma'aseroth*, II, 1 (p. 82); P. *Ma'aseroth* II,3; 49d.

[31] *Qoheleth Rabbah* VII,7.

[32] See Bacher, op. cit., I,17 ff.

[33] See, for example, Tos. *Pes.* II (III), 11 (p. 159); ibid. X,12 (p. 173).

[34] B. *B. M.* 59a,b. Cf. *HUCA* 20:374 ff.

[35] Cf. Allon, op. cit., p. 67.

[36] Closest to regular prayer services come the services of the מעמדות *Ma'amadoth*. A brief survey of the history of this institution is the following: At the time of the Temple in Jerusalem there were twenty-four sacrificial units. I Chron. 24:7–18 lists the names of twenty-four priestly families constituting or heading these units. Tos. *Ta'anith* IV (III), 2 states that originally there were eight priestly משמרות *Mishmaroth* and eight *Mishmaroth* of Levites. Later (since David and Samuel) these numbers were increased to twenty-four *Mishmaroth* of priests, twenty-four *Mishmaroth* of Levites, and twenty-four *Ma'amadoth* of Israelites. In our Mishnah, however, these three groups (priests, Levites, and Israelites) appear as members of the same twenty-four *Mishmaroth* (M. *Ta'anith* IV,2). These units functioned at the Temple sacrifices in weekly rotation.

Originally, only priests were members of the *Mishmar*. See Chron. loc. cit. and Mishnah *Ta'anith* II,6 (see commentaries). Later the Levites were also included (see Tosefta, loc. cit.) and, to some extent, even the Israelites (see M. *Ta'anith* IV,2 and Tosefta, ibid. 3).

The lay members of each unit constituted a *Ma'amad*. However, in M. *Ta'anith* IV,2 "*Ma'amad*" is also used for a group composed of priests, Levites, and laymen, attached to the *Mishmar*. (This *Ma'amad* stood by while the *Mishmar* did the sacrificing.)

Probably the majority of these units lived in Palestinian localities outside of Jerusalem. When the time came for a given unit to function, its priests and Levites and some of the Israelites (this is clearly implied in Tosefta, ibid.) went to Jerusalem, while most of the Israelites remained in their home towns and held gatherings, i.e., daily services and read in these Gen. 1.

[37] See B. *Ber.* 27b–28a; P. *Ber.* IV,1; 7cd; P. *Ta'aniyyoth* IV,1; 67d., a Baraitha: "It happened that a student came before R. Joshua and asked him, 'Is the evening *Tefillah* optional or compulsory?' He said to him, 'It is optional.' He came to Rabban Gamaliel and said to him, 'Is the evening Tefillah optional or compulsory?' He said, 'It is compulsory'. . . When the scholars came to the academy, Gamaliel asked whether there was a dissenting opinion.

Rabbi Joshua said to him, 'no.' He said to him, 'Behold in your name I was told that it is optional?' . . . Rabban Gamaliel kept sitting and expounding and R. Joshua remained standing, until the people began to clamor and say to Huzpith, the speaker, 'Stop!' and he stopped. They then said: 'How long is he to go on annoying him? On New Year last year he annoyed him; he annoyed him in the matter of the first-born in the matter of R. Zadok (B. *Bekhoroth* 63a); now he annoys him again. Come, let us depose him. Whom shall we appoint instead? . . . R. Eleazar ben Azariah' . . ."

One of the significant implications of this incident is that the members of the *Beth Din Ha-Gadol* of Javneh possessed the right of electing and deposing the head of the *Beth Din Ha-Gadol*.

[38] Cf. Elbogen, *Der jüdische Gottesdienst*, pp. 250 ff; Allon, op. cit., pp. 167 ff.

39
שמעון הפקולי הסדיר י״ח ברכות לפני רבן גמליאל על הסדר ביבנה

B. *Ber.* 28b; B. *Meg.* 17b; (Baraitha).

40 Cf., e.g., J. Mann, in *HUCA* 2:269 ff.; Schechter in *JQR* 10:6.

41 Cf. *HUCA*, 20:384 f.

42 R. Gordis concludes, by comparing our Bible with the texts of the Dead Sea Scrolls, that masoretic activity existed already at that early time. See *Jewish Frontier* (April 1957), pp. 17 ff.

43 *Judaism*, I,86 f.

44 See B. *Shabbath* 115 ff.; Tosefta ibid. XIII(XIV),5; P. *Shab.* XVI,1; 15bc. See further L. Ginzberg in *JBL* (1922), p. 122, n. 19. Allon's reasoning (op. cit., pp. 172–73) that גליונים or עון גליון in the above passages means "margins" of the Holy Books is not convincing.

45 *Devarim Rabbah* I,1.

46 See commentaries on B. *Shab.* 115a.

47 Cf. M. Guttmann ארץ ישראל במדרש ותלמוד pp. 35–36; Allon, op. cit., pp. 159–60.

48 For example: B. *Giṭ.* 55b; ibid. 56a; ibid. 88a; B. *B. M.* 30b.

49 *Sifre Deut.*

50 Ed. Lauterbach, II, p. 188.

51 To the priests, not to the Levites. This change was made already at the time of the Temple. See B. *Yev.* 86b.

52 P. *Sheqalim* VIII,4; 51b.
דתני אין מקדישין ולא מעריכין ולא מחרימין ולא מביאין תרומות ומעשרות בזמן הזה.

53 A term for the produce under the suspicion of being untithed. The etymology of the word דמאי is uncertain.

54 See Tractate *Demai.*

55 See *HUCA*, 27:115 ff., "Hillelites and Shammaites, a Clarification."

56 See *HUCA* 20:370 ff.

57 See also Tosefta *B. Q.* VIII,10–12 where more exceptions are listed and the reason is given why no prohibition was issued against the raising of cattle; see also a Baraitha in B. *B. Q.* 79b.

58 See Tosefta *B. M.* II,33 and parallels: "Gentiles and shepherds of 'small animals' shall neither be raised nor lowered."

59 Tosefta *Yev.* III,3.

60 Cf. also A. Gulak, *Tarbiz* 12:181–89.

61 See Allon, op. cit., I,164 ff.

62 See, e.g., Tos. *Yom Tov* II,15.
אמר ר' יוסי תודוס איש רומי הנהיג את בני רומי להיות לוקחין טלאים ועושין אותן מקולסין בלילי פסחים אמרו לו אף הוא קרוב להאכיל קדשים בחוץ מפני שקוראין אותן פסחים.

R. Jose said, Thodos of Rome instructed the [Jewish] people of Rome to get lambs and prepare them as whole roasts in the Passover nights. They replied to him: He [Thodos] came close to making people eat holy meat outside [of the Temple area] since they call them "Paschal sacrifices."

See also M. *Pes.* IV,4: מקום שנהגו לאכול צלי בלילי פסחים אוכלין

"Where the custom is to eat roast on the nights of Passover they may eat so."
The purpose of this custom is certainly to commemorate the Paschal sacrifice
though the roast here does not necessarily refer to a whole roasted lamb.
According to Allon, *Toledoth*, I,165; M. *Pes.* X,4 "but this night roast only"
does not refer to the time of the Temple as generally believed, but to the
custom of the tannaitic period to eat roast in remembrance of the Paschal
sacrifice of the past. He supports his view by citing a Genizah fragment (Abrahams in *JQR* 1:44,47,49) in which the Seder ritual includes the question
regarding the roast and even prescribes a benediction over it (ibid., p. 46).
However in view of the fact that the eating of roast was merely a local custom
in tannaitic times the conjecture that Judah I considered this one custom in
his "Mah Nishtannah . . ." is not acceptable.

[63] See Allon, op. cit., pp. 165 ff.

[64] For example, A. Sammter in the Itzkowski ed. of the Mishnah (Berlin,
1887), ad loc. Friedman, מאיר עין להגדה של פסח p. 55.

[65] See E. D. Goldschmidt, *The Passover Haggadah: Its Sources and History*,
pp. 51–52.

[66] Tos. *Pes.* X,12:

מעשה ברבן גמליאל וזקנים שהיו מסובין בביתו של בייתוס בן זונין בלוד
והיו עסוקין בהילכות הפסח כל אותו הלילה עד קרות הגבר הגביהו מלפניהם
ונועדו והלכו להם לבית המדרש.

It happened that Rabban Gamaliel and the sages were partaking of the Passover meal in the house of Boethos, son of Zonan, in Lud, and they discussed
the laws of Passover all the night till the rooster crowed. Then they [the
tables and blinds of the windows] were removed before them, and they went
jointly to the *Beth Ha-Midrash*.

[67] See, e.g., J. Fischer, *Hazofeh*, X (Budapest, 1926), 238 ff. Sulzbach,
Jeschurun 4 (1917): 216.

[68] See particularly Graetz, *Geschichte* 4, n. 21, pp. 441 ff.; H. Vogelstein,
"Die Entstehung und Entwicklung des Apostolats im Judentum," *MGWJ* 49
(1905): 427–49. Same, "The Development of the Apostolate in Judaism and
its Transformation in Christianity," *HUCA* 2 (1925): 100–23; S. Krauss, "Die
jüdischen Apostel," *JQR* o.s. 17 (1904–1905): 370–83; A. Büchler, "Apostole,
Apostoli," *JE* 2:20; J. S. Zuri שני ספר, שלטון הנשיאות והועד pp. 124 ff.;
G. Allon תולדות היהודים בארץ ישראל I,146–147, H. Mantel, *Studies in
the History of the Sanhedrin*, pp. 188 ff.

[69] B. *Ta'anith* 29a. See also Midrash Ekhah Rabbathi 2.2.

[70] Op. cit., IV,131,433,445.

[71] Op. cit., p. 445.

[72] Op. cit., IV,131.

[73] See Halevy, op. cit., I.e.,362 ff.; Zuri, *Rabbi Akiba* [Hebrew], pp. 110 f.

[74] See Tos. *Sanh.* II,8:

אמר ר' שמעון מעשה בר' עקיבא שהיה חבוש בבית האסורין ועיבר שלש
שנים זו אחר זו

"Rabbi Simon [a disciple of Akiba] said: It happened that Akiba, while in
prison, intercalated three consecutive years."

[75] See, for example, B. *R. H.* 26a.

[76] See particularly L. Ginzberg, **פירושים וחדושים בירושלמי** III,174 ff.

[77] See T. Mommsen, loc. cit.

[78] See, e.g., G. Allon **א ,תולדות היהודים בא״י** pp. 201 f.

[79] See particularly Ch. Tchernowitz, op. cit., IV,271 ff.

[80] **תנא עדיות בו בים נשנית וכל היכא דאמרינן בו ביום ההוא יומא הוה**

[81]

אמר רבי שמעון בן עזאי מקובל אני מפי ע״ב זקן ביום שהושיבו את רבי
אלעזר בן עזריה בישיבה ששיר השירים וקהלת מטמאים את הידים...

[82] See *Diqduqe Soferim* on B. *Ber.* 28a. Some versions, as for example the current printed editions, read that Gamaliel was to lead the sessions for three Sabbaths and Eleazar ben Azariah for only one.

[83] See W. Bacher, *Die Agada der Tannaiten*, I,219 ff.

[84] *Sifre Deut.*, ed. Finkelstein, p. 112:

...מה אילו לא עמד שפן בשעתו עזרא בשעתו לא היתה תורה משתכחת
Had Shafan not risen in his time, Ezra in his time, Rabbi Akiba in his time, would the Torah not have been forgotten ? etc.

[85] B. *Sanh.* 14a; B. *A. Z.* 17b–18a, etc.

[86] *Sifre*, loc. cit., p. 113:

... ר' שמעון בן יוחי אומר אם לומר שהתורה עתידה להשתכח מישראל
והלא כבר נאמר כי לא תשכח מפי זרעו אלא איש פלוני אוסר איש פלוני
מתיר איש פלוני מטמא איש פלוני מטהר ולא ימצאו דבר ברור.

. . . R. Simon ben Yohai says: Can this mean that the Torah will be [literally] forgotten by [the people of] Israel? Yet, behold it is said, "for it shall not be forgotten out of the mouths of their seed" [Deut. 31:21]; but [it means]: One man prohibits what the other man permits, one man declares for unclean what another man declares for clean, and no clear matter [non-controversial law] will be found.

[87]

... שלא תאמר למדתי הלכות דיי תלמוד לומר   מצוה   הצה   כל
המצוה   למוד מדרש הלכות והגדות.

Lest you say, it is enough for me that I studied Halakhoth, therefore Scripture says [Deut. 11:22] "all the commandment" instead of "the commandment" or "commandment" meaning: Study Midrash, Halakhoth and Haggadoth.

[88] "Torah" is used here in its broader meaning which includes the oral law

תורה שבעל פה

[89] Similiar praise was uttered occasionally in regard to other singularly eminent personalities for their great accomplishments in the field of Jewish learning, e.g. in B. *Sukkah* 20a Ezra, Hillel I and Rabbi Ḥiyya and his sons are praised for rescuing the Torah; in B. *B. B.* 21a Joshua ben Gamla, the high priest, is praised because he introduced all over the country attendance at school for every boy of six or seven.

[90] *ARN* I:18, p. 66–67:

וכנגדן היה ר' יהודה הנשיא מונה שבחן של חכמים של רבי טפון של ר'
עקיבא ושל ר״א בן עזריה ושל ר' יוחנן בן נורי ושל ר' יוסי הגלילי. לרבי
טרפון קרא לו גל אבנים. וי״א גל של אגוזים כיון שנוטל אדם אחד מהן כולן
מתקשקשין ובאין זה לזה. כך היה ר' טרפון דומה בשעה שת״ח נכנס אצלו
וא״ל שנה לי. מביא לו מקרא ומשנה מדרש הלכות והגדות. כיון שיצא מלפניו
היה יוצא מלא ברכה וטוב.

לר' עקיבא קרא לו אוצר בלום. למה רבי עקיבא דומה לפועל שנטל
קופתו ויצא לחוץ מצא חטים מניח בה מצא שעורים מניח בה כוסמין מניח
בה פולין מניח בה עדשים מניח בה כיון שנכנס לביתו מברר חטים בפני
עצמן שעורים בפני עצמן (כוסמין בפני עצמן) פולין בפני עצמן עדשים בפני
עצמן. כך עשה ר' עקיבא ועשה כל התורה טבעות טבעות.
לר"א בן עזריה קרא לו קופה של רוכלים. ולמה היה ר"א דומה לרוכל
שנטל קופתו ונכנס למדינה ובאו בני המדינה ואמרו לו שמן טוב יש עמך.
פלייטון יש עמך. אפרסמון יש עמך ומוצאין הכל עמו. כך היה ר"א בן עזריה
בזמן שת"ח נכנס אצלו. שאלו במקרא אומר לו במשנה אומר לו במדרש
אומר לו בהלכות אומר לו באגדות אומר לו. כיון שיצא מלפניו הוא מלא
טוב וברכה.

B. Git. 67a contains a parallel passage:

איסי בן יהודה מנה שבחן של חכמים... ר"ע אוצר בלום

Rashi, s.v. בלום gives a different *ARN* version which, however, does not change the essence.

[91] The readings vary, some versions reading בלום while others have בלוס. We are inclined to accept the reading בלוס = βλύω, βλύσω meaning "completely filled warehouse." The emphasis is on the "warehouse" because its goods are well arranged in contrast with the heap of stones and the peddler's basket (see Rashi, loc. cit.)

[92] See Rashi, loc. cit.

[93] Ed. Horovitz-Rabin, p. 246.

[94] *Mekhilta DeRabbi Simon*, ed. Hoffmann, p. 117, has a different version but this does not change the essence.

[95] While the probable meaning of סדר here is "arranged," it also may mean "as he lectured in proper order [systematically]" just as the phrase סדר אגדתא is understood to mean "he recited Aggadoth in proper order." See references and literature in Strack, *Introduction*, p. 197.

[96] See A. Guttmann, *HUCA* 17 (1942–43): 395 ff.

[97] A. Guttmann, *HUCA* 16 (1941): 137 ff.

[98] *Shir R.* VIII,2; *Eccl. R.* VI,2.

[99] Cf. L. Ginzberg, *JE*, 1:306.

[100] The exaggeration is obvious if we realize how many circumstances from within and without influenced the fate of the Torah. See particularly M. Guttmann, *Zur Einleitung in die Halacha*, and Ch. Tchernowitz, *Toledoth*. The natural basis for the exaggeration was Akiba's extraordinary personality.

[101] A short version of this Baraitha is also given in *Sifre Deut.*, ibid.

[102] Examples of tractates which were arranged according to subject matter already at the time of the Temple (totally or partially) are: *Tamid, Middoth, Yoma*.

[103] Cf. Zuri, *Rabbi Akiba* (Hebrew), p. 266.

[104] See *Sifra*, beginning.

[105] See W. Bacher, *Die exegetische Terminologie der jüdischen Traditionsliteratur*; Mielziner, *Introduction*, pp. 182 ff.; H. L. Strack, *Introduction*, pp. 285 ff.; and particularly the books on hermeneutic rules by Adolf Schwarz.

[106] *Sifre Num.* 15:31 (112), p. 121.

[107] See Z. Frankel, *Darkhe*, p. 210.

[108] The rabbis named in *Shir Ha-Shirim Rabbah* II,5 are: Judah, Nehemiah, Meir, Jose, Simon ben Johai, Eliezer (son of Jose Ha-Gelili), and Eleazar ben Jacob. The disciples of Akiba who survived the Hadrianic persecutions, according to *Ber. Rabbah* 61:3, are: Meir, Judah, Jose, Simon, Eleazar ben Shamua, Johanan, Ha-Sandlar, and Eliezer ben Jacob. Another list, ibid., names: Judah, Nehemiah, Jose, Simon, Haninah ben Hakinai, and Johanan Ha-Sandlar. None of the variant readings includes the name of Simon, son of Gamaliel.

[109] B. *Ket.* 49b–50a.

[110] B. *Shab.* 15b.

[111] Tosefta *Shevi'ith* IV, 21; B. *R. H.* 15a.

[112] See M. Guttmann, op. cit., II,161 ff.

[113] P. *Ḥag.* III,1; 78d.

[114] *Qoheleth Rabbah* I,4.

[115] B. *Ber.* 63a,b; P. *Ned.* VI,8;40a,

Rav Safra said: Rabbi Abbahu said the following: When Hananiah the son of Rabbi Joshua's brother went down to the Diaspora [Babylonia], he intercalated the years and fixed new moons outside of the Land [Palestine]. They [the Palestinian Jewish authorities] sent to him two scholars, R. Jose ben Kipper and R. Zekhariah ben Kevuttal. When he saw them, he said to them: Why have you come? They said: We have come to study Torah . . . Soon they began to declare clean what he declared unclean and to permit what he prohibited . . . He said to them: "Why do you declare clean what I declare unclean, why do you permit what I prohibit?" They said to him: "Because you intercalate years and fix new moons outside of Palestine." He said to them: "Did not Akiba son of Joseph intercalate years and fix new moons outside of Palestine?" They said to him: "Don't mention Rabbi Akiba who left none equal to him in the land of Israel." He said to them: "I also left no equal in the land of Israel." They said to him: "The kids which you left behind have become goats with horns, and they have sent us to you saying, 'Go and tell him in our name: If he listens, that is good; if not, he should be in ban.' "

In this incident no name of a Nasi is mentioned. It obviously occurred at a time of interregnum, probably after the Bar Kokhba uprising.

[116] B. *R. H.* 32a; P. ibid. IV,6;59c; Tosefta, ibid. IV,5,

[117] See B. *R. H.* 31a. H. Mantel, op. cit., pp. 140 ff. reconstructs Johanan's statement and suggests that there was only one removal from Javneh to Usha, and this took place after the Bar Kokhba war. It never met in Javneh after this war, nor did it meet in Usha before it.

[118] B. *Shab.* 33b.

[119] B. *Ber.* 63b.

[120] Z. Frankel, op. cit., p. 179, believes that the reference to the Vineyard of Javneh here is correct. Questionable is merely the identity of the place where the sermons were given, whether it was the Vineyard of Javneh or Usha.

[121] B. *Shab.* 33b.

[122] *Sifre Berakhah* on 33:3. No. 344 (3), p. 401.

[123] See Rashi, B. *R. H.* 31b.

[124] See the full discussion of this point in M. Guttmann מפתח התלמוד II,161 f.

[125] B. *Horayoth* 13b.

[126] See Tos. *Demai* III,14 (50).

[127] See e.g. B. *B. M.* 84b.

[128] See B. *Sukkah* 26a and P. *Sukkah* II,5;53a.

[129] See B. *B. M.* 84b and B. *Ned.* 66b.

[130] See B. *Horayoth* 13b.

[131] Ibid.

[132] Tos. *Sanh.* VII,1 (425).

[133] M. *Ket.* VI,4 and elsewhere.

[134] See A. Guttmann לשאלת היחס: מנהג־הלכה בתקופת התלמוד in *Bitzaron* VII,8 pp. 95 ff. and VII,9 pp. 192 ff.

[135] Mishnah *B. B.* VIII,5.

[136] M. *Ket.* IX,1.

[137] B. *Shab.* 151b.

[138] See M. *Ket.* XI,5.

[139] B. *Hag.* 5b and parallels.

[140] M. *Meg.* I,8.

[141] P. *Meg.* I,9;71c; B. *Bava Qamma* 83a.

[142] M. *Ket.* XIII,11; B. *Git.* 41a; M. *Ket.* V,8; ibid. VII,9, etc.

[143] That he issued this ruling in conjunction with R. Eleazar son of Zadok (who may have been his *Av Beth Din*) is given in Tosefta *Sanh.* 2:13 (418) with reference to a specific instance; in B. *A. Z.* 36a and parallels in a general way.

[144] See A. Guttmann "The Patriarch Judah I," *HUCA* 25:239 ff.

[145] גובאי may mean here, as in B. *Qid.* 70b, Persians (Ghebre) and refer to a war between Persians and Romans. According to Krochmal, החלוץ II, pp. 72,92, n. 9 our passage refers to the invasion of the Parthians in 161 under Vologeses. Graetz, op. cit., I,438 admits that our passage may have reference to the Persians, but not to the Parthians. He also notes that the passage is too vague to be utilized for chronological purposes.

[146] See A. Guttmann, "The Patriarch Judah I," *HUCA* 25:239 ff.

[147] See Graetz, *Geschichte*, IV,204 ff.; Krochmal, *He-Chaluz*, II,71 ff.; S. Krauss, *Antoninus und Rabbi*, pp. 33 ff.; pp. 122 ff.

[148] B. *Git.* 17a

והתני רבי חייא... יודע הקב"ה בישראל שאין יכולין לקבל גזירת ארומיים עמד והגלה אותם לבבל

[149] Graetz, loc. cit., maintains that Hiyya had the persecutions of Marcus Aurelius (161–180) in mind. This is a conjecture.

[150] J. S. Zuri, *Rab*, p. 21 claims, without sufficient support, that Hiyya stayed there for twenty-five years.

[151] B. *Ned.* 41a:

מתניתא... כי הוה גמיר רבי תלת עשרי אפי הילכתא אגמריה לרבי חייא שבעה מנהון לסוף חלש רבי אהדר ר' חייא קמיה הנהו שבעה אפי דאמריה שיתא אד

[152] B. *Ket.* 103b (and parallels):

אייל ר' חייא אנא עבדי דלא משתכחה תורה מישראל דאייתינא כיתנא
ושדיינא ומגדלנא נישבי וצייידנא טביא ומאכילנא בישרא ליתמי ואריכנא
מגילתא ממשכי דטביא וסליקנא למתא דלית בה מקרי דרדיקנא וכתיבנא
חמשה חומשי לחמשה ינוקי ומתנינא שיתא סידרי לשיתא ינוקי לכל חד וחד
אמרי ליה אתצי סידרך לחברך והיינו דאמר רבי כמה גדולים מעשי חייא

[153] *Die Agada der Tannaiten*, II,521, n. 3.

[154] B. *Meg.* 11a:

במתניתא תנא לא מאסתים בימי כשדים שהעמדתי להם דניאל חנניה
מישאל ועזריה ולא געלתים בימי יוונים שהעמדתי להם שמעון הצדיק וחשמונאי
ובניו ומתתיחו כה״ג לכלותם בימי המן שהעמדתי להם מרדכי ואסתר להפר
בריתי אתם בימי פרסיים שהעמדתי להם של בית רבי וחכמי דורות

It was taught [in a Baraitha]: "I have not rejected them" [Lev. 26:44] — in
the days of the Chaldeans, when I raised up for them Daniel, Hananiah,
Mishael and Azariah; "neither did I abhor them" [Lev., ibid] — in the days
of the Greeks, when I raised up for them Simon the Righteous and Hasmonai
and his sons, and Mattathias the high priest; "to destroy them utterly" [Lev.,
loc. cit.] — in the days of Haman, when I raised up for them Mordecai and
Esther; "to break my covenant with them" [Lev., loc. cit.] — in the days of
the Romans [reading of MS M; other texts read: Persians], when I raised up
for them the members of the house of Rabbi and the sages of the various
generations.

[155] For example, by R. Meir, R. Hiyya, Bar Kappara.

[156] See literature and brief discussion in Strack, *Introduction*, pp. 12 ff.;
Mielziner, *Introduction*, pp. 5,6,281.

[157] See A. Guttmann *Mischna*, giving a complete synopsis of Mishnah and
Tosefta. Much of the supplementary material of the Tosefta and fragmentary
repetition of numerous mishnaic statements are obviously based on a written
Mishnah text.

[158] See Zuri. תולדות המשפט הצבורי העברי 11,29.

[159] He considered most of the existing Mishnah collections, see P. *Horayoth*
III,48bc and parallels.

[160] See numerous references and discussion of their significance A. Guttmann
op. cit.; summary of the conclusions pp. 181 ff.

[161] B. *Ḥul.* 85a.

[162] Example: M. *Ḥul.* IX,3c and Tos. ibid. VIII,18b. Cf. A. Guttmann,
Das Problem der Mischnaredaktion, pp. 108, 109.

[163] See, e.g., B. *Sanh.* 86a.

[164] B. *Yev.* 64b: מכדי מתניתין מאן תקן רבי

[165] P. *Meg.* I,1; 70b; P. *Pes.* IV,1; 30d: מי שסידר את המשנה

[166] Tosefta *Giṭ.* V(III),1 (328):

... רבי הושיב בית דין ונמנו שאם שהתו בפני סיקריקון שנים עשר חודשכל
הקודם לליקח נותן לבעלים רביע בקרקע ריע במעות ויד הבעלים על
העליונה אם יש בידן ליקח הן קודמין לכל אדם.

[167] Tos. *Ahiluth* XVIII,18 (617). (See also P. *Shevi'ith* VI,1; 36c):

מעשה ברבי ור' ישמעאל בר'יוסי ור' אליעזר הקפר ששבתו בחנות של
פזי בלוד והיה ר' פנחס בן יאיר יושב לפניהן אמרו לו אשקלון מה אתם

בה... אמרו לו אם כן בואו ונמנו עליה לפוטרה מן המעשרות ולא נמנה
עמהם ר' ישמעאל בר' יוסי כשיצא אמר רבי מפני מה לא נמנית עמנו

[168] M. *'Ohaloth*, XVIII,9.

[169] Tos. *Shevi'ith* IV,17.

[170] Tchernowitz, *Toledoth*, IV,339,340.

[171] See, for example, Zuri, op. cit., I,11,54 showing that not merely *Taq-qanoth* and *Gezeroth*, but other laws as well had been passed by vote. See also A. Guttmann, *Das Problem der Mischnaredaktion*, pp. 110 ff.

[172] Op. cit., I,54 ff.; see also ibid., II,103.

[173] See M. *Sanh*. V,5; Tos. ibid. VII,1,2; additional details ibid. IX,4; see also Tos. *Nega'im* I,11.

[174] See A. Guttmann, op. cit., pp. 103 ff.

[175] Tos. *Ḥag*. I,1:

הטמא פטור מן הראייה... יוחנן בן דהבאי או' משום ר' יהודה אף הסומא...
השיב רבי על דברי יוחנן בן דהבאי והכריעו חכמים לסייע לדברי ר יהודה

A defiled man is exempt from the command to *appear* [before the Lord; see Exod. 23:14; Deut. 16:16]. Johanan, son of Dahbai, said in the name of R. Judah: also a blind man. . . . Rabbi replied to Johanan ben Dahbai, and the sages decided the matter in favor of R. Judah.

[176] See M. *Men*. VI,3; Tos. ibid. VII,7.

[177] See P. *A. Z.* II,2;41a. P. *Shab*. VI,1; 7d.

ג' דברים התירו לבית רבי שיהו רואין במראה. ושיהו מספרין קומי ושילמדו
את בניהם יוונית שהיו זקוקין למלכות

They [the sages] permitted to the House of Rabbi three matters: to use a mirror; to wear a special hair-do [κόμη, customary among high class Romans]; because they have to deal with the [Roman] authorities; and to teach Greek to their children.

[178] See Robert Wilde, *The Treatment of the Jews in the Greek Christian Writers*, p. 158, "St. Irenaeus (140–200) was . . . for the first time presenting Christianity in a systematic form, in an effort to make rapprochements with the learned circles to whom Gnosticism made its appeal." Ibid., p. 149, "His great work *The Manifestation* . . . was probably written about 180 in successive stages." See also Strack's conjecture (*Introduction*, p. 12) that "the Jews were led to codify in a definitive form and thus also to commit to writing their oral traditions with a view, in part at least, to the New Testament canon then in process of formation."

[179] See A. Guttmann, "The Problem of the Anonymous Mishnah," *HUCA* 16 (1941): 137 ff.

[180] See L. Blau, in ספר זכרון לכבוד... p. 16, where he points out that משניות "*Mishnajoth*" (in old sources) means: a complete edited פוזנסקי collection of Mishnahs and not just individual Mishnahs.

[181]
לעולם הוי רץ אחר המשנה יותר מן התלמוד. הדא דתמר עד שלא שיקע
בן רבי רוב משניות. אבל מששיקע רבי רוב משניות לעולם הוי רץ אחר
התלמוד יותר מן המשנה.
Cf. Zuri, op. cit., II,29.

[182] They spoke Hebrew and Aramaic. See B. *Meg*. 18a (*R. H.* 26b):
לא הוו ידעי רבנן מאי סירוגין שמעוה לאמתא דבי רבי דקאמרה להו

לרבנן דהוו עיילי פיסקי פיסקי לבי רבי עד מתי אתם נכנסין סירוגין סירוגין
וכו' עד מתי אתה מסלסל בשערך וכו'

The rabbis did not know what was meant by סרוגין *serugin*, until they heard
the maid of Rabbi's house, on seeing the rabbis enter at intervals, say to them,
How long are you going to come in *serugin?*

Subsequently several more instances of similar nature are cited which all
show that Judah's learning and teaching was not limited to the halls of the
academy but encompassed his entire household to the extent that casual remarks of his maid servants enlightened the rabbis in regard to the meaning
of some uncommon Hebrew words.

183 B. *Soṭah* 49b:

והאמר רבי בארץ ישראל לשון סורסי למה אלא אי לשון הקודש אי לשון
יוונית.

It is possible that Judah objected to the Aramaic title רבן *Rabban*, the title
of the Princes that preceded him, and insisted on the Hebrew title *Rabbi*.

184 B. *Giṭ.* 59a; B. *Sanh.* 36a:

מימות משה ועד רבי לא מצינו תורה וגדולה במקום אחד

185 See M. *Horayoth* III,1:

... וכן נשיא שחטא ואחר כך עבר מגדולתו... מביא שעיר

"If the Nasi (Ruler) sinned and afterward passed from his greatness (ruler-
ship)." Similarly ibid. III,2. Cf. Zuri, op. cit., I,43,44.

186

א״ר בא בראשונה היה כל אחד ואחד ממנה את תלמידיו. כגון רבן יוחנן
בן זכיי מינה את רבי ליעזר ואת רבי יהושע. ורבי יהושע את רבי עקיבא.
ורבי עקיבא את רבי מאיר ואת רבי שמעון. ... חזרו וחלקו כבוד לבית הזה
(בית רבי). אמרו בית דין דין שמינה שלא לדעת הנשיא אין מינויי מינוי. ונשיא
שמינה שלא לדעת בית דין מינויי מינוי. חזרו והתקינו שלא יהו בית דין ממנין
אלא מדעת הנשיא. ושלא יהא הנשיא ממנה אלא מדעת ב״ד.

Some sources speak of ordination by three men (*Beth Din*), and even by a
single sage without any reference to the Nasi's consent. See, e.g., B. *Sanh.*
13b–14a.

187 P. *Ta'anith* IV,2; 68a; *Qoheleth Rabbah*, VII:

רבי הוה ממני תרין מינויין [בכל שנה (ק״ר)] אין הוון כדיי היו מתקיימין
ואין לא הוון מסתלקין. מדדמך פקיד לבריה אמר לא תעביד כן אלא מני
כולהון כחדא. ומני לר' חנינא (ק״ר) קדמאי.

Rabbi used to make two appointments [ordained two men] every year; if they
proved worthy they were retained, and if not they were demoted. When
Rabbi was close to death, he commanded his son saying: "You should not
act so, but appoint them all together [at once], and appoint R. Ḥanina first."

188 See P. *Ta'anith* IV, loc. cit.:

ולמה לא מניתיה הוא. אמר רבי דרוסא בגין דצווחין עלויי בציפורין
ציפוראיי. ובגין צווחה עבדין. אמר רבי לעזר בי ר' יוסה על שהשיבו טעם
ברבים: רבי הוה יתיב מתני וזכרו
פליטיהם אותי והיו אל ההרים כיוני הגיאיות כולם הומיות
(יחזקאל ז, ט״ז). א״ל הומות. א״ל הן קריתה. אמר ליה קדם רב המנונא
דבבל. אמר ליה כד תיחות לתמן אמור ליה דמנייתך חכים. וידע דלא מיתמני
ביומוי.

Cf. Krochmal, *He-Chaluz*, II,85 ff.

[189] It is conceivable that the loud complaint of the people of Sepphoris was the primary reason for Judah's action.

[190] P. *Ta'anith*, ibid. See also B. *Ket.* 103b, B. *Shab.* 29b, where the wording is: חנינא בר חמא ישב בראש The words ישב בראש here unquestionably mean, as pointed out already by Graetz (op. cit., IV,446) that Ḥaninah should be ordained first. The B. Talmud, however, misunderstood these words and assumed that they meant that Ḥaninah should be the head of the *Beth Din Ha-Gadol*.

[191] P. *Shevi'ith* VI,1; 36b,c. P. *Giṭ.* I,2; 43c (Cf. B. *Sanh.* 5b):

רבי הוה בעכו... אמר רבי יעקב בר אידי מאותה שעה גזרו שלא יהא
תלמיד מורה הורייה. רבי חייא בשם רבי הונא תלמיד שהורה אפילו כהלכה
אין הוראתו הורייה. תני תלמיד שהורה הלכה לפני רבו חייב מיתה.

Rabbi was in Akko . . . said R. Jacob son of Idi: At that time a decree was issued stating that a student must not render a decision. R. Ḥiyya said in the name of R. Huna: A decision rendered by a student, even if it is in accordance with the Halakhah, has no validity. It was taught [in a Baraitha]: A student who decides a Halakhah in the presence of his teacher is guilty of a death penalty.

[192]

בעא מיניה רבי מרבי חייא כגון אני מהו בשעיר אמר ליה הרי צרתך בבל

[193] Cf. A. Büchler, *Synedrion*, pp. 156 ff.

[194] B. *Shab.* 156a:

כתיב אפינקסיה דלוי אמרית קדם רבי ומנו רבינו הקדוש על דהוו גבלין
שתיתאב בבל והוה צוח רבי ומנו רבינו הקדוש על דהוו גבלין שתיתא ולית
דשמיע ליה ולית חילא בידיה למיסר וכו'

It was written in Levi's note book: I spoke to my teacher, i.e., our holy Master, about those who mix *shatitha* in Babylonia, and my teacher, i.e., our holy Master, protested vehemently against the practice of mixing *shatitha*, but none heeded him, and he lacked the power to forbid it, etc.

[195] See A. Büchler, *JQR* 13:683 ff. Krauss, op. cit., p. 26.

[196] P. *Demai* II,1; 22c. Ibid., III,3; 23c;. Tos. *Shevi'ith* IV,10 (665). B. *Ḥul.* 6b,7a.

[197] B. *Ḥul.* 6b,7a:

העיד ר' יהושע בן זרוז בן חמיו של ר' מאיר לפני רבי על ר"מ שאכל
עלה של ירק בבית שאן והתיר רבי את בית שאן כולה על ידו. חברו עליו
אחיו ובית אביו אמרו לו מקום שאבותיך ואבות אבותיך נהגו בו איסור אתה
תנהוג בו היתר? דרש להן מקרא זה " וכתת נחש הנחשת אשר עשה משה כי
עד הימים ההמה היו בני ישראל מקטרים לו ויקרא לו נחשתן (מ"ב, יח,
ד) « אפשר בא אסא ולא ביערו בא יהושפט ולא ביערו והלא כל עבודה
זרה שבעולם אסא ויהושפט ביערום? אלא מקום הניחו לו אבותיו להתגדר
בו. אף אני מקום הניחו לי אבותי להתגדר בו.

[198] P. *Demai* I,3; 22a. P. *Ta'anith* III,1; 66c:

רבי בעא מישרי שמיטתא סלק רבי פנחס בן יאיר לגביה. א"ל מה עיבוריא
עבידין. אמר ליה עולשין יפות. מה עיבוריא עבידין. א"ל עולשין יפות.
וידע ר' דלית הוא מסכמה עימיה.

Rabbi wanted to suspend the sabbatical year. R. Pinḥas ben Ja'ir visited him. Rabbi asked him: How is the crop doing? R. Pinḥas replied: The endives are good. — How is the crop doing? Pinhas again replied: The endives are good. Then Rabbi knew that R. Pinḥas would not agree with him.

[199] P. *Pe'ah* V,1; 18d. See details in *P. Shevi'ith* VI,3; 37a:

בראשונה היה הירק אסור בספרי ארץ ישראל שהתקינו שיהא הירק מותר בספרי ארץ ישראל. אע״פ כן היה אסור להביא ירק מחוץ לארץ לארץ. התקינו שיהא מותר להביא ירק מחוץ לארץ לארץ. אע״פ כן היה אסור ליקח ירק במוצאי שביעית מיד. ר' התיר ליקח ירק במוצאי שביעית מיד.

In former times vegetables were prohibited [immediately after the sabbatical year] in towns near the border of the Land of Israel [since they may have come from the prohibited crop grown in the Land of Israel during the sabbatical year]; later they ordained that vegetables be permitted in towns near the border of Israel. Nevertheless it was prohibited to import vegetables from the outside to the Land of Israel. Now they ordained that the import of vegetables from the outside to the Land of Israel be permitted. Nonetheless it was prohibited to buy greens immediately after the Sabbatical year. Rabbi permitted to buy vegetables immediately after the Sabbatical year.

[200] M. *Shevi'ith* VI,4: רבי התיר ליקח ירק במוצאי שביעית מיד.

[201] P. *Pe'ah* VII,3; 20b: אייתון קומי תרין פיגלין מבין

ריש שתא לצומא רבא והוה אפיקי שמיתטא והוה בהון טעוניה דגמלא אמר לון ולית אסיר ולאו ספחין אינון. א״ל בפוקי ריש שתא איזדרען. באותה שעה התיר רבי ליקח ירק במוצאי שביעית מיד.

Two radishes were brought before Rabbi between Rosh Ha-Shanah and the Great Fast after the sabbatical year. They were enough for a camel's load [i.e., they were very big]. He asked: Did they not grow [during the sabbatical year] and are, therefore, prohibited? They replied to him: They were planted after the New Year. At that time Rabbi permitted to buy vegetables immediately after the sabbatical year.

[202] See Krauss, op. cit., pp. 17 ff.

[203] B. *B. B.* 90b–91a. According to the parallel version in Tos. *A. Z.* IV(V),2 (465–466) Judah the Nasi permitted the export of wine to Syria, while in the Talmud this was done by Judah, the son of Bathyra. On the other hand, the Tosefta has Rabbi Judah (i.e., the son of Ilai) in place of Rabbi (i.e., Judah, the Nasi) of the Talmud version.

[204] Tos. *'Eruvin* VI(V),13 (145–146). B. *'Eruvin* 61a. P. ibid. V,7;22d. Zuri, op. cit., II,152, n. 18 points to the contradiction between Tosefta and P. Talmud regarding the geographical location of חמתה, חמתא, חמתן Hamta(n).

[205] M. *Shab.* VI,5: שן תותבת ושן של זהב ר' מתיר וחכמים אוסרים.
Rabbi permits a false tooth or a gold tooth; but the sages forbid it.

[206] *'Eruvin* 32b,33a:

... ורבי היא דאמר כל דבר שהוא משום שבות לא גזרו עליו בין השמשות וכו'.

[This Mishnah] represents the view of Rabbi who said: Any act that is forbidden by the rabbinical measure *shevuth* is not subject to that prohibition during twilight [of the Sabbath eve], etc.

[207] P. *Shab.* XVIII,1; 16c.

[208] B. *Shab.* 64ab. B. *Beẓah* 40ab. Some other cases of Judah's leniency regarding the Sabbath: B. *Shab.* 51a. Ibid. 60b.

[209] P. *Ta'anith* IV,9; 69c. P. *Meg.* I,4; 70c. P. *Yev.* VI,6; 7d. B. *Meg.* 5b:

רבי... ובקש לעקור תשעה באב ולא הודו לו. אמר לפניו רבי אבא בר
זבדא רבי לא כך היה מעשה אלא תשעה באב שחל להיות בשבת הוה
ודחינוהו לאחר השבת ואמר רבי הואיל ונדחה ידחה ולא הודו חכמים.

Rabbi . . . wanted to abolish [the fast of] the Ninth of Ab but the sages did not agree with him. Rabbi Abba son of Zevada said: Master, this was not the case, but it happened that the Ninth of Ab fell on a Sabbath and it was postponed to the day after the Sabbath. Then Rabbi said: Since we postpone it, let us postpone it altogether (i.e., not observe it this year); but the sages did not agree with him.

[210] Krauss, op. cit., p. 133.

[211] B. *Ta'anith* 14b:

דתניא אין גוזרין יותר משלש עשרה תעניות על הצבור לפי שאין מטריחין
את הצבור יותר מדאי דברי רבי וכו'

It was taught [in a Baraitha]: Not more than thirteen fasts are ordained upon the community because we should not trouble the community unduly; this is the opinion of Rabbi.

[212] Cf. I. H. Weiss, op. cit., II,180.

[213] P. *Meg.* I,1; 70b. B. *Meg.* 5ab:

רבי... רחץ בקרונה של צפורי בשבעה עשר בתמוז

[214] B. *Ta'anith* 12a:

תנו רבנן עד מתי אוכל ושותה עד שיעלה עמוד השחר דברי רבי

Our rabbis taught [in a Baraitha]: Until when may one eat and drink [on the night preceding a fast]? Until the rise of dawn; this is the opinion of Rabbi.

[215] B. *Ber.* 27b:

והאמר רבי אבין פעם אחת התפלל רבי של שבת בערב שבת ונכנס
למרחץ ויצא ושנה לן פרקין ועדיין לא חשכה. אמר רבא ההוא דנכנס
להזיע וקודם גזירה הוה, וכו'

Has not R. Abin related that once Rabbi said the Sabbath *Tefillah* on the eve of Sabbath and he went into the bath and came out and taught us our section while it was not yet dark? — Rabba said: He went in merely to perspire, and it happened before the prohibition was issued [against bathing and perspiring on Sabbath].

[216] Ibid.:

פעם אחת נתקשרו שמים בעבים כסבורים העם לומר חשכה הוא ונכנסו
לבית הכנסת והתפללו של מוצאי שבת בשבת ונתפזרו העבים וזרחה החמה
ובאו ושאלו את רבי ואמר הואיל והתפללו התפללו

Once [on Sabbath] the sky became overcast with clouds and the congregation thought that it was night time. They went into the Synagogue and said the prayers for the termination of Sabbath; then the clouds scattered and the sun came out. The people came and asked Rabbi, and he said to them: Since they prayed, they have prayed [i.e., fulfilled their obligation].

[217] M. *R. H.* II,2–4. Tos. ibid. II(I),2:

בראשונה היו משיאין משואות. משקלקלו המינים (חילופי נוסחאות: צדוקים,
כותים) התקינו שיהו שלוחין יוצאין. כיצד היו משיאין, וכו'

Beforetime they used to kindle flares, but after the evil doings of the *minim* [sectarians; or *ḳuthim*, Samaritans; or *zeduqim*, Sadducees] [who kindled flares at the wrong time] they ordained that messengers should go forth. How did they kindle the flares?, etc.

[218] P. R. H. II,1; 58a: מי ביטל את המשואות רבי ביטל את המשואות

Who abolished the flares? Rabbi abolished the flares.

G. Allon, *Toledoth*, I,149–50 argues that this change was made long before Judah's time, who merely completed the change.

[219] E. Mahler, *Handbuch der Jüdischen Chronologie*. See detailed literature at the end of U. Cassuto's article in *Encyclopaedia Judaica*. IX,813.

[220] P. R. H. II,1; 58a:

והתיר רוצח. והתיר עד מפי עד. והתיר שיהו יוצאין עליו מבערב בחזקת שנתקדש.

Cf. Graetz, *Geschichte*, IV,198, n. 3.

[221] B. Qid. 63a:

דתניא האומר לאשה הרי את מקודשת לי לאחר שאתגייר... לאחר שימות בעלך וכו' רבי יהודה הנשיא אומר מקודשת ומה טעם אמרו אינה מקודשת משום איבה.

It was taught [in a Baraitha]: If he says to a woman: Be thou betrothed unto me after my conversion [to Judaism] . . . after the death of your husband, etc., Rabbi Judah the Prince holds that she is betrothed; but why did they say that she is not betrothed? Because of enmity [that may be the consequence of such betrothals].

[222] B. Qid. 64a:

דתניא בשעת קידושין אמר יש לו בנים בשעת מיתה אמר אין לו בנים בשעת קידושין אמר אין לו אחים בשעת מיתה אמר יש לו אחים נאמן להתיר ואין נאמן לאסור וכו'

It was taught [in a Baraitha]: If he says at the time of betrothal that he has children; at the time of death he says that he has no children; at the time of betrothal he says that he has no brothers; at the time of death he says that he has brothers; he is believed to free [her from legal ties] but is not believed to restrict her [marital rights].

[223] B. Git. 84b: ת"ר כל התנאין פסולין בגט דברי רבי וכו'

Our rabbis taught [in a Baraitha]: All conditions [written] in a bill of divorcement make it invalid. This is the view of Rabbi, etc.

[224] B. Yev. 60b:

דאמר ר' יהושע בן לוי עיר אחת היתה בארץ ישראל שקרא עליה ערער ושגר רבי את רבי רומנוס ובדקה ומצא בה גיורת פחותה מבת שלש שנים ויום אחד והכשירה רבי לכהונה

As R. Joshua ben Levi related: There was a certain town in the Land of Israel the legitimacy [pedigree] of whose inhabitants was disputed, and Rabbi sent R. Romanos who conducted an inquiry and found in it the daughter of a proselyte who was under the age of three years and one day [married to a priest], and Rabbi declared her eligible to live with a priest [her husband].

[225] B. Yev. 59b:

מעשה בריבה אחת בהיתלו שהיתה מכבדת את הבית ורבעה כלב כופרי מאחריה והכשירה רבי לכהונה

It once happened in Hitalu that while a young woman was sweeping the floor

294

a village dog [Rashi: big hunting dog] raped her from the rear, and Rabbi permitted her to marry a priest.

[226] Tos. *Shab.* XV(XVI),14. B. *Yoma,* 83b:

מי שנשכו נחש קורין לו רופא ממקום למקום ושוחטין לו תרנגולת וגוזזין
לו כרישין ואינו צריך לעשר לעשר דברי רבי ר' שמעון בן אלעזר אומר צריך
לעשר.

If a person is bitten by a snake, one may call a physician for him from one place into another, or tear open a hen for him, or cut leek from the ground for him, give it to him to eat, without having separated the tithe thereof; this is the view of Rabbi. R. Simon ben Eleazar said: He must tithe it.

[227] B. *Yev.* 64b. (P. *Yev.* VI,6; 7d does not give names):

דתניא מלה מלה הראשון ומת שני ומת שלישי לא תמול דברי רבי. רבן שמעון
בן גמליאל אומר שלישי תמול רביעי לא תמול

It was taught [in a Baraitha]: If one circumcised the first son and he died, the second son and he too died, the third one should not be circumcised, this is the opinion of Rabbi. Rabban Simon ben Gamaliel says: The third one should be circumcised but not the fourth one.

Judah changed his opinion on other occasions, too. See for example, B. *B. M.* 44a; B. *A. Z.* 52b. These and similar passages are considered by some scholars, among them Z. Frankel (*Mevo Ha-Yerushalmi,* p. 20ab), Rappoport (*Kerem Ḥemed,* part II) as evidence that Judah made a second edition of the Mishnah in his old age. However, the fact that Judah changed his opinion in several instances does not prove conclusively that his former opinions were part of an edited Mishnah.

[228] B. *Ta'anith* 17a:

רבי אומר אומר אני אסור לשתות יין לעולם אבל מה אעשה שתקנתו
קלקלתו. אמר אביי כמאן שתו האידנא כהני חמרא כרבי

Rabbi says: I say a [priest] should not at any time drink wine, but what can I do seeing that his misfortune [destruction of the Temple] resulted in an advantage to him [i.e., he is now permitted to drink wine].

[229] B. *Ḥul.* 95a:

... אמר רבי בשביל שוטה זה שעשה שלא כהוגן אנו נאסור כל המקולין
וכו'

[230] See also S. Zeitlin, "The Second Day of Rosh Ha-Shanah in Israel," *JQR* 44 (1954): 362 ff.

[231] Examples: M. *Shab.* XII,3; M. *Nazir* I,4; M. *B. Q.* V,3; M. *'Arakhin* IV,2; M. *Middoth* III,4. Tos. *Shab.* X(XI),19; Tos. *Pes.* III,9; Tos. *B. B.* XI,1.

[232] Examples: M. *'Arakhin* I,5. Tos. *Demai* I,9. Tos. *Shevi'ith* VIII, 3; Tos. *Shab.* IX,20; Tos. *M. Q.* I,3; I,8; II,2; Tos. *Soṭah* XV,1; Tos. *Qid.* IV,7; Tos. *Ḥul.* II,5; VIII,6; Tos. *'Arakhin* IV,33; Tos. *Temurah* I,8; Tos. *Nega'im* I,8; Tos. *Niddah* III,4; Tos. *Makhshirin* III,14; Tos. *Ṭevul Yom* II,12.

[233] See Zuri, op. cit., II,62–63.

[234] Occasionally other sages, too, were called *qadosh,* "holy", but not other Princes. Examples: R. Meir (P. *Ber.* II,7; 5b). Judah was given the epithet *qadosh* in his life time, see B. *Shab.* 118b, not after his death as stated by I. H. Weiss, *Dor.* II,178.

[235] For the former view, see Krochmal, op. cit., II,93. For the latter see

S. Krauss, op. cit., p. 134. See Krauss, loc. cit., n. 1, and p. 94, n. 2 for further literature on this matter.

[236] See particularly W. Bacher in *JE* 7,333 and and A. Hyman, *Toledoth*, II,600 ff.

[237] P. *Shab.* XVI,1; 15c; *Lev. R.* 15:4; *Ekha R.* on *Lamentations* 4:20 (77a in ed. Buber). See Krauss, op. cit., pp. 131 ff. and literature there cited.

While Ḥiyya compared Judah to the Messiah, Judah and Hezekiah, Ḥiyya's sons said something entirely different. B. *Sanh.* 38a:

יהודה וחזקיה בני רבי חייא הוו יתבי בסעודתא קמי רבי ולא הוו קא
אמרי ולא מידי אמר להו אגברו חמרא אדרדקי כי היכי דלימרו מילתא
כיון דאיבסום פתחו ואמרו אין בן דוד בא עד שיכלו שני בתי אבות מישראל
ואלו הן ראש גולה שבבבל ונשיא שבארץ ישראל וכו'

This attitude of Ḥiyya's sons toward the House of the Nasi may be rooted in their tense relationship to the sons of Judah. Zuri, *Rab.*, p. 99 suggests, without sufficient evidence, that the reason for this tense relationship was their competition in trade.

[238] See L. Wallach in *JQR* 31 (1941).

[239] P. *Kil.* IX,3; 32b (cf. *Ber. Rabba* 98:8):

אין סליק רב הונא ריש גלותא להכא אנא מותיב ליה לעיל מיניי דהוא
מן יהודה ואנא מבנימן דהוא מן דכריא ואנא מן נוקבתא.

Should Exilarch Rav Huna come here, I will place him above me because he is a descendant of Judah while I am a descendant of Benjamin; he is a descendant of [King David's] male lineage while I am a descendant of [his] female lineage.

[240] B. *Ket.* 103b (and parallels): והושיבו ישיבה אחר שלשים יום

[241] P. *Sanh.* I,2; 18c:

רבי לעזר בשם ר' חנינה מעשה בעשרים וארבע קרנות של בית ר' שנכנסו
לעבר שנה בלוד ונכנסה בהן עין רע ומתו כולם בפרק אחד. מאותה שעה
עקרוה מיהודה וקבעוה בגליל.

[242] B. *Ket.* 103b. B. *Sanh.* 32b:

ת"ר צדק צדק תרדוף הלך אחר... רבי לבית שערים

Our rabbis taught [in a Baraitha]: 'Justice, justice shalt thou follow' [Deut. 16:20]. Follow . . . Rabbi to Beth She'arim.

[243] P. *Kil.* IX,3; 32b; P. *Ket.* XII,3; 35a:

רבי הוה יתיב ליה בציפורין שבע עשרה שנין

[244] B. *Meg.* 5b: והא רבי בטבריא הוה

[245] See discussion in A. Hyman, *Toledoth* II,603 f.

[246] B. *Niddah* 47b.

[247] P. *Shevi'ith* VI,1; 36b.

[248] *Sifre Deut.* 32,46.

[249] B. *Shab.* 46a.

[250] See Zuri, op. cit., II,76, n. 29.

[251] M. *Soṭah* IX,15: משמת רבי בטלה ענוה ויראת חטא

This statement and the numerous other expressions of deep affection and veneration are not refuted or invalidated by a few exceptional incidents. To judge Judah's personality according to the exceptional incidents, as done, for

example, by Krochmal, op. cit., pp. 84 ff., is to distort history. Besides, some
of these incidents merely show that Judah was psychologically a normal human
being unable (or unwilling) to suppress his emotions. An example: P. *Kil.*
IX,3; 32b:

רבי הוה ענוון סגין והוה אמר כל מה דיימי לי בר נשא אנא עביד חוץ
ממה שעשו זקני בתירה לזקני דשרון גרמון מנשיאותיה ומנוניה. אין סליק
רב הונא ריש גלותא להכא אנא מותיב ליה לעיל מיניי... חד זמן אעל רבי
חייא רובא לגביה אמר ליה הא רב הונא לבר נתכרכמו פניו של רבי. אמר
ליה ארונו בא. אמר ליה פוק וחמי מאן בעי לך לבר. ונפק ולא אשכח בר
נש וידע דהוא כעיס עלוי וכו'

Rabbi was very humble and said, 'Whatever a man may say to me [pertaining
to humility] I would do, with the exception of that which the Elders of
Bathyra did to the Elders of Sharon: They resigned their leadership and
appointed him [Hillel; see B. *Pes.* 66b and parallels]. However, if the Exilarch
Rav Huna would come here, I would place him above me. . . .' Once Rabbi
Ḥiyya the Great visited Judah and said to him: 'Rav Huna is outside.' Hereupon Rabbi's face turned pale [remembering his promise to place Rav Huna
above himself]. Then Ḥiyya said: 'His coffin came.' Rabbi now said: 'Go
and see who wants you outside.' He went, but did not find anybody and
knew that he [Judah] was angry at him.

It is quite understandable that a practical joke like this upset Judah and
he was, therefore, unable to suppress his feelings. This incident and others of
this type prove that the editors of the Talmud did not suppress facts uncom-
plimentary to the great and venerated leaders of Judaism. This fact enhances
the value of the Talmud as a source of Jewish history.

Bibliography

PRIMARY SOURCES

Including Translations

PRE-TALMUDIC LITERATURE

Apocrypha. Revised Standard Version. New York, 1952.

The Apocrypha and Pseudepigrapha of the Old Testament in English. Edited by R. H. Charles. 2 vols. London, 1913.

Bible, Masoretic text.

The Dead Sea Scriptures. English translation by T. H. Gaster. New York, 1956.

Flavius Josephus. Editio Major by B. Niese. Berlin, 1887–89.

Josephus. Works. With English translation by H. St. J. Thackeray, R. Marcus, A. Wikgren, and L. H. Feldman. Loeb Classical Library. 9 vols. London, 1926–65.

Maccabees, First Book. Translated by S. Tedesche. Introduction and Commentary by S. Zeitlin. New York, 1950.

Maccabees, Second Book. Translated by S. Tedesche. Edited by S. Zeitlin. New York, 1954.

Maccabees, Third and Fourth Books. Edited and translated by M. Hadas. New York, 1953.

Megilloth Midbar Yehudah. Hebrew edition by A. M. Haberman. Jerusalem, 1959.

Philo. Works. With English translation by F. H. Colson, H. Whitaker, J. W. Earp. Loeb Classical Library. 10 vols. London, 1929–62.

The Zadokite Documents. Edited by C. Rabin. New York, 1954 and Oxford, 1958 (2nd ed.).

LITERATURE OF THE TALMUDIC AND GEONIC PERIOD

Avoth De-Rabbi Nathan. Edited by S. Schechter. Vienna, 1887. Translated by J. Goldin, *The Fathers According to Rabbi Nathan.* New Haven, 1955.

Iggereth Rav Sherira Gaon. Edited by B. M. Lewin. Haifa, 1921.

Mechilta D'Rabbi Ishmael. Edited by H. S. Horowitz and I. A. Rabin. Breslau, 1930 and Jerusalem, 1960.

Megillath Ta'anith. Die Fastenrolle. Edited and translated by H. Lichtenstein. *HUCA* 8-9 (1932).

Megillath Ta'anith with Introductions and Notes. B. Z. Zurie. Jerusalem, 1964.

Mekilta de-Rabbi Ishmael. Edited and translated by J. Z. Lauterbach. 3 vols. Philadelphia, 1933–35.

Mekhilta de-Rabbi Simon ben Yohai. Edited by J. N. Epstein and E. Z. Melamed. Jerusalem, 1955.

Midrash Bereshith Rabbah. Edited by Theodor-Albeck. Berlin, 1912–36; 3 vols. Jerusalem, 1965 (reprint).

Midrash Devarim Rabbah. Edited by S. Lieberman. Jerusalem, 1940 and 1964.

Midrash Ha-Gadol on Genesis. Edited by M. Margulies. Jerusalem, 1947; *on Exodus,* Jerusalem, 1956.

Midrash Ha-Gadol on Leviticus. Edited by E. N. Rabinowitz. New York, 1932.

Midrash Ha-Gadol on Numbers. Edited by S. Fish. London, 1957.

Midrash Rabbah. With commentary by M. A. Mirkin. 9 vols. Tel-Aviv, 1956–64.

Midrash Tanhuma. Edited by S. Buber. Wilna, 1885. Reprint, New York, 1946.

Midrash Tannaim on Deuteronomy. Edited by D. Hoffmann. 2 vols. Berlin, 1908–9.

Midrash Tehillim. Edited by S. Buber. Wilna, 1891. Reprint, New York, 1947.

Midrash Wayyiqra Rabbah. Edited by M. Margulies. 5 vols. Jerusalem, 1953–60.

The Minor Tractates. Edited by M. Higger, some with translation. New York, 1930–37.

The Minor Tractates of the Talmud. Translated by A. Cohen 2 vols. London, 1965.

Mishnah, standard text. English translation by H. Danby. London, 1933 (used with changes).

The Mishnah of the Palestinian Talmud. Edited by W. H. Lowe. Cambridge, 1883.

The Mishnah of Rabbi Eliezer. Edited by H. G. Enelow. New York, 1933.

Otzar ha-Geonim. Edited by B. M. Lewin. 13 vols. Haifa-Jerusalem, 1928–62.

Ozar ha-Baraithoth. Compiled by M. Higger. 10 vols. New York, 1938–48.

Pesiqta de-Rav Kahana. Edited by D. Mandelbaum. 2 vols. New York, 1962.

Pesiqta Rabbathi. Edited by M. Friedmann. Vienna, 1885.

Pirqe Avoth. Edited by R. T. Herford. New York, 1925.

Seder 'Olam Rabba. Edited by B. Ratner. Wilna, 1897.

Seder Tannaim we-Amoraim. Edited by K. Kahan. Frankfurt a.M., 1935.

Sifra. Edited by I. H. Weiss. Vienna, 1862.

Sifre Deuteronomy. Edited by Horowitz-Finkelstein. Berlin, 1939.

Sifre Numbers and *Sifre Zutta.* Edited by H. S. Horowitz. Leipzig, 1917.

Sifre on Numbers and Deuteronomy. Edited by M. Friedmann. Vienna, 1864 and 1924; New York, 1948.

Talmud, Babylonian. Edited by L. B. Goldschmidt. Critical text and German translation. 8 vols. Berlin, 1897–1933. 9th vol., Haag, 1935.

Talmud, Babylonian (Bavli), standard edition. Translated and edited by I. Epstein. London, 1935–52 (used with changes).

BIBLIOGRAPHY

Talmud, Palestinian ("Yerushalmi"). Used both the "majority" ed. (e.g., Zhitomir, 1860–67), and the Krotoschin ed. (which follows the Cracow ed.), 1866.
Tosefta. Edited by S. Lieberman. *Zera'im*. New York, 1955. *Mo'ed*. New York, 1962. *Nashim*. New York, 1967.
Tosefta. Edited by M. S. Zukermandel. Pasewalk, 1881. 2d ed. Jerusalem, 1937.
Yalqut Shim'oni. Warsaw, 1876; New York, 1944; Jerusalem, 1952.

NON-JEWISH SOURCES

Ammianus Marcellinus. Edited and translated by J. C. Rolfe. Loeb Classical Library. 3 vols. London, 1951–52.
Caesar, Gaius Julius. *Civil Wars*. Edited and translated by A. G. Peskett. Loeb Classical Library. London, 1938.
Dio Cassius (Cassius Dio). *Dio's Roman History*. Edited and translated by E. Cary. Loeb Classical Library. London–New York, 1914–27.
Eusebius of Caesarea. *Historia ecclesiastica*. Loeb Classical Library. London, 1926–32.
Gospels Parallels: A Synopsis of the First Three Gospels. Edited by B. H. Throckmorton. New York, 1949 (and later reprints).
Hegesippus. Edited by J. Caesar and F. Weber. Marburg, 1864.
Herodotus. *Histories*. Edited and translated by A. D. Godley. Loeb Classical Library. 4 vols. New York, 1920–24.
Justin Martyr. *Dialogus cum Tryphone*. Edited by A. Hemman and François Garnier. Paris, 1958. Translated by A. L. Williams. London, 1930.
Libanius. *Opera*. Edited by R. Forster. Leipzig, 1903–22.
Livy, Titus. *History of Rome*. Edited and translated by B. O. Foster (and others). Loeb Classical Library. 14 vols. Cambridge, 1960–61.
The New Testament. *The Four Translation New Testament*. New York, 1966.
Strabo. *Geography*. Edited and translated by H. L. Jones. Loeb Classical Library. 8 vols. London, 1917–32.
Tacitus, Cornelius. *The Annals of Tacitus*. Translated by J. Jackson. Vol. 1. Cambridge, Mass., 1951–52.
Theodosius II. *The Theodosian Code*. Translated by C. Pharr. Princeton, 1952.

SECONDARY (POST-GEONIC) SOURCES

Abrahams, I. *Studies in Pharisaism and the Gospels*. 2nd ser. Cambridge, 1924.
Albeck, C., מבוא למשנה (*Introduction to the Mishnah*) Jerusalem-Tel Aviv, 1959.
———. *Untersuchungen über die halakischen Midraschim*. Berlin, 1927.
Allon, G. מחקרים בתולדות ישראל (Studies in Jewish History) 2 vols. Tel Aviv, 1957.
———. תולדות היהודים בארץ ישראל בתקופת המשנה והתלמוד (*History of the Jews in the Land of Israel during the Period of the Mishnah and the Talmud*) 2 vols. Tel Aviv, 1952.

300

———. נשיאותו של רבן יוחנן בן זכאי   In *Klausner Volume*. Tel Aviv, 1937.

———. "How Yabneh Became R. Johanan ben Zakkai's Residence" (Hebrew), *Zion* 3 (April 1938).

———. "The Attitude of the Pharisees toward the Roman Rule and the Herodian Dynasty" (Hebrew), *Zion* 4 (July, 1938).

Aptowitzer, V. *Parteipolitik der Hasmonäerzeit, in rabbinischem und pseudepigraphischem Schrifttum*. Vienna and Leipzig, 1927.

Atlas, S. להתפתחות הסוגיא וההלכה *HUCA* 17 (1942–43).

———. הערמה משפטית בתלמוד *Ginzberg Festschrift*. New York, 1946.

Avi-Yonah, M. בימי רומא וביזאנטיון 3rd ed. Jerusalem, 1962. German translation, *Geschichte der Juden im Zeitalter des Talmud in den Tagen von Rom und Byzanz*. Berlin, 1962.

———. *The Holy Land: from the Persian to the Arab Conquests*. (536 B.C. to A.D. 640); a historical geography. Grand Rapids, 1966. Translated from Hebrew, גיאוגרפיה היסטורית

Bacher, W. *Die Agada der Tannaiten*. 2 vols. Strassburg, 1884–90.

———. Hebrew translation by A. Z. Rabinowitz, אגדות התנאים Jerusalem-Berlin, 1922.

———. *Die exegetische Terminologie der jüdischen Traditions-literatur*. Leipzig, 1905.

———. *Traditionen und Tradenten in den Schulen Palästinas und Babyloniens*. Leipzig, 1914.

Baeck, L. *Aus drei Jahrtausenden*. Berlin, 1938. (See especially the article, "Die Pharisär," pp. 188–235).

———. *Judaism and Christianity*. Translated by W. Kaufmann. Philadelphia, 1958.

Baer, Y. F. ישראל בעמים Jerusalem, 1955.

Bamberger, B. J. "The Dating of Aggadic Materials." *JBL* 68 (1949): 115–23.

Baneth, E. *Ursprung der Saddokäer*. Leipzig, 1882.

Baron, S. W. *A Social and Religious History of the Jews*. 12 vols. Revised ed. New York–Philadelphia, 1952–67.

Beer, M. "The Exilarchate in Talmudic Times." *Zion* 27 (1963): 1–33.

Belkin, S. *Philo and the Oral Law*. Cambridge, 1940.

Bickermann, E. *Der Gott der Makkabäer*. Berlin, 1937.

———. "The Historical Foundations of Postbiblical Judaism." In *The Jews*, edited by L. Finkelstein. New York, 1949, I, 70–114.

———. *From Ezra to the Last of the Maccabees*. New York, 1962.

Blau, L. "Jochanan ben Zakkai in christlicher Beleuchtung." *MGWJ*, n.s., 8:548–61.

Bloch, M. A. שערי תורת התקנות 3 vols. Vienna–Przemysl–Budapest, 1879–1906.

Bonsirven, J. *Palestinian Judaism in the Time of Jesus Christ*. New York, 1964.

Brandon, S. G. F. *Jesus and the Zealots*. Cambridge, 1967.

Brody, A. *Der Mišna-Traktat Tamid*. Uppsala, 1936.

Büchler, A. *Das Synedrion in Jerusalem*. Vienna, 1902.

————. *Die Priester und der Cultus im letzten Jahrzehnt des jerusalemischen Tempels.* Vienna, 1895.

————. *Der Galiläische 'Am-ha'areṣ des zweiten Jahrhunderts. Vienna,* 1906.

————. "Apostole, Apostoli." *JE* 2:20.

————. *The Economic Conditions of Judaea after the Destruction of the Second Temple.* London, 1912.

————. *Studies in Sin and Atonement in the Rabbinic Literature of the First Century.* London, 1928.

Cohen, B. "Letter and Spirit in Jewish and Roman Law." *M. M. Kaplan Jubilee Volume.* New York, 1953.

————. *Law and Tradition in Judaism.* New York, 1959.

————. *Jewish and Roman Law.* 2 vols. New York, 1966.

Cowley, A. *Aramaic Papyri of the Fifth Century B.C.* Oxford, 1923.

Danby, H. *The Mishnah.* English translation. London, 1933.

Daube, D. "Rabbinic Methods of Interpretation and Hellenistic Rhetoric." *HUCA* 22 (1949): 239–64.

————. *The New Testament and Rabbinic Judaism.* London, 1956.

————. *Collaboration with Tyranny in Rabbinic Law.* London, 1965.

————. "Alexandrian Methods of Interpretation and the Rabbis." *Festschrift Hans Lewald.* Basel, 1953.

Davies, W. D. *Paul and Rabbinic Judaism.* London, 1948.

————. *Christian Origins and Judaism.* Philadelphia, 1962.

————. and D. Daube. *The Background of the New Testament and its Eschatology.* Cambridge, 1956.

Derenbourg, J. *Essai sur l'histoire et la géographie de la Palestine.* Paris, 1867.

De Vries, B. תולדות ההלכה התלמודית Tel Aviv, 1962.

Dinur, B. Z. תולדות ישראל 2nd ed. Tel Aviv. 1958–66.

Dubnow, S. *Weltgeschichte des jüdischen Volkes.* Translated from the Russian manuscript by A. Steinberg. 10 vols. Berlin, 1925. Hebrew translation, Tel Aviv, 1958–59.

Dupont-Sommer, A. *The Jewish Sect of the Qumran and the Essenes.* Translated by R. D. Barnett. London, 1954.

Elbogen, I. *Der jüdische Gottesdienst in seiner geschichtlichen Entwicklung.* 4th ed. Hildesheim, 1962.

Elon, M. מבוא למשפט העברי 3 vols. Jerusalem, 1964.

Englander, H. "The Men in the Great Synagogue." *HUCA Jubilee Volume.* New York, 1925.

Epstein, J. N. מבוא לנוסח המשנה Jerusalem, 1948.

————. מבואות לספרות התנאים (*Introduction to Tannaitic Literature*) Jerusalem, 1957.

Epstein, L. *Marriage Laws in Bible and Talmud.* Cambridge, Mass., 1942.

————. *Sex Laws and Customs in Judaism.* New York, 1948. Hebrew translation, Tel-Aviv, 1959.

Falk, Z. *Current Bibliography of Hebrew Law.* Published annually in Tel-Aviv.

Federbush, S. בנתיבות התלמוד (Essays) Jerusalem, 1957.

Feldman, W. M. *Rabbinical Mathematics and Astronomy.* 2nd ed. New York, 1965.

Finkel, A. *The Pharisees and the Teacher of Nazareth*. Leiden–Köln, 1964.

Finkelstein, L. *Akiba: Scholar, Saint and Martyr*. New York, 1936.

———. *The Pharisees: The Sociological Background of Their Faith*. 2 vols. Philadelphia, 1938. 3rd revised ed., 1962.

———. מבוא למסכתות אבות ואבות דרבי נתן New York, 1951.

———. Editor of *The Jews: Their History, Culture and Religion*. 3rd ed. Philadelphia, 1960.

Fischel, H. A. *The First Book of Maccabees* (with a Commentary). New York, 1948.

Flusser, D. האמונות והדעות של הכנסיה הנוצרית הקדומה הראשונה Jerusalem, 1964.

Frank, E. *Talmudic and Rabbinical Chronology: The System of Counting Years in Jewish Literature*. New York, 1956.

Frankel, Z. דרכי המשנה (*Darkhe Ha-Mishna. Hodegetica in Mischnam*). Leipzig, 1867. With revisions, Warsaw, 1923 and later.

———. *Der gerichtliche Beweis nach Mosaisch-talmudischem Rechte*. Berlin, 1846.

———. "Über Lapidarstyl der talmudischen Historik." *MGWJ* 1 (1851–52).

———. "Die Gemeindeordnung nach talmudischem Rechte." *MGWJ* 2 (1853).

———. מבוא הירושלמי *Einleitung in den Jerusalemischen Talmud*. Breslau, 1870.

Frey, J. B. *Corpus inscriptionum judaicarum*. Vol. 1. Rome, 1936.

Friedman, M. מאיר עין על סדר והגדה של פסח Vienna, 1895.

Gandz, S. *Monumenta Talmudica*. Vol. 2. Vienna–Leipzig, 1913.

———. "Studies in the Hebrew Calendar." *JQR* 11 (1949–50).

Gavin, F. "Rabbinic Parallels in Early Church Orders." *HUCA* 6 (1929).

Geiger, A. *Urschrift und Uebersetzungen der Bibel*. Breslau, 1857. Hebrew translation, Jerusalem, 1948–49.

———. *Das Judentum und seine Geschichte*. 2nd ed., vols. 1, 2, Breslau, 1865.

———. *Nachgelassene Schriften*. 5 vols. Breslau, 1885.

Gerhardsson, B. *Memory and Manuscript*. Uppsala, 1961.

Ginzberg, L. *Geonica*. 2 vols. New York, 1909.

———. *The Legends of the Jews*. 7 vols. Philadelphia, 1909–38.

———. "The Mishnah Tamid." *Journal of Jewish Lore and Philosophy* 1 (1919).

———. *Eine unbekannte jüdische Sekte*. New York, 1922.

———. מקומה של ההלכה בחכמת ישראל Jerusalem, 1931. English translation, Philadelphia, 1955.

———. פירושים וחידושים בירושלמי (*A Commentary on the Palestinian Talmud*). 4 vols. New York, 1941 and 1961 (4th vol. edited by D. Halivni).

———. *On Jewish Law and Lore*. (Essays) Philadelphia, 1955.

Glatzer, N. N. *Untersuchungen zur Geschichtslehre der Tannaiten*. Berlin, 1933.

Glueck, N. *The River Jordan*. New York, 1968.

Goldberger, J. המקורות בדבר עלית הלל לנשיאות *Hazofeh Lehokhmath Yisrael* 10 (1926).

Goldin, J. "Three Pillars of Simeon the Righteous." *PAAJR* 27 (1957).

———. "The Two Versions of Avot de R. Natan." *HUCA* 19 (1945).

Goldschmidt, E. D. *The Passover Haggadah: Its Sources and History.* (Hebrew) Jerusalem, 1960.

Goldstein, M. *Jesus in the Jewish Tradition.* New York, 1950.

Goodenough, E. R. *Jewish Symbols in the Greco-Roman Period.* 12 vols. New York, 1953–65.

———. *The Jurisprudence of the Jewish Courts in Egypt.* New Haven–London, 1929.

Graetz, H. *Geschichte der Juden.* 11 vols. 5th ed. of vol. 3, pt. 1, edited by Brann. Leipzig, 1905; of vol. 3, pt. 2, 1906. 4th ed. of vol. 4 edited by S. Horowitz. Leipzig, 1908. Hebrew ed. of vol. 2, Warsaw, 1893.

———. *Gnosticismus und Judenthum.* Krotoschin, 1846.

Guignebert, C. *The Jewish World in the Time of Jesus.* Translated London, 1939 and New York, 1959.

Gulak, A. יסודי המשפט העברי 4 vols. Jerusalem–Berlin, 1922.

Guttmann, A. *Mišna und Tosephta.* Breslau, 1938.

———. "Pharisaism in Transition." *Essays in Honor of Solomon B. Freehof.* Pittsburgh, 1964.

———. "Foundations of Rabbinic Judaism." *HUCA* 23 (1950–51).

———. "Hillelites and Shammaites: A Clarification." *HUCA* 28 (1957).

———. "Tractate Abot — Its Place in Rabbinic Literature." *JQR* 41, No. 2 (1950).

———. "The End of the Jewish Sacrificial Cult." *HUCA* 38 (1967).

Guttmann, H. *Darstellung der jüdischen Religion bei Flavius Josephus.* Breslau, 1928.

Guttmann, M. מפתח התלמוד (*Clavis Talmudis*) 4 vols. Csongrad–Budapest–Breslau, 1906–30.

———. *Das Judentum und seine Umwelt.* Berlin, 1927.

———. *Zur Einleitung in die Halacha.* Budapest, 1909, 1913.

———. היהדות וסביבתה *Jewish Studies in Memory of M. Guttmann.* Budapest, 1946.

Hadas, M. *Hellenistic Culture: Fusion and Diffusion.* New York, 1960.

Halevy, I. *Dorot Harischonim* דורות הראשונים 5 vols. Frankfurt a.M., 1898–1937.

Harnack, C. G. A. von. *Die Mission und Ausbreitung des Christentums in den ersten drei Jahrhunderten.* Leipzig, 1902. English translation, 2nd ed., London–New York, 1908.

Haroy, J. L. *The Jews of Ancient Rome.* Philadelphia, 1960.

Heinemann, I. *Philons griechische und jüdische Bildung.* Breslau, 1932.

———. "Die Lehre vom ungeschriebenen Gesetz im küdischen Schrifttum." *HUCA* 4 (1927).

———. דרכי האגדה Jerusalem, 1953.

Heinemann, J. "The Status of the Labourer in Jewish Law and Society in the Tannaitic Period." *HUCA* 25 (1954).

Helfgott, B. W. *The Doctrine of Election in Tannaitic Literature.* New York, 1954.

Herford, R. T. *Christianity in Talmud and Midrasch.* London, 1903.

———. *The Pharisees*. London, 1924. Last printing, Boston, 1962. German translation, W. Fischel. Leipzig, 1928.

Herzfeld, L. *Geschichte des Volkes Jisrael*. 2nd ed. 2 vols. Leipzig, 1863.

Herzog, I. *Main Institutions of Jewish Law*. 2 vols. London, 1936–39.

Hirschberg, H. "Allusions to the Apostle Paul in the Talmud." *JBL* 63 (1943).

Hoenig, S. *The Great Sanhedrin*. Philadelphia, 1953.

Hoffmann, D. *Der oberste Gerichtshof in der Stadt des Heiligtums*. Berlin, 1878.

———. *Die erste Mischna und die Controversen der Tannaim*. Berlin, 1882. Hebrew translation, Berlin, 1914.

———. *Mishnajot IV, Neziqin*. With translation and commentary. Berlin, 1898.

Hyman, A. תולדות תנאים ואמוראים (*Toldoth Tannaim Ve'Amoraim*) 3 vols. London, 1910.

———. תורה הכתובה והמסורה 3 vols. Tel Aviv, 1936–39.

Jacobs, L. *Studies in Talmudic Logic and Methodology*. London, 1961.

Jeremias, J. *Jerusalem zur Zeit Jesu*. 3 vols. Leipzig and Göttingen, 1923–37.

Joel, M. *Blicke in die Religionsgeschichte*. 2 vols. Breslau, 1880, 1883.

Jost, J. M. *Geschichte des Judenthums und seiner Sekten*. 3 vols. Leipzig, 1857–59.

Juster, J. *Les Juifs dans l'empire romain*. 2 vols. Paris, 1914.

Kadushin, M. *The Rabbinic Mind*. 2nd ed. New York, 1965.

Kagan, K. K. *Three Great Systems of Jurisprudence*. London, 1955.

Kahle, P. *The Cairo Geniza*. London, 1947.

Kaminka, A. הלל הזקן ומפעלו ("Hillel and his Works") *Zion* 3 (1939).

———. פרצופו המוסרי של שמאי *Bitzaron* (1940), No. 9.

Kassovsky, H. J. אוצר לשון המשנה (*Concordantiae Totius Mischnae*) 2 vols. Frankfurt a.M., 1927. 2nd ed. 4 vols. Jerusalem, 1956–60.

———. אוצר לשון התוספתא (*Thesaurus Thosephtae*) (6 vols. Jerusalem, 1932–61.

———. אוצר לשון התלמוד *Thesaurus Talmudis Concordantiae Verborum*) Jerusalem, 1954–67. 17 vols. Incomplete.

Katsh, A. I. *Judaism in Islam: Biblical and Talmudic Backgrounds of the Koran*. New York, 1954.

Katz, B. פרושים, צדוקים, קנאים, נוצרים Tel Aviv, 1957.

Kennard, J. S., Jr. "The Jewish Provincial Assembly." *Zeitschrift für Neutestamentliche Wissenschaft* 53 (1962).

Klausner, J. הסטוריה של הבית השני 3rd ed. 5 vols. Jerusalem, 1952.

———. הרעיון המשיחי בישראל 2nd ed. Jerusalem, 1927. English translation by W. F. Stinespring, *The Messianic Idea in Israel*. New York, 1955.

Klein, S. ארץ יהודה Tel Aviv, 1939.

———. ארץ הגליל Jerusalem, 1945.

Kosovsky, B. *Concordance to the Mekhilta of R. Jishmael*. 4 vols. Jerusalem, 1965–66.

———. אוצר השמות של מכילתא דרבי ישמעאל. שמות פרטיים Jerusalem, 1965.

Krauss, S. *Griechische und lateinische Lehnwörter im Talmud*. 2 vols. Berlin, 1898–99.

————. "Die jüdischen Apostel." *JQR*, o.s., 17 (1904–05).

————. *Antoninus und Rabbi*. Frankfurt a.M., 1910.

————. *Monumenta Talmudica*. vol. V. Vienna and Leipzig, 1914.

————. *Talmudische Archäologie*. 3 vols. Leipzig, 1910–12. Hebrew translation, קדמוניות התלמוד Vienna, 1924. Incomplete.

————. *Synagogale Altertümer*. Berlin–Vienna, 1922.

Krochmal, A. תולדות רבי יהודה הנשיא He-Ḥaluẓ 2 (1852).

Krochmal, N. מורה נבוכי הזמן Edited by S. Rawidowicz. Berlin, 1924.

Kuenen, A. "Über die Männer der grossen Synagoge." *Gesammelte Abhandlungen zur biblischen Wissenschaft*. Translated by Budde. Freiburg–Leipzig, 1894.

Lauterbach, J. Z. "The Pharisees and their Teachings." *HUCA* 6 (1929).

————. *Midrash and Mishnah*. New York, 1916.

————. *Rabbinic Essays*. Cincinnati, 1951.

Leon, H. J. *The Jews of Ancient Rome*. Philadelphia, 1960.

Levi, I. "De l'origine davidique de Hillel." *REJ* 31 (1895).

Levy, A. "Geschichte der jüdischen Münzen; Hyrcanus." *JQR* 37 (1947).

Lieberman, S. *Greek in Jewish Palestine*. New York, 1942.

————. *Hellenism in Jewish Palestine*. 2nd ed. New York, 1962.

————. "Light on the Cave Scrolls from Rabbinic Sources." *PAAJR* 20 (1951).

Liver, J. תולדות בית דוד (*The House of David*) Jerusalem, 1959.

Löw, L. *Gesammelte Schriften*. Szegedin, 1889–98.

————. *Die Lebensalter in der jüdischen Literatur*. Szegedin, 1875.

Löwinger, S. "Entwicklung unserer Traditionsliteratur." *Jewish Studies in Memory of Michael Guttmann*. Budapest, 1946.

Mann, J. "The Office of the Exilarch in Babylonia and its Development at the end of the Gaonic Period" (Hebrew). *Poznanski Memorial Volume*. Warsaw, 1927.

————. "Rabbinic Studies in the Synoptic Gospels." *HUCA* 1 (1924).

————. "Genizah Fragments of the Palestinian Order of Service." *HUCA* 2 (1925).

Mantel, H. *Studies in the History of the Sanhedrin*. Cambridge, Mass., 1961.

————. "Ordination and Appointment in the Days of the Temple" (Hebrew). *Tarbiz* 32 (January, 1963).

Marcus, J. R. and A. T. Bilgray. *Index to Jewish Festschriften*. Cincinnati, 1937.

Marcus, R. *Law in the Apocrypha*. New York, 1927.

————. "The Pharisees in the Light of Modern Scholarship." *Journal of Religion* 32 (1952).

————. "Pharisees, Essenes and Gnostics." *JBL* 73 (1954).

Marmorstein, A. *The Old Rabbinic Doctrine of God*. 2 vols. London, 1927, 1937.

————. *Studies in Jewish Theology*. Edited by J. Rabbinowitz and H. S. Lew, Oxford, 1950.

Meyer, E. *Ursprung und Anfänge des Chritentums*. Berlin, 1921.

Mielziner, M. *Introduction to the Talmud*. 4th ed. New York, 1968.

Mihaly, E. "A Rabbinic Defense of the Election of Israel." *HUCA* 35 (1964).

Mommsen, T. *Römische Geschichte*. Vol. 5. Berlin, 1885.

———. *Judaea und die Juden: Mit einem Nachwort von E. Taeubler*. Berlin, 1936 (reprint).

Montefiore, C. G. *Rabbinic Literature and Gospel Teachings*. London, 1930.

Moore, G. F. *Judaism in the First Centuries of the Christian Era*. 3 vols. Cambridge, Mass., 1927–30.

Nemoy, L., ed. *Kirkisani, Abu Yusuf Yakub al-, Karaite, Kitāb al-anwār wal-marāqib. Code of Karaite law*. 5 vols. New York, 1939–43.

———. "Al-Qirqisani's Account of the Jewish Sects." *HUCA* 7 (1930).

Neufeld, E. *Ancient Jewish Marriage Laws*. London, 1944.

Neusner, J. *A Life of Rabban Yohanan ben Zakkai*. Leiden, 1962.

———. *A History of the Jews in Babylonia*. Vol. 1: *The Parthian Period*. Leiden, 1965. Vol. 2: *The Early Sassanian Period*. Leiden, 1966.

Obermeyer, J. *Die Landschaft Babylonien*. Frankfurt a.M., 1929.

Oesterley, W. O. E., H. Loewe, and E. Rosenthal, eds. *Judaism and Christianity*. 3 vols. London–New York, 1937–38.

Parkes, J. *The Foundations of Judaism and Christianity*. Chicago, 1960.

Passamaneck, S. "Traces of Rabbinical Maritime Law and Custom." *Revue d'histoire du droit* 34 (1966).

Petuchowski, J. J. "Halakhah in the Church Fathers." *Essays in Honor of Solomon B. Freehof*. Pittsburgh, 1964.

———. "*Mumar*: A Study in Rabbinic Psychology." *HUCA* 30 (1959).

Poznanski, S. "Jacob ben Ephraim." *D. Kaufmann Memorial Volume*. Breslau, 1900.

———. "Die Anfänge des palästinensischen Gaonats." *Adolf Schwarz Festchrift*. Berlin–Vienna, 1917.

Rabbinowicz, R. N. דקדוקי סופרים 16 vols. Munich, 1867–97.

Rabin, C. *Qumran Studies*. London, 1957.

Reifenberg, A. *Ancient Jewish Coins*. 3rd ed. Jerusalem, 1963.

Rosenthal, J. Studies and Sources in the Time of the Second Temple (Hebrew). 2 vols. Jerusalem, 1967.

de Rossi, Azariah. מאור עינים Wilna, 1886.

Rostovtzeff, M. *The Social and Economic History of the Roman Empire*. 2nd ed. Oxford, 1957.

———. *Social and Economic History of the Hellenistic World*. Oxford, 1941.

Roth, E. לתולדות המונוגמיה אצל היהודים *M. Guttmann Memorial Volume*. Budapest, 1946.

Sandmel, S. *Judaism, Jesus and Paul: Some Problems of Method in Scholarly Research*. Nashville, 1951.

———. *A Jewish Understanding of the New Testament*. Cincinnati, 1956.

———. "Myths, Genealogies, and Jewish Myths and the Writings of the Gospels." *HUCA* 27 (1956).

———. *Philo's Place in Judaism*. Cincinnati, 1956.

Schaeder, H. H. *Esra der Schreiber*. Tübingen, 1930.

Schoeps, H. J. *Aus frühchristlicher Zeit*. Tübingen, 1950.

———. *Paul: The Theology of the Apostle in the Light of Jewish Religious History*. London, 1961.

Schürer, E. *Geschichte des jüdischen Volkes im Zeitalter Jesu Christi.* 4th ed. 3 vols. Leipzig, 1901–9.

Schwarz, A. *Die Erleichterungen der Schammaiten und die Erschwerungen der Hilleliten.* Vienna, 1893.

Shalit, A. הורדוס המלך Jerusalem, 1960.

Silberg, M. כך דרכו של תלמוד (*Principia Talmudica*) Jerusalem, 1961.

Smith, M. *Tannaitic Parallels to the Gospels.* Philadelphia, 1951.

Smith, R. W. *The Religion of the Semites.* New ed. London, 1914.

Sonne, I. "The Newly Discovered Bar Kokeba Letter." *PAAJR* 23 (1954).

———. "The Use of Rabbinic Literature as Historical Sources," *JQR* 36 (1945).

Spicehandler, E. בי דואר and דינא דמגיסתא בי ("Notes on Gentile Courts in Talmudic Babylonia") *HUCA* 26 (1955).

Stein, M. תן לי יבנה וחכמיה ("Yabneh and her Scholars") *Zion* 2 (1938).

Stendahl, K. *The Scrolls and the New Testament.* New York, 1957.

Strack, H. L. *Einleitung in Talmud und Midraš.* 5th ed. Munich, 1921.

——— and P. Billerbeck. *Kommentar zum Neuen Testament aus Talmud und Midrasch.* 5 vols. Munich, 1922–28. 2 index vols. by J. Jeremias and K. Adolph, 1956, 1961.

Sukenik, E. L. "A Hoard of Coins of John Hyrcanus." *JQR* 37 (1946–47).

Taeubler, E. "Palästina in der hellenistisch-römischen Zeit." In *Tyche.* Berlin, 1926.

Tcherikover, V. *Hellenistic Civilization and the Jews.* Philadelphia, 1959.

———. היהודים והיוונים בתקופה ההלניסתית Tel Aviv, 1963.

Tchernowitz, C. (Rav Zair) תולדות ההלכה (*Toledoth Ha-Halakah*) 4 vols. New York, 1934–50.

———. הזוגות ומקדש חוניו *Ginzberg Jubilee Volume.* New York, 1946.

Thackeray, H. S. T. *Josephus the Man and the Historian.* New York, 1929.

Urbach, E. בעלי התוספות (*The Tosaphists: Their History, Writings and Methods*) 2nd ed. Jerusalem, 1955.

———. הלכה ונבואה *Tarbiz* 18 (1946–47).

Vermes, G. *Scripture and Tradition in Judaism.* Leiden, 1961.

Vogelstein, H. "The Development of the Apostolate in Judaism and its Transformation in Christianity." *HUCA* 2 (1925).

Wacholder, B. Z. *Nicolaus of Damascus.* Berkeley and Los Angeles, 1962.

Wallach, L. "The Colloquy of Marcus Aurelius with Patriarch Judah I." *JQR* 3 (1941).

Weinberg, J. J. מחקרים בתלמוד Berlin, 1937–38.

Weiss, A. *The Talmud and its Development* (Hebrew). New York, 1954.

———. סדר הדין (*Court Procedure: Studies in Talmudic Law*). New York, 1957.

Weiss, I. H. דור דור ודורשיו 5 vols. 4th ed., Wilna, 1904.

Wellhausen J. *Die Pharisäer und Sadducäer.* 2nd ed. Hannover, 1924.

Wilde, R. *The Treatment of the Jews in the Greek Christian Writers.* Washington, 1949.

Winter, P. *On the Trial of Jesus.* Berlin, 1961.

Wolfson, H. A. "Synedrion in Greek Jewish Literature and Philo." *JQR* 36 (1945–46).

————. *Philo: Foundations of Religious Philosophy.* 2 vols. Cambridge, Mass., 1947.

Ya'viz (Jawitz), Z. תולדות ישראל 4th ed., vols. 4–7. Jerusalem–Tel Aviv, 1933–36.

Zeitlin, S. *Megillat Ta'anit as a Source for Jewish Chronology.* Philadelphia, 1922.

————. הצדוקים והפרושים (*The Sadducees and Pharisees*) New York, 1936.

————. "The Am Haarez." *JQR* 23 (1932–33).

————. "The Pharisees and the Gospels." *Essays and Studies in Memory of Linda R. Miller.* New York, 1938.

————. *The Rise and Fall of the Judaean State.* 2 vols. Philadelphia, 1962, 1967.

————. *Who Crucified Jesus?* New York–London, 1942.

————. "The Political Synedrion and the Religious Sanhedrin." *JQR* 36 (1945).

Zucker, H. *Studien zur jüdischen Selbstverwaltung im Altertum.* Berlin, 1936.

Zunz, L. *Gottesdienstliche Vorträge der Juden.* 2nd ed. Frankfurt a.M., 1892. Hebrew translation by M. A. Zek, הדרשות בישראל Jerusalem, 1954.

Zuri, J. S. רב Jerusalem, 1925.

————. תולדות המשפט הצבורי העברי, א, שלטון הנשיאות והועד Paris, 1931.

————. עקיבא Jerusalem, 1924.

addendum

Urbach, E. E. *The Sages, Their Concepts and Beliefs* (Hebrew). Jerusalem, 1969.

Index

CONCISE INDEX OF SOURCES

311

INDEX OF PERSONS AND PLACES

315

GENERAL INDEX

Martyr, 230, 254
Menorah, immersion of, 154–55
Messiah, 296
Messianic ideas, 250
Metal vessels, 44
Min, minim, 160, 165, 206–7, 219, 251, 293; *birkath haminim*, 169, 206
Mirror, 289
Muqzeh, 250
Mysticism, 196

Nasi, 27, 39, 59, 201, 203, 206, 246, 248, 254, 290
Nathin, 26
New moon, 204
Nizzoq, 153–54
Noachide Laws, 181, 278
Nomocracy, 3

"Old law" (*mishnah rishonah*), 229
Omer, harvesting on Sabbath, 144–45
Onias Temple, 42–43
Oral law, tradition, 127, 136, 158, 228, 284
Ordination, 290
Ozar Balus, 225

Palmyrians, 58
Parthians, 28, 287
Paschal sacrifice, 217
Passover, 283
Patriarchate, 19
Peace, 181
Peneh Mosheh, 252
Persians, 287
Pharisees, Sadducees, Essenes, 3, 12, 46, 180, 183, 207; Josephus' view, 124–29; talmudic, rabbinic, New Testament views, 129–30; designations of parties, 130–33; political role of Pharisees, 133–36; controversies between Pharisees and Sadducees, 136–56; various aspects of controversies, 156–58; inconsistent use of, 158–59; post-classical Sadducees, 160–61; post-classical Pharisees, 161–175
Prayers, 204–6, 213, 281; error in, 293
"Price control," 182–83

Priest, 3–5, 49, 55, 192–94, 281; drunk, 253
Priestly dues, 209–10
Prophets, prophetism, 3–4; false, 23
Proselyte, 26, 192
Prozbul, 71, 72
Puppet kings, 20–21
Purim, 6, 251

Qadosh, 295
Qal vehomer, 108
Qorban Ha-Edah, 252
Qumran, Damascus covenanters, 271; sect, 276

Rabban, *see* Titles
Rabbanites, 175
Recalcitrant elder, 21–22
Red heifer, 150–51
Resurrection, 137–38
Romanos, R., 294
Romans, 128, 135, 136, 189, 198–99, 211-12, 219, 221, 224, 234, 237–38, 248, 254, 287
Rosh Ha-Shanah, 250
"Rulers" (*seganim*), 258

Sabbath, 250, 293; "committee", 59; prayers, 251
Sabbatical year, 211, 249–50, 291–92
Sacrificial cult, 193, 209–10, 281
Sadducees, 251, 259, 293; *see also* Pharisees
Sages (*hakhamim*), 7
Samaritans, 145–46, 251, 293
Sanhedrin, Court, Great Court, etc., 13, 47, 50–54 pass., 113, 135, 200–201, 203, 233, 234–35, 242, 246–47, 259, 260, 281, 291; designation, synonyms, 17–18; history, changing authority, 18–21; functions, 21–25; membership, 25–27; location, 27–28; sessions, 28–29
Satrap, vice-satrap, 258
Scribes, 4, 7, 8, 130, 172
Sectarians, sectarianism, 203, 219, 251
Seder, 216–17; *see also* Paschal sacrifice
Sefer Gezeratha, 143
Semikhah, 34–39 *pass.*, 63–66, 115

Alexander Guttmann is professor of Talmud and Rabbinics at the Hebrew Union College-Jewish Institute of Religion, Cincinnati. Formerly he was professor of Hochschule (Lehranstalt) für die Wissenschaft des Judentums, Berlin. He attended the University of Budapest, University of Breslau, University of Berlin, Jewish Theological Seminaries of Budapest and Breslau and received his Ph.D. from the University of Breslau.

The manuscript was edited by Robert H. Tennenhouse. The book was designed by S. R. Tenenbaum. The type face for the text is Linotype Granjon designed by George W. Jones in 1924. The display face is Daphnis designed by Walter Tiemann in 1931.

The book is printed on S. D. Warren's Olde Style Antique paper and bound in Elephant Hide paper over boards. Manufactured in the United States of America.